Lecture Notes in Computer Science 15458

Founding Editors

Gerhard Goos

Juris Hartmanis

Editorial Board Members

Elisa Bertino, *Purdue University, West Lafayette, IN, USA*
Wen Gao, *Peking University, Beijing, China*
Bernhard Steffen ⓘ, *TU Dortmund University, Dortmund, Germany*
Moti Yung ⓘ, *Columbia University, New York, NY, USA*

The series Lecture Notes in Computer Science (LNCS), including its subseries Lecture Notes in Artificial Intelligence (LNAI) and Lecture Notes in Bioinformatics (LNBI), has established itself as a medium for the publication of new developments in computer science and information technology research, teaching, and education.

LNCS enjoys close cooperation with the computer science R & D community, the series counts many renowned academics among its volume editors and paper authors, and collaborates with prestigious societies. Its mission is to serve this international community by providing an invaluable service, mainly focused on the publication of conference and workshop proceedings and postproceedings. LNCS commenced publication in 1973.

Jun Ma · Yuyin Zhou · Bo Wang
Editors

Medical Image Segmentation Foundation Models

CVPR 2024 Challenge: Segment Anything in Medical Images on Laptop

MedSAM on Laptop 2024, Held in Conjunction with CVPR 2024
Seattle, WA, USA, June 17–21, 2024
Proceedings

Editors
Jun Ma
University of Toronto
Toronto, ON, Canada

University Health Network
Toronto, ON, Canada

Vector Institute
Toronto, ON, Canada

Bo Wang
University of Toronto
Toronto, ON, Canada

University Health Network
Toronto, ON, Canada

Vector Institute
Toronto, ON, Canada

Yuyin Zhou
University of California
Santa Cruz, CA, USA

ISSN 0302-9743   ISSN 1611-3349 (electronic)
Lecture Notes in Computer Science
ISBN 978-3-031-81853-0   ISBN 978-3-031-81854-7 (eBook)
https://doi.org/10.1007/978-3-031-81854-7

© The Editor(s) (if applicable) and The Author(s), under exclusive license to Springer Nature Switzerland AG 2025

This work is subject to copyright. All rights are solely and exclusively licensed by the Publisher, whether the whole or part of the material is concerned, specifically the rights of translation, reprinting, reuse of illustrations, recitation, broadcasting, reproduction on microfilms or in any other physical way, and transmission or information storage and retrieval, electronic adaptation, computer software, or by similar or dissimilar methodology now known or hereafter developed.
The use of general descriptive names, registered names, trademarks, service marks, etc. in this publication does not imply, even in the absence of a specific statement, that such names are exempt from the relevant protective laws and regulations and therefore free for general use.
The publisher, the authors and the editors are safe to assume that the advice and information in this book are believed to be true and accurate at the date of publication. Neither the publisher nor the authors or the editors give a warranty, expressed or implied, with respect to the material contained herein or for any errors or omissions that may have been made. The publisher remains neutral with regard to jurisdictional claims in published maps and institutional affiliations.

This Springer imprint is published by the registered company Springer Nature Switzerland AG
The registered company address is: Gewerbestrasse 11, 6330 Cham, Switzerland

If disposing of this product, please recycle the paper.

Preface

This volume contains the proceedings of the International Challenge on Segment Anything in Medical Images on Laptop held in conjunction with the IEEE/CVF Conference on Computer Vision and Pattern Recognition (CVPR) in 2024. By "proceedings", we refer to the collection of papers authored by participants, detailing their solutions for general medical image segmentation models using the official training dataset curated for this challenge.

Medical image segmentation is a pivotal step in clinical practice, serving to accurately quantify anatomical structures and pathological regions. This field is currently experiencing a paradigm shift, moving from specialized models designed for individual tasks to foundation models capable of managing a multitude of segmentation scenarios. However, most existing segmentation foundation models are primarily tailored for natural images or often necessitate substantial computational resources during inference. This limitation poses a significant barrier to their widespread implementation in clinical settings.

This challenge aimed to promote the development of universal promptable medical image segmentation foundation models that are deployable on laptops or other edge devices without reliance on GPUs. Specifically, the challenge task was to develop a lightweight bounding box-based segmentation model, and we provided a large-scale training dataset with 1,000,000+ image-mask pairs, covering 10 medical image modalities and more than 20 cancer types. The evaluation metrics related to both segmentation accuracy and efficiency, including Dice Similarity Coefficient (DSC) and Normalized Surface Dice (NSD), and the inference speed (runtime).

The challenge was hosted on the CodaBench platform and we received 1000+ submissions from more than 200 participants (https://www.codabench.org/competitions/1847/). We finally invited the top 20 teams to submit their algorithm Docker containers during the testing phase. Participants also submitted their methodology papers on the OpenReview platform. Each paper received was single-blind reviewed by three to five reviewers. Based on the initial reviews and the authors' revisions, we accepted 16 papers. These proceedings provide state-of-the-art algorithms for efficient and promptable medical image segmentation. We thank all the participants, reviewers, and the program committee whose incredible work made this possible.

November 2024

Jun Ma
Yuyin Zhou
Bo Wang

Organization

Organizing Committee

Jun Ma	University of Toronto; University Health Network; Vector Institute, Canada
Yuyin Zhou	University of California, Santa Cruz, USA
Bo Wang	University of Toronto; University Health Network; Vector Institute, Canada

Program Committee

Challenge Coordinators

Feifei Li	University Health Network, Canada
Sumin Kim	University of Toronto; University Health Network; Vector Institute, Canada

Data Contributors

Gianluca Brugnara	Heidelberg University Hospital, Germany
Philipp Vollmuth	Heidelberg University Hospital, Germany
Martha Foltyn-Dumitru	Heidelberg University Hospital, Germany
Jaeyoung Cho	Heidelberg University Hospital, Germany
Mustafa A. Mahmutoglu	Heidelberg University Hospital, Germany
Martin Bendszus	Heidelberg University Hospital, Germany
Irada Pflüger	Heidelberg University Hospital, Germany
Aditya Rastogi	Heidelberg University Hospital, Germany
Dong Ni	Shenzhen University, China
Xin Yang	Shenzhen University, China
Guangquan Zhou	Southeast University, China
Kaini Wang	Southeast University, China
Nicholas Heller	Cleveland Clinic, USA
Nikolaos Papanikolopoulos	University of Minnesota, Minneapolis, USA
Christopher Weight	Cleveland Clinic, USA
Yubing Tong	University of Pennsylvania, USA
Jayaram K. Udupa	University of Pennsylvania, USA
Patrick J. Cahill	Children's Hospital of Philadelphia, USA

Robert Haase — University Hospital Bonn, Germany
Inga Krause — University Hospital Bonn, Germany
Erich Kobler — University Hospital Bonn, Germany
Thomas Pinetz — University Hospital Bonn, Germany
Alexander Radbruch — University Hospital Bonn, Germany
Yaqi Wang — Communication University of Zhejiang, China
Yifan Zhang — Hangzhou Dental Hospital Group, China
Francisco Contijoch — University of California, San Diego, USA
Elliot McVeigh — University of California, San Diego, USA
Xin Ye — Zhejiang Provincial People's Hospital, China
Shucheng He — Zhejiang Provincial People's Hospital, China
Yucheng Tang — NVIDIA, USA
Haichun Yang — Vanderbilt University Medical Center, USA
Yuankai Huo — Vanderbilt University, USA
Gongning Luo — King Abdullah University of Science and Technology, Kingdom of Saudi Arabia
Kaisar Kushibar — Universitat de Barcelona, Spain
Jandos Amankulov — Kazakh Institute of Oncology and Radiology, Kazakhstan
Amangeldi Mukhamejan — Kazakh Institute of Oncology and Radiology, Kazakhstan
Dias Toleshbayev — Kazakh Institute of Oncology and Radiology, Kazakhstan
Jan Egger — University Hospital Essen, Germany
Antonio Pepe — Graz University of Technology, Austria
Christina Gsaxner — Graz University of Technology, Austria
Gijs Luijten — University Hospital Essen, Germany
Shohei Fujita — University of Tokyo, Japan
Tomohiro Kikuchi — Jichi Medical University, Japan
Benedikt Wiestler — Technical University of Munich, Germany
Jan S. Kirschke — Technical University of Munich, Germany
Ezequiel de la Rosa — University of Zurich, Switzerland
Federico Bolelli — Technical University of Munich, Germany
Luca Lumetti — Technical University of Munich, Germany
Costantino Grana — University of Zurich, Switzerland
Carlos Martín-Isla — Universitat de Barcelona, Spain
Karim Lekadir — Universitat de Barcelona, Spain
Victor M. Campello — Universitat de Barcelona, Spain
Behrus Puladi — RWTH Aachen University, Germany
Guomin Wu — Hospital of Stomatology, Jilin University, China
Kunpeng Xie — RWTH Aachen University, Germany; Hospital of Stomatology, Jilin University, China

Wei Shao	University of Florida, USA
Wayne Brisbane	University of California, Los Angeles, USA
Hongxu Jiang	University of Florida, USA
Hao Wei	Chinese University of Hong Kong, China
Wu Yuan	Chinese University of Hong Kong, China
Shuangle Li	Zigong First People's Hospital, China

Contents

MedficientSAM: A Robust Medical Segmentation Model with Optimized
Inference Pipeline for Limited Clinical Settings 1
   *Bao-Hiep Le, Dang-Khoa Nguyen-Vu, Trong-Hieu Nguyen-Mau,
Hai-Dang Nguyen, and Minh-Triet Tran*

DAFT: Data-Aware Fine-Tuning of Foundation Models for Efficient
and Effective Medical Image Segmentation 15
   Alexander Pfefferle, Lennart Purucker, and Frank Hutter

Filters, Thresholds, and Geodesic Distances for Scribble-Based Interactive
Segmentation of Medical Images 39
   Zdravko Marinov, Alexander Jaus, Jens Kleesiek, and Rainer Stiefelhagen

Rep-MedSAM: Towards Real-Time and Universal Medical Image
Segmentation 57
   Muxin Wei, Shuqing Chen, Silin Wu, and Dabin Xu

Swin-LiteMedSAM: A Lightweight Box-Based Segment Anything Model
for Large-Scale Medical Image Datasets 70
   Ruochen Gao, Donghang Lyu, and Marius Staring

A Light-Weight Universal Medical Segmentation Network for Laptops
Based on Knowledge Distillation 83
   Songxiao Yang, Yizhou Li, Ye Chen, Zhuofeng Wu, and Masatoshi Okutomi

Taking a Step Back: Revisiting Classical Approaches for Efficient
Interactive Segmentation of Medical Images 101
   Zdravko Marinov, Alexander Jaus, Jens Kleesiek, and Rainer Stiefelhagen

ExpertsMedSAM: Faster Medical Image Segment Anything
with Mixture-of-Experts 126
   Li Zhi, Yaqi Wang, and Shuai Wang

Efficient Quantization-Aware Training on Segment Anything Model
in Medical Images and Its Deployment 137
   Haisheng Lu, Yujie Fu, Fan Zhang, and Le Zhang

Lite Class-Prompt Tiny-ViT for Multi-modality Medical Image
Segmentation 151
   Haotian Guan, Bingze Dai, and Jiajing Zhang

Segment Anything in Medical Images with nnUNet 167
    Raphael Stock, Yannick Kirchhoff, Maximilian R. Rokuss,
    Ashis Ravindran, and Klaus Maier-Hein

SwiftMedSAM: An Ultra-lightweight Prompt-Based Universal Medical
Image Segmentation Model for Highly Constrained Environments 180
    Youngbin Kong, Kwangtai Kim, Seoi Jeong, Kyu Eun Lee,
    and Hyoun-Joong Kong

RepViT-MedSAM: Efficient Segment Anything in the Medical Images 195
    Qasim Ali, Yuhao Chen, and Alex Wong

U-MedSAM: Uncertainty-Aware MedSAM for Medical Image
Segmentation 206
    Xin Wang, Xiaoyu Liu, Peng Huang, Pu Huang, Shu Hu, and Hongtu Zhu

Modality-Specific Strategies for Medical Image Segmentation Using
Lightweight SAM Architectures 218
    Thuy Dao, Xincheng Ye, Joshua Scarsbrook,
    Gowrienanthan Balarupan, Fernanda L. Ribeiro, and Steffen Bollmann

Gray's Anatomy for Segment Anything Model: Optimizing Grayscale
Medical Images for Fast and Lightweight Segmentation 232
    In Kyu Lee, Jonghoe Ku, and YoungHwan Choi

Author Index 247

MedficientSAM: A Robust Medical Segmentation Model with Optimized Inference Pipeline for Limited Clinical Settings

Bao-Hiep Le[1,2]✉, Dang-Khoa Nguyen-Vu[1,2], Trong-Hieu Nguyen-Mau[1,2], Hai-Dang Nguyen[1,2], and Minh-Triet Tran[1,2,3]

[1] University of Science, Ho Chi Minh City, Vietnam
nvdkhoa20@apcs.fitus.edu.vn, 20120081@student.hcmus.edu.vn,
nhdang@selab.hcmus.edu.vn, tmtriet@fit.hcmus.edu.vn
[2] Vietnam National University, Ho Chi Minh City, Vietnam
lbhiep20@apcs.fitus.edu.vn
[3] John von Neumann Institute, Ho Chi Minh City, Vietnam

Abstract. Medical image segmentation plays a crucial role in clinical practice, aiding in identifying tumors, delineating organs, and monitoring disease progression. The advent of the Segment Anything Model (SAM) has enabled the development of universal medical image segmentation models that generalize across different modalities. However, the accessibility of such deep learning models in clinical settings is still limited by the reliance on powerful computing devices. In this paper, we propose MedficientSAM, which adopts the EfficientViT model to replace the heavy image encoder in SAM and then distills the knowledge from the MedSAM model on the challenge's training set. To further improve inference time, we re-implement the inference pipeline in the C++ programming language, optimizing the runtime on edge devices. MedficientSAM outperforms MedSAM in both accuracy and efficiency, achieving average DSC and NSD scores of **0.8642** and **0.8795**, respectively, on the public validation set. The average inference time is **1.0083 s** for 2D images and **8.9585 s** for 3D images. Our code and models are publicly available at https://github.com/hieplpvip/medficientsam.

Keywords: Medical image segmentation · Distillation · Embeddings Caching · C++ Implementation · Edge AI

1 Introduction

Medical image segmentation is a crucial clinical practice component, enabling precise diagnosis, treatment planning, and disease monitoring. Segmentation

---

The first two authors share equal contribution.

facilitates a deeper understanding of anatomical structures and abnormalities by delineating the boundaries of organs and pathological regions within images. Early segmentation models for medical images were often based on the nnU-Net structure [7]. While effective, these models were limited to specific datasets, each tailored to a particular segmentation task. The emergence of the Segment Anything Model (SAM) [9], a generalized 2D segmentation model, has marked a significant paradigm shift in the segmentation task. A straightforward way to leverage the SAM model for medical images is to train it on a large-scale medical dataset [15]. Additionally, other approaches have been proposed, such as using adapters that allow the model to incorporate medical knowledge [3,5,10,22]. However, these efforts focus on adapting SAM to medical data while maintaining high computational demands. In most healthcare facilities, powerful computational devices are not available, and quick results are required, making it challenging to deploy these models in practice.

The "Segment Anything In Medical Images On Laptop" challenge aims to develop universal promptable medical image segmentation models that can be deployed on laptops or edge devices without relying on GPUs. Specifically, participants are tasked with creating a lightweight, bounding box-based segmentation model. The challenge also introduces a baseline model, LiteMedSAM, which replaces the heavy image encoder in MedSAM with TinyViT [23], a scaled-down vision transformer model using a progressive contraction approach [4]. The challenge provides a large training dataset with over one million image-mask pairs, covering 11 types of medical images, including Computed Tomography (CT), Magnetic Resonance Imaging (MRI), Positron Emission Tomography (PET), X-ray, ultrasound, mammography, Optical Coherence Tomography (OCT), endoscopy, fundus, dermoscopy, and microscopy, along with more than 20 types of cancer.

Many works have introduced lighter models to address computational constraints by replacing the heavy image encoder of SAM. In natural image processing, notable examples include MobileSAM [26] and EfficientViT-SAM [27]. MobileSAM utilizes TinyViT as a lightweight image encoder, similar to LiteMedSAM. EfficientViT-SAM, on the other hand, replaces traditional softmax attention [21] with lightweight ReLU linear attention [8], reducing computational complexity from quadratic to linear while maintaining functionality. The benchmarks in [27] indicate that EfficientViT-SAM offers higher throughput than MobileSAM, despite having more parameters, and also delivers superior segmentation accuracy, even outperforming the original SAM.

Given the advantages of EfficientViT-SAM over other lightweight models, we choose it as the student model and perform knowledge distillation from the MedSAM teacher model. The distillation focuses on the image encoder, employing the L2 loss function to align the outputs of the student and teacher encoders. The entire pipeline, called MedficientSAM, is then fine-tuned using a compound loss function, combining Focal loss [11] and Dice loss [18] in a 20:1 ratio. To further improve inference speed, we re-implement the inference process in C++. While Python is widely recognized for its ease of use and extensive libraries, it is relatively slow compared to lower-level programming languages. The optimized inference pipeline in C++ ensures that MedficientSAM can deliver high-speed and accurate segmentation results even on resource-constrained devices, making it highly applicable in real-time clinical settings.

Our main contributions can be summarized as follows:

- We introduce MedficientSAM, utilizing knowledge distillation from the state-of-the-art segmentation model in medical images, MedSAM, and fine-tune it on a large-scale medical dataset to further improve accuracy.
- We implement a C++ inference pipeline to significantly reduce execution time on edge devices, offering a substantial performance boost over traditional Python-based pipelines.
- We propose the caching mechanism to reduce unnecessary recomputation of embeddings.

2 Method

2.1 Preprocessing

We follow the preprocessing in MedSAM implementation. For input images, we resize their longest dimension to align with the input size of EfficientViT-SAM's image encoder using bilinear interpolation, apply min-max scaling, and pad the resized images with zero values to create square dimensions (e.g., 512×512). The preprocessing steps for ground-truth masks are similar, except for the interpolation method and scaling approach. Specifically, we resize their longest dimension to match the input size of the image encoder using nearest-exact interpolation, then padding the resized masks with zeros to achieve square dimensions.

Additionally, since SAM only works on 2D images, for 3D volumes, we opt to slice them along the third dimension, creating 2D slices. These slices are then processed as described above.

2.2 Proposed Method

MedficientSAM is based on EfficientViT-SAM. We replace the image encoder from MedSAM with EfficientViT, a family of vision transformer models, while retaining the prompt encoder and mask decoder. Like EfficientViT-SAM, MedficientSAM has three variants, L0, L1, and L2, listed in increasing order of model sizes. Section 3 presents the speed-accuracy trade-offs analysis. Figure 1 demonstrates the macro architecture of EfficientViT-SAM-L1, which we use for official submission in the challenge. The model is trained in two stages: distillation and fine-tuning.

Distillation. To initialize the image encoder, we transfer the knowledge of MedSAM's image encoder (ViT-B) into EfficientViT through distillation. The goal is to align EfficientViT's and MedSAM-ViT-B's image embeddings by minimizing an L2 loss function.

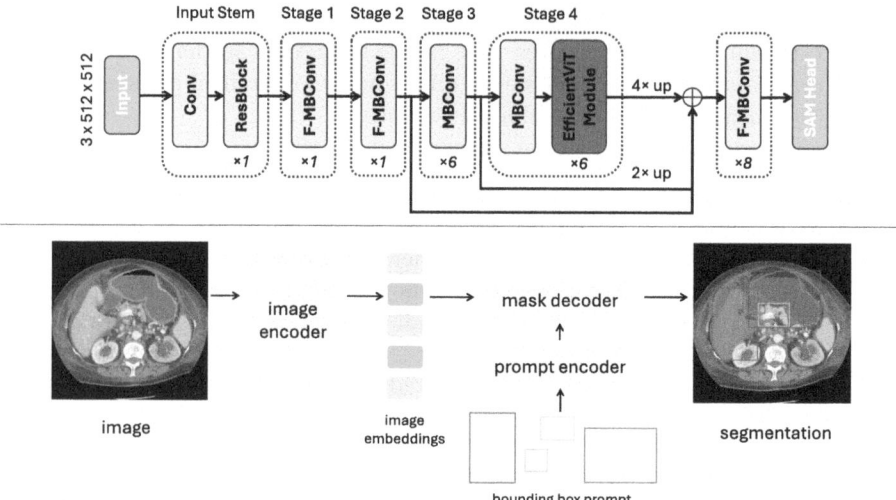

Fig. 1. EfficientViT-SAM-L1's macro architecture (top) and MedficientSAM (bottom). *Top:* "ResBlock" refers to the basic building block from ResNet34 [6]. "F-MBConv" refers to the fused MBConv block from [20]. "EfficientViT Module" is the building block from [2]. *Bottom:* MedficientSAM is a promptable segmentation model that allows users to specify segmentation targets using bounding boxes.

Fine-Tuning. We integrate the distilled EfficientViT with MedSAM's pre-trained prompt encoder and mask decoder to create MedficientSAM. Subsequently, we perform end-to-end training to enhance performance further. To prompt the model, we generate box prompts by determining the smallest rectangles that cover the binary masks, introducing random shifts to improve the model's robustness.

Loss Function. Recently, compound loss functions have proven robust in various medical image segmentation tasks [14]. During fine-tuning, we use the weighted summation between Focal loss [11] and Dice loss [18] at a ratio of 20:1. Specifically, let S and G denote the result masks and ground truth, respectively. N is the number of voxels in the image I. The focal loss is defined as

$$s_{t,i} = \begin{cases} s_i & \text{if } g_i = 1 \\ 1 - s_i & \text{otherwise} \end{cases} \tag{1}$$

$$L_{Focal} = -\frac{1}{N} \sum_{i=1}^{N} (1 - s_{t,i})^{\gamma} \log(s_{t,i}) \tag{2}$$

and dice loss is defined as

$$L_{Dice} = 1 - \frac{2\sum_{i=1}^{N} s_i g_i}{\sum_{i=1}^{N} s_i^2 + \sum_{i=1}^{N} g_i^2} \tag{3}$$

The final loss L is defined as

$$L = 20 \times L_{Focal} + L_{Dice} \tag{4}$$

3D Inference. Inspired by LiteMedSAM, for 3D volume inference, we start at the middle slice and propagate towards the ends, using the previously predicted mask slice as a guided prompt. We employ the idea of mask propagation as used in our previous work for organ segmentation [19]. If a binary mask is found in the previous slice, we obtain the bounding box that covers the binary mask and use it as the box prompt for the current slice instead of the box prompt from the input.

2.3 Post-processing

The binary masks output by MedficientSAM have a fixed size of 256 × 256. We first resize these output masks to match the input size of the image encoder, then crop out the padded zeros, and finally resize them back to their original resolution.

2.4 Inference Optimization

While very convenient for model prototyping, Python is unsuitable for deployment due to its interpreting nature. We propose porting the pipeline to C++, a compiled language, and using OpenVINO as the model runtime to reduce inference time. Specifically, our inference optimization includes four parts:

- **Export model to OpenVINO format:** OpenVINO is an open-source deployment toolkit optimized to run on CPU. With OpenVINO's excellent support for PyTorch, we can easily export our model from PyTorch to OpenVINO format and run it in C++.
- **Port pre/post-processing stages to C++:** Unlike the model, the pre- and post-processing stages have to be ported to C++ manually. For image resizing, we use the OpenCV library [1]. For working with tensors, we use the xtensor library [16], which is inspired by NumPy.
- **Further optimization for compiled code:** To squeeze even more performance, we compile everything from source code to take advantage of optimizations like Advanced Vector Extensions and Link Time Optimization.
- **Embeddings caching for 3D volumes:** When inferring on 3D volumes with different prompting boxes, we need to iterate over the 2D slices and compute their embeddings repeatedly. Since the image encoder is the heaviest component of MedficientSAM, we propose caching the embeddings to avoid unnecessary recomputation.

3 Experiments

3.1 Dataset and Evaluation Measures

The dataset from the challenge is curated from publicly available sources, including some well-known datasets such as AbdomenCT-1K, AMOS, KiTS23, and COVID-19-20. The segmentation covers 11 medical image modalities (CT, MRI, PET, X-ray, ultrasound, mammography, OCT, endoscopy, fundus, dermoscopy, and microscopy) and targets more than 20 cancer types. The training set comprises over one million image-mask pairs, and the validation set includes about 30,000 image-prompt pairs.

The evaluation metrics include two accuracy measures: Dice Similarity Coefficient (DSC) and Normalized Surface Dice (NSD), alongside running time as an efficiency measure. These metrics collectively contribute to the ranking computation. The evaluation platform is CPU-only to simulate edge devices, running on an Intel(R) Xeon(R) W-2133 at 3.60GHz with 6 cores. Furthermore, the memory usage is constrained to a maximum of 8 GB. Participants are required to submit the solutions as Docker [17] containers.

3.2 Implementation Details

Environment Settings: Table 1 presents the development environments and requirements.

Table 1. Development environments and requirements.

System	Ubuntu 22.04.3 LTS
CPU	AMD EPYC 7742 64-Core Processor
RAM	256 GB
GPU	One NVIDIA A100 40G
CUDA version	12.0
Programming language	Python 3.10
Deep learning framework	torch 2.2.2, torchvision 0.17.2

Docker containers are locally evaluated for their memory and time usage. The platform is detailed in Table 2. Constraints are set to simulate the official evaluation platform.

Table 2. Local evaluation platform.

System	Ubuntu 22.04.3 LTS
CPU	Intel(R) Core(TM) i9-10900K
RAM	8 GB
Docker version	26.1.3

Table 3. Training protocols for distillation stage.

Teacher Model	MedSAM-ViT-B [15]
Student Model	EfficientViT-L1 [15]
Data augmentation	Horizontal Flipping and Vertical Flipping
Patch size	512 × 512 × 3
Batch size	8
Total epochs	8
Optimizer	AdamW [13] with weight decay set to 0.0005
Initial learning rate (lr)	0.075
Lr decay schedule	decay the Lr by 0.5 every epoch
Training time	68 h
Loss function	L2
Number of model parameters	43.59M
Number of flops	49.23G

Training Protocols: We apply random horizontal and vertical flipping during the distillation stage for data augmentation. During fine-tuning, we apply Shift Scale Rotate in addition to flipping. We find that applying color-related augmentation techniques (such as RGB shift) reduces the accuracy. This is possibly due to medical image segmentation being sensitive to changes in color.

When distilling from MedSAM-Vit-B to EfficientViT, we need to repeatedly compute the output embeddings of MedSAM-Vit-B to use as labels for training EfficientViT. Since MedSAM-Vit-B is a very heavy model, this computation significantly contributes to the training time. One way to solve this is to precompute and save these embeddings to disk. However, due to the large size of the MedSAM dataset, precomputing the whole dataset would generate approximately 6 TB of embeddings, a very large amount of disk storage. Therefore, we resort to computing the embeddings on the fly and reducing the number of training samples to 400,000 randomly chosen image-mask pairs.

For the fine-tuning stage, the whole MedSAM dataset is used. Tables 3 and 4 detail the training protocols for the distillation and fine-tuning stages, respectively.

4 Results and Discussion

4.1 Quantitative Results

Table 5 compares the performance of the proposed model (MedficientSAM-L1) with the baseline model (LiteMedSAM) on the public validation set. We conduct ablation studies regarding the two-stage training process and the use of data augmentation.

Overall, LiteMedSAM scores highest on most targets, including CT, MR, US, and Fundus. In particular, MR and US showed significant gaps, with differences of 3% and 10%, respectively. However, LiteMedSAM falls far behind

Table 4. Training protocols for fine-tuning stage.

Model	MedficientSAM-L1
Data augmentation	Horizontal Flipping, Vertical Flipping, and Shift Scale Rotate
Patch size	512 × 512 × 3
Batch size	32
Total epochs	8
Optimizer	AdamW [13] with default settings
Initial learning rate (lr)	0.000002
Lr decay schedule	Cosine Annealing [12]
Training time	50.5 h
Number of model parameters	47.65M
Number of flops	51.05G

MedficientSAM and its variants for the remaining targets. Notably, with PET, LiteMedSAM achieved DSC and NSD scores of only 51.58% and 25.17%, respectively, while MedficientSAM achieved 73.00% and 58.03%, outperforming its ablated versions as well.

MedficientSAM has shown its effectiveness immediately after distillation, achieving DSC and NSD scores of 85.57% and 86.99% respectively, both higher than LiteMedSAM. Fine-tuning the whole pipeline improves the model's performance by 1–3% in several targets, except for ultrasound, which decreases by about 2% after fine-tuning. There is no significant difference in the version without augmentation; the two targets where it achieves the highest results, dermoscopy and microscopy, are only approximately equal to the randomly augmented MedficientSAM.

Generally, MedficientSAM achieves the highest average scores compared to the other methods, with DSC and NSD scores of 86.42% and 87.95%, respectively. The version without augmentation performs slightly better than the distillation-only version, and all three variants perform better than LiteMedSAM.

4.2 Qualitative Results

Figure 2 illustrates several examples where the MedficientSAM performs well and some examples where it performs poorly. Specifically, in cases of good segmentation, selected examples include cell microscopy, chest x-ray, and abdominal endoscopy. The model performed very well in these examples, achieving DSC scores of 94%–98%, above the average. This may be because these images have high resolution, clear boundaries, and large object regions. Additionally, RGB images can be better segmented due to better color distinction than grayscale images.

Table 5. Quantitative evaluation results on the public validation set (top-1 scores are bolded). Ablation studies are performed to investigate the effectiveness of the fine-tuning stage and data augmentation.

Target	LiteMedSAM		Only Distillation		No Augmentation		MedficientSAM-L1	
	DSC(%)	NSD(%)	DSC(%)	NSD(%)	DSC(%)	NSD (%)	DSC(%)	NSD (%)
CT	**92.26**	**94.90**	91.13	93.75	92.24	94.71	92.15	94.80
MR	**89.63**	**93.37**	85.73	89.75	87.25	90.88	86.98	90.77
PET	51.58	25.17	70.49	54.52	72.05	56.26	**73.00**	**58.03**
US	**94.77**	**96.81**	84.43	89.29	81.99	86.74	82.50	87.24
X-Ray	75.83	80.39	78.92	84.64	79.88	85.73	**80.47**	**86.23**
Dermoscopy	92.47	93.85	92.84	94.16	**94.24**	**95.62**	94.16	95.54
Endoscopy	96.04	98.11	**96.88**	**98.81**	96.05	98.33	96.10	98.37
Fundus	**94.81**	**96.41**	94.10	95.83	94.16	95.89	94.32	96.05
Microscopy	61.63	65.38	75.63	82.15	**78.76**	**85.22**	78.09	84.47
Average	83.23	82.71	85.57	86.99	86.29	87.71	**86.42**	**87.95**

In cases of challenging segmentation, the model performs much below average, at only 64%–68%. Selected examples include lesion PET scans, organ CT scans, and brain tumor MR scans. The poor performance of the model in these examples may be due to the characteristics of the image modality; for example, PET has a quite different color scale compared to other types. Additionally, in the second example, the segmented regions are separate from each other instead of being a single part, which can confuse the model. Furthermore, a low resolution can also make segmentation less effective, as the image will be blurry after resizing, and the boundaries will not be clear.

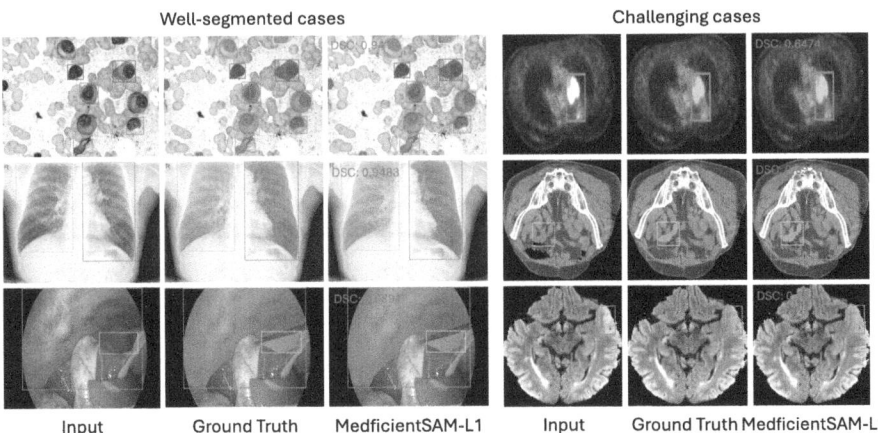

Fig. 2. Qualitative results from various public datasets. We illustrate both well-segmented and challenging examples for our proposed segmentation pipeline.

4.3 Segmentation Efficiency Results on Validation Set

Table 6 compares the efficiency of MedficientSAM against MedSAM and its smaller variant, LiteMedSAM, on the validation set. The average running time and memory usage are reported in seconds and megabytes. Although MedficientSAM has a higher resolution than LiteMedSAM (512 compared to 256), a higher number of FLOPs, and significantly more parameters, MedficientSAM still runs 5 times faster than LiteMedSAM. Regarding memory usage, MedficientSAM uses only half the amount of memory that LiteMedSAM requires. Moreover, MedficientSAM does not suffer from performance drops when switching to a lighter architecture, unlike LiteMedSAM. In fact, it even outperforms MedSAM, which is a heavier model with high resolution (1024×1024). The supe-

Table 6. Segmentation efficiency results on the public validation set. The computational metrics are obtained on an Intel(R) Core(TM) i9-10900K, except for MedSAM, which can not run on CPU.

Method	Res.	#Params	#FLOPs	Accuracy(%)		Runtime		Memory Usage	
				DSC	NSD	2D	3D	2D	3D
MedSAM	1024	93.74M	488.24G	84.91	86.46	N/A	N/A	N/A	N/A
LiteMedSAM	256	9.79M	39.98G	83.23	82.71	5.1	42.6	1135	1241
MedficientSAM-L0	512	34.79M	36.80G	85.85	87.05	**0.9**	**7.4**	**448**	**687**
MedficientSAM-L1	512	47.65M	51.05G	**86.42**	**87.95**	1.0	9.0	553	793
MedficientSAM-L2	512	61.33M	70.71G	86.08	87.53	1.1	11.1	663	903

Table 7. Running time (s) of some validation cases, measured on an Intel(R) Core(TM) i9-10900K. "Baseline" refers to LiteMedSAM. "Proposed" refers to MedficientSAM-L1. "Ablation" refers to MedficientSAM-L1 running in Python. Embeddings caching is not used for "Baseline" and "Ablation".

Case ID	Size	Num. Objects	Baseline	Ablation	Proposed
3DBox_CT_0566	(287, 512, 512)	6	247.5	136.1	40.6
3DBox_CT_0888	(237, 512, 512)	6	70.1	37.8	15.0
3DBox_CT_0860	(246, 512, 512)	1	12.8	8.0	4.4
3DBox_MR_0621	(115, 400, 400)	6	107.0	56.8	14.9
3DBox_MR_0121	(64, 290, 320)	6	70.0	36.8	9.0
3DBox_MR_0179	(84, 512, 512)	1	12.5	7.3	3.9
3DBox_PET_0001	(264, 200, 200)	1	8.9	5.9	2.6
2DBox_US_0525	(256, 256, 3)	1	3.8	2.8	0.9
2DBox_X-Ray_0053	(320, 640, 3)	34	8.9	3.6	1.3
2DBox_Dermoscopy_0003	(3024, 4032, 3)	1	6.9	3.0	1.1
2DBox_Endoscopy_0086	(480, 560, 3)	1	4.3	2.8	1.0
2DBox_Fundus_0003	(2048, 2048, 3)	1	5.1	2.8	1.0
2DBox_Microscope_0008	(1536, 2040, 3)	19	14.2	3.4	1.3
2DBox_Microscope_0016	(1920, 2560, 3)	241	21.3	9.8	6.6

rior performance of MedficientSAM demonstrates the effectiveness and robustness of our method.

For more detailed analysis, Table 7 presents the running time of various cases from the public validation set. We conduct an ablation study on the speed-up of the C++ inference pipeline compared to Python. Note that LiteMedSAM, the baseline, is also running in Python. The ablation study also demonstrates the superiority over LiteMedSAM, with runtime reduced by more than half. This indicates that MedficientSAM's robustness is not only due to the optimized inference pipeline but also the architecture itself. Reimplementing the inference process in C++ further halves the running time.

4.4 Results on Final Testing Set

Table 8. Ranking on the final testing set. Our team, "seno", achieved the top rank in the challenge. For each modality, the numbers denote the ranks of DSC, NSD, and Runtime, respectively.

Team	Rank	Score	CT	MR	Endo	US
seno	1	4.74	9/2/2	8/6/2	1/1/1	1/1/1
automlfreiburg	2	7.04	1/1/1	2/4/1	9/9/2	19/20/2
skippinglegday	3	7.11	2/3/6	7/12/6	12/12/7	2/2/7
lkeb	4	9.19	3/6/8	6/1/8	10/10/11	6/7/9
yangspalworld	5	9.22	8/9/3	16/18/3	15/15/4	9/9/3
cvhci	6	9.28	18/19/5	18/15/5	2/2/6	12/12/6
organagent	7	9.39	17/18/12	13/16/13	4/2/9	4/5/11
hmi306	8	10.26	6/8/17	15/19/22	7/7/14	3/4/12
hawken50	9	10.37	21/20/11	4/21/14	5/5/3	17/17/4
uestcsd	9	10.37	4/5/4	3/2/4	21/21/5	14/15/5

Team	X-Ray	Fundus	Microscope	PET	OCT
seno	8/8/2	1/1/1	7/8/1	18/16/3	9/8/2
automlfreiburg	15/15/1	15/15/2	11/11/2	5/7/2	7/7/4
skippinglegday	9/9/7	9/9/8	4/5/7	14/14/7	2/2/7
lkeb	19/19/10	12/12/12	10/10/9	4/4/11	11/11/9
yangspalworld	12/12/3	13/13/4	17/17/3	8/9/4	8/9/5
cvhci	1/1/6	4/4/6	13/14/6	12/15/1	23/23/1
organagent	6/5/9	3/3/9	1/1/11	23/22/14	5/6/11
hmi306	5/6/11	5/5/14	3/3/15	22/23/19	1/1/10
hawken50	10/11/4	8/8/3	2/2/5	3/3/23	18/17/3
uestcsd	21/21/5	20/20/5	19/19/4	2/1/5	14/14/6

On the final testing set, MedficientSAM ranks highest, outperforming all other teams in both segmentation accuracy and runtime. Our method achieved an average rank of 4.74, significantly ahead of the second-ranked team, which had an average rank of 7.04. Table 8 clearly demonstrates our dominance, particularly in the critical metric of runtime efficiency. Except for PET, we ranked 1st or 2nd in terms of running time across modalities, competing closely with the second-ranked team. However, unlike the second-ranked team, MedficientSAM maintains high accuracy across most targets (except for PET) on DSC and NSD metrics. While the second-ranked team falls to rank 20 in some targets, our method consistently performs well. MedficientSAM has set a new benchmark for speed and performance, significantly reducing computational time while maintaining high accuracy across various medical imaging modalities.

4.5 Limitation and Future Work

MedficientSAM has shown significant improvements but still has limitations and areas for future work. Currently, 3D volumes are processed independently on each slice, resulting in longer processing times and ignoring the spatial relationships between adjacent slices. This could potentially impact the accuracy of segmentations in 3D medical imaging. Besides, training with larger datasets, such as SA-Med2D-20M [25], could improve robustness and generalizability. Moreover, implementing model pruning and quantization could further reduce computational requirements. Finally, expanding MedficientSAM to segment all relevant structures within a medical image (i.e., Segment Everything) will enhance its applicability in diverse clinical scenarios.

5 Conclusion

In this work, we present MedficientSAM, leveraging EfficientViT to enhance both the efficiency and accuracy of MedSAM. Our method employs a two-stage training process, resulting in improved segmentation accuracy compared to MedSAM while substantially lowering computational demands. Additionally, we have developed a novel C++ inference pipeline, enabling MedficientSAM to operate on resource-constrained devices commonly found in clinical environments. We have open-sourced our code and models on GitHub to foster further research and collaboration.

Acknowledgements. We thank all the data owners for making the medical images publicly available and Codabench [24] for hosting the challenge platform. This research is supported by Vingroup Innovation Foundation (VINIF) in project code VINIF.2019.DA19. We thank University of Science, VNU-HCM, for providing access to the DGX A100 server used in this work.

Disclosure of Interests. The authors have no competing interests to declare that are relevant to the content of this article.

References

1. Bradski, G.: The OpenCV library. Dr. Dobb's J. Softw. Tools (2000)
2. Cai, H., Li, J., Hu, M., Gan, C., Han, S.: Efficientvit: multi-scale linear attention for high-resolution dense prediction (2024). https://arxiv.org/abs/2205.14756
3. Chen, C., et al.: MA-SAM: modality-agnostic SAM adaptation for 3D medical image segmentation (2023). https://arxiv.org/abs/2309.08842
4. Feichtenhofer, C.: X3D: expanding architectures for efficient video recognition (2020)
5. Gong, S., et al.: 3DSAM-adapter: holistic adaptation of SAM from 2D to 3D for promptable tumor segmentation. Med. Image Anal. **98**, 103324 (2024). https://doi.org/10.1016/j.media.2024.103324
6. He, K., Zhang, X., Ren, S., Sun, J.: Deep residual learning for image recognition. In: 2016 IEEE Conference on Computer Vision and Pattern Recognition (CVPR), pp. 770–778 (2016). https://doi.org/10.1109/CVPR.2016.90
7. Isensee, F., Jaeger, P.F., Kohl, S.A.A., Petersen, J., Maier-Hein, K.H.: nnU-Net: a self-configuring method for deep learning-based biomedical image segmentation. Nat. Methods **18**(2), 203–211 (2021). https://doi.org/10.1038/s41592-020-01008-z
8. Katharopoulos, A., Vyas, A., Pappas, N., Fleuret, F.: Transformers are RNNs: fast autoregressive transformers with linear attention (2020)
9. Kirillov, A., et al.: Segment anything. arXiv:2304.02643 (2023)
10. Li, H., Liu, H., Hu, D., Wang, J., Oguz, I.: Promise: prompt-driven 3D medical image segmentation using pretrained image foundation models (2023). https://arxiv.org/abs/2310.19721
11. Lin, T.Y., Goyal, P., Girshick, R., He, K., Dollár, P.: Focal loss for dense object detection. In: 2017 IEEE International Conference on Computer Vision (ICCV), pp. 2999–3007 (2017). https://doi.org/10.1109/ICCV.2017.324
12. Loshchilov, I., Hutter, F.: SGDR: stochastic gradient descent with warm restarts. In: International Conference on Learning Representations (2017). https://openreview.net/forum?id=Skq89Scxx
13. Loshchilov, I., Hutter, F.: Decoupled weight decay regularization. In: International Conference on Learning Representations (2019). https://openreview.net/forum?id=Bkg6RiCqY7
14. Ma, J., et al.: Loss odyssey in medical image segmentation. Med. Image Anal. **71**, 102035 (2021)
15. Ma, J., He, Y., Li, F., Han, L., You, C., Wang, B.: Segment anything in medical images. Nat. Commun. **15**(1), 654 (2024)
16. Mabille, J., Corlay, S., Vollprecht, W.: xtensor: multi-dimensional arrays with broadcasting and lazy computing (2016). https://github.com/xtensor-stack/xtensor
17. Merkel, D.: Docker: lightweight linux containers for consistent development and deployment. Linux J. **2014**(239), 2 (2014)
18. Milletari, F., Navab, N., Ahmadi, S.A.: V-net: fully convolutional neural networks for volumetric medical image segmentation. In: 2016 Fourth International Conference on 3D Vision (3DV), pp. 565–571 (2016). https://doi.org/10.1109/3DV.2016.79
19. Pham, M., Nguyen-Ho, T., Dao, T.T.P., Nguyen, T., Tran, M.: Semi-supervised organ segmentation with mask propagation refinement and uncertainty estimation

for data generation. In: Ma, J., Wang, B. (eds.) Fast and Low-Resource Semi-supervised Abdominal Organ Segmentation - MICCAI 2022 Challenge, FLARE 2022, Held in Conjunction with MICCAI 2022, Singapore, September 22, 2022, Proceedings. Lecture Notes in Computer Science, vol. 13816, pp. 163–177. Springer, Cham (2022). https://doi.org/10.1007/978-3-031-23911-3_15
20. Tan, M., Le, Q.: Efficientnetv2: smaller models and faster training. In: Meila, M., Zhang, T. (eds.) Proceedings of the 38th International Conference on Machine Learning. Proceedings of Machine Learning Research, vol. 139, pp. 10096–10106. PMLR (2021). https://proceedings.mlr.press/v139/tan21a.html
21. Vaswani, A., et al.: Attention is all you need (2023)
22. Wu, J., et al.: Medical SAM adapter: adapting segment anything model for medical image segmentation (2023)
23. Wu, K., et al.: Tinyvit: fast pretraining distillation for small vision transformers. In: European Conference on Computer Vision (ECCV) (2022)
24. Xu, Z., et al.: Codabench: flexible, easy-to-use, and reproducible meta-benchmark platform. Patterns **3**(7), 100543 (2022)
25. Ye, J., et al.: SA-Med2D-20M dataset: segment anything in 2D medical imaging with 20 million masks (2023)
26. Zhang, C., et al.: Faster segment anything: towards lightweight SAM for mobile applications (2023). https://arxiv.org/abs/2306.14289
27. Zhang, Z., Cai, H., Han, S.: Efficientvit-SAM: accelerated segment anything model without accuracy loss (2024)

DAFT: Data-Aware Fine-Tuning of Foundation Models for Efficient and Effective Medical Image Segmentation

Alexander Pfefferle[1](✉)[iD], Lennart Purucker[1][iD], and Frank Hutter[1,2][iD]

[1] University of Freiburg, Freiburg, Germany
{pfeffera,purucker,fh}@cs.uni-freiburg.de
[2] ELLIS Institute Tübingen, Tübingen, Germany

Abstract. Efficient and effective medical image segmentation supports faster and better decision-making of medical experts. In this work, we propose data-aware fine-tuning (DAFT), a method for enabling efficient and effective inference with foundation models, and apply it to medical image segmentation tasks. Following concepts from meta-learning for algorithm selection and dynamic selection, DAFT aims to fine-tune several versions of a foundation model on subsets of all available data instead of fine-tuning just one larger model. Then, at inference time, we select which fine-tuned model to use for the prediction depending on the distribution of the input data. DAFT enables us to create more efficient and effective models for each subset than when creating one model for all data. In our implementation of DAFT for the "Segment Anything In Medical Images On Laptop" competition as part of the CVPR24 Workshop on "Foundation Models for Medical Vision", we use the EfficientViT architecture, knowledge distillation, and OpenVINO runtime to further improve the inference. Additionally, we optimized the efficiency of our method through a flood of improvements, including an optimized inference runtime, caching, optimizing the Docker deployment container, and better inference code. DAFT improved the average dice similarity coefficient from 78.64% to 83.29% and the normalized surface distance from 80.58% to 85.59% compared to the LiteMedSAM baseline on the test data. Our final submission secured first place on the post-challenge leaderboard. Finally, and more importantly, we improved the average inference speed over the baseline by a factor of 6.5 (14.69 to 2.25 s) on the test set.

Keywords: Data Aware · Fine Tuning · Efficient · Image Segmentation

1 Introduction

Medical experts in various medical applications have to spot and detect patterns in medical images from Computer Tomography (CT), Microscopy, and X-Ray on a daily basis. Clinical applications that rely on image segmentation to detect regions of interest in medical images enable experts to make faster and better decisions. Such clinical applications can be powered by state-of-the-art image segmentation foundation models like SAM [16] or MedSAM [20].

The problem with foundation models for image segmentation is that they often are large, expensive models, e.g., MedSAM has more than 93 Million parameters and requires more than 10GB RAM when run on CPU. Furthermore, trends like the ever-increasing size of foundation models, as seen in the field of large language models[1], will likely make new image segmentation models only more expensive to use in real-world inference in a clinical application. Yet, critically, medical images are always sensitive patient data. Such images are not easily shared with others and often cannot leave the hospital's network or *even leave an expert's laptop*.

Therefore, it is crucial for the viability and usability of clinical applications to enable image segmentation models that are resource-efficient and effective in supporting the decisions of experts. Our goal is to enable even the most resource-constrained experts to benefit from image segmentation models.

Our goal perfectly aligns with the challenge `Segment Anything In Medical Images On Laptop`, organized by Jun Ma, Yuyin Zhou, Bo Wang, Feifei Li, and Sumin Kim as a part of the CVPR24 Workshop on Foundation Models for Medical Vision. In this manuscript, we, the `automlfreiburg` Team from the University of Freiburg, present *data-aware fine-tuning* (`DAFT`), our proposed method to enable efficient and effective inference with foundation models applied to medical image segmentation tasks to solve the challenge.

`DAFT` aims to fine-tune *several versions* of a foundation model on *subsets* of all available fine-tuning data to produce models that need to understand and remember less, while also being more effective for their specific subset's distribution. Then, at inference time, we *select* which fine-tuned model to use for the prediction depending on the distribution of the input data. `DAFT` follows traditional concepts from meta-learning algorithm selection [3,17,19,27,30] and dynamic selection [4,6,9], which we adapted to the age of foundation models.

The rest of this manuscript is structured as follows: the remainder of this Section introduces the challenge's background, the approach we used, and related work. In Sect. 2, we present our method in more detail, describing our fine-tuning pipeline and how we improved the runtime speed of our approach. Section 3 contains the implementation details and our protocol for evaluating submissions. Our results are demonstrated in Sect. 4. Finally, we present our improvements for the post-challenge "performance booster" in Sect. 5 before concluding our manuscript.

1.1 Competition Background

The `Segment Anything In Medical Images On Laptop` competition challenges participants to create a universal promptable medical image segmentation

---

[1] https://ai.meta.com/blog/meta-llama-3/.

predictor, that is deployable on a laptop. Hereby, deployable on a laptop means that we *do not* have access to a GPU and only 8GB of RAM and an Intel CPU with 6 cores.

The desired universal promptable medical image segmentation predictor must be able to produce predictions for a wide variety of medical imaging modalities, including 3D modalities, such as Computer Tomography (CT), Magnetic Resonance Tomography (MR), Positron Emission Tomography (PET), 2D greyscale images like Ultrasonic (US), X-Ray, Optical Coherence Tomography (OCT), Mammography and 2D RGB images like Dermoscopy, Endoscopy, Fundus and Microscopy. The prompts are boxes (2D or 3D) surrounding the to-be-segmented area of the image.

The universal predictor, deployed in a Docker [22] container, is evaluated through a multi-step process. For each data point, the Dice Similarity Coefficient (DSC), Normalized Surface Distance (NSD), and running time are computed. These metrics are averaged within each modality. All submissions are then ranked according to their performance in each metric across all modalities. In the final step, the average rank of each submission across all metrics and modalities is computed to obtain the overall evaluation score.

The organizers provided a preprocessed dataset we could use for training. Furthermore, they shared a list of additional datasets and a list of pretrained models that we were allowed to use. Both lists were extended and curated by the community up until one month before the submission deadline. Moreover, the challenge was hosted on Codabench [33] with a validation leaderboard with up to 6 submissions per day. The organizers also supported up to six Docker submissions on the validation data in total.

When submitting to Codabench, participants would upload the predictions of their model and receive the average DSC and NSD for each modality. The organizers would execute Docker submissions in the evaluation environment, and participants received the predictions and runtime for each data point as well as any error messages.

1.2 Our Approach

We implemented DAFT for this challenge by following a training protocol of 1) knowledge distillation, 2) general fine-tuning, and 3) data-aware fine-tuning for 11 subsets of the data.

In detail, we defined 11 subsets by separating the data based on the origin of the image, like Dermoscopy or Mammography. Then for each subset, we 1) created an EfficientViT [5] backbone for our foundation model by knowledge-distilling and using pre-trained weights; 2) fine-tuned the model on all available data; and 3) fine-tuned only on the training data of the respective subset. Then, at inference, we associated the input image with one of our 11 subsets and selected the respective fine-tuned foundation model for segmenting the input image.

Besides DAFT, we implemented a flood of improvements for inference efficiency over the baseline: using EfficientViT as a faster neural network architecture, an optimized inference runtime based on OpenVINO, caching, optimizing the Docker deployment container, and enhancing the inference code.

On the test data, we show that DAFT improved the average across all modalities for the dice similarity coefficient from 78.64% to 83.29% and for the normalized surface distance from 80.58% to 85.59% compared to the baseline. Our performance booster submission secured first place on the post-challenge leaderboard. Finally, and more importantly, we improved the average inference speed over the baseline by a factor of 6.5 (14.69 to 2.25 s) on the test set.

1.3 Related Work

In general, fine-tuning [8,13,29,31] has become more important in recent years due to the prevalence of large and expensive foundation models that need to be adjusted for specific applications at hand. Parameter Efficient Fine-Tuning (PEFT) [8] techniques, have been developed to make fine-tuning more resource efficient, by reducing the number of parameters getting trained. One such PEFT technique is Low Rank Adaption (LoRA) [13], in which the original weights are frozen and the weight updates are decomposed into low-rank matrices that are added and fine-tuned during training, thereby reducing the number of parameters that need to be updated.

Fine-tuning in general has shown to be extremely powerful for medical image segmentation tasks. MedSAM [20] is a segmentation foundation model for medical images created by the organizers of the competition. It was created by fine-tuning the Segment Anything Model (SAM) [16] on over 1 million medical images. The creators of MedSAM also released LiteMedSAM[2], a lightweight version of MedSAM that was used as a baseline in the competition.

At the same time, there has been research into making segmentation foundation models faster. One area of research in this regard focuses on finding more efficient architectures, e.g. EfficientViT-SAM [35] or MobileSAM [34] for SAM. Speeding up inference of a model can also be achieved by using a runtime that is better optimized for deployment on certain hardware, e.g. OpenVINO [1,10,36] or the ONNXRuntime [7].

Besides fine-tuning, knowledge distillation [11] enables a model that is being trained to leverage knowledge gained by other models that have been trained before. LiteMedSAM was created by distilling the vision transformer in MedSAM to a TinyViT [32] and performing additional fine-tuning afterward.

Furthermore, DAFT is highly related to meta-learning for algorithm selection [3,17,19,27,30] and dynamic selection [4,6,9]. In the former, a meta-model is learned to select one algorithm from a fixed set of potential algorithms to solve a problem. For example, a specific SAT solver is selected to solve a specific SAT instance. This motivated our approach in that we treat different subsets of the data as different problems that certain foundation models might solve better than others. In dynamic selection, a meta-model selects which model is used to

---

[2] https://github.com/bowang-lab/MedSAM/tree/0c044e9b4a6da58775cb4eb4b483a ba3f2df5a45.

obtain predictions *per data point* of a machine learning task. This specifically motivated our inference setup. So far, to the best of our knowledge, no one applied the concepts of dynamic selection or meta-learning algorithm selection to fine-tuning.

A mixture of experts (MoE) model [21,23] is the closest related work for DAFT with foundation models [15]. But MoE models differ fundamentally as the selection, i.e., routing, happens during the inference and training but not before, as we propose with DAFT.

2 Method: Data-Aware Fine-Tuning

The concept of data-aware fine-tuning (DAFT) is to select differently fine-tuned foundation models for different *foundation modalities*.

Foundation modalities are subsets of the data that differ in their distribution for the application of a foundation model. Generally, foundation modalities can be understood as different clusters of data points in the data for which a foundation model would be used. In other words, a collection of data points that are sufficiently similar based on their intrinsic characteristics. For this challenge and the application of medical images, we chose the origins of medical images, e.g., Dermoscopy or Mammography, as our foundation modalities.

To then decide which fine-tuned foundation model to select given a new input image, we created a *meta-model*. The meta-model predicts which foundation modality the input image belongs to, which in turn decides which fine-tuned foundation model we select to segment the image. Due to our choice of foundation modalities, the meta-model was extremely simple in this challenge, as detailed in the following Subsection. Figure 1 provides a general overview of our method.

2.1 Data Subset Selection for Data-Aware Fine-Tuning

For this challenge and the application of medical images, we chose the origins of medical images, e.g., Dermoscopy or Mammography, as our 11 foundation modalities. This choice is based on our hypothesis that fine-tuning a foundation model that, for example, focuses only on learning Dermoscopy data might perform better on Dermoscopy data than a model that was trained on both Mammography and Dermoscopy data. Likewise, we hypothesize that the model fine-tuned only on a subset of the data can be made more efficient at inference as it also only requires a subset of the capacity, enabling us, in principle, to use smaller models or prune fine-tuned models more aggressively.

We shortly investigated subdividing X-ray images into X-ray upper extremity, lower extremity, etc. but stopped due to time constraints. Likewise, we considered creating more general foundation modalities by splitting images by {3D modalities, 2D greyscale, 2D RGB}, {3D, 2D}, or {RGB, not RGB}. For the sake of simplicity, we stick with our original choice and leave it to future work to further subdivide these foundation modalities for medical images. Still, we

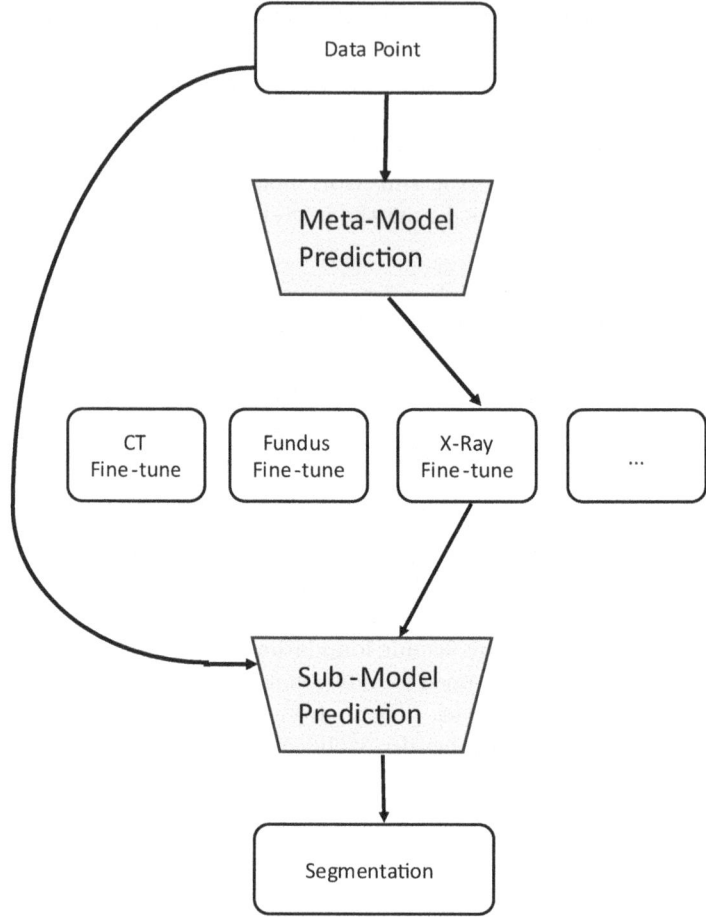

Fig. 1. Overview of our implementation of DAFT for medical image segmentation.

would like to highlight that more general foundation modalities are likely useful to avoid overfitting.

For data modalities with less obvious human-perceivable differences in the data, like with foundation models for tabular data [12] and time series [2], we suggest using unsupervised learning to cluster the data into foundation modalities, or compute meta-features of the data and cluster according to these meta-features.

Given a set of foundation modalities, we require a foundation model selector to determine when to use which fine-tuned foundation model for an image. To this end, we initially created a selector for medical images by training a tabular meta-model to predict the modality of an input image. We also considered training an image classifier to predict the modality but decided that the increase in runtime would be too expensive. To create a meta-dataset for training the selector, we computed meta-features (like height, width, number of boxes, or percentage of black pixels) of all data points in the training data and stored their modalities (like CT or MR) as target labels. We decided to create two meta-models since the meta-features for 2D and 3D data points can be different. Our model selector checked whether we have a 2D or 3D data point at hand and used the corresponding meta-model afterward. We used a scikit-learn MLP-Classifier[3] for both meta-models and achieved an accuracy score of 64% on 2D and 88% on 3D when training on the dataset provided by the organizers and evaluating on the official validation set. This shows that we are able to differentiate the modalities reasonably well with our straightforward meta-features and meta-models.

While the selector was working as intended, we realized that the modality would always be known in any realistic use case for the medical domain. In real-world settings where medical image segmentation is used, we would know the modality within our software, as the different modalities are clearly separable medical applications (and software products). With this in mind, we instead opted to select the foundation model based on the file name of the image during inference, since the file names of all images in the challenge followed a naming convention that indicated their origin (e.g., 3D images start with 3DBox_ and 2D images start with 2DBox_ followed by the modality and case number: 3DBox_PET_0001). We confirmed with the organizers that this approach is allowed and in the spirit of the competition before focusing on it as our final meta-model to predict the foundation modality.

The final implementation of our meta-model is a tree of if-else cases based on parsing the file name and mapping a leaf in the tree to a foundation model fine-tuned on a subset of the data. As the naming conventions were not always consistent and since we believed that there might be unknown naming conventions at test time, we devised several additional naming checks and a general fallback case. The fallback case would use the provided LiteMedSAM baseline model to segment an image.

2.2 Fine-Tuning Based on Data-Aware Subsets

To obtain a fine-tuned foundation model for each of the foundation modalities, we set up a fine-tuning pipeline including model distillation [11,25], re-using weights of pre-trained models, general fine-tuning and data-aware fine-tuning.

In detail, our fine-tuning pipeline was a three-step process. Ideally the first two steps would have been executed once and the last step once per foundation modality. The pipeline is visualized in Fig. 2 and consisted of the following steps:

1. **Knowledge Distillation:** Distill the TinyViT [32] image encoder of LiteMedSAM[4] to EfficientViT [5] and copy the weights of the prompt encoder/mask decoder.

---

[3] https://scikit-learn.org/stable/modules/generated/sklearn.neural_network.MLPClassifier.html.
[4] https://github.com/bowang-lab/MedSAM/tree/LiteMedSAM.

2. **General Fine-Tuning:** Fine-tune the initial foundation model from the previous step on the entire dataset of images provided by the organizers. This step makes up for errors or forgetting during knowledge distillation and provides us with a pre-trained-like model.
3. **Data-Aware Fine-Tuning:** Further fine-tune the foundation model from general fine-tuning on a subset of the dataset based on the origin of the image.

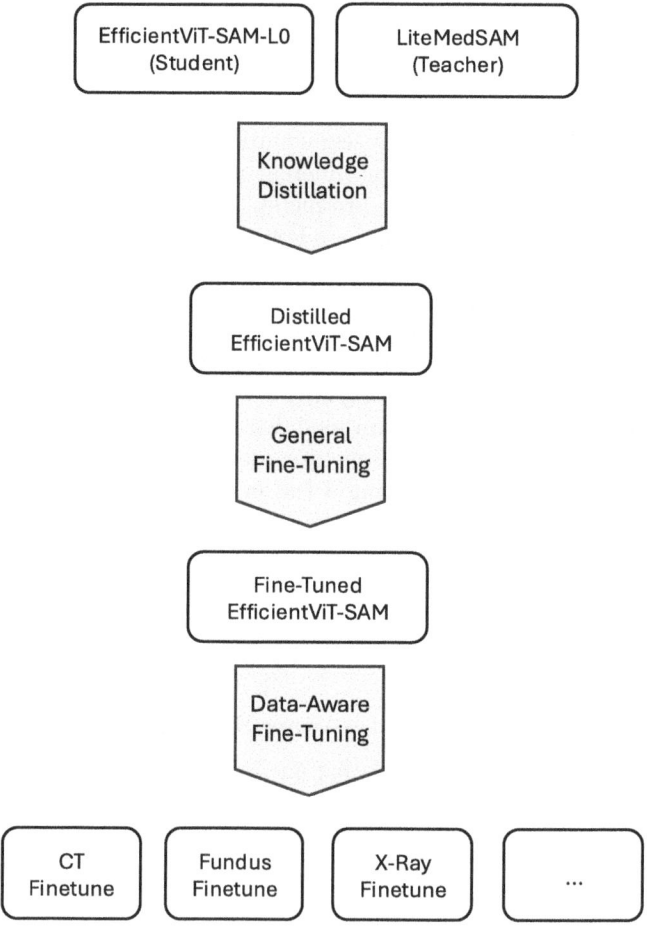

Fig. 2. Overview of our fine-tuning pipeline.

We initialized EfficientViT-SAM [35] with its pretrained weights[5] and leveraged the training done for LiteMedSAM by distilling the image encoder of

---
[5] Specifically, we used: https://huggingface.co/han-cai/efficientvit-sam/resolve/main/l0.pt.

LiteMedSAM to the image encoder of EfficientViT-SAM. Since the architecture of the prompt encoder and mask decoder were the same in both architectures, we were able to copy the corresponding weights after knowledge distillation. We used EfficientViT since we found it to be faster at inference speed than TinyViT. All available data was used for the distillation step. We also considered using MedSAM as a teacher network but decided that the distillation process would take too long.

We added the general fine-tuning, the second step in our pipeline, because we used the EfficientViT-SAM architecture as a backbone. Since the EfficientViT-SAM was not pre-trained on medical images, we first need to guarantee that our distilled model achieves similar general performance on medical images to LiteMedSAM. Thus, we also fine-tuned (or, depending on your perspective, retrained) the distilled model on the entire dataset. For general and data-aware fine-tuning runs, we froze the prompt encoder and only updated the image encoder and mask decoder. Data-aware fine-tuning directly after distillation would likely perform worse as the foundation model might not be properly adjusted to the general distribution of medical images.

During steps one and two, we only trained on a single random slice of each 3D data point in an epoch. This reduced the training time significantly and also ensured that modalities with deep 3D data points that contained many slices did not dominate the training. In the last step, we trained on all slices of each 3D data point in each epoch if the corresponding subset contained 3D data. Thus, `DAFT` also enabled us to have a more efficient fine-tuning pipeline, especially reducing the time required to obtain production-ready foundation models for the foundation modalities with 2D images or only a small number of data points in their respective subset.

Pre-processing, Post-processing, and Loss Function. For pre-processing, we resized and padded images to a size of $(256, 256)$ and normalized the intensities. In all three steps of our pipeline, we augmented images by flipping them horizontally with a probability of 50% and vertically with a probability of 50%. Following the training code for LiteMedSAM, we also randomly increased the size of the prompt's bounding boxes in all directions by up to five pixels. Additionally, for inference, we post-process our prediction by resizing the logits predicted by our model to the original size of the image using bilinear interpolation with a threshold of 0 afterward. Our loss function depended on the step of our pipeline. During knowledge distillation, we minimized the mean squared error between the embeddings predicted by both image encoders. For general fine-tuning and data-aware fine-tuning, we optimized the unweighted sum of the binary cross-entropy loss, dice loss, and intersection over union loss.

2.3 Inference Optimization for CPU

We optimized the runtime of our model through a flood of improvements, including using a faster neural network architecture, an optimized inference runtime, caching, optimizing the Docker deployment container, and inference code. All our improvements were specifically for CPU or would apply to CPU and GPU.

Architecture. We used EfficientViT instead of TinyViT as an image encoder, which made computing image embeddings faster, which is particularly important for 3D images, where we need to compute image embeddings for multiple slices.

Optimized Inference Runtime. We replaced PyTorch [14,24] by using the OpenVINO[6] runtime, which made inference faster and also reduced the latency of loading the execution environment before inference. OpenVINO achieves the latter by reducing the number of imports and import dependencies used at inference, avoiding loading the entire PyTorch library, which takes a considerable amount of time. Specifically, this allows us to avoid loading dependencies required only for training. For this challenge, we noticed that reducing loading the execution environment before inference is very important because the Docker container will be run once per data point. Hence, if we manage to speed up the latency to the first inference, we save time on every single data point.

Caching. Moreover, we used OpenVINO Model Caching[7] to speed up loading our models. This increases the runtime the first time a model is loaded since the cache needs to be created, but all subsequent runs using the same model will be faster since it will be loaded from cache.

Optimized Docker Container. We optimized the Docker container by reducing its size and the number of layers to increase the efficiency of running commands with the Docker container. In detail, we used `python:3.11-slim` instead of `pytorch/pytorch:latest` as a parent image to avoid loading code irrelevant for inference. Using newer Python versions, especially 3.11[8], increases the speed of Python itself. Besides, using a more lightweight version of Python, we opted for the headless version of OpenCV[9] to reduce the number of default packages installed. To further reduce the image size, we specifically removed caching for `apt` and `pip` while building the image. Finally, we combined multiple `RUN` commands and further made sure with docker-squash[10], to get a container that only consisted of a single layer.

The training checkpoints used in the Docker image were also converted to more optimized deployment artifacts beforehand. In detail, we converted training checkpoints of all fine-tuned models to ONNX[11] and only then to OpenVINO artifacts.

---

[6] https://github.com/openvinotoolkit/openvino.
[7] https://docs.openvino.ai/2024/openvino-workflow/running-inference/optimize-inference/optimizing-latency/model-caching-overview.html.
[8] https://docs.python.org/3/whatsnew/3.11.html#whatsnew311-faster-cpython.
[9] https://github.com/opencv/opencv-python.
[10] https://github.com/goldmann/docker-squash/tree/fec66e1659e0137d72ea7df57c38a6e36c0fba0b.
[11] https://github.com/onnx/onnx.

Optimized Inference Code. Last but not least, we improved the inference code of LiteMedSAM. In LiteMedSAM, if given a 3D image, the code first sliced it into multiple 2D images before segmenting each 2D image individually. It would segment each 2D image for each input prompt box *individually* going from the midpoint of the z-dimensions outward in both directions. Thereby, it would use the prediction for the prior 2D image to compute the prompt box for the next 2D image, by fitting the smallest box that encompasses the predicted area and increasing it by 3 pixels in each direction for robustness. As a result, the original pipeline would re-compute the image embedding for every 2D image and every prompt box. If two or more provided prompt boxes span across the same sliced 2D images (the same z-dimension of the 3D image), these shared slices would be re-computed for each such prompt box. To optimize this when predicting for 3D images, we avoid redundant computation by caching the image embeddings computed for each sliced 2D image. Thus, we guarantee to compute the image embedding at most once per sliced 2D image across all prompt boxes, i.e., segmentation tasks.

Additionally, we adjusted the original training pipeline for loading 2D or 3D images to work directly on `.npz` files[12]. Without this adjustment, we would need to convert 2D images to `.npy` files and extract and store the sliced 2D images as `.npy` files from the original 3D image `.npz` files.

3 Experimental Setup

We follow the experimental design provided by the organizers to obtain results. Additionally, we explain the process behind our development protocol and any remaining implementation details in the following.

3.1 Model Development Evaluation Protocol

For all training runs during development, we restricted ourselves to the dataset prepared by the competition organizers and did not include any other external public datasets. Thus, we also did not include any of the allowed public datasets gathered by the community during the competition's initial phase.

During development, we evaluated the accuracy of our approach by submitting its predictions to the validation leaderboard, treating the leaderboard as our validation data to obtain validation performance. Like in traditional hyperparameter optimization, our evaluation might have overfitted to the validation data as a result of re-using a fixed validation set over the course of the challenge.

To evaluate the runtime during development in a realistic setting, we used the organizer's evaluation script[13] with our Docker container on a basic DigitalOcean droplet with 4 vCPUs with 8GB RAM[14]; simulating deployment on a laptop.

---

[12] https://numpy.org/devdocs/reference/generated/numpy.lib.format.html.
[13] https://github.com/bowang-lab/MedSAM/blob/0c044e9b4a6da58775cb4eb4b483aba3f2df5a45/CVPR24_time_eval.py.
[14] https://www.digitalocean.com/pricing/droplets#basic-droplets.

3.2 Implementation Details

Our development code is available on the *finalsubmission* branch of our GitHub repository[15]. The rest of this Section details the used environment settings and training protocols, concluding with the results of our training protocol: an overview of the final set of data-aware fine-tuned foundation models.

Environment Settings. The training environment and requirements are presented in Table 1. We used this specific environment since it was available on our compute cluster, the JUWELS Hardware Booster[16], which we used for training. Table 2 details the environment we used to create the final model artifacts for deployment in the Docker image; we executed this conversion locally on a consumer-grade personal computer. Finally, Table 3 details the requirements used as part of our Docker image.

Table 1. Training Environment and Requirements

System	Rocky Linux release 8.9 (Green Obsidian)
CPU	AMD EPYC Rome 7402 CPU, 2× 24 cores, 2,7 GHz
RAM	100 GB of 512 GB DDR4, 3200 MHz
GPU (number and type)	Four NVIDIA A100 40GB
CUDA version	12.0
Programming language	Python 3.11.3
Deep learning framework	torch 2.1.2
Specific dependencies	monai 1.3.0, numpy 1.25.1, opencv-python 4.9.0.80 Branch of efficientvit[a]

[a] Link to specific branch

Table 2. Model Conversion Environment

Python Version	3.10.13
Specific dependencies	numpy 1.24.1, openvino 2024.0.0, torch 2.2.0, onnxruntime 1.17.1 efficientvit[a]

[a] Link to specific branch

Table 3. Docker Image Requirements

Parent image	python:3.11-slim
Specific dependencies	numpy 1.26.4, openvino 2024.0.0, opencv-python-headless 4.9.0.80

---

[15] https://github.com/automl/CVPR24-MedSAM-on-Laptop/tree/finalsubmission.
[16] https://www.fz-juelich.de/en/ias/jsc/systems/supercomputers/juwels.

Training Protocols. We followed the workflow presented in Fig. 1 and described in Sect. 2.2. Within each step, we optimized for training performance as described in Sect. 2.2. Finally, we selected the best-fine-tuned model per foundation modality by optimizing for validation performance across all steps of our pipeline. As a result, if general fine-tuning does not improve over knowledge distillation, we stick to the model from knowledge distillation. Likewise, if data-aware fine-tuning does not improve over general fine-tuning, we stick to the model from general fine-tuning.

The details of our training protocols are shown in the following tables: Table 4 presents the protocol for knowledge distillation; Table 5 presents the protocol used for general fine-tuning and data-aware fine-tuning (DAFT), we used the same protocol and only changed the input data for DAFT; and finally Table 6 presents the results of our DAFT-based training protocol.

In detail, Table 6 shows how we obtained the final fine-tuned foundation model per foundation modality and the respective number of training epochs. For all but X-ray, Ultrasonic, Dermoscopy, and Endoscopy, DAFT improved validation performance. For Endoscopy, not even general fine-tuning improved validation performance in the first place. Likewise, we noticed that if we use only MR or PET data, we start to overfit for MR and PET, respectively. Hence, we used a larger subset of data, merging several foundation modalities for DAFT in these two cases. We note that CT, MR, and PET are similar in the images they produce and their application, which motivated merging these specific foundation modalities. Furthermore, we found that none of the models we trained were able to beat LiteMedSAM, the baseline, on ultrasonic data. Thus, we decided to use the LiteMedSAM version provided by the organizers for ultrasonic data instead of our fine-tuned EfficientViT-SAM models.

Furthermore, for X-ray, we trained knowledge distillation and general fine-tuning only on 80% of all data for only 20 epochs and 46 epochs, respectively, due to using an older version of our code for training. We did not use the l0-checkpoint of EfficientViT-SAM during knowledge distillation of Microscopy for the same reason.

4 Results and Discussion

We first present the quantitative results in Sect. 4.1; next, the qualitative results in Sect. 4.2; followed by the efficiency results in Sect. 4.3. The quantitative and efficiency results were obtained on the validation set provided by the organizers. Finally we present the results on the final test set in Sect. 4.4.

4.1 Quantitative Results

We present the quantitative results on validation data for the baseline (i.e., LightMedSAM[17]), an ablation study, and our final submission based on DAFT.

---

[17] https://github.com/bowang-lab/MedSAM/tree/2a5a0556cabee8a62c8c1ec7e7cd821909adcb0c.

Table 4. Training Protocol for Knowledge Distillation

Pre-trained Model	EfficientViT l0, LiteMedSAM
Batch size	7
Patch size	$256 \times 256 \times 3$
Total epochs	24
Optimizer	AdamW ($\beta = (0.9, 0.999)$, $\epsilon = 10^{-8}$)
Initial learning rate (lr)	$5 \cdot 10^{-5}$
Lr decay schedule	ReduceLROnPlateau ($mode = min$, $factor = 0.9$, $patience = 5$, $cooldown = 5$)
Training time	13.7 h
Loss function	mean squared error
Number of model parameters	30M

Table 5. Training Protocol for Fine-Tuning

Pre-trained Model	Output Model from Knowledge Distillation or General Fine-Tuning
Batch size	96
Patch size	$256 \times 256 \times 3$
Total epochs	24 (in edge cases 20, see Text and Table 6)
Optimizer	AdamW ($\beta = (0.9, 0.999)$, $\epsilon = 10^{-8}$)
Initial learning rate (lr)	$5 \cdot 10^{-5}$
Lr decay schedule	ReduceLROnPlateau ($mode = min$, $factor = 0.9$, $patience = 5$, $cooldown = 5$)
Training time	7.3 h for general fine-tuning
Loss function	cross-entropy loss + dice loss + inter. over union loss
Number of model parameters	34.8M

Table 6. Number of Epochs per Pipeline Step and Selected Data-Aware Subsets for DAFT per Foundation Modality. To avoid overfitting, we combined several modalities for MR and PET. For X-ray, Dermoscopy, and Endoscopy, we did not perform DAFT as it did not increase the validation score. The table does not include the ultrasonic foundation modality because we used the baseline LiteMedSAM model without DAFT for ultrasonic data. Note that we were not able to train more epochs for CT, MR, and PET due to time-constrained resources. These modalities are particularly expensive during training.

Foundation Modality	CT	MR	PET	X-Ray	Dermoscopy	Endoscopy	Fundus	Microscopy	OCT	Mammography
Knowledge Distillation	24	24	24	20	24	24	24	20	24	24
General Fine-Tuning	24	24	24	46	24	0	24	50	24	24
Data-Aware Fine-Tuning	4	3	3	0	0	0	24	50	24	24
Used Data-Aware Subsets	CT	CT, MR, PET	CT, MR, PET	-	-	-	Fundus	Microscopy	OCT	Mammography

Our ablation study consists of an EfficientViT-SAM model *without* `DAFT`, that is, we created one general, large foundation model for all foundation modalities by performing knowledge distillation for 24 epochs and general fine-tuning for 24 epochs on the whole dataset. For the ablation study, we used a PyTorch runtime. The ablation study provides insights across our presented results into how well our method would have been without `DAFT`.

Table 7 shows the results on validation data. `DAFT` improved the average dice similarity coefficient from 82.6% to 88.07% and the normalized surface distance from 81.61% to 89.16% compared to the baseline. Our EfficientViT+`DAFT` approach is specifically effective for Microscopy (65.39% to 87.14% NSD) and PET (16.07% to 56.31% NSD). Our proposed method made no improvements for ultrasonic (US) data as we used the baseline model for this data (the observed differences are noise). Yet, the ablation study shows that our EfficientViT model performs much worse for this data, which explains why we failed to improve over the baseline with `DAFT` for EfficientViT. For all other data modalities, we noticed that our ablation study, EfficientViT backbone, improved over the baseline. And `DAFT` further improves over our EfficientViT backbone.

Table 7. Quantitative Evaluation Results On Validation Data. The baseline is LiteMedSAM, the ablation study a knowledge-distilled and fine-tuned version of EfficientViT, and our proposed method uses `DAFT` in addition.

Target	Baseline		Ablation Study		Proposed	
	DSC(%)	NSD(%)	DSC(%)	NSD(%)	DSC(%)	NSD(%)
CT	92.19	94.77	91.09	94.58	93.14	95.48
MR	89.13	92.66	86.98	91.28	88.21	91.73
PET	46.54	16.07	70.46	55.24	71.46	56.31
US	94.78	96.81	83.89	88.63	94.77	96.81
X-Ray	75.83	80.39	71.98	77.7	77.07	82.83
Dermoscopy	92.47	93.85	94.94	96.38	94.97	96.41
Endoscopy	96.04	98.11	95.24	97.94	96.60	98.61
Fundus	94.8	96.41	94.75	96.4	95.59	97.16
Microscopy	61.63	65.39	78.12	84.62	80.86	87.14
Average	82.6	81.61	85.27	86.98	88.07	89.16

4.2 Qualitative Results

Figure 3 contains examples of good segmentation results on Dermoscopy, Endoscopy, and Fundus data. The corresponding DSC and NSD scores were 97.28% and 98.16% for Dermoscopy, 97.83% and 98.29% for Endoscopy, and

97.96% and 98.7% for Fundus. Figure 4 depicts two examples with bad segmentation results. The Mammography example had a DSC of 81.37% and a NSD of 84.58%. The whole 3D CT data point had scores of 76.77% and 91.63%. The bad segmentation results show that our predictions are too large and convex, which our model did not seem to expect for these data points.

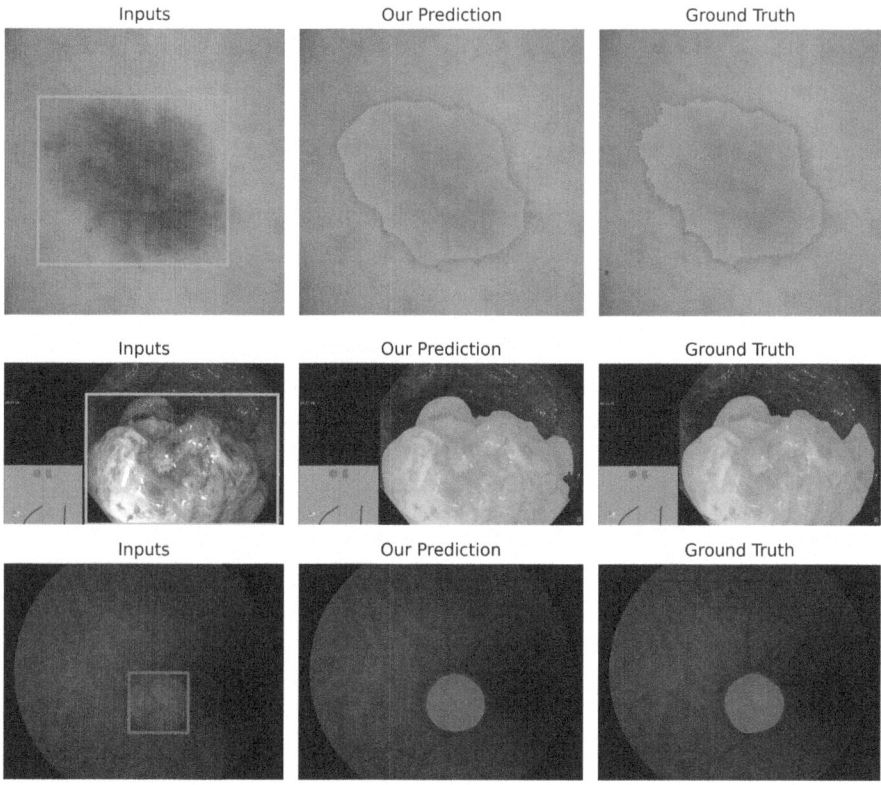

Fig. 3. Examples of Good Segmentation Results: The first row contains a Dermoscopy data point, the second row is an Endoscopy data point, and the last row is a Fundus data point.

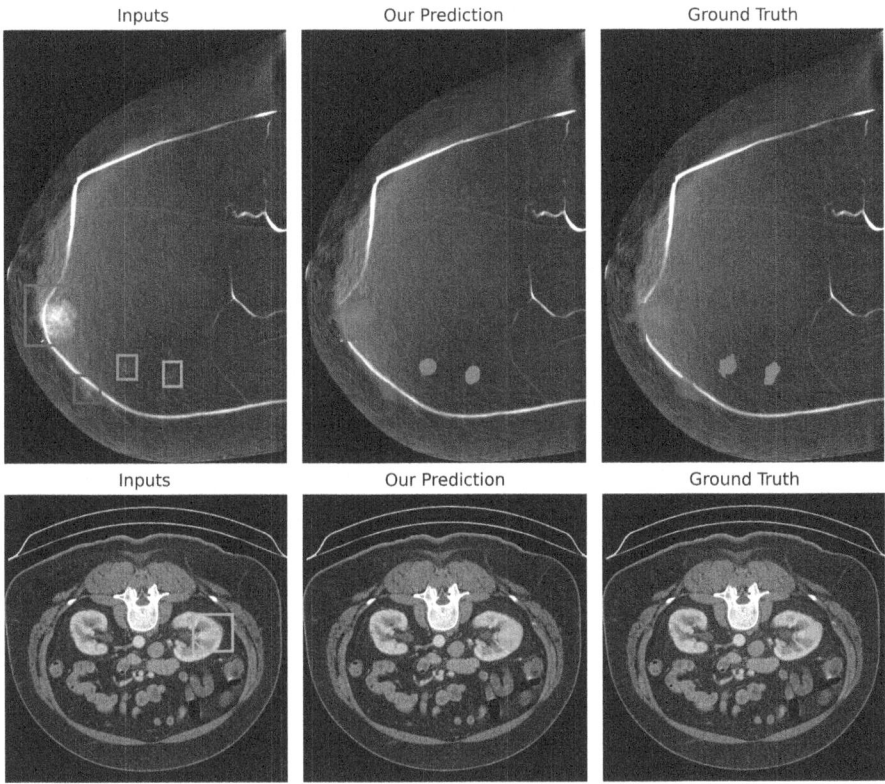

Fig. 4. Examples of Bad Segmentation Results: The first row contains a Mammography example, and the second row a slice of a CT example.

4.3 Inference Efficiency Results

Table 8 records the runtime of the baseline and our final submission for a list of example data points from the validation set. We observe the biggest relative improvements for 3D images. This likely follows from caching the computation of the image embeddings and using EfficientViT instead of TinyViT as the backbone, since the image embedding is the most expensive part of the network architecture.

We are also significantly faster on 2D data points. This is likely because our code initializes faster since we replaced the heavy PyTorch library with OpenVINO; this drastically reduced the latency to the first inference. This is more important for 2D data points than for 3D data points, as the inference time of the image encoder is the dominating factor for 3D data points. Our results for ultrasonic (US) 2D data points, where we used the baseline model, also show that our improvements do not only come from using EfficientViT but from the flood of our improvements described in Sect. 2.3.

For the presented ablation study w.r.t. inference efficiency, we ran our proposed model but replaced OpenVINO with ONNXRuntime[18]. ONNXRuntime is over two times slower on all 3D data points except 3DBox_MR_0121 and also slightly slower on all 2D data points. This shows that OpenVINO with caching dominates the ONNXRuntime for this application.

Table 8. Quantitative evaluation of segmentation efficiency in terms of running time (s). We used our own evaluation on CPU, as described in Sect. 3.1, to obtain the running time per method.

Case ID	Size	Num. Objects	Baseline[a]	Ablation Study	Proposed
3DBox_CT_0566	(287, 512, 512)	6	814.9	266.2	113.9
3DBox_CT_0888	(237, 512, 512)	6	219.8	89.6	38.2
3DBox_CT_0860	(246, 512, 512)	1	40.2	22.6	10.2
3DBox_MR_0621	(115, 400, 400)	6	389.0	96.6	45.5
3DBox_MR_0121	(64, 290, 320)	6	247.6	56.1	42.5
3DBox_MR_0179	(84, 512, 512)	1	38.3	24.2	11.1
3DBox_PET_0001	(264, 200, 200)	1	30.5	16.8	7.8
2DBox_US_0525	(256, 256, 3)	1	11.3	3.7	3.5
2DBox_X-Ray_0053	(320, 640, 3)	34	13.1	5.9	5.0
2DBox_Dermoscopy_0003	(3024, 4032, 3)	1	10.8	4.7	3.3
2DBox_Endoscopy_0086	(480, 560, 3)	1	11.0	4.0	2.7
2DBox_Fundus_0003	(2048, 2048, 3)	1	11.4	3.8	3.0
2DBox_Microscope_0008	(1536, 2040, 3)	19	13.1	5.3	4.1
2DBox_Microscope_0016	(1920, 2560, 3)	241	35.8	29.4	27.5
Average Runtime	-	-	134.8	44.9	22.7

[a] We used the code at https://github.com/bowang-lab/MedSAM/tree/2a5a0556cabee8a62c8c1ec7e7cd821909adcb0c and fixed a bug that caused overlays to be saved no matter whether -save_overlay was present

4.4 Results on Final Testing Set

Table 9 contains our results on the final testing set. The average DSC across all modalities improved from 76.1% to 79.84% and the NSD from 78.63% to 82.35%. The runtime decreased significantly across all modalities. The average runtime improved from 22.81 to 4.01, which demonstrates a speedup of factor 5.7. When looking at the specific modalities, we observe the biggest increases in accuracy for CT and OCT. We can also observe significant improvements in both DSC and NSD for MR, PET and Microscopy data. We see a significant decrease in accuracy for X-Ray data. Our final submission achieved second place on the testing leaderboard.

---

[18] https://onnxruntime.ai/.

Table 9. Quantitative Evaluation Results on final testing set. The baseline is LiteMed-SAM, and our proposed method uses **DAFT**. The results were generated by executing the Docker container on an Ubuntu 20.04 desktop, powered by an Intel Xeon(R) W-2133 CPU at 3.6 GHz, with 8 GB of RAM.

Target	Baseline			Proposed		
	DSC(%)	NSD(%)	Runtime	DSC(%)	NSD (%)	Runtime
CT	55.4	58.34	43.58	74.92	80.41	7.33
MR	64.83	62.84	18.75	73.5	69.22	3.58
PET	61.35	57.93	84.4	66.96	60.33	10.62
US	85.25	89.73	10.72	85.29	89.73	3.72
X-Ray	85.75	94.03	9.07	71.42	81.84	2.21
OCT	67.23	73.33	7.74	79.05	85.71	2.42
Endoscopy	94.41	96.95	6.8	94.08	96.68	1.91
Fundus	86.33	88.39	8.05	86.74	88.79	1.98
Microscopy	84.36	86.15	16.19	86.6	88.48	2.32
Average	76.1	78.63	22.81	79.84	82.35	4.01

4.5 Limitations and Future Work

The biggest limitation of our final submission is the amount of training and validation data we used in our model development protocol. The validation dataset was missing Mammography and OCT data and only had a few data points for certain modalities (e.g., ten for Fundus, or only three for 3D PET); since we used the validation scores to pick our final set of models, we are likely overfitting to the validation data. Likewise, we might overfit to our training data, as our training data was quite limited (e.g., Microscopy had only 1000 data points during training). Furthermore, due to our focus on **DAFT**, we did not perform large-scale re-training or fine-tuning runs across a collection of all publicly shared training datasets, which would likely have resulted in further improvements.

An interesting area for further research would be to automatically determine the subsets used for data-aware fine-tuning. We hope that by automating the subset selection we would be able to find more sensible subsets compared to picking them manually. This would also enable us to use **DAFT** for applications where we can not easily divide the data into conceptually different subsets ourselves. We could determine these subsets by clustering the data points according to their meta-features, or the latent representation of an auto-encoder or by using Visual DNA [26]. The number of clusters could be determined automatically by using the silhouette score [28]. We would iterate over the number of clusters, and pick the one that achieves the highest silhouette score. The data points corresponding to a cluster would make up a subset for **DAFT**. Since the data points inside the same cluster are similar, the **DAFT** models would not need to learn as complex relations and representations as a universal model would, which means that we could reduce their complexity, e.g. by pruning them, and thereby further improve the inference speed of our approach. Furthermore, we think that exploring the use of DAFT in other application areas, such as tabular data, time series, or NLP seems like a promising area for future research.

5 Post-challenge Performance Booster

Following the announcement of the competition results, the organizers invited participants to retrain their models on an enlarged dataset and incorporate potential improvements to try and beat their old submission. They also added data to the validation and test set.

5.1 Changes

We incorporated early stopping into all three training steps to avoid overfitting. The provided dataset was split into 80% for training and 20% for validation for each foundation modality. Then, we used a patience of 7 for early stopping and selected the checkpoint with the lowest validation loss. Additionally, we decided to use a shared model for all 3D modalities, including CT. In Sect. 4.4 we saw that LiteMedSAM ranked bad in accuracy on ultrasonic data in the final test set, so we decided to also use the EfficientViT architecture and DAFT for ultrasonic images. Details about the number of epochs trained are provided in Table 10 and Table 11. Lastly, we wrote the inference code in C++ instead of Python to further improve inference speed. To this end we used the C++ implementation of the winner of the competition, MedficientSAM [18], and modified it to work with our approach. Our updated code is available on the *main* branch of our GitHub repository[19].

Table 10. Epochs and CO_2eq (g) of Knowledge Distillation and General Fine Tuning. CO_2eq is based on 475g CO_2/kWh.

Pipeline Step	Total Epochs	CO_2eq	Best Epoch
Knowledge Distillation	25	4050.97	17
General Fine-Tuning	25	2020.39	17

5.2 Results

We compare the results of our booster submission to the LiteMedSAM baseline in Table 12. We observe that our runtime improved across all modalities, bringing the average down from 14.69 to 2.25, which equals a speedup of factor 6.5. We improved the average DSC from 78.64% to 83.29% and the average NSD from 80.58% to 85.59%. The biggest change in accuracy happened for the CT modality, the DSC increased from 55.75% to 73.53% and the NSD from 58.48% to 78.4%. Our performance booster submission achieved first place on the post-challenge leaderboard.

---

[19] https://github.com/automl/CVPR24-MedSAM-on-Laptop.

Table 11. Epochs and CO_2eq (g) of the Data-Aware Fine Tuning step and Selected Data-Aware Subsets for `DAFT` per Foundation Modality. CO_2eq is based on 475g CO_2/kWh.

Foundation Modality	Total Epochs	CO_2eq	Best Epoch	Used Data-Aware Subsets
3D	13	26277.3	5	CT, MR, PET
X-Ray	17	580.96	9	X-Ray
Dermoscopy	11	126.96	3	Dermoscopy
Endoscopy	9	394.69	1	Endoscopy
Fundus	13	39.38	5	Fundus
Microscopy	25	52.71	17	Microscopy
OCT	15	28.44	7	OCT
Mammography	10	24.44	2	Mammography
US	13	30.91	5	US

Table 12. Quantitative Evaluation Results of the LiteMedSAM baseline and our Booster Submission on the final testing set. The results were generated by executing the Docker container on an Ubuntu 20.04 desktop, powered by an Intel Xeon(R) W-2133 CPU at 3.6 GHz, with 8 GB of RAM.

Target	Baseline			Booster Submission		
	DSC(%)	NSD(%)	Runtime	DSC(%)	NSD (%)	Runtime
CT	55.75	58.48	38.78	73.53	78.4	5.59
MR	64.80	62.75	18.57	72.84	70.36	2.81
PET	76.94	66.98	14.90	78.75	69.38	2.4
US	85.24	89.73	8.96	89.32	93.34	1.6
X-Ray	85.51	94.40	9.95	83.94	93.87	2.08
OCT	73.31	80.20	8.39	81.64	88.75	1.32
Endoscopy	94.41	96.95	7.56	94.24	96.85	1.25
Fundus	87.47	89.58	8.77	86.36	88.53	1.38
Microscopy	84.36	86.15	16.34	89	90.84	1.84
Average	78.64	80.58	14.69	83.29	85.59	2.25

6 Conclusion

We proposed data-aware fine-tuning (`DAFT`), a method for enabling efficient and effective inference with foundation models, and applied it to medical image segmentation tasks as part of the "Segment Anything In Medical Images On Laptop" competition. Following concepts from meta-learning for algorithm selection and dynamic selection, `DAFT` aims to fine-tune several versions of a foundation model on subsets of all available data instead of fine-tuning just one larger model. Then, at inference time, we select which fine-tuned model to use for the prediction depending on the distribution of the input data. In our implementation of DAFT we use the EfficientViT architecture, knowledge distillation, and OpenVINO runtime to further improve the efficiency and effectiveness of inference.

Our results on the test data show that DAFT enables us to create more effective models for most modalities than when creating one model for all modalities. Moreover, we show that we can outperform the baseline by a wide margin. Likewise, we detail the large improvement in inference obtained by our implementation. Our results demonstrate the potential of DAFT and optimizing foundation models for inference. Both concepts enable us to deploy efficient and effective segmentation foundation models on the laptops of medical experts.

Acknowledgments. We thank all the data owners for making the medical images publicly available and CodaLab [33] for hosting the challenge platform. We also thank all authors of prior work for making their weights and code public. The authors gratefully acknowledge funding by the Deutsche Forschungsgemeinschaft (DFG, German Research Foundation) under SFB 1597 (SmallData), grant number 499552394. Furthermore, the authors gratefully acknowledge the Gauss Center for Supercomputing eV (www.gauss-centre.eu) for funding this project by providing computing time through the John von Neumann Institute for Computing (NIC) on the GCS Supercomputer JUWELS at Jülich Supercomputing Center (JSC). Lastly, the authors gratefully acknowledge funding by the Deutsche Forschungsgemeinschaft (DFG, German Research Foundation) under grant number 417962828. We are additionally grateful to the organizers for setting up the challenge and for the great effort and time put into running the competition.

Disclosure of Interests. The authors have no competing interests to declare that are relevant to the content of this article.

References

1. Andriyanov, N.: Analysis of the acceleration of neural networks inference on intel processors based on openvino toolkit. In: 2020 Systems of Signal Synchronization, Generating and Processing in Telecommunications (SYNCHROINFO), pp. 1–5. IEEE (2020)
2. Ansari, A.F., et al.: Chronos: learning the language of time series. arXiv preprint arXiv:2403.07815 (2024)
3. Bischl, B., et al.: ASlib: a benchmark library for algorithm selection. Artif. Intell. **237**, 41–58 (2016)
4. Britto, A.S., Jr., Sabourin, R., Oliveira, L.E.: Dynamic selection of classifiersa comprehensive review. Pattern Recogn. **47**(11), 3665–3680 (2014)
5. Cai, H., Li, J., Hu, M., Gan, C., Han, S.: Efficientvit: multi-scale linear attention for high-resolution dense prediction (2024)
6. Cruz, R.M., Sabourin, R., Cavalcanti, G.D.: Dynamic classifier selection: recent advances and perspectives. Inf. Fusion **41**, 195–216 (2018)
7. Onnx runtime (2021), version: 1.18.0. https://onnxruntime.ai/
8. Ding, N., et al.: Parameter-efficient fine-tuning of large-scale pre-trained language models. Nat. Mach. Intell. **5**(3), 220–235 (2023)

9. Giacinto, G., Roli, F.: Methods for dynamic classifier selection. In: Proceedings 10th International Conference on Image Analysis and Processing, pp. 659–664. IEEE (1999)
10. Gorbachev, Y., Fedorov, M., Slavutin, I., Tugarev, A., Fatekhov, M., Tarkan, Y.: Openvino deep learning workbench: comprehensive analysis and tuning of neural networks inference. In: Proceedings of the IEEE/CVF International Conference on Computer Vision Workshops (2019)
11. Gou, J., Yu, B., Maybank, S.J., Tao, D.: Knowledge distillation: a survey. Int. J. Comput. Vision **129**(6), 1789–1819 (2021)
12. Hollmann, N., Müller, S., Eggensperger, K., Hutter, F.: TabPFN: a transformer that solves small tabular classification problems in a second. arXiv preprint arXiv:2207.01848 (2022)
13. Hu, E.J., et al.: Lora: low-rank adaptation of large language models. arXiv preprint arXiv:2106.09685 (2021)
14. Imambi, S., Prakash, K.B., Kanagachidambaresan, G.: Pytorch. Programming with TensorFlow: Solution for Edge Computing Applications, pp. 87–104 (2021)
15. Jiang, A.Q., et al.: Mixtral of experts. arXiv preprint arXiv:2401.04088 (2024)
16. Kirillov, A., et al.: Segment anything. In: Proceedings of the International Conference on Computer Vision, pp. 4015–4026 (2023)
17. Kotthoff, L.: Algorithm selection for combinatorial search problems: a survey. In: Data Mining and Constraint Programming: Foundations of a Cross-Disciplinary Approach, pp. 149–190 (2016)
18. Le, B.H., Nguyen-Vu, D.K., Nguyen-Mau, T.H., Nguyen, H.D., Tran, M.T.: MedficientSAM: a robust medical segmentation model with optimized inference pipeline for limited clinical settings. In: Submitted to CVPR 2024: Segment Anything in Medical Images on Laptop (2024, under review). https://openreview.net/forum?id=aa0f77RKI0
19. Lindauer, M., Hoos, H.H., Hutter, F., Schaub, T.: Autofolio: an automatically configured algorithm selector. J. Artif. Intell. Res. **53**, 745–778 (2015)
20. Ma, J., He, Y., Li, F., Han, L., You, C., Wang, B.: Segment anything in medical images. Nat. Commun. **15**(1), 654 (2024)
21. Masoudnia, S., Ebrahimpour, R.: Mixture of experts: a literature survey. Artif. Intell. Rev. **42**, 275–293 (2014)
22. Merkel, D.: Docker: lightweight linux containers for consistent development and deployment. Linux J. **2014**(239), 2 (2014)
23. Miller, D.J., Uyar, H.: A mixture of experts classifier with learning based on both labelled and unlabelled data. In: Advances in Neural Information Processing Systems, vol. 9 (1996)
24. Paszke, A., et al.: Pytorch: an imperative style, high-performance deep learning library. In: Advances in Neural Information Processing Systems 32, pp. 8024–8035. Curran Associates, Inc. (2019). http://papers.neurips.cc/paper/9015-pytorch-an-imperative-style-high-performance-deep-learning-library.pdf
25. Polino, A., Pascanu, R., Alistarh, D.: Model compression via distillation and quantization. arXiv preprint arXiv:1802.05668 (2018)
26. Ramtoula, B., Gadd, M., Newman, P., De Martini, D.: Visual DNA: representing and comparing images using distributions of neuron activations. In: CVPR (2023)
27. Rice, J.R.: The algorithm selection problem. In: Advances in Computers, vol. 15, pp. 65–118. Elsevier (1976)
28. Shahapure, K.R., Nicholas, C.: Cluster quality analysis using silhouette score. In: 2020 IEEE 7th International Conference on Data Science and Advanced Analytics (DSAA), pp. 747–748 (2020). https://doi.org/10.1109/DSAA49011.2020.00096

29. Too, E.C., Yujian, L., Njuki, S., Yingchun, L.: A comparative study of fine-tuning deep learning models for plant disease identification. Comput. Electron. Agric. **161**, 272–279 (2019)
30. Tornede, A., Gehring, L., Tornede, T., Wever, M., Hüllermeier, E.: Algorithm selection on a meta level. Mach. Learn. **112**(4), 1253–1286 (2023)
31. Wang, G., et al.: Interactive medical image segmentation using deep learning with image-specific fine tuning. IEEE Trans. Med. Imaging **37**(7), 1562–1573 (2018)
32. Wu, K., et al.: Tinyvit: fast pretraining distillation for small vision transformers (2022)
33. Xu, Z., et al.: Codabench: flexible, easy-to-use, and reproducible meta-benchmark platform. Patterns **3**(7), 100543 (2022)
34. Zhang, C., et al.: Faster segment anything: towards lightweight SAM for mobile applications. arXiv preprint arXiv:2306.14289 (2023)
35. Zhang, Z., Cai, H., Han, S.: Efficientvit-SAM: accelerated segment anything model without performance loss. In: CVPR Workshop: Efficient Large Vision Models (2024)
36. Zunin, V.: Intel openvino toolkit for computer vision: object detection and semantic segmentation. In: 2021 International Russian Automation Conference (RusAutoCon), pp. 847–851. IEEE (2021)

Filters, Thresholds, and Geodesic Distances for Scribble-Based Interactive Segmentation of Medical Images

Zdravko Marinov[1,2] ✉ , Alexander Jaus[1,2], Jens Kleesiek[3,4], and Rainer Stiefelhagen[1]

[1] Karlsruhe Institute of Technology, Karlsruhe, Germany
zdravko.marinov@kit.edu
[2] HIDSS4Health - Helmholtz Information and Data Science School for Health, Karlsruhe/Heidelberg, Germany
[3] Institute for AI in Medicine, University Hospital Essen, Essen, Germany
[4] Cancer Research Center Cologne Essen (CCCE), University Medicine Essen, Essen, Germany

Abstract. Interactive segmentation plays a vital role in medical image analysis, facilitating accurate diagnosis and treatment planning through real-time interaction and rapid annotations. Scribble-based methods, where users draw over target structures, are particularly effective for delineating thin structures like vessels, providing precise pixel-level detail compared to bounding boxes. MedSAM, introduced in 2023, is optimized for bounding box inputs, which limits its effectiveness for precise interaction types such as scribbles. Additionally, it exhibits a slower inference due to its large size. To address these limitations, we evaluated simpler models such as thresholding, Meijering filters, and Geodesic Distance Transforms. These models outperformed MedSAM in segmentation accuracy and efficiency across fundus, microscopy, PET, and OCT, achieving a Dice Score of 62.31 and a Normalized Surface Dice of 67.01 on the validation set. Our findings highlight the effectiveness of traditional methods and reveal the current limitations of emerging foundation models. This comparative analysis aims to improve MedSAM's robustness and efficiency, contributing to the development of a more reliable general model for medical image segmentation.

1 Introduction

Background. Deep learning advancements have significantly enhanced the segmentation of anatomical structures and lesions in medical images. These models, however, often depend on manually annotated datasets, which are labor-intensive to create [2,10,17,21,32,41]. To reduce this burden, interactive segmentation methods have been developed, utilizing simpler annotations like clicks or bounding boxes instead of detailed voxelwise labels [3,14,15,25,29,30,39,40,44]. These methods combine user inputs with image data to make predictions, which, once verified by medical professionals, can be used as new annotations [29]. However, scribbles provide a more intuitive and versatile annotation method, allowing users to specify exact pixels of the target object. Various studies have employed freehand strokes to initiate segmentation masks [6,13,40,42] and to refine existing ones [13,42], significantly speeding up the annotation process. Interactive models leveraging scribbles can therefore facilitate quicker and more precise data annotation.

Related Work. MedSAM [26] is a fine-tuned version of the Segment Anything Model (SAM) [24] that has been trained on 11 imaging modalities and over 1.5 million image-mask pairs, showcasing impressive generalizability across various segmentation tasks [26,29]. However, MedSAM is limited to processing bounding boxes or clicks and does not support scribble-based inputs. Adaptations like ScribblePrompt [42] have optimized MedSAM for scribble guidance, maintaining its generalization across multiple modalities. Despite these advancements, the research on scribble-based interactions remains relatively sparse. To address this gap, Ma et al. [26] organized the Segment Anything in Medical Images on Laptop Challenge (Task 2: Scribble)[1] to develop and evaluate efficient scribble-based methods for interactive segmentation. This paper presents our submission to this challenge, aiming to contribute further to the exploration of scribble-based interactive segmentation techniques.

Motivation. Our motivation stems from the efficacy of classical methods in addressing segmentation tasks with simplicity and efficiency. By comparing these methods against recent generalist models like MedSAM, we seek to unravel insights into how such straightforward models can surpass large, pre-trained vision models. Furthermore, we aim to initiate discourse on enhancing MedSAM for future iterations. Our study offers the following contributions:

1. We investigate classical approaches for the fundus, microscopy, PET, and OCT modalities and investigate if they can outperform MedSAM's lightweight implementation (LiteMedSAM-Scribble[2]) in terms of segmentation accuracy and efficiency
2. We examine the failure cases and discuss why MedSAM silently fails on certain modalities and propose how to tackle this in future fine-tuning iterations
3. We make all our code and trained models publicly available to the community

2 Method

We go over the fundus, OCT, PET, and microscopy imaging modalities one-by-one and examine which classical approaches are able to outperform MedSAM and propose techniques to make MedSAM more efficient on modalities on which we could not outperform it. For the rest of the modalities in the challenge, we use MedSAM's lightweight implementation LiteMedSAM-Scribble.

---
[1] https://www.codabench.org/competitions/2566/.
[2] https://github.com/bowang-lab/MedSAM/tree/LiteMedSAMScribble.

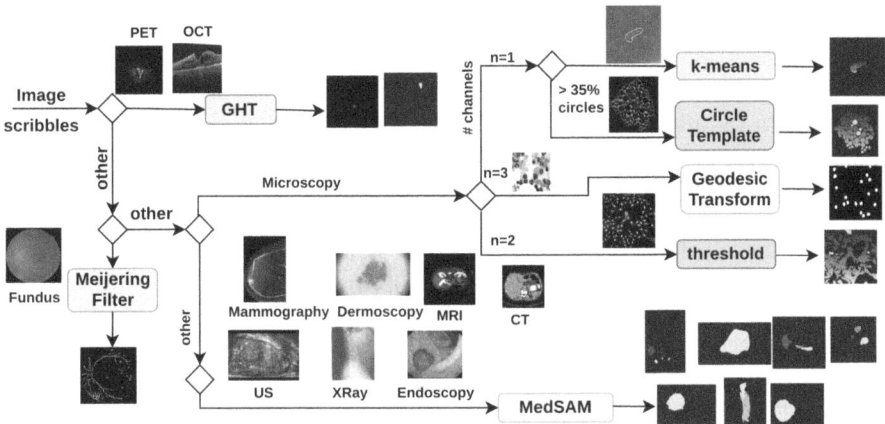

Fig. 1. Overview of our pipeline. We apply a different model for the various imaging modalities. For PET and OCT, we use the generalized histogram threshold (GHT) [4]. For microscopy, we check the number of channels and apply: (1) Geodesic Distance Transform [7] for $n = 3$; (2) a threshold, set to the mean image intensity for $n = 2$; (3) k-means clustering [28] for $n = 1$ if less than 35% of the bounding boxes contain circular objects, otherwise we apply a circle template matching. For fundus images, we apply a Meijering filter [31]. For the rest of the modalities, we use MedSAM.

Note: We only focus on the segmentation tasks seen in the MedSAM training dataset, e.g., only FDG-PET lesions segmentation and only vessel segmentation on fundus images. We also always use LiteMedSAM-Scribble as a lightweight MedSAM implementation and refer to it as MedSAM for brevity (Fig. 1).

2.1 PET and OCT

Tasks: The challenge presents PET data exclusively sourced from the AutoPET dataset [10], which is dedicated to the delineation of active tumor lesions across the whole body using Fludeoxyglucose (FDG) as the imaging agent. Similarly, the OCT data is drawn solely from a single dataset [1], concentrating on the segmentation of intraretinal cystoid fluid.

Challenges: The scarcity of public PET datasets for tumor segmentation [10,12,35] hampers the development of large-scale foundational models in this field. In the AutoPET dataset [11], PET lesions exhibit low contrast against surrounding tissues, and other healthy anatomical structures, such as the heart, brain, and bladder, also show high physiological uptake. Moreover, the top results from AutoPET 2023[3] are modest, with the highest Dice Score being 0.36, highlighting the difficulty of the task. For OCT, the images have high resolution but feature tiny target structures, resulting in a pronounced class imbalance.

---

[3] https://autopet-ii.grand-challenge.org/leaderboard/.

Classical Approaches: Thresholding techniques are commonly employed for tumor segmentation in PET scans [20,22,33], delivering promising results due to their simplicity and intuitive application. Scribble-based methods enhance this approach by allowing thresholds to be applied within the local context of the scribble, effectively excluding healthy tissues like the heart and brain that lie outside the defined boundaries. This is in contrast to previous methods that globally excluded regions such as the brain and bladder from the whole-body context [10,16,34]. Furthermore, using scribbles in OCT images helps mitigate class imbalance by focusing on the local area around the scribble, rather than the entire high-resolution image.

To effectively utilize the context around the scribbles for thresholding, we first convert the scribbles into bounding boxes by expanding them by 50 pixels in all directions. The bounding box B is computed as:

$$B = \{\min(S_x) - 50, \min(S_y) - 50, \max(S_x) + 50, \max(S_y) + 50\} \quad (1)$$

where S_x, S_y are the sets of x and y coordinates of all the provided scribbles.

Next, we calculate the Generalized Histogram Threshold (GHT) [4] by aggregating PET or OCT values from all expanded bounding boxes. This threshold is then applied to the entire volume to generate a unified prediction, with instance indices matching their respective scribble indices. For PET images, we retain values exceeding the threshold, as tumors exhibit high FDG uptake. In contrast, for OCT images, we keep values below the threshold due to the darker appearance of cystoid fluids.

2.2 Microscopy

Tasks: MedSAM's microscopy training data is exclusively derived from the NeurIPS 2022 CellSeg dataset [27]. This dataset poses significant challenges due to its diversity, containing images captured with various microscope types such as brightfield, fluorescent, phase-contrast (PC), and differential interference contrast (DIC). Additionally, the dataset includes a variety of cell types as segmentation targets, further increasing the complexity of the task.

Challenges: The microscopy imaging modality presents several significant challenges: (1) The number of instances per image can be exceptionally high, sometimes exceeding 1000, leading to substantial computational overhead when processing each bounding box individually. (2) The diversity of microscope types requires either a highly robust generalist model or multiple specialized models to handle the varying imaging characteristics effectively. (3) The high-resolution nature of the images is problematic, as critical details may be lost when resizing to smaller resolutions, such as MedSAM's resizing to 256 × 256.

Classical Approaches: We employ different classical methods based on the number of channels in the image. Additionally, we convert all scribbles into bounding boxes by expanding the scribble coordinates by 50 pixels in all directions, as described in Eq. 1.

Grayscale: When processing grayscale images, we apply a k-means clustering algorithm [28] with $k = 2$. To identify the foreground class, we analyze the pixel frequency for each class within a 10×10 window at the center of the bounding box, selecting the class with the higher pixel count. We use the Hough circle transform [23] to detect circles of various radii within each bounding box and for images where $> 35\%$ of the bounding boxes contain circular objects the largest detected circle serves as the prediction for that bounding box.

Two-Channel: For images with two channels (commonly three channels in practice, where one channel is filled with zeros, as seen in fluorescent microscopy), we employ the mean image intensity as a threshold. This simple yet effective method enables reliable segmentation.

RGB: For RGB images, we opt to utilize the scribbles as seeds for a Geodesic Distance Transform (GDT) [7]. For each scribble, we first transform it into a bounding box B and then apply the GDT within the bounding-box cropped image I_B with the scribble S used as seeds:

$$\text{GDT}(x, S, I_B)_{x \in I_B} = \min_{x' \in S} d(x, x') \qquad (2)$$

where $d(x, x')$ is the Geodesic distance as described in [7]. We utilize the GeodisTK[4] implementation for computing the Geodesic distance. The Geodesic distance quantifies the minimum cost of traversing from one pixel to another, considering the intensity gradients along the path, which aids in edge-aware segmentation. To apply it for segmentation, we assign all pixels x above the 70th percentile GDT_{70} as background and the rest as foreground.

$$\text{seg}(x) = \begin{cases} 0 & \text{if } \text{GDT}(x, S, I_B) > \text{GDT}_{70}, \\ 1 & \text{otherwise.} \end{cases} \qquad (3)$$

2.3 Fundus

Tasks: Fundus tasks concentrate on optic discs and cups [37] as well as more intricate structures such as retinal vessels [8,38]. In the case of vessels, bounding-box interaction signals prove inadequate for highlighting relevant context, however, scribbles are precise enough to indicate the underlying tubular segmentation targets.

Challenges: Fundus image datasets focusing on retinal vessels exhibit a large diversity in terms of labeling protocols and imaging characteristics, leading to a large domain shift between datasets [9]. In particular, MedSAM struggles with thin structures such as vessels as it has only been trained on optic disc and cups in the fundus domain and bounding boxes are a suboptimal guidance signal for such structures.

---

[4] https://github.com/taigw/GeodisTK.

Classical Approaches: To detect tubular-like structures, we apply a Meijering filter [31] over the whole image I and assign all pixel values x between the 90th and 95th percentile to the "foreground" as:

$$\text{seg}(x) = \begin{cases} 1 & \text{if Meijering}(I)_{90} < x < \text{Meijering}(I)_{95}, \\ 0 & \text{otherwise.} \end{cases}$$

We chose this interval as values above the 90th percentile have a high enough filter response to be considered tubular structures, but we observed that values above the 95th percentile correspond to noise.

2.4 Other Modalities

For the rest of the modalities (CT, MRI, X-Ray, Mammography, Endoscopy, Dermoscopy, Ultrasound), due to time constraints, we simply utilized MedSAM's lightweight pre-trained implementation LiteMedSAM-Scribble[5]. Note, that for this challenge, only 2D images from the CT and MRI domain were used (Table 1).

Table 1. Summary of our used models for the final submission.

Modality	Used Model
PET and OCT	Generalized Histogram Threshold [4]
Fundus	Meijering Filter [31]
Microscopy	k-means, Thresholding, Geodesic Distance [7], Circle Templates [23]
Other	LiteMedSAM [26]

2.5 Preprocessing

We re-used the code provided by LiteMedSAM-Scribble[6] for loading the data and inferring predictions and added more functions to the script for our methods. We avoid loading LiteMedSAM's weights for tasks which do not need it and import modules only immediately before they are used. The image loading and preprocessing is done as follows:

LiteMedSAM: The image is resized to a common size of 256×256 and padded to the shorter side to keep the original aspect ratio. Then, the image is min-max normalized and fed to the model. The model performs a forward pass for each scribble.

---

[5] https://github.com/bowang-lab/MedSAM/tree/LiteMedSAMScribble.
[6] https://github.com/bowang-lab/MedSAM/blob/LiteMedSAMScribble/CVPR24_LiteMedSAM_infer_scribble.py.

k-means and Geodesic Distance Transform (GDT): When applying k-means clustering or GDT, we use the unnormalized values within each transformed bounding box (computing via Eq. 1 for each scribble) and apply k-means/GDT for each instance.

Thresholding: Thresholds are always computed using the combination of all image values in the bounding boxes and then applied to the whole unnormalized image. Instance indices are then assigned according to the scribble indices.

Meijering Filter: The Meijering filter is applied on the whole unnormalized image. However, the image is first converted to grayscale by computing the mean over all of its channels.

2.6 Post-processing

After each forward pass, we perform only one post-processing transformation. For all images, we keep the largest connected component and fill all the holes within it.

3 Experiments

3.1 Dataset and Evaluation Measures

We used only the challenge dataset for model development and validation. The evaluation metrics include two accuracy measures-Dice Similarity Coefficient (DSC) and Normalized Surface Dice (NSD), alongside one efficiency measure: running time. These metrics collectively contribute to the ranking computation.

3.2 Implementation Details

Environment Settings. The development environments and requirements for all our methods are presented in Table 2.

Table 2. Development environments and requirements for all our methods.

System	Ubuntu 22.04.4 LTS
CPU[a]	Intel(R) Core(TM) i7-13700H CPU@5.00GHz
RAM	8 × 4 GB; 5200MT/s
GPU (number and type)	None
CUDA version	11.8
Programming language	Python 3.10.14
Deep learning framework	torch 2.2.1
Specific dependencies	None
Code	https://github.com/Zrrr1997/medsam_cvhci_scribble

[a] https://ark.intel.com/content/www/us/en/ark/products/232128/intel-core-i7-13700h-processor-24m-cache-up-to-5-00-ghz.html

Training Protocols. For MedSAM, we use the provided pre-trained LiteMedSAM-Scribble model whose training is described in [26]. As such, we did no training or fine-tuning whatsoever since we implemented only classical non-deep learning methods for our submission (Table 3).

Table 3. Training protocol for LiteMedSAM.

Pre-trained Model	LiteMedSAM [26]
Batch size	No further fine-tuning
Patch size	$256 \times 256 \times 3$
Total epochs	No further fine-tuning
Optimizer	No further fine-tuning
Initial learning rate (lr)	No further fine-tuning
Lr decay schedule	No further fine-tuning
Training time	No further fine-tuning
Loss function	No further fine-tuning
Number of model parameters	9.79M[a]
Number of flops	1.81G[b]
CO_2eq	No further fine-tuning

[a] https://github.com/sksq96/pytorch-summary
[b] https://github.com/facebookresearch/fvcore

4 Results and Discussion

We discuss the results of the individual modalities one-by-one as we propose different models for the OCT, PET, fundus, and micrsocopy imaging modalities.

4.1 PET and OCT

Efficiency Strategies: Thresholding eliminates the need for slow forward passes as the threshold is applied directly on the whole image in a single binary operation. Table 4 shows that the thresholding is extremely fast for both the PET and OCT modalities although it sacrifices some of the performance on the PET modality. We do not report the Dice and NSD for OCT as it is not part of the validation set but we report its efficiency on the training data. For this, we simply simulate empty OCT scribbles to measure the inference time.

How to Improve MedSAM on PET and OCT? The findings are alarming, as simple thresholding outperforms MedSAM in the PET task. We hypothesize that this discrepancy stems from the insufficiency of available data to enhance MedSAM's capacity for generalization and feature extraction sufficiently. Moreover, PET data could benefit from augmentation with anatomical labels derived

Table 4. Results on the validation stage of the challenge for PET. We cannot report results for OCT as there are no validation images for that domain but we do report the time per image on the training set [1].

Model	Dice	NSD	Time per Image
LiteMedSAM (PET)	66.80	49.42	0.01 s
Thresholding (PET)	49.00	67.00	0.77 s
LiteMedSAM (OCT)	-	-	1.78 s
Thresholding (OCT)	-	-	0.005 s

from paired CT scans [19,34], which was the winning approach in AutoPET 2023. This approach supplements the model with expert knowledge regarding affected anatomical regions, thereby enriching its understanding. Similarly, in the OCT domain, incorporating additional anatomical labels, such as those corresponding to various retinal layers, could lead to substantial improvements.

4.2 Microscopy

Efficiency Strategies: The classical approaches that we apply improve MedSAM's efficiency 15-fold. The segmentation results on the validation set are also x3 higher as seen in Table 5.

Table 5. Results on the validation stage of the challenge for Microscopy images

Model	Dice	NSD	Time per Image
LiteMedSAM	12.00	9.00	38.2 s
k-means OR threshold OR LiteMedSAM	31.81	32.55	2.4 s

How to Improve MedSAM on Microscopy? It appears that MedSAM encounters challenges with miniature scribbles, particularly when they are resized to fit its input size of 256 × 256. We believe that adopting a crop-then-infer approach could enhance MedSAM's performance. By cropping the image before inference, only the crop would require resizing, ensuring that the scribbles retain their detail and enabling MedSAM to focus more effectively on the local instance. However, further research is warranted to validate this hypothesis thoroughly.

4.3 Fundus

Efficiency Strategies: We focus on segmentation accuracy rather than efficiency in this domain. Thus, our model based on the Meijering filter [31] is

Table 6. Results on the validation stage of the challenge for Fundus images

Model	Dice	NSD	Time per Image
LiteMedSAM	5.00	0.00	1.2 s
Meijering filter	38.00	49.00	9.7 s

slower than the baseline (LiteMedSAM-Scribble), but achieves a much higher Dice score and NSD as seen in Table 6.

How to Improve MedSAM on Fundus? MedSAM is only trained on the tasks of optic disc and optic cup segmentation for fundus images [26]. As such, there is a domain/task gap when it is asked to segment thin vessel-like structures. However, there are many public fundus datasets with annotated retinal vessels [5,8,9,18,36,38] that could be used to fine-tune MedSAM on this specific task in future iterations.

4.4 Quantitative Results on Validation Set

Table 7 shows that our approach outperforms (on average) the baseline (LiteMed-SAM). However, we also show in Tables 4 and 5 that we are able to significantly improve the efficiency of the baseline on OCT, PET, and microscopy images.

Table 7. Quantitative evaluation results. Baseline: LiteMedSAM-Scribble. Ablations were done on the Geodesic percentile threshold in Eq. 3.

Target	Baseline		Ablation GDT_{10}		Ablation GDT_{90}		Proposed GDT_{70}	
	DSC(%)	NSD(%)	DSC(%)	NSD(%)	DSC(%)	NSD (%)	DSC(%)	NSD (%)
CT	81.00	83.00	81.00	83.00	81.00	83.00	81.00	83.00
MR	70.00	77.00	70.00	77.00	70.00	77.00	70.00	77.00
PET	67.00	90.00	49.00	67.00	49.00	67.00	49.00	67.00
US	85.00	88.00	85.00	88.00	85.00	88.00	85.00	88.00
X-Ray	22.00	19.00	22.00	19.00	22.00	19.00	22.00	19.00
Dermoscopy	90.00	91.00	90.00	91.00	90.00	91.00	90.00	91.00
Endoscopy	94.00	97.00	94.00	97.00	94.00	97.00	94.00	97.00
Fundus	5.00	0.00	38.00	49.00	38.00	49.00	38.00	49.00
Microscopy	12.00	9.00	22.44	24.12	30.22	30.78	31.81	32.55
Average	58.00	62.00	61.27	66.12	62.14	66.86	62.31	67.01

4.5 Segmentation Efficiency Results on Validation Set

The efficiency on a few samples from the validation set are listed in Table 8. Our optimization on the PET and microscopy modalities contributes to a much more efficient prediction time, especially when there are many instances in the image such as for 2D_Microscope_0016 where the inference is reduced from 127 s to only 6 s with our approach. Our ablation regarding the Geodesic percentile also demonstrates negligible differences in terms of efficiency.

Table 8. Quantitative evaluation of segmentation efficiency in terms of running time (s) on the hardware specified in Table 2. Abl.: Ablation

Case ID	Size	#Objects	Baseline	Abl. GDT_{90}	Ours GDT_{70}
2D_US_0525	(256, 256, 3)	1	1.9	1.9	1.9
2D_X-Ray_0001	(2487, 2048, 3)	7	6.0	6.0	6.0
2D_Dermoscopy_0003	(3024, 4032, 3)	1	3.7	3.7	3.7
2D_Endoscopy_0086	(480, 560, 3)	1	2.1	2.1	2.1
2D_Fundus_0003	(2048, 2048, 3)	1	2.5	9.9	9.9
2D_Microscope_0008	(1536, 2040, 3)	19	2.6	1.9	1.8
2D_Microscope_0016	(1920, 2560, 3)	241	126.8	6.3	5.7
2D_PET_0001	(200, 200, 3)	1	1.9	0.06	0.06
2D_PET_0002	(192, 192, 3)	1	1.9	0.08	0.08

4.6 Qualitative Results on Validation Set

We show some qualitative image examples for the predictions of our models on various modalities.

PET and OCT Threshold-Based Methods. Figure 2 shows examples of predictions on OCT and PET images. Although thresholds are more efficient than MedSAM, they do produce noisier predictions.

Microscopy Classical Approaches. Figure 3 demonstrate failure cases of MedSAM in the microscopy domain. It seems that MedSAM struggles with small structures with ambiguous boundaries. MedSAM also struggles with multiple instances indicated with scribbles and focuses only on a small subset of them, or even only on one (last two rows). In contrast, classical approaches perform quite well in these domains, landing a spot in our methodology for our final submission to the challenge.

Fundus. Figure 4 shows examples for predictions on fundus images. Although the filter produces noisy artifacts, it does segment a large portion of the retinal vessels. MedSAM, on the other hand, clearly focuses on the optic disc and cup as the model has no notion of what the target task is since it has only been trained on segmenting discs and cups. This bias can be alleviated by either fine-tuning MedSAM on more datasets, containing new tasks, such as vessel segmentation, or to provide contextual information on what is supposed to be segmented in the image, e.g., with an additional "task prompt".

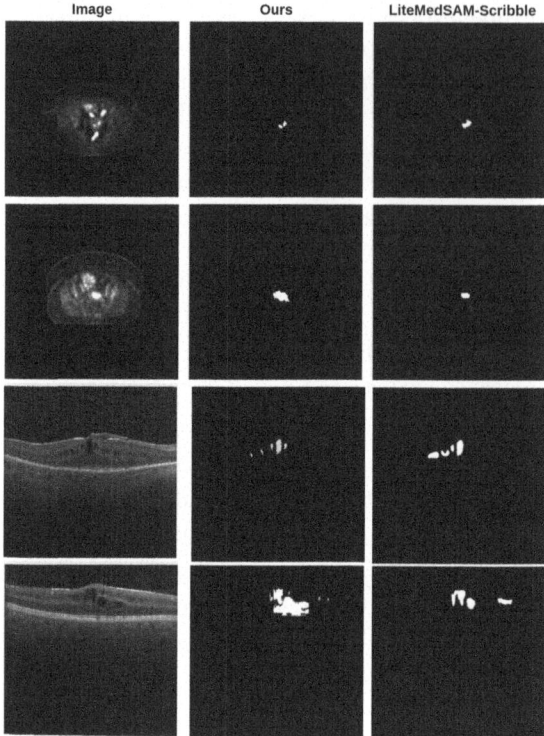

Fig. 2. Examples for OCT and PET predictions.

4.7 Results on Final Testing Set

The results on the final test set are presented in Table 9. Our focus on classical methods is evident in the leading runtimes on the leaderboard, where we secured 1st place across all modalities. By making only minor adjustments to the post-processing pipeline of LiteMedSAMScribble, our submission significantly outperforms the baseline in the CT and X-Ray domains. However, this improvement is not observed in the MR, Endoscopy, and Ultrasound modalities. We ranked last in the Fundus domain, possibly due to our assumption that all images contain vessel-like structures as targets, thereby overlooking other features, such as optic discs. Overall, our method achieved 2nd place on the final leaderboard out of a total of four methods.

4.8 Post-challenge Analysis

During the post-challenge phase, we have participated in the **Performance Booster** track without the use of any external datasets. Here, we describe how we have improved our methods.

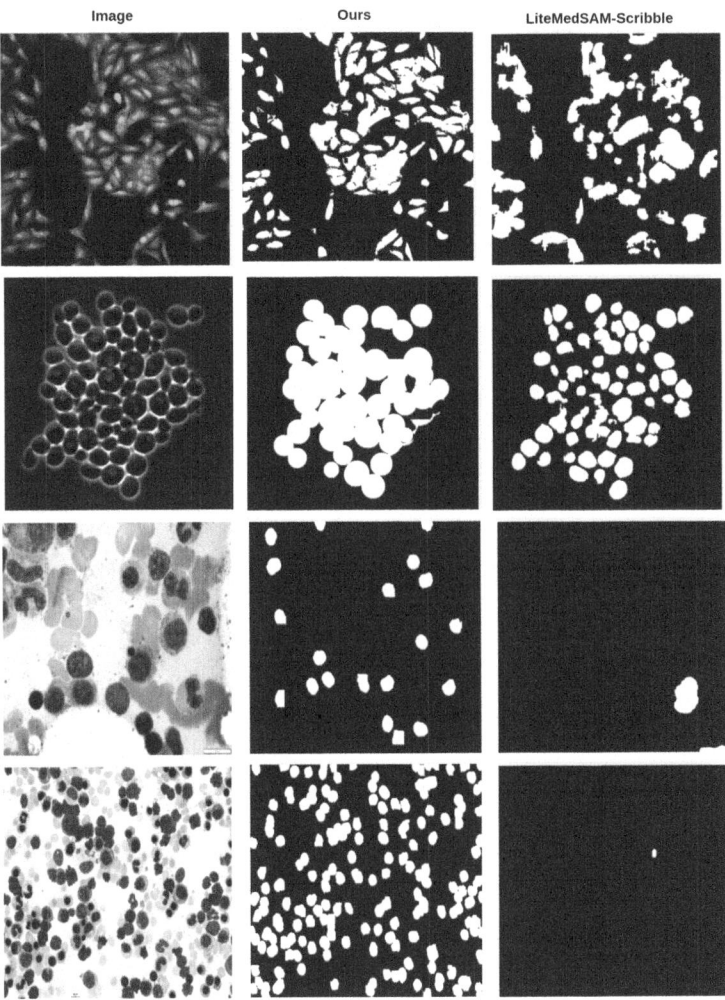

Fig. 3. Examples of microscopy predictions from the validation set.

Changed Methodology. We made only a few adjustments to our methods, focusing on incremental improvements. For MR, Endoscopy, and Ultrasound, we remove all of our previous post-processing as we observed as decline in performance in Table 7. Fo the Fundus domain, we distinguish between vessels and optic discs as a segmentation target by counting the number of scribbles. If the count is below 4, we simply use the baseline (LiteMedSAMScribble), otherwise, we use our Meijering filtering approach.

Results from Post-challenge Analysis. The changes in the code led to an improvement in the runtime for the MR, Endoscopy, and Ultrasound domains

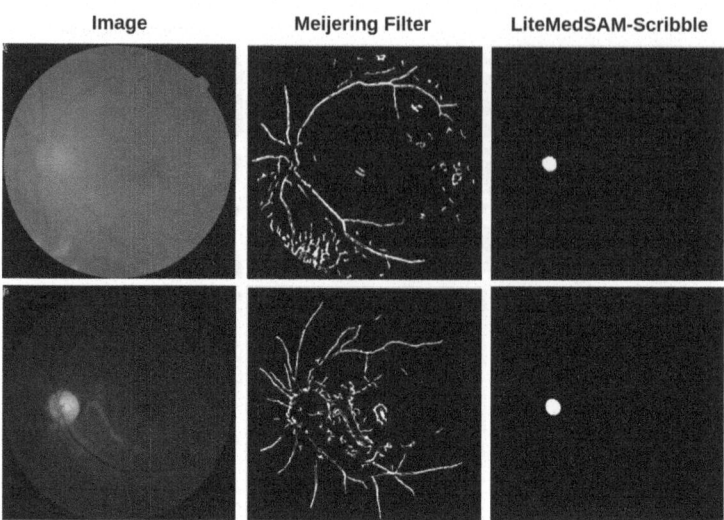

Fig. 4. Examples for Fundus predictions

Table 9. Results on the testing stage of the challenge. Worst rank is 4

Modality	Dice (Rank)	NSD (Rank)	Runtime (Rank)
CT	68.86 (1)	74.87 (1)	5.37 (1)
MR	49.60 (3)	53.88 (3)	5.08 (1)
X-Ray	56.07 (1)	64.48 (2)	5.80 (1)
Endoscopy	83.69 (3)	85.78 (3)	5.09 (1)
Fundus	0.00 (4)	0.00 (4)	15.48 (1)
Microscopy	37.03 (2)	38.29 (2)	1.36 (1)
OCT	22.11 (1)	23.12 (3)	1.08 (1)
PET	65.17 (3)	77.80 (3)	0.97 (1)
US	60.89 (3)	61.36 (3)	5.26 (1)

in terms of runtime as we omitted the postprocessing. For Fundus, we see a dramatic improvement of 79% Dice and 81% NSD. The changes in performance are listed in Table 10.

Table 10. Post-challenge changes in performance

Modality	Dice	NSD	Runtime
US	60.89	61.36	5.04
MR	49.60	53.88	5.00
Endoscopy	83.69	85.78	4.94
Fundus	79.46	81.43	6.05

4.9 Limitation and Future Work

Our methodology has two primary limitations: (1) it concentrates on specialized models tailored to individual modalities rather than developing a model capable of reasoning and segmenting structures across any modality, thus restricting our approach's generalizability; (2) our models rely on strong assumptions about the underlying task, such as vessel segmentation in fundus images, and if the task on the test set changes, our models are likely to fail completely, as observed with MedSAM in Fig. 2. However, we deliberately use this segmented approach to identify and understand the weaknesses in MedSAM, with the goal of improving it in future iterations. Our findings indicate that incorporating explicit assumptions about imaging modalities can provide a robust signal, sometimes outperforming MedSAM in specific cases, but it needs to be applied adaptively.

A promising future direction involves adding an adaptive task prompt to MedSAM. This would act as a model or an additional input that provides information about the underlying task, such as "fundus vessel segmentation" or "fundus optic cup segmentation." This can potentially adjust MedSAM's mode to the specific task, producing more accurate predictions and avoiding the training biases seen in Fig. 2. In essence, informing the model about the specific segmentation task should enhance its adaptability and performance. This approach allows the integration of domain knowledge directly into the model, potentially tailoring it to specific domains and tasks.

5 Conclusion

Our results suggest that MedSAM needs further fine-tuning on scribble-based data and a method for adapting to new tasks it has not encountered, such as vessel segmentation. Our findings reveal the importance of integrating explicit task knowledge to surpass MedSAM's current performance. We propose for future iterations that a task adapter, which supplies information about the target structure and imaging modality, could boost MedSAM's effectiveness in these challenging areas.

Acknowledgements. We thank all the data owners for making the medical images publicly available and CodaLab [43] for hosting the challenge platform. The present contribution is supported by the Helmholtz Association under the joint research school "HIDSS4Health - Helmholtz Information and Data Science School for Health. Parts of this work were performed on the HoreKa supercomputer funded by the Ministry of Science, Research and the Arts Baden-Württemberg and by the Federal Ministry of Education and Research.

Disclosure of Interests. The authors have no competing interests to declare that are relevant to the content of this article.

References

1. Ahmed, Z., Ahmed, M., Baqai, A., Umrani, F.A.: Intraretinal cystoid fluid (2022). https://doi.org/10.34740/KAGGLE/DS/2277068. https://www.kaggle.com/ds/2277068
2. Antonelli, M., et al.: The medical segmentation decathlon. Nat. Commun. **13**(1), 4128 (2022)
3. Asad, M., et al.: Adaptive multi-scale online likelihood network for AI-assisted interactive segmentation. In: International Conference on Medical Image Computing and Computer-Assisted Intervention, pp. 564–574. Springer, Cham (2023)
4. Barron, J.T.: A generalization of otsu's method and minimum error thresholding. In: Computer Vision–ECCV 2020: 16th European Conference, Glasgow, UK, 23–28 August 2020, Proceedings, Part V 16, pp. 455–470. Springer, Cham (2020)
5. Budai, A., Bock, R., Maier, A., Hornegger, J., Michelson, G., et al.: Robust vessel segmentation in fundus images. Int. J. Biomed. Imaging **2013** (2013)
6. Chen, X., Cheung, Y.S.J., Lim, S.N., Zhao, H.: Scribbleseg: scribble-based interactive image segmentation. arXiv preprint arXiv:2303.11320 (2023)
7. Criminisi, A., Sharp, T., Blake, A.: Geos: geodesic image segmentation. In: Computer Vision–ECCV 2008: 10th European Conference on Computer Vision, Marseille, France, 12–18 October 2008, Proceedings, Part I 10, pp. 99–112. Springer (2008)
8. Fraz, M.M., et al.: An ensemble classification-based approach applied to retinal blood vessel segmentation. IEEE Trans. Biomed. Eng. **59**(9), 2538–2548 (2012)
9. Galdran, A., Anjos, A., Dolz, J., Chakor, H., Lombaert, H., Ayed, I.B.: State-of-the-art retinal vessel segmentation with minimalistic models. Sci. Rep. **12**(1), 6174 (2022)
10. Gatidis, S., et al.: The autopet challenge: towards fully automated lesion segmentation in oncologic PET/CT imaging (2023)
11. Gatidis, S., et al.: The autopet challenge: towards fully automated lesion segmentation in oncologic PET/CT imaging. Preprint at Research Square (Nature Portfolio) (2023). https://doi.org/10.21203/rs.3.rs-2572595/v1
12. Gatidis, S., et al.: A whole-body FDG-PET/CT dataset with manually annotated tumor lesions. Sci. Data **9**(1), 601 (2022)
13. Gotkowski, K., Gonzalez, C., Kaltenborn, I., Fischbach, R., Bucher, A., Mukhopadhyay, A.: i3deep: efficient 3D interactive segmentation with the NNU-Net. In: International Conference on Medical Imaging with Deep Learning, pp. 441–456. PMLR (2022)

14. Hadlich, M., Marinov, Z., Kim, M., Nasca, E., Kleesiek, J., Stiefelhagen, R.: Sliding window fastedit: a framework for lesion annotation in whole-body pet images. arXiv preprint arXiv:2311.14482 (2023)
15. Hallitschke, V.J., et al.: Multimodal interactive lung lesion segmentation: a framework for annotating PET/CT images based on physiological and anatomical cues. In: 2023 IEEE 20th International Symposium on Biomedical Imaging (ISBI), pp. 1–5. IEEE (2023)
16. Heiliger, L., et al.: Autopet challenge: combining nn-unet with swin unetr augmented by maximum intensity projection classifier. arXiv preprint arXiv:2209.01112 (2022)
17. Hernandez Petzsche, M.R., et al.: ISLES 2022: a multi-center magnetic resonance imaging stroke lesion segmentation dataset. Sci. Data **9**(1), 762 (2022)
18. Hoover, A., Kouznetsova, V., Goldbaum, M.: Locating blood vessels in retinal images by piecewise threshold probing of a matched filter response. IEEE Trans. Med. Imaging **19**(3), 203–210 (2000)
19. Jaus, A., et al.: Towards unifying anatomy segmentation: automated generation of a full-body CT dataset via knowledge aggregation and anatomical guidelines. arXiv preprint arXiv:2307.13375 (2023)
20. Jentzen, W., Freudenberg, L., Eising, E.G., Heinze, M., Brandau, W., Bockisch, A.: Segmentation of pet volumes by iterative image thresholding. J. Nucl. Med. **48**(1), 108–114 (2007)
21. Ji, Y., et al.: Amos: a large-scale abdominal multi-organ benchmark for versatile medical image segmentation. Adv. Neural. Inf. Process. Syst. **35**, 36722–36732 (2022)
22. Kim, M., et al.: Evaluation of thresholding methods for the quantification of [68GA] Ga-PSMA-11 PET molecular tumor volume and their effect on survival prediction in patients with advanced prostate cancer undergoing [177LU] LU-PSMA-617 radioligand therapy. Eur. J. Nucl. Med. Mol. Imaging **50**(7), 2196–2209 (2023)
23. Kimme, C., Ballard, D., Sklansky, J.: Finding circles by an array of accumulators. Commun. ACM **18**(2), 120–122 (1975)
24. Kirillov, A., et al.: Segment anything. In: Proceedings of the IEEE/CVF International Conference on Computer Vision, pp. 4015–4026 (2023)
25. Luo, X., et al.: Mideepseg: minimally interactive segmentation of unseen objects from medical images using deep learning. Med. Image Anal. **72**, 102102 (2021)
26. Ma, J., He, Y., Li, F., Han, L., You, C., Wang, B.: Segment anything in medical images. Nat. Commun. **15**(1), 654 (2024)
27. Ma, J., et al.: The multi-modality cell segmentation challenge: towards universal solutions. Nat. Methods (2024). https://doi.org/10.1038/s41592-024-02233-6
28. MacQueen, J., et al.: Some methods for classification and analysis of multivariate observations. In: Proceedings of the Fifth Berkeley Symposium on Mathematical Statistics and Probability, vol. 1, pp. 281–297. Oakland, CA, USA (1967)
29. Marinov, Z., Jäger, P.F., Egger, J., Kleesiek, J., Stiefelhagen, R.: Deep interactive segmentation of medical images: a systematic review and taxonomy. arXiv preprint arXiv:2311.13964 (2023)
30. Marinov, Z., Stiefelhagen, R., Kleesiek, J.: Guiding the guidance: a comparative analysis of user guidance signals for interactive segmentation of volumetric images. In: International Conference on Medical Image Computing and Computer-Assisted Intervention, pp. 637–647. Springer (2023)
31. Meijering, E., Jacob, M., Sarria, J.C., Steiner, P., Hirling, H., Unser, E.M.: Design and validation of a tool for neurite tracing and analysis in fluorescence microscopy images. Cytometry Part A J. Int. Soc. Anal. Cytol. **58**(2), 167–176 (2004)

32. Menze, B.H., et al.: The multimodal brain tumor image segmentation benchmark (brats). IEEE Trans. Med. Imaging **34**(10), 1993–2024 (2014)
33. Moussallem, M., Valette, P.J., Traverse-Glehen, A., Houzard, C., Jegou, C., Giammarile, F.: New strategy for automatic tumor segmentation by adaptive thresholding on PET/CT images. J. Appl. Clin. Med. Phys. **13**(5), 236–251 (2012)
34. Murugesan, G.K., et al.: Improving lesion segmentation in FDG-18 whole-body PET/CT scans using multilabel approach: Autopet II challenge. arXiv preprint arXiv:2311.01574 (2023)
35. Oreiller, V., et al.: Head and neck tumor segmentation in PET/CT: the hecktor challenge. Med. Image Anal. **77**, 102336 (2022)
36. Orlando, J.I., Barbosa Breda, J., Van Keer, K., Blaschko, M.B., Blanco, P.J., Bulant, C.A.: Towards a glaucoma risk index based on simulated hemodynamics from fundus images. In: Medical Image Computing and Computer Assisted Intervention–MICCAI 2018: 21st International Conference, Granada, Spain, 16–20 September 2018, Proceedings, Part II 11, pp. 65–73. Springer (2018)
37. Porwal, P., et al.: Indian diabetic retinopathy image dataset (IDRID): a database for diabetic retinopathy screening research. Data **3**(3), 25 (2018)
38. Staal, J., Abràmoff, M.D., Niemeijer, M., Viergever, M.A., Van Ginneken, B.: Ridge-based vessel segmentation in color images of the retina. IEEE Trans. Med. Imaging **23**(4), 501–509 (2004)
39. Wang, G., et al.: Interactive medical image segmentation using deep learning with image-specific fine tuning. IEEE Trans. Med. Imaging **37**(7), 1562–1573 (2018)
40. Wang, G., et al.: Deepigeos: a deep interactive geodesic framework for medical image segmentation. IEEE Trans. Pattern Anal. Mach. Intell. **41**(7), 1559–1572 (2018)
41. Wasserthal, J., et al.: Totalsegmentator: robust segmentation of 104 anatomic structures in CT images. Radiol. Artif. Intell. **5**(5) (2023)
42. Wong, H.E., Rakic, M., Guttag, J., Dalca, A.V.: Scribbleprompt: fast and flexible interactive segmentation for any medical image. arXiv preprint arXiv:2312.07381 (2023)
43. Xu, Z., et al.: Codabench: flexible, easy-to-use, and reproducible meta-benchmark platform. Patterns **3**(7), 100543 (2022)
44. Zhao, F., Xie, X.: An overview of interactive medical image segmentation. Ann. BMVA **2013**(7), 1–22 (2013)

Rep-MedSAM: Towards Real-Time and Universal Medical Image Segmentation

Muxin Wei⬤, Shuqing Chen(✉), Silin Wu, and Dabin Xu

School of Medicine and Health, Harbin Institute of Technology, Harbin, China
chenshuqing@hit.edu.cn

Abstract. Medical image segmentation has been a pivotal step in clinical practice, enabling more precise analysis of medical images. MedSAM, as a medical image segmentation foundation model, has significantly extended the ability of SAM to segment a broad spectrum of different modalities of medical images and achieves excellent performance comparing specialist models. However, with a heavy image encoder, MedSAM falls short of clinical usage in terms of time efficiency. Therefore, the CVPR 2024: Segment Anything In Medical Images On Laptop Challenge addresses performance and efficiency in a task, where the model infers with only CPU. To this end, we propose Rep-MedSAM, which integrates RepViT, a mobile-friendly CNN with efficient designs of lightweight ViTs, by replacing the image encoder in MedSAM. Our method is simple but effective, including knowledge distillation from pretrained MedSAM, whole-pipeline training and fine-tuning with extra datasets. We conduct all experiments on the challenge. Our method achieved an average DSC of 85.90% and an average NSD of 87.07% on validation. As for time cost, our method shows thrilling results compared to the baseline on validation. The average time for 2D and 3D cases is 0.47 s and 22.47 s, respectively, with an average of 2.41 s for each case. Our code is available at GitHub.

Keywords: MedSAM · Rep-ViT · Medical Images

1 Introduction

Accurate and efficient segmentation is an indispensable part of clinical analysis, which entails the identifying and delineating of regions of interest (ROIs) involving various of medical targets, across an extensive spectrum of modalities. In recent years, deep learning-based methods have been widely adopted to segment medical images automatically. Specifically, many important baseline methods like U-Net [23], limited to their task-specific nature, their performance on new tasks or different data modalities, are prone to decrease. To address this lack of generality, prompt-based foundation models such as the segment anything model (SAM) [15] render few-shot or even zero-shot learning in medical images possible. Nevertheless, trained with a large amount of natural images, SAM can hardly be applied to medical images, as natural images are significantly different from medical images. Following SAM, MedSAM [18] performs excellently in medical images with prompts. The original MedSAM is built with three main components, including an image encoder, a prompt encoder, and a mask decoder. However, with an inadequate inference speed, primarily due to the heavy image encoder, Vision Transformer [6] MedSAM falls short of clinical usage on real-time requirements. Inspired by MobileSAM [28], the proposed baseline was distilled and replaced with a lightweight image encoder TinyViT [26] from the MedSAM image encoder ViT by imposing the image embedding outputs to be the same as MedSAM, after which we fine-tune the whole model pipeline. Despite a remarkable improvement in inference speed, the baseline still stumbles over limited computational budgets. Therefore, the CVPR 2024: SEGMENT ANYTHING IN MEDICAL IMAGES ON LAPTOP Challenge aims at efficient and well-performing semi-automatic segmentations for multimodal medical images with bounding box prompts. During the validation and test phase, the model runs in a docker environment, where only CPU and 8G of RAM are available for inference.

Recent works for downsizing ViT have shown promising inference speed in mobile devices (e.g., TinyViT, MobileViT [20]). However, carrying a large number of parameters, many ViT-based models fail to meet resource-constrained mobile devices. To this end, we propose a simple but effective method based on RepViT [25], a pure CNN architecture utilizing a lightweight structure from both CNN and ViT. RepViT has demonstrated state-of-the-art performance on various tasks versus lightweight CNNs and ViTs, showing favourable performance and inference speed. Therefore, we use RepViT as the image encoder, replacing TinyViT in the baseline.

Our main contributions of this work can be summarized as follows:

- We propose a simple but effective pipeline using a teacher-student framework to distil knowledge from a well-trained MedSAM.
- With some small architecture and preprocessing adaptations, we significantly reduce computational and time costs during distillation.
- We evaluate the effectiveness of the proposed method in context of the challenge, where we realize performance and efficiency improvement over baseline.

2 Method

As illustrated in Fig. 1, our framework consist of the MedSAM model (i.e., the teacher model for distillation) and our Rep-MedSAM model (i.e., the student model) to achieve efficient learning and inference.

2.1 Preprocessing

The challenge dataset contains over one millions image-mask pairs, covering 11 medical image modalities and more than 20 cancer types. To attain fast,

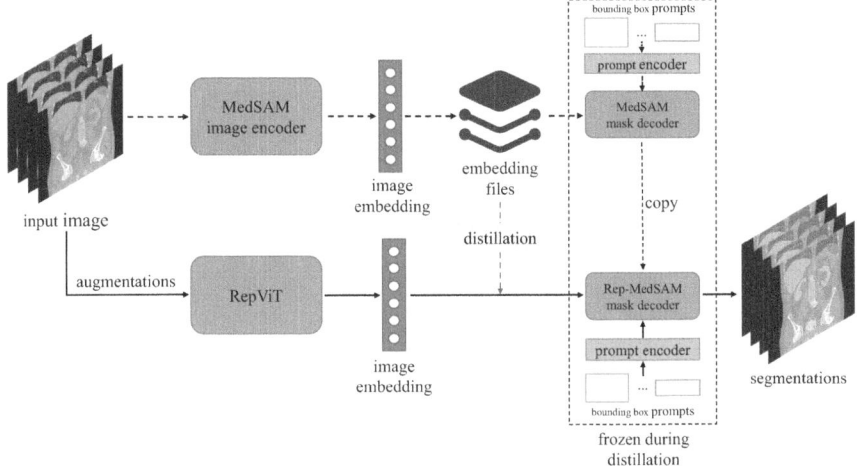

Fig. 1. Overview of our proposed framework.

consistent and compatible preprocessing and data loading, following [18], we make use of the following preprocessing steps:

- Dataset format conversion.
- Image intensity clipping and normalization.
- Identify non-zero slices for annotations, then crop images to non-zero regions with annotations.
- Resize all images to a uniform size of 256 × 256 × 3.
- To promote distillation efficiency, we store image embeddings from the MedSAM image encoder.

During intensity clipping, we perform specific strategies for different modalities. Notably, we normalize the Hounsfield units for CT images using typical window width and level values for specific anatomy. For grayscale images (e.g., MR, X-ray, Ultrasound, Mammography and OCT), intensity values are clipped between the 0.5th and 99.5th percentiles. As for RGB images (e.g., Dermoscopy, Endoscopy, Fundus and Pathology), if images with intensities that were within the range of [0, 255], their intensities remained unaltered, otherwise normalized to the range of [0, 255]. In addition, for CT and MR images, we use axial slices as training inputs. Finally, to train efficiently, we resize all images to a uniform size of 256 × 256 × 3.

2.2 Network Architecture

We inherit the mask decoder and prompt encoder from MedSAM while replacing the bulky image encoder with RepViT-M1.0. Figure 2 shows the macro designs of our image encoder. Our image encoder is composed of a stem, two downsampling layers and an encoding layer. Between each layer, we adopt a ratio

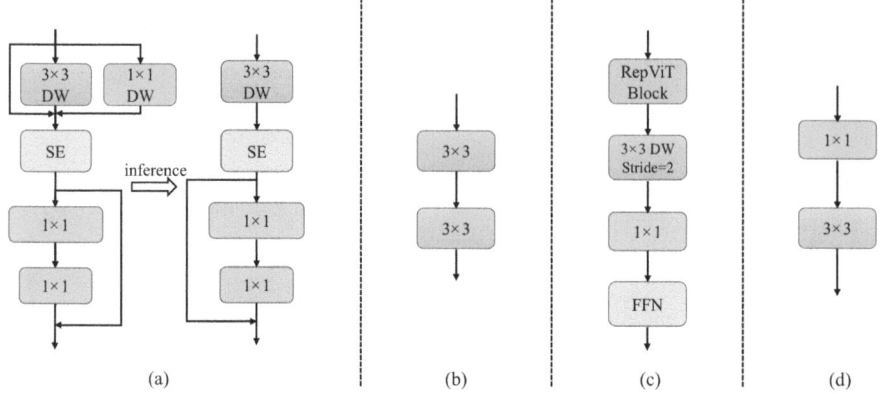

Fig. 2. Macro designs. (a), (b), (c) and (d) are designs of the RepViT block, stem, downsampling layer and encoding layer, respectively. Convolutional layers are simply denoted by the kernel size. The norm layer and nonlinearity are omitted.

of 1:1:8 to insert multiple RepViT blocks. RepViT reduces computational and memory costs using the structural re-parameterization technique [5], accelerating inference speed with limited computational resources. Such a technique can reduce time cost during inference while maintaining performance. Table 6 shows the time cost with and without structural re-parameterization on the validation set.

2.3 Pretraining Distillation

Inspired by [26], instead of finetune-stage distillation, we pay most attention to pretraining distillation. Pretraining with distillation is insufficient and resources costly, as passing training data through the teacher model in each iteration and each epoch takes up a fair portion of computational resources. Meanwhile, a large teacher model may occupy most GPU memory, dragging the training speed down as a result of smaller batch size. To address this problem, we propose a pretraining distillation framework similar to [26,28]. However, no data augmentation is applied to training images when acquiring image embeddings from MedSAM. By contrast, we applied vertical and horizontal flipping to input images of our student model, so as to align the teacher model with better generality.

Mathematically, for an input image x, we store image embedding prediction $\hat{\mathbf{y}} = T(x)$ from the teacher image encoder, where $T(\cdot)$ is the teacher image encoder model. Correspondingly, we have $S(\mathcal{A}(x))$, where $S(\cdot)$ is the student image encoder and $\mathcal{A}(x)$ is the input image with data augmentation $\mathcal{A}$. During pretraining, we only need to recover $\hat{\mathbf{y}}$ from stored files, and optimize the following objective function for student model distillation:

$$\mathcal{L} = MSE(\hat{\mathbf{y}}, S(\mathcal{A}(x))), \tag{1}$$

where $MSE(\cdot)$ is the mean squared error. It is to be observed that our strategy to distil the image encoder is label-free, which enables large-scale pretraining. As depicted in Fig. 1, we copied and frozen the mask decoder from MedSAM. This is because image embeddings generated from the student image encoder are sufficiently close to the original teacher model. We conducted pretraining distillation with challenge datasets, except for the CT modality. We use only 20% of CT images, due to insufficient space, uniformly sampling from the challenge dataset to preserve data diversity.

2.4 Post-processing

We do not make use of any post-processing in the context of this challenge.

3 Experiments

3.1 Dataset and Evaluation Measures

We used the challenge dataset and supplementary public datasets for model development. To learn more about the supplementary datasets we used, please refer to Table 8. The evaluation metrics include two accuracy measures: Dice Similarity Coefficient (DSC) and Normalized Surface Dice (NSD)-alongside one efficiency measure-running time. These metrics collectively contribute to the ranking computation.

Table 1. Development environments and requirements.

System	Ubuntu 20.04.4 LTS
CPU	Intel(R) Xeon(R) Gold 6248R@3.0GHz
RAM	29GB
GPU (number and type)	One Nvidia Tesla V100S PCIe 32GB
CUDA version	12.2
Programming language	Python 3.9
Deep learning framework	PyTorch (torch 2.0, torchvision 0.15.1)
Code	GitHub

3.2 Implementation Details

Environment Settings. The development environments and requirements are outlined in Table 1.

Training Protocols. The training protocols for pretraining distillation, pipeline training and fine-tuning with supplementary datasets are listed in Table 2, Table 3 and Table 4. During pretraining distillation, no data augmentation is applied the to teacher model. We applied data augmentation of vertical and horizontal flipping for student model during distillation and pipeline training, combining color jitter during fine-tuning with supplementary datasets.

During pipeline training, we use all challenge datasets, while for the fine-tuning stage, we abandon CT images in the challenge dataset and train with

Table 2. Pretraining distillation protocols.

Pre-trained Model	MedSAM [18]
Student Model	Rep-MedSAM
Data augmentation	Vertical and Horizontal Flip
Batch size	16
Patch size	$3 \times 256 \times 256$
Total epochs	5
Optimizer	AdamW
Initial learning rate (lr)	5E−4
Lr decay schedule	ReduceLROnPlateau
Training time	60 h
Loss function	Mean squared error
Number of model parameters	10.57M[a]
Number of flops	468G[b]

[a] https://github.com/sksq96/pytorch-summary
[b] https://github.com/facebookresearch/fvcore

Table 3. Pipeline training protocols.

Network architecture	Rep-MedSAM
Data augmentation	Vertical and Horizontal Flip
Batch size	16
Patch size	$3 \times 256 \times 256$
Total epochs	8
Optimizer	AdamW
Initial learning rate (lr)	3E−4
Lr decay schedule	ReduceLROnPlateau
Training time	128 h
Loss function	Dice loss, BCE loss and IoU loss
Number of model parameters	10.57M
Number of flops	468G

Table 4. Fine-tuning protocols.

Network architecture	Rep-MedSAM
Data augmentation	Flip and Color Jitter
Batch size	16
Patch size	$3 \times 256 \times 256$
Total epochs	12
Optimizer	AdamW
Initial learning rate (lr)	2E−5
Lr decay schedule	ReduceLROnPlateau
Training time	54 h
Loss function	Dice loss, BCE loss and IoU loss
Number of model parameters	10.57M
Number of flops	468G

supplementary CT datasets only. For other modalities, we trained both challenge datasets and supplementary datasets.

As mentioned in Sect. 2.3, we use MSE as the loss function during pretraining distillation. However, for the pipeline training and fine-tuning stages, we follow the loss function in baseline, using the combination of Dice loss and BCE loss for mask loss, while IoU loss for IoU between prediction and ground truth.

4 Results and Discussion

4.1 Quantitative Results on Validation Set

Table 5 presents the results of our Rep-MedSAM compared to the baseline on validation set at different stage. Our method manifests outstanding performance on most modalities. It is noteworthy that our method excels in Microscopy and PET images compared to the baseline. However, our method exhibits mediocre performance on PET and US images.

We conducted ablation studies on efficiency between the baseline and our Rep-MedSAM with and without structural re-parameterization technique in terms of time. We built Docker images for different methods and ran under the same environment for fair comparison. The last two columns refer to the time cost of our method without and with the structural re-parameterization technique. Compared to the baseline, both methods significantly decrease inference time by a large margin, especially in 3D cases with large volumes. Notably, when encountering multiple targets, like pathological images, it is the mask decoder which contributes the most to time cost, rather than the image encoder.

Figure 3 shows 4 representative segmentation results of Rep-MedSAM on unseen data, covering both large and small targets. Our method successfully segments targets in CT and MR cases. In OCT and US cases, blue arrows in

Table 5. Quantitative evaluation results on the validation set.

Modality	Baseline		Distillation		Pipeline Training		Fine-tuning	
	DSC(%)	NSD(%)	DSC(%)	NSD(%)	DSC(%)	NSD(%)	DSC(%)	NSD(%)
CT	92.26	94.90	69.33	71.96	89.47	91.66	**92.89**	**95.34**
MR	**89.63**	**93.37**	78.97	80.78	81.34	84.25	87.30	91.06
PET	51.58	25.17	61.46	42.22	**69.91**	**52.33**	66.15	47.09
US	**94.77**	**96.81**	80.03	84.73	83.77	89.14	80.67	86.18
X-Ray	75.83	80.39	76.36	82.12	78.33	84.29	**81.51**	**87.38**
Dermatology	92.47	93.85	92.62	94.13	92.72	94.26	**93.98**	**95.48**
Endoscopy	**96.04**	98.11	93.54	96.31	85.77	89.99	95.67	**98.16**
Fundus	94.81	96.41	93.47	95.13	91.46	93.23	**94.93**	**96.57**
Microscopy	61.63	65.38	75.00	81.63	76.26	82.79	**80.04**	**86.35**
Average	83.22	82.71	80.08	81.00	83.23	84.66	**85.90**	**87.07**

Table 6. Quantitative evaluation of efficiency regarding running time(s).

Case ID	Size	Num. Objects	Baseline	w/o	w/
3DBox_CT_0566	(287, 512, 512)	6	436.97	247.97	194.22
3DBox_CT_0888	(237, 512, 512)	6	115.53	66.78	53.44
3DBox_CT_0860	(246, 512, 512)	1	16.60	9.95	7.96
3DBox_MR_0621	(115, 400, 400)	6	174.80	102.65	80.45
3DBox_MR_0121	(64, 290, 320)	6	119.09	66.01	54.62
3DBox_MR_0179	(84, 512, 512)	1	14.89	8.79	7.22
3DBox_PET_0001	(264, 200, 200)	1	8.94	5.56	4.86
2DBox_US_0525	(256, 256, 3)	1	0.88	0.47	0.37
2DBox_X-Ray_0053	(320, 640, 3)	34	2.19	1.77	1.59
2DBox_Dermoscopy_0003	(3024, 4032, 3)	1	1.50	1.15	0.98
2DBox_Endoscopy_0086	(480, 560, 3)	1	0.88	0.50	0.42
2DBox_Fundus_0003	(2048, 2048, 3)	1	0.89	0.62	0.48
2DBox_Microscope_0008	(1536, 2040, 3)	19	1.81	1.50	1.44
2DBox_Microscope_0016	(1920, 2560, 3)	241	14.47	13.79	13.66

the figure indicate over- and under-segmentation errors. This may be due to our model focusing too much on strong differences in intensities around ROI, neglecting ROI as a whole (e.g., the yellow box in the US case), and images losing some details after resampling.

4.2 Results on the Final Testing Set

Table 7 shows the comparative analysis of the baseline and our proposed method across various modalities on the test set. Notably, Rep-MedSAM demonstrates significant improvements in both DSC and NSD metrics for CT scans, with an increase of approximately 17.5% and 18.5%, respectively, indicating a marked enhancement in segmentation accuracy. This trend of improved performance is consistent across most modalities, with the most substantial reduction in runtime observed in Microscopy, where our model reduces the time by over 10 s compared to the baseline. However, the results also highlight certain deficiencies in specific modalities, especially the X-Ray. Despite the runtime improvements in our model, the repeated computation image embeddings for 3D modalities and the start time of the bulky docker still dominate the overall runtime, suggesting there is still room for a boost in inference and docker deployment.

Table 7. Quantitative evaluation results on the test set.

Modality	Baseline			Rep-MedSAM		
	DSC(%)	NSD(%)	Time (s)	DSC(%)	NSD (%)	Time (s)
CT	55.75	58.48	38.78	**73.21**	**76.95**	**20.65**
MR	64.80	62.75	18.57	**71.24**	**66.44**	**10.48**
PET	76.94	66.98	14.9	**80.09**	**70.59**	**9.57**
US	85.24	89.73	8.96	**89.25**	**93.48**	**5.93**
X-Ray	**85.51**	**94.40**	9.95	78.45	89.25	**5.72**
Endoscopy	**94.41**	**96.95**	7.56	93.87	96.60	**5.21**
Fundus	87.47	89.58	8.77	**84.63**	**86.87**	**5.33**
Microscopy	84.36	86.15	16.34	**88.12**	**90.02**	**5.71**
OCT	73.31	80.20	8.39	**83.11**	**89.66**	**5.4**
Average	78.64	80.58	14.69	**82.44**	**84.43**	**8.22**

4.3 Limitation and Future Work

While our model outperforms the baseline in segmentation results, there is still room for further improvement. Regarding inference speed, the image encoder is the most time-consuming component when inferencing with fewer objects, whereas the mask decoder becomes the bottleneck when processing a larger number of objects. Additionally, segmenting each slice in 3D images independently leads to higher time costs and the potential loss of spatial information, which may impact segmentation accuracy. We will refer to the updated research progress to improve the quality and speed of 3D image segmentations in our future work.

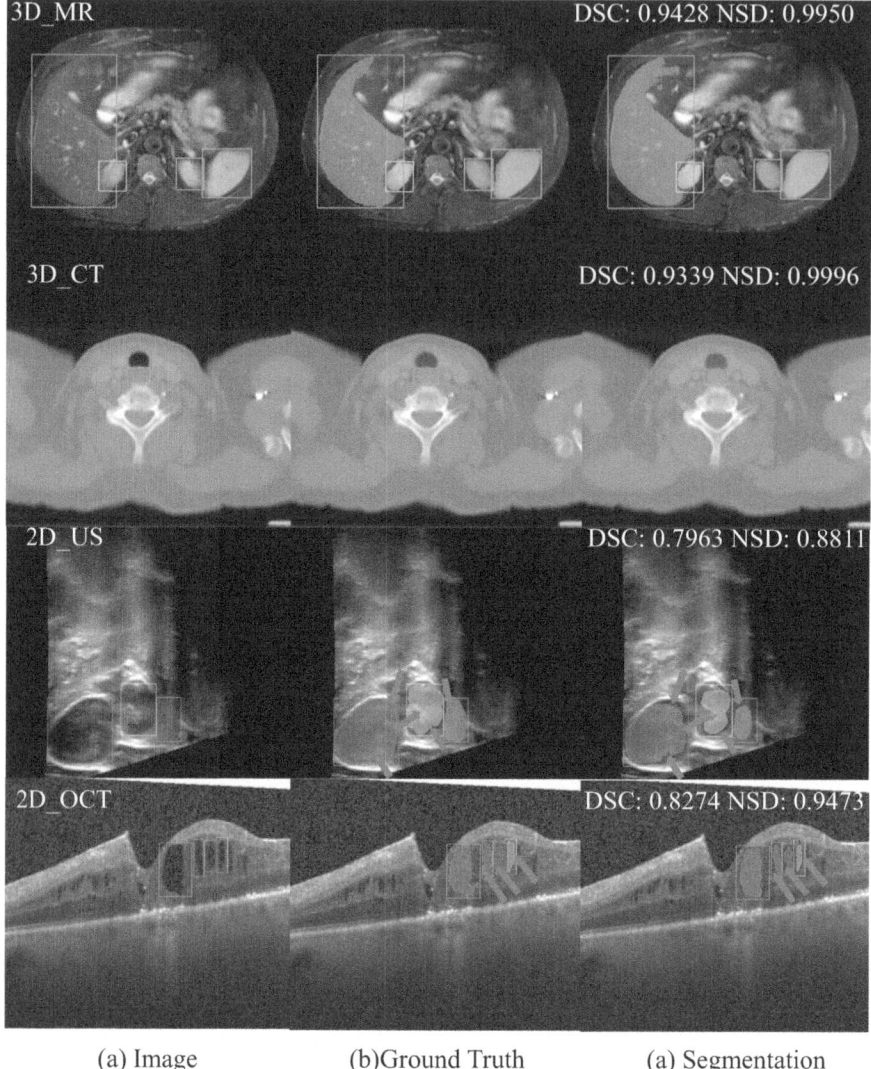

Fig. 3. Qualitative results of our Rep-MedSAM on two easy cases (MR and CT) and two hard cases (US and OCT).

5 Conclusion

In this paper, we proposed a framework based on knowledge distillation to leverage large pre-trained MedSAM for more efficient semi-automatic segmentations based on bounding boxes. Our method demonstrates excellent results in both efficiency and performance. Our proposed framework can serve as a robust tool for medical image segmentation in clinical practice.

Acknowledgements. We thank all the data owners for making the medical images publicly available and CodaLab [27] for hosting the challenge platform.

Disclosure of Interests. The authors have no competing interests to declare that are relevant to the content of this article.

Appendix

Table 8. External public datasets in fine-tuning.

Modality	Dataset Name
CT	CT-Org [22], ULS23 [11], FLARE22 [19], HaN-Seg [21]
Dermoscopy	None
Endoscopy	BKAI-IGH NeoPolyp [2,7,16]
Fundus	E-ophtha [4]
Mammography	None
Microscopy	PanNuke [8] [9]
MR	ARC [10], ACDC [3], CDEMRIS [14]
PET	None
Ultrasound	CAMUS [17], MicroSegNet [13], CT2US [24]
X-Ray	Panoramic X-ray [1], Hip joint X-ray [12],

References

1. Abdi, A.H., Kasaei, S., Mehdizadeh, M.: Automatic segmentation of mandible in panoramic X-ray. J. Med. Imaging **2**(4), 044003 (2015)
2. An, N.S., et al.: Blazeneo: blazing fast polyp segmentation and neoplasm detection. IEEE Access **10**, 43669–43684 (2022)
3. Bernard, O., et al.: Deep learning techniques for automatic MRI cardiac multi-structures segmentation and diagnosis: is the problem solved? IEEE Trans. Med. Imaging **37**(11), 2514–2525 (2018)
4. Decencière, E., et al.: TeleOphta: machine learning and image processing methods for teleophthalmology. IRBM **34**(2), 196–203 (2013)
5. Ding, X., Zhang, X., Ma, N., Han, J., Ding, G., Sun, J.: Repvgg: making VGG-style convnets great again. arXiv preprint arXiv:2101.03697 (2021)
6. Dosovitskiy, A., et al.: An image is worth 16x16 words: transformers for image recognition at scale. In: International Conference on Learning Representations (2021)
7. Duc, N.T., Oanh, N.T., Thuy, N.T., Triet, T.M., Dinh, V.S.: Colonformer: an efficient transformer based method for colon polyp segmentation. IEEE Access **10**, 80575–80586 (2022)

8. Gamper, J., Koohbanani, N.A., Benet, K., Khuram, A., Rajpoot, N.: Pannuke: an open pan-cancer histology dataset for nuclei instance segmentation and classification. In: European Congress on Digital Pathology, pp. 11–19. Springer (2019)
9. Gamper, J., et al.: Pannuke dataset extension, insights and baselines. arXiv preprint arXiv:2003.10778 (2020)
10. Gibson, M., et al.: Aphasia recovery cohort (ARC) dataset (2023)
11. de Grauw, M., Alves, N., Schuurmans, M., Huisman, H., van Ginneken, B., Hering, A.: The ULS23 challenge public training dataset (2023)
12. Gut, D.: X-ray images of the hip joints (2021)
13. Jiang, H., et al.: MicroSegNet: a deep learning approach for prostate segmentation on micro-ultrasound images. Comput. Med. Imaging Graph. **112**, 102326 (2024)
14. Karim, R., et al.: Evaluation of current algorithms for segmentation of scar tissue from late Gadolinium enhancement cardiovascular magnetic resonance of the left atrium: an open-access grand challenge. J. Cardiovasc. Magn. Reson. **15**(1), 105 (2013)
15. Kirillov, A., et al.: Segment anything. In: Proceedings of the International Conference on Computer Vision, pp. 4015–4026 (2023)
16. Lan, P.N., et al.: Neounet: towards accurate colon polyp segmentation and neoplasm detection. arXiv preprint arXiv:2107.05023 (2021)
17. Leclerc, S., et al.: Deep learning for segmentation using an open large-scale dataset in 2D echocardiography. IEEE Trans. Med. Imaging **38**(9), 2198–2210 (2019)
18. Ma, J., He, Y., Li, F., Han, L., You, C., Wang, B.: Segment anything in medical images. Nat. Commun. **15**(1), 654 (2024)
19. Ma, J., et al.: Unleashing the strengths of unlabeled data in pan-cancer abdominal organ quantification: the flare22 challenge. arXiv preprint arXiv:2308.05862 (2023)
20. Mehta, S., Rastegari, M.: Mobilevit: light-weight, general-purpose, and mobile-friendly vision transformer. In: International Conference on Learning Representations (2022)
21. Podobnik, G., Strojan, P., Peterlin, P., Ibragimov, B., Vrtovec, T.: HaN-Seg: the head and neck organ-at-risk CT and MR segmentation dataset. Med. Phys. **50**(3), 1917–1927 (2023)
22. Rister, B., Shivakumar, K., Nobashi, T., Rubin, D.L.: CT-ORG: a dataset of CT volumes with multiple organ segmentations (2019)
23. Ronneberger, O., Fischer, P., Brox, T.: U-net: convolutional networks for biomedical image segmentation (2015)
24. Song, Y., Zheng, J., Lei, L., Ni, Z., Zhao, B., Hu, Y.: CT2US: cross-modal transfer learning for kidney segmentation in ultrasound images with synthesized data. Ultrasonics **122**, 106706 (2022)
25. Wang, A., Chen, H., Lin, Z., Han, J., Ding, G.: Repvit: revisiting mobile CNN from VIT perspective (2023)

26. Wu, K., et al.: Tinyvit: fast pretraining distillation for small vision transformers. In: European Conference on Computer Vision (2022)
27. Xu, Z., et al.: Codabench: flexible, easy-to-use, and reproducible meta-benchmark platform. Patterns **3**(7), 100543 (2022)
28. Zhang, C., et al.: Faster segment anything: towards lightweight SAM for mobile applications. arXiv preprint arXiv:2306.14289 (2023)

Swin-LiteMedSAM: A Lightweight Box-Based Segment Anything Model for Large-Scale Medical Image Datasets

Ruochen Gao[ID], Donghang Lyu[✉][ID], and Marius Staring[ID]

Division of Image Processing, Department of Radiology, Leiden University Medical Center, Leiden, The Netherlands
d.lyu@lumc.nl

Abstract. Medical imaging is essential for the diagnosis and treatment of diseases, with medical image segmentation as a subtask receiving high attention. However, automatic medical image segmentation models are typically task-specific and struggle to handle multiple scenarios, such as different imaging modalities and regions of interest. With the introduction of the Segment Anything Model (SAM), training a universal model for various clinical scenarios has become feasible. Recently, several Medical SAM (MedSAM) methods have been proposed, but these models often rely on heavy image encoders to achieve high performance, which may not be practical for real-world applications due to their high computational demands and slow inference speed. To address this issue, a lightweight version of the MedSAM (LiteMedSAM) can provide a viable solution, achieving high performance while requiring fewer resources and less time. In this work, we introduce Swin-LiteMedSAM, a new variant of LiteMedSAM. This model integrates the tiny Swin Transformer as the image encoder, incorporates multiple types of prompts, including box-based points and scribble generated from a given bounding box, and establishes skip connections between the image encoder and the mask decoder. In the *Segment Anything in Medical Images on Laptop* challenge (CVPR 2024), our approach strikes a good balance between segmentation performance and speed, demonstrating significantly improved overall results across multiple modalities compared to the LiteMedSAM baseline provided by the challenge organizers. Our proposed model achieved a DSC score of **0.8678** and an NSD score of **0.8844** on the validation set. On the final test set, it attained a DSC score of **0.8193** and an NSD score of **0.8461**, securing fourth place in the challenge. The code and trained model are available at https://github.com/RuochenGao/Swin_LiteMedSAM.

Keywords: LiteMedSAM · Swin Transformer · Multiple Prompts

R. Gao and D. Lyu—These authors contributed equally to this work.

1 Introduction

Medical imaging diagnosis is fundamental for evaluating diseases, and medical image segmentation, which involves the extraction of specific structures such as tumors and organs from medical images, consistently receives significant attention. Deep learning methods have demonstrated effectiveness in this field, leading to the development of numerous models tailored for specific scenarios. However, each scenario typically requires training a dedicated segmentation model, demanding substantial effort. In recent years, inspired by the rapid development of large language models (LLMs) in the natural language processing (NLP) field, researchers have begun exploring the application of large models in computer vision. Segment Anything Model (SAM) [5] is one such innovation, aiming to unify the segmentation task for general images by training with a huge amount of data. while SAM holds potential, the distinct features of medical images can hinder its performance in medical image segmentation. Therefore, recent works [8,10] focus on adapting the SAM model for medical applications by re-training with a large volume of medical images. Despite achieving high performance in various medical image segmentation tasks, SAM models' large parameter volume and the high spatial resolution of medical images require substantial computational resources and processing time. This poses challenges for practical deployment of SAM models in real-world applications, or even for non-industry academic groups conducting research on them. Consequently, lite SAM models are gaining more attention as a solution to this problem.

The original SAM model is composed of three main components: an image encoder, a prompt encoder, and a mask decoder. Among these, the image encoder is the primary factor contributing to high computational and memory costs due to the usage of ViT-H [3]. To mitigate resource consumption and accelerate processing, various studies have aimed to make the image encoder more lightweight. For instance, FastSAM [15] introduces a CNN-based framework, while Mobile-SAM [13] tackles this issue by distilling knowledge from the ViT-H image encoder into a tiny ViT-based encoder. Additionally, EfficientSAM [11] employs the Masked Autoencoders (MAE) [4] framework to efficiently transfer knowledge from a large image encoder to a small one, resulting in a more resource-efficient design with better performance. EfficientViT-SAM [14] further enhances this approach by incorporating EfficientViT [1] with fused MBConv blocks [9] to create a lightweight image encoder. Recently, the challenge *Segment Anything in Medical Images on Laptop*[1], hosted at CVPR 2024, sought universal promptable medical image segmentation models deployable on laptops or edge devices without GPU reliance. The organizers developed LiteMedSAM[2] as a baseline, using the distillation strategy described in [13]. Although LiteMedSAM focuses on optimizing the image encoder to reduce resource usage, segmentation performance is compromised. Therefore, our goal is to enhance performance without highly sacrificing efficiency. To achieve this, we use a lightweight Swin Trans-

---

[1] https://www.codabench.org/competitions/1847/.
[2] https://github.com/bowang-lab/MedSAM/tree/LiteMedSAM.

former as image encoder and also introduce two additional prompts, box-based points and box-based scribble, except the original box prompt. To this end, we introduce our model, Swin-LiteMedSAM. The key contributions of our model are as follows:

- Instead of transferring knowledge to a tiny ViT, we employ a tiny Swin Transformer [6] as the image encoder. The Swin Transformer is designed to handle large images more efficiently, both in terms of computation and memory usage compared to ViT. Moreover, skip connections are established between the image encoder and mask decoder to enhance feature integration.
- We introduce additional types of prompts beyond boxes, including box-based points and box-based scribble. These prompts are automatically generated from the given bounding box and effectively improve model performance without significantly increasing resource costs.
- Overall, Swin-LiteMedSAM achieves substantial improvements in performance over LiteMedSAM while maintaining high inference speed.

2 Method

2.1 Data Preprocessing

To accelerate the model's training and inference stages and reduce memory consumption, we resize the input image to 256×256. This is achieved by first resizing the images while maintaining their original aspect ratio based on the longest side, and then do zero padding to reach the final size of 256×256. For data normalization, we use the method described in [8]. Please refer to [8] for more details.

Note that gray-scale images such as CT, MR, US, and PET typically have only one channel, whereas RGB images from modalities like endoscopy, dermoscopy, and fundus imaging usually have three channels. To maintain consistency during model training, we replicated the channel dimension for gray-scale images, converting them from one channel to three channels.

2.2 Proposed Method

Our model's structure is shown in Fig. 1. It mainly comprises three components: an image encoder, a prompt decoder, and a mask decoder. The function of these three components are detailed below.

The image encoder architecture is inspired by the original tiny ViT design of LiteMedSAM. The input first passes through two convolutional layers, which capture low-level spatial features and adjust the number of channels to 64. Following this, the encoder consists of four stages, with their depths arranged according to the tiny ViT configuration as (2, 2, 6, 2). The structure of the Swin block used in our encoder is illustrated in Fig. 2. We have slightly modified the standard Swin block by adding a convolutional block with batch normalization between the windowed multi-head self-attention (W-MSA) module and

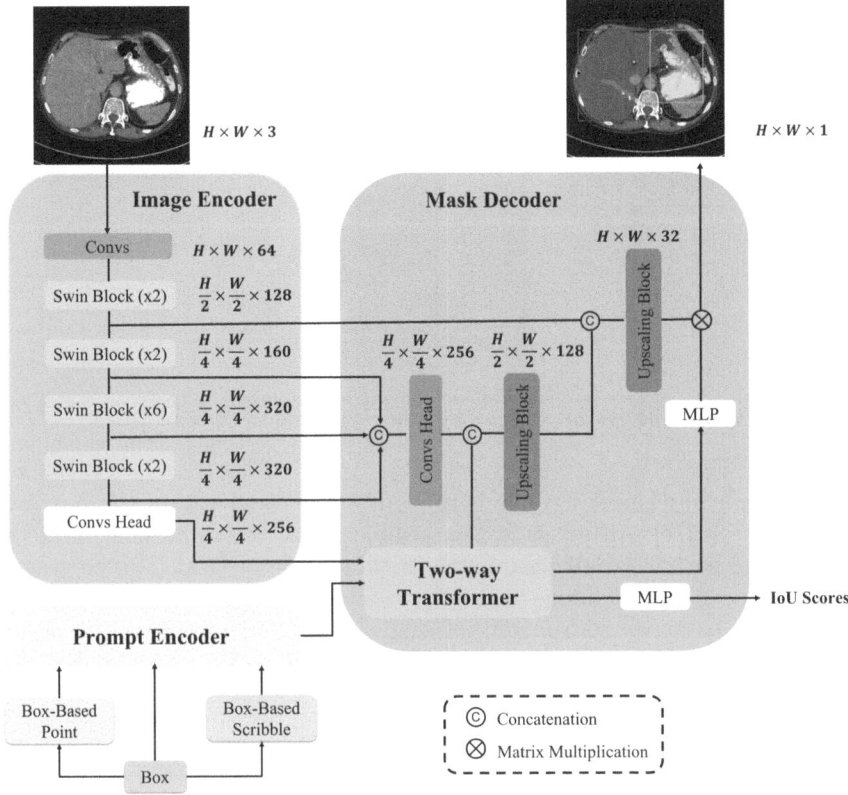

Fig. 1. Overview of the Swin-LiteMedSAM architecture.

the Multi-Layer Perceptron (MLP). This modification enables our encoder to effectively capturing both global and local features. Furthermore, the number of channels and spatial resolution across four stages remain consistent with the original design. Finally, a head branch consisting of several convolutional layers and layer normalization adjusts the channel number to 256.

In the prompt encoder, we introduce two additional types of prompts: box-based points and a box-based scribble, alongside the original box prompt. The box-based points and the box are combined to form a sparse embedding, while the box-based scribble is used for dense embedding. For the box-based prompt, drawing from insights provided by [10] and [2], which demonstrate the effectiveness of using multiple points over a single point, we opt to utilize four points in our prompt encoder. To achieve this, we divide the bounding box area into four equivalent sub-parts based on the central point. We then randomly generate one point in the non-zero area of each sub-part, resulting in four points distributed inside the box. If a sub-part contains only zeros, we select the central point. This approach ensures a relatively sparse distribution of points covering more area.

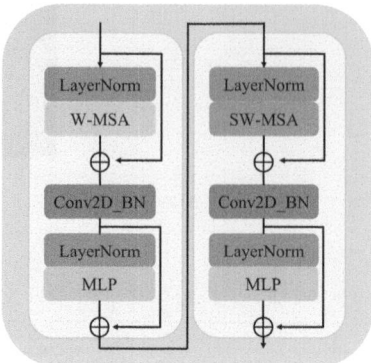

Fig. 2. The overall structure of the Swin Transformer block.

Furthermore, a box-based scribble is randomly generated within the box using the algorithm in [16]. All pixels in the scribble are set to 1 and placed into the corresponding part of an all-zero matrix with a shape of (256, 256) to create a mask for the dense embedding. Similarly, if all pixels in the box are zeros, the scribble is set to an all-zero matrix of shape (256, 256) to ensure the prompt encoder focuses on the sparse prompt embedding part, as illustrated in Fig. 3(a).

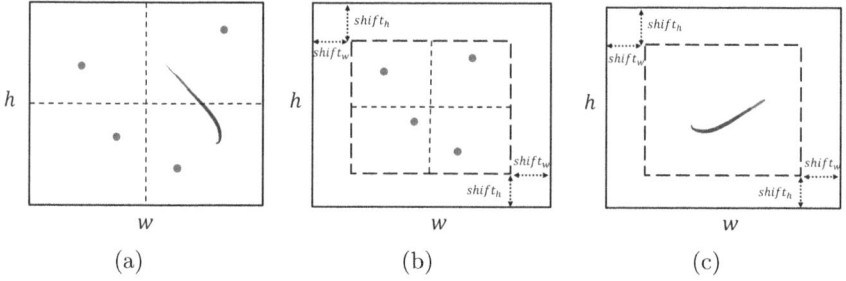

Fig. 3. (a) Box-based points and scribble generation strategies during the training stage. (b) Box-based points generation strategy during the inference stage. (c) Box-based scribble generation strategy during inference stage.

Then in the mask decoder, we follow the SAM original design by using a two-way transformer to process embeddings from the prompt encoder and image encoder. Moreover, we build skip connections between the image encoder and mask decoder, concatenating outputs from the last three stages and fusing them with several convolutional layers. This output is then combined with the two-way transformer's output and passed through an upscaling block to double the image resolution. Similarly, the upscaled output is concatenated with the first stage's output from the image encoder, and the resulting output is further upsampled to return back to the original spatial resolution.

For the loss function, it consists of a mask prediction loss L_{mask} and a IoU score prediction loss L_{iou}:

$$L = L_{mask} + L_{iou}, \tag{1}$$

where L_{mask} is the summation of the Dice loss and binary cross-entropy by comparing the predicted mask with the ground truth mask, while L_{iou} is the MSE loss between the predicted and actual IoU scores.

2.3 Inference Strategy for Box-Based Points and Box-Based Scribble

The strategy for generating box-based points and box-based scribble has some difference between the training and inference stages. During the training stage, the range for generating four points is within the entire bounding box, which aims to expose the model to diverse cases and helps improve its generalization capabilities. However, randomly generating points within the whole box might not be ideal during the inference stage, as objects are typically located near the central part of the box. Random generation can easily place some points near the boundary, which is less effective and even negatively impact performance. Furthermore, for the situation of a single point prompt, the central point of the box is always the first choice [2]. Likewise, the two corner points of the box already provide some external and surrounding information of objects. Therefore, points should be better distributed in the relatively central part of the box. For a given bounding box, represented by its upper left point (x_{min}, y_{min}) and bottom right point (x_{max}, y_{max}), we introduce two variables, shift_h and shift_w, to adjust the coordinates along height and width directions so that four points do not occur in the peripheral area, as shown in Fig. 3(b). This adjustment is denoted as follows:

$$x'_{min} = x_{min} + \text{shift}_w,$$
$$y'_{min} = y_{min} + \text{shift}_h,$$
$$x'_{max} = x_{max} - \text{shift}_w,$$
$$y'_{max} = y_{max} - \text{shift}_h.$$

Here, the new upper left point (x'_{min}, y'_{min}) and bottom right point (x'_{max}, y'_{max}) form a new box and randomly generate four points within it. The range of shift_w is $(0, \frac{1}{2}w)$, and the range of shift_h is $(0, \frac{1}{2}h)$, where w and h are the width and height of the image, respectively. In this study, we adjusted the range of shift_w to $(\frac{1}{5}w, \frac{2}{5}w)$ and the range of shift_h to $(\frac{1}{5}h, \frac{2}{5}h)$ to ensure that the distribution of points is closer to the center. Additionally, shift_w and shift_h are randomly adjusted within their ranges for each sample to achieve better overall performance. We also follow the same points distribution strategy as in the training stage to ensure that the four points are positioned in the four quadrants of the image.

Then Fig. 3(c) illustrates the strategy of generating a scribble in the inference stage. Considering the empirical distribution of points, we believe that placing

Table 1. Evaluation Platform environment settings.

System	Ubuntu 20.04 Desktop
CPU	Intel Xeon(R) W-2133 @3.60GHz
RAM	8GB
Docker version	20.10.13

Table 2. Training environment settings.

System	Red Hat 9
CPU	AMD EPYC 7513 @2.60GHz
RAM	256GB
GPU (number and type)	One NVIDIA A100 40G
CUDA version	12.4
Programming language	Python 3.10
Deep learning framework	PyTorch 2.2.2
Specific dependencies	Monai, Einops, Timm and Transformers

the scribble closer to the edges is more effective than points for capturing contour information. Therefore, we adjusted the range of shift$_w$ to $(\frac{1}{8}w, \frac{1}{6}w)$ and the range of shift$_h$ to $(\frac{1}{8}h, \frac{1}{6}h)$ to expand the area for generating a scribble. Note that we generate the scribble in non-zero areas, based on the prior knowledge that people typically avoid drawing scribble in regions with zero pixel values.

3 Experiments

3.1 Dataset and Evaluation Metrics

Training and Validation Dataset. We only use the provided challenge dataset, without additional public datasets. This dataset includes 11 modalities: CT, MRI, PET, X-ray, ultrasound, mammography, OCT, endoscopy, fundus, dermoscopy, and microscopy, totaling more than one million 2D image-mask pairs.

Testing Dataset. The testing set in this challenge is hidden, with all testing images newly collected from 20+ different institutions worldwide.

Evaluation Metrics. The evaluation metrics are the Dice Similarity Coefficient (DSC) and Normalized Surface Dice (NSD) for accuracy, and Docker container running time for efficiency. These metrics together determine the ranking. Note that only mean results are available. The evaluation platform environment is presented in Table 1.

3.2 Implementation Details

Training Environment Settings. The training environments are presented in Table 2.

Training Protocols. Our training strategy consists of two stages. In the first stage, we utilize knowledge distillation to transfer information from the large ViT-B image encoder to the tiny Swin Transformer as our image encoder. To note, we pre-saved the output image embeddings from the ViT-B encoder to speed up the distillation process. In the second stage, we take the pre-trained image encoder from the first stage and proceed to train the entire model. The training details of these two stages are listed in Table 3.

Data Sampling Strategy. During the training, we randomly sample image cases from the dataset. If the case is 3D, such as a CT, MR, or PET scan, we randomly sample a slice from the 3D image. If the case is 2D, such as an X-ray or microscopy image, we use the image directly. This strategy significantly reduces training time and ensures a more balanced distribution of training samples across different modalities.

Data Augmentation. We apply vertical and horizontal flips to the image, each with a 50% probability.

Inference Environment Settings. During the inference stage, the running environment differs from the training stage. A docker container is built, starting with a 'python:3.10-slim' image and installing the CPU version of PyTorch 2.2.2. All other aspects still remain same with the training stage.

Table 3. Training protocols of the first stage and the second stage.

	The first stage	The second stage
Pre-trained Model	MedSAM ViT-B	Tiny Swin Transformer
Batch size	64	16
Patch size	$256 \times 256 \times 3$	$256 \times 256 \times 3$
Total epochs	10	25
Optimizer	AdamW	AdamW
Initial learning rate (lr)	2e-4	2e-4
Lr decay schedule	ReducedLROnPlateau	ReducedLROnPlateau
Training time	60.8 h	46 h
Loss function	L1 Loss	MSE Loss+Dice Loss+BCE Loss
Number of model parameters	10.51M	36.77M
Number of flops	47.70G	55.20G

4 Results and Discussion

4.1 Quantitative Results on Validation Set

Table 4 shows that Swin-LiteMedSAM achieves higher average DSC (86.70%) and NSD (88.55%) scores compared to LiteMedSAM, which recorded 83.81% for DSC and 83.26% for NSD. In general, Swin-LiteMedSAM achieved a more balanced and comprehensive performance across the nine modalities compared to LiteMedSAM. It showed significant improvement in PET and Microscopy while maintaining strong performance in most modalities. However, the model experienced a noticeable drop in DSC and NSD scores for the US modality.

Then Table 5 further highlights the importance of each component in our proposed method, particularly the inclusion of skip connections, as well as both box-based points and scribble, in achieving superior segmentation performance. Here, the introduction of two additional box-based prompts provide limited improvement. This could be due to two factors. First, some prompts may have been placed in sub-optimal positions due to the random way, negatively impacting overall performance. Second, inadequate training can be a contributing factor. Although the data sampling strategy helped balance the distribution of modalities and accelerated the training process, it significantly reduced the number of

Table 4. Comparison between LiteMedSAM and our proposed Swin-LiteMedSAM.

Target	LiteMedSAM		Swin-LiteMedSAM	
	DSC (%)	NSD (%)	DSC (%)	NSD (%)
CT	**92.26**	**94.90**	91.46	94.70
MR	**89.63**	**93.37**	87.12	91.19
PET	51.58	25.17	**69.43**	**56.99**
US	**94.77**	**96.81**	85.57	90.63
X-ray	81.05	85.35	**83.98**	**88.88**
Dermoscopy	92.47	93.85	**94.20**	**95.65**
Endoscopy	**96.04**	**98.11**	95.29	97.63
Fundus	94.81	96.41	**95.83**	**97.39**
Microscopy	61.63	65.38	**77.45**	**83.91**
Average	83.81	83.26	**86.70**	**88.55**

Table 5. Ablation study of the proposed method. The check mark shows including the module in the method. Here, Swin-T indicates tiny Swin Transformer.

Swin-T	Skip connection	Box-based points	Box-based scribble	DSC (%)	NSD (%)
✓				85.79	86.75
✓	✓			86.48	87.74
✓	✓	✓		86.22	87.79
✓	✓	✓	✓	**86.70**	**88.55**

training samples. This reduction can hinder the effective training of the prompts, which require a high volume of diverse cases to perform optimally.

4.2 Quantitative Results on Testing Set

As shown in Table 6, our proposed method significantly outperforms LiteMedSAM across most imaging modalities in terms of DSC and NSD, while also reducing runtime of all the modalities. Specifically, for CT images, our method achieved an absolute DSC improvement of 17.15%, corresponding to a relative improvement of 30.76%, and an NSD increase of 18.51%, corresponding to a relative improvement of 31.75%, compared to LiteMedSAM, also with a faster runtime. For PET and X-ray modalities, our method demonstrated competitive DSC and NSD results. In PET, it achieved a marginal NSD improvement while maintaining similar DSC performance, and significantly reduced runtime. For X-ray, despite a slightly lower DSC compared to LiteMedSAM, the difference is minimal, demonstrating a still competitive result.

Furthermore, we observed significant instability in the original LiteMedSAM. Taking CT modality as an example, LiteMedSAM performed exceptionally well on the validation set, surpassing Swin-LiteMedSAM. However, when evaluated on the testing set, performance of CT experienced a significant performance drop, with DSC falling from 92.26% to 55.75% and NSD dropping from 94.90% to 58.48%. Although Swin-LiteMedSAM encounters a similar issue with the CT modality, the performance drop is much less severe. Furthermore, this issue is observed in other modalities as well, further approving that the Swin-LiteMedSAM model offers better stability and generalization, which are essential for the real world applications.

Table 6. Quantitative evaluation results for final testing set

Target	LiteMedSAM[a]			Proposed Swin-LiteMedSAM		
	DSC (%)	NSD (%)	Runtime (s)	DSC (%)	NSD (%)	Runtime (s)
CT	55.75	58.48	32.68	**72.90**	**76.99**	**25.14**
MR	64.80	62.75	15.91	**68.61**	**70.13**	**13.44**
PET	**76.94**	66.98	12.99	76.50	**67.63**	**10.52**
US	85.24	89.73	8.27	**88.01**	**92.43**	**7.58**
X-ray	**85.51**	**94.40**	8.79	84.58	94.32	**6.89**
Endoscopy	94.41	96.95	13.85	**94.58**	**97.17**	**11.36**
Fundus	**87.47**	**89.58**	11.72	80.71	82.93	**9.85**
Microscopy	84.36	86.15	11.85	**87.08**	**88.94**	**10.48**
OCT	73.31	80.20	8.39	**84.39**	**90.97**	**6.87**
Average	78.64	80.58	13.99	**81.93**	**84.61**	**11.01**

[a] The model weights and results are released by the challenge organizer.

4.3 Qualitative Results on External Public Dataset

Since the ground truth for the challenge validation and testing set is not available, we select SegRap2023 [7], a public head and neck CT dataset containing annotations for multiple organs, to verify the model's performance.

As depicted in Fig. 4, we showcase three representative examples from SegRap2023 to visually check our model's performance. In the first case, our model demonstrates strong performance in brain segmentation. This is primarily attributed to the brain's large size and distinct contrast with surrounding tissues. Moving to the second case, we observed that our model maintains good performance even with smaller targets such as the spinal cord, esophagus, and trachea. However, in the third case, our model's performance falls short compared to the ground truth. The main issue arises from the ambiguous semantics in medical images. For instance, when aiming to segment the oral cavity, our method only identifies the teeth. This discrepancy stems from the fact that the box prompt for the oral cavity can also be interpreted as segmenting teeth. It is hard to provide a more precise prompt in this case to specify the intended target for segmentation.

4.4 Limitation and Future Work

One main limitation of our method for this challenge is that our model is using 2D images for training and validation, whereas medical imaging data, such as CT, MRI, and PET, are typically in 3D format. Currently, we process these 3D images by making predictions on individual 2D slices, which does not fully utilize the 3D anatomical information and might hinder the performance improvement. The key issue is that the prompts input to the model are generally based on 2D information, such as bounding boxes and points. In the future, we aim to explore how to provide effective prompt information in 3D and adapt the model to handle 3D images directly.

Additionally, we applied certain manual rules to control the distribution of box-based points and the scribble, which is impossible to find the optimal setting and can easily do harm to the overall performance if not set properly. Furthermore, due to variations in medical modalities and the shapes of segmentation targets, the distribution of points and scribble should be adjusted accordingly. Therefore, developing a learning-based method for generating box-based points and scribble would be highly beneficial and could further enhance the model's performance.

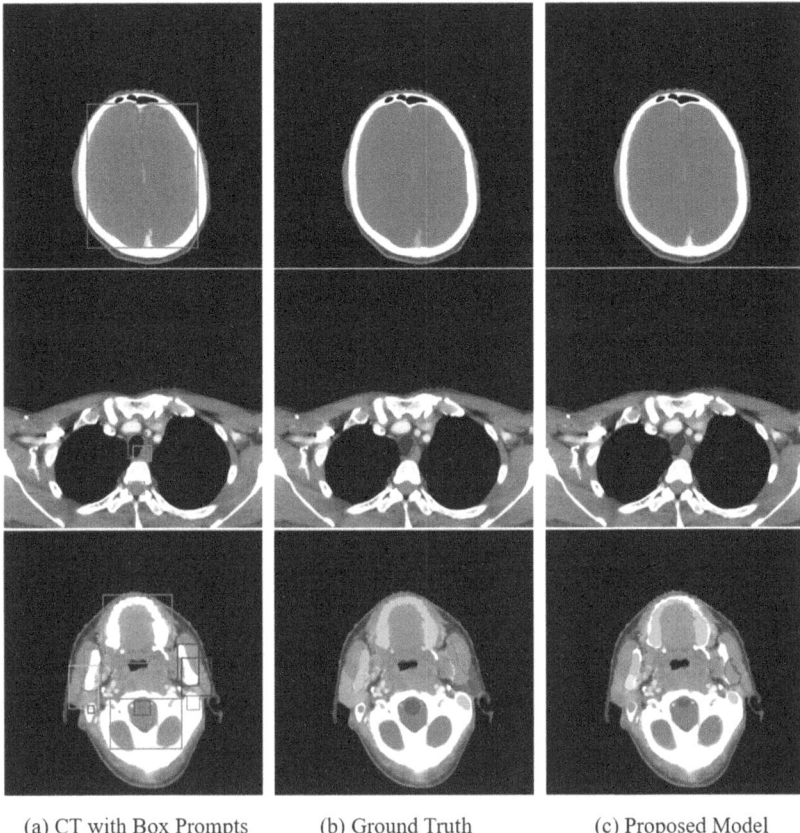

(a) CT with Box Prompts (b) Ground Truth (c) Proposed Model

Fig. 4. Visual comparison between ground truth and our proposed method, with each row representing one case from SegRap2023. (a), (b), and (c) represent the original image with box prompts, ground truth, and the prediction results of our proposed model, respectively.

5 Conclusion

In this paper, we introduce Swin-LiteMedSAM, a lightweight box-based segment anything model. Our model utilizes the tiny Swin Transformer as image encoder, enabling it to extracts high-level features more effectively. Additionally, the introduction of box-based points and box-based scribble provide more spatial cues, which improve segmentation accuracy without substantially increasing computational costs or demanding extensive manual annotation. Overall, our approach achieves stronger and more stable performance across different medical imaging modalities while maintaining fast inference speed, outperforming the LiteMedSAM model.

Acknowledgements. We thank all the data owners for making the medical images publicly available and CodaLab [12] for hosting the challenge platform. This study utilized computing resources from the Academic Leiden Interdisciplinary Cluster Environment (ALICE) provided by Leiden University. This study was supported by the China Scholarship Council (No. 202207720085) and the project ROBUST: Trustworthy AI-based Systems for Sustainable Growth with project number KICH3.LTP.20.006, which is (partly) financed by the Dutch Research Council (NWO), Philips Research, and the Dutch Ministry of Economic Affairs and Climate Policy (EZK) under the program LTP KIC 2020-2023.

Disclosure of Interests. The authors have no competing interests to declare that are relevant to the content of this article.

References

1. Cai, H., Gan, C., Han, S.: Efficientvit: enhanced linear attention for high-resolution low-computation visual recognition. arXiv preprint arXiv:2205.14756 (2022)
2. Cheng, D., Qin, Z., Jiang, Z., Zhang, S., Lao, Q., Li, K.: Sam on medical images: a comprehensive study on three prompt modes. arXiv preprint arXiv:2305.00035 (2023)
3. Dosovitskiy, A., et al.: An image is worth 16x16 words: transformers for image recognition at scale. arXiv preprint arXiv:2010.11929 (2020)
4. He, K., Chen, X., Xie, S., Li, Y., Dollár, P., Girshick, R.: Masked autoencoders are scalable vision learners. In: Proceedings of the IEEE/CVF Conference on Computer Vision and Pattern Recognition, pp. 16000–16009 (2022)
5. Kirillov, A., et al.: Segment anything. In: Proceedings of the International Conference on Computer Vision, pp. 4015–4026 (2023)
6. Liu, Z., et al.: Swin transformer: hierarchical vision transformer using shifted windows. In: Proceedings of the IEEE/CVF International Conference on Computer Vision, pp. 10012–10022 (2021)
7. Luo, X., et al.: Segrap2023: a benchmark of organs-at-risk and gross tumor volume segmentation for radiotherapy planning of nasopharyngeal carcinoma. arXiv preprint arXiv:2312.09576 (2023)
8. Ma, J., He, Y., Li, F., Han, L., You, C., Wang, B.: Segment anything in medical images. Nat. Commun. **15**(1), 654 (2024)
9. Tan, M., Le, Q.: Efficientnetv2: smaller models and faster training. In: International Conference on Machine Learning, pp. 10096–10106. PMLR (2021)
10. Wu, J., et al.: Medical SAM adapter: adapting segment anything model for medical image segmentation. arXiv preprint arXiv:2304.12620 (2023)
11. Xiong, Y., et al.: Efficientsam: leveraged masked image pretraining for efficient segment anything. arXiv preprint arXiv:2312.00863 (2023)
12. Xu, Z., et al.: Codabench: flexible, easy-to-use, and reproducible meta-benchmark platform. Patterns **3**(7), 100543 (2022)
13. Zhang, C., et al.: Faster segment anything: towards lightweight SAM for mobile applications. arXiv preprint arXiv:2306.14289 (2023)
14. Zhang, Z., Cai, H., Han, S.: Efficientvit-SAM: accelerated segment anything model without performance loss. In: CVPR Workshop: Efficient Large Vision Models (2024)
15. Zhao, X., et al.: Fast segment anything. arXiv preprint arXiv:2306.12156 (2023)
16. Zou, X., et al.: Segment everything everywhere all at once. In: Advances in Neural Information Processing Systems, vol. 36 (2024)

A Light-Weight Universal Medical Segmentation Network for Laptops Based on Knowledge Distillation

Songxiao Yang[1](✉), Yizhou Li[1], Ye Chen[2], Zhuofeng Wu[1], and Masatoshi Okutomi[1]

[1] Tokyo Institute of Technology, Ookayama 2-12-1, Meguro, Tokyo, Japan
{syang,yli,zwu}@ok.sc.e.titech.ac.jp, mxo@sc.e.titech.ac.jp
[2] The University of Tokyo, Kashiwanoha 5-1-5, Chiba, Japan
chenye@g.ecc.u-tokyo.ac.jp

Abstract. In medical imaging, accurate and efficient segmentation is crucial for diagnostics, treatment planning, and monitoring disease progression. Traditional methods, while capable of providing reliable results, often require substantial computational resources, which may not be feasible on devices with limited capabilities such as standard CPUs and limited RAM. To address this challenge, we present an optimized universal segmentation framework that leverages a lightweight image encoder RepViT-M0.6, distilled from Swin-T. Our comprehensive analysis of the online validation set shows that our method surpasses the baseline LiteMedSAM model. We achieve a Dice Similarity Coefficient (DSC) of 84.68% and a Normalized Surface Dice (NSD) of 85.28%. Furthermore, the method achieves a more than threefold increase in inference speed, making it viable for real-time applications on devices with limited computational power. This demonstrates that our adaptation significantly enhances processing speed and resource efficiency without sacrificing accuracy.

Keywords: Segment Anything · Lightweight Model · Medical Imaging Segmentation · Computational Efficiency

1 Introduction

Segmentation plays a crucial role in medical imaging analysis, involving the identification and delineation of regions of interest (ROI) within medical images. The precision of segmentation is crucial for numerous clinical tasks, including disease diagnosis, treatment planning, and monitoring disease progression [13,50]. Traditionally, manual segmentation has been regarded as the standard for precisely defining anatomical and pathological regions. However, this method is highly time and labor-consuming and demands significant expertise. To overcome these limitations, automatic segmentation techniques have been introduced. These advanced methods greatly reduce the required time and effort, improve consistency, and enable the efficient analysis of large-scale medical datasets [63].

Recently, deep-learning techniques for image segmentation have shown promising results by training networks to understand intricate image features and produce accurate segmentations [7]. However, many existing models designed for medical image segmentation face a significant limitation that they are tailored for specific tasks and may not perform well when applied to new tasks or different datasets [47]. This task-specific nature poses a challenge to the widespread use of these models in clinical settings. Conversely, recent advancements in natural image segmentation have introduced foundation models, like the segment anything (SAM) [34] and segment everything everywhere all at once [72], showing exceptional adaptability and performance across a range of segmentation tasks. Moreover, the development of MedSAM [42] aims to address the challenge of limited generalizability in medical image segmentation by facilitating universal segmentation across diverse medical imaging tasks.

Despite their strong performance, these methods often utilize large-scale image encoders, leading to high computational demands that limit their practicality. To address this issue and speed up inference while conserving resources, various approaches have been explored to replace the image encoder of SAM with lightweight models. For instance, MobileSAM [69] distills the knowledge of SAM's ViT-H model into a compact vision transformer, while EdgeSAM [71] employs a CNN-based model trained to mimic ViT-H, incorporating a meticulous distillation strategy with the prompt encoder and mask decoder. Additionally, EfficientSAM [66] leverages the MAE pretraining method to enhance performance. However, these methods typically suffer from significant performance drops.

In our work, we propose a solution to further accelerate inference and reduce resource usage while maintaining high performance. Firstly, we enhance the performance of the original LiteMedSAM by replacing its image encoder with Swin-T. Subsequently, to make the encoder lightweight, we distill a RepViT-M0.6 from Swin-T and substitute the encoder of Swin-T with the distilled RepViT-M0.6 image encoder, achieving higher speed and reduced resource consumption while preserving performance.

We extensively evaluate our proposal on the online validation set and compare it with the baseline model (LiteMedSAM). Our results demonstrate improved performance, with the evaluation metric DSC increasing by approximately 2% and NSD by around 1%. Furthermore, we achieve over three times faster inference speed on devices equipped with a CPU and 8 GB of RAM.

2 Method

2.1 Pre-processing

We first conducted a statistical analysis of the challenge dataset. As shown in Table 1, Computed Tomography (CT) is the predominant modality, comprising 76.70% of the dataset with 1,219,765 slices. Magnetic Resonance (MR) images are also well-represented, making up 13.55% with 214,454 slices. Positron Emission Tomography (PET) accounts for 4.03%, contributing 64,163 slices. Endoscopy and X-Ray images constitute smaller portions at 2.82% and 1.91% respectively, providing 44,804 and 30,360 slices. Other modalities such as Ultrasound(US), Dermoscopy, Microscopy, Optical Coherence Tomography (OCT), Mammography, and Fundus Photography each contribute less than 1%.

During the pre-processing of the external public datasets (the list of external public datasets is shown in Table 8), we initially excluded all slices or images lacking targets or containing extremely small targets (smaller than 20 pixels) to ensure each slice or image had at least one target for segmentation. Subsequently, we normalized all slices/images to a range of [0, 1] and stored each slice/image along with its corresponding ground truth in a single npy file to facilitate faster I/O operations.

In the training phase, all grayscale images were converted to 3-channel images by replicating the image three times along the channel dimension. We resized the longer side of all images to 256 pixels while maintaining the original aspect ratio and then padded them to 256 × 256 pixels to meet the input requirements of the encoder. If an image had multiple labels, one label was randomly selected. Random data augmentation was applied to both images and their corresponding ground truths. Additionally, we utilized multiple worker processes to accelerate data loading.

Table 1. Statistical analysis of the dataset.

Modality	Proportion	Num. Slices
CT	76.70%	1219765
MR	13.55%	215454
PET	4.03%	64163
Endoscopy	2.82%	44804
X-Ray	1.91%	30360
US	0.40%	6318
Dermoscopy	0.24%	3874
Microscopy	0.11%	1627
OCT	0.09%	1436
Mammography	0.08%	1233
Fundus	0.07%	1100
Total		1590134

2.2 Proposed Method

The proposed method employs a 2-stage training protocol for a teacher-student model. In the first stage, we train a strong teacher model by replacing MedSAM's image encoder with a Swin-T-based encoder. In the second stage, we distill the features to a RepViT-M0.6-based MedSAM. The following sections will provide details of our model structures and the training & inference strategies.

Teacher Model. As previous studies have shown [66,69,70], the image encoder is the heaviest and most parameter-intensive part of the SAM [34], significantly affecting segmentation performance. Thus, selecting a strong yet efficient image encoder is crucial. The default encoder for SAM is ViT-H [17], known for its strong capabilities. However, training SAM with ViT-H requires 68 h on 256 A100 GPUs as mentioned in [34], posing a significant challenge for reproducibility or improvement.

To address this, we opt for the Swin-T image encoder [39], a small but effective hierarchical Transformer that uses shifted windows to limit self-attention computation to non-overlapping local windows while allowing cross-window connections. This architecture is efficient, modeling at various scales with linear computational complexity relative to image size, thus reducing the computational burden compared to ViT.

We replace lightweight MedSAM's original image encoder with Swin-T and train the entire pipeline from scratch. The Swin-T-based lightweight MedSAM shows significant improvement over the TinyViT-based lightweight MedSAM provided by the competition. Although Swin-T is the smallest Swin Transformer, it is still not efficient enough for fast inference on a laptop CPU. Therefore, we will use this model as a strong teacher model in the next section and distill its features into a smaller student model for much faster inference on a laptop CPU.

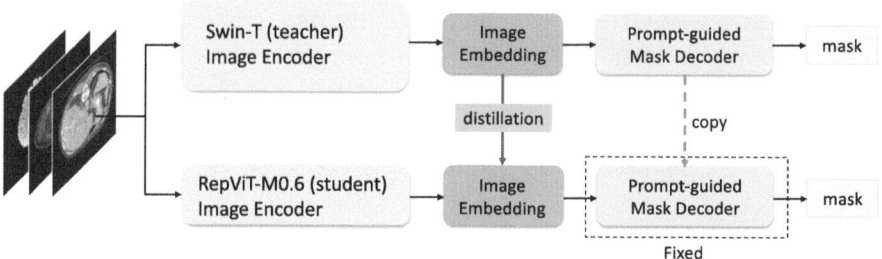

Fig. 1. Proposed teacher-student model architecture. For the teacher model (top), we use a Swin-T image encoder to replace the image encoder in the MedSAM and train the entire pipeline from scratch. For the student model (bottom), which is based on the RepViT-M0.6 image encoder, we distill the features from the teacher image encoder to the student image encoder. The prompt-guided mask decoder is directly copied from the teacher model and not finetuned.

Student Model. With a well-trained teacher model, our next step is to select an efficient student model and effectively distill the teacher model's features into it. For the student model, we choose RepViT-M0.6 [62], the smallest version of RepViT, as the image encoder for the student MedSAM model. RepViT is a series of lightweight CNNs redesigned from a ViT perspective, emphasizing their suitability for mobile devices. It builds on the mobile-friendly design of MobileNetV3 [28] and incorporates efficient architectural features of lightweight ViTs.

RepViT, being purely CNN-based, achieves very low latency and memory usage without the computational burden of attentions. After testing various RepViT variants, we found that RepViT-M0.6 offers sufficient performance for feature distillation with the highest inference speed on a CPU.

Feature Distillation to Student Model. Next, we discuss the feature distillation from the teacher model to the student model. Following the practice in [69], SAM model distillation methods are classified into fully-coupled, semi-coupled, and decoupled distillation. The first two methods add supervision to the model's final output, i.e., the mask output, while decoupled distillation only distills the image encoder part.

Since the performance bottleneck mainly depends on the image encoder, it is reasonable to fix the prompt-guided mask decoder, which has a small number of parameters, and only distill the image encoder from the feature level. Therefore, we follow this practice and distill the image encoder part, as shown in Fig. 1, using a simple MSE loss between the outputs of the Swin-T encoder and the RepViT encoder. This simple distillation method works surprisingly well, with the student model's performance being comparable to the teacher model.

As mentioned in [69], finetuning the prompt-guided mask decoder after distilling the image encoder might potentially improve overall performance. However, in our case, the small image encoder with RepViT-M0.6 sufficiently matches the Swin-T in the feature level. Thus, finetuning the prompt-guided mask decoder with mask loss did not provide a performance boost.

Loss Functions. For the teacher MedSAM model with Swin-T, we train the entire pipeline from scratch using a combination of Dice loss, cross-entropy loss, and MSE loss. This compound loss function is robust for various medical image segmentation tasks [41]. For the student MedSAM model with RepViT-M0.6, we distill only the image encoder part. We compute the MSE loss between the feature outputs of the teacher and student models' image encoders.

Strategies to Accelerate CPU Inference. Our student model with RepViT-M0.6 is already fast on CPU inference. However, we explored quantization for potential benefits. We tried Pytorch FX Graph Quantization [6] and ONNX Runtime [15] for Int8 quantization, but observed significant performance loss even after calibration. Therefore, we abandoned quantization. Instead, we used "torch.jit" to increase the model loading speed, contributing to the speed boost in the Docker test.

2.3 Post-processing

First, as the model outputs are logits, we first convert the logits to probabilities using a sigmoid function. The masks are then cropped to match the shape of the image, which has been resized to have a longest side of 256 pixels, without being padded to 256 × 256 pixels. Following this, the masks are resized back to the original image dimensions using bilinear interpolation, ensuring proper alignment and smooth transitions. The resulting tensor is then converted to a NumPy array on the CPU. Finally, a threshold is applied to generate a binary segmentation mask, where values greater than 0.5 indicate the presence of the target object. This comprehensive process ensures that the model's raw outputs are accurately transformed into a practical segmentation format.

3 Experiments

3.1 Dataset and Evaluation Measures

We use the challenge dataset and external public datasets for network training, as shown in the supplementary Table 8.

The evaluation metrics include two accuracy measures-Dice Similarity Coefficient (DSC) and Normalized Surface Dice (NSD)-and the running time for efficiency measurement. These metrics collectively contribute to the ranking computation.

3.2 Environment Settings

The details of our environment are presented in Table 2. We use Ubuntu 22.04.4 LTS as our operating system. Our system is equipped with an Intel(R) Core(TM) i9-13900KF CPU and 64 GB of RAM. Additionally, we utilize an NVIDIA RTX 4090 GPU with 24 GB of memory.

Table 2. Development environments and requirements.

System	Ubuntu 22.04.4 LTS
CPU	Intel(R) Core(TM) i9-13900KF CPU@3.00 GHz
RAM	4 × 16 GB; 2.67MT/s
GPU (number and type)	One NVIDIA RTX 4090 24G
CUDA version	12.1
Programming language	Python 3.10
Deep learning framework	torch 2.1.2, torchvision 0.16.2
Specific dependencies	N/A
Code	GitHub

3.3 Training Protocols of LiteMedSAM with Swin-T Image Encoder

In training LiteMedSAM with the Swin-T image encoder, we initially apply data augmentation techniques to enhance model robustness. These techniques include random horizontal and vertical flips. To avoid overfitting to the data sequence, we randomly select images from the dataset. For images with multiple labels, we randomly choose one label per image. The bounding box is generated by calculating the coordinates of the top-left and bottom-right corners of the label and applying a slight perturbation to them. A validation set is constructed by randomly selecting approximately 5% of the entire training dataset.

As shown in Table 3, during training, images are pre-processed to 3×256×256. The network is trained from scratch over 100 epochs. We employ a combination of Dice Loss, Cross Entropy Loss, and Mean Squared Error Loss (MSELoss) as the loss function. The initial learning rate is set to 0.005. We use AdamW as the optimizer and ReduceLROnPlateau as the learning rate scheduler, which reduces the learning rate by a factor of 0.9 whenever the validation loss does not decrease for five consecutive epochs. We assess the model's performance on the validation set at the end of each epoch and save the model that records the best performance on the validation set.

Table 3. Training protocols of LiteMedSAM with Swin-T image encoder.

Pre-trained Model	N/A
Batch size	8
Patch size	3 × 256 × 256
Total epochs	100
Optimizer	AdamW
Initial learning rate (lr)	0.005
Lr decay schedule	ReduceLROnPlateau(reduction ratio 0.9)
Training time	1200 h
Loss function	Dice Loss, Cross Entropy Loss, MSE Loss
Number of model parameters	14.55M
Number of flops	42.85G
CO_2eq	848 Kg

3.4 Training Protocols for the Knowledge Distillation of RepViT-M0.6 Image Encoder from Swin-T Image Encoder

For the knowledge distillation of the RepViT-M0.6 image encoder from the Swin-T image encoder, the training process is similar to the training of LiteMedSAM with Swin-T. The data is processed by data augmentation and shuffled before input into the network. We maintain the same dataset split as used in the training of LiteMedSAM with Swin-T. During training, images are pre-processed to $3 \times 256 \times 256$ and we conduct the distillation of the RepViT-M0.6 from the Swin-T image encoder over 50 epochs, as illustrated in Table 4. To minimize the difference in the image embedding outputs between RepViT-M0.6 and Swin-T, we calculate MSELoss. We utilize AdamW as the optimizer with an initial learning rate of 0.005 and ReduceLROnPlateau as the learning rate scheduler, which reduces the learning rate by a factor of 0.9 whenever the validation loss does not decrease for five epochs. We evaluate the model on the validation set after each epoch and save the model version that achieved the lowest validation loss.

Table 4. Training protocols for the knowledge distillation of RepViT-M0.6 image encoder from Swin-T image encoder.

Pre-trained Teacher Model	Swin-T Image Encoder
Pre-trained Student Model	N/A
Batch size	8
Patch size	$3 \times 256 \times 256$
Total epochs	50
Optimizer	AdamW
Initial learning rate (lr)	0.005
Lr decay schedule	ReduceLROnPlateau(reduction ratio 0.9)
Training time	400 h
Loss function	MSE Loss
Number of model parameters	2.32M
Number of flops	9.00G
CO_2eq	99 Kg

4 Results and Discussion

4.1 Quantitative Results on Online Validation Set

In Table 5, we compare three methods: the baseline, LiteMedSAM with Swin-T, and our proposed LiteMedSAM with RepViT-M0.6 image encoder, which is distilled from the Swin-T model. We evaluate their performance on the online validation set using the DSC and NSD evaluation metrics.

The LiteMedSAM with Swin-T (without knowledge distillation) demonstrates an average improvement of approximately 2% in both DSC and NSD compared to the baseline. This improvement is observed across most modalities, with the exception of a slight decrease in Endoscopy and Fundus. Furthermore, when employing knowledge distillation, there is only a minor decline in the average DSC and NSD, yet still shows a clear improvement compared to the baseline.

Table 5. Quantitative evaluation results on online validation set.

Target	Baseline DSC(%)	Baseline NSD(%)	w/o Knowledge Distillation DSC(%)	w/o Knowledge Distillation NSD(%)	Proposed DSC(%)	Proposed NSD (%)
CT	89.53	91.82	89.94	91.85	**92.65**	**95.06**
MR	78.75	81.87	81.35	84.36	**86.09**	**89.34**
PET	68.91	55.43	**71.00**	**55.95**	62.38	38.58
US	81.34	87.12	81.60	86.74	**82.45**	**87.54**
X-Ray	70.23	76.58	78.39	**84.49**	**79.13**	85.11
Dermoscopy	92.65	94.14	**93.58**	**95.08**	93.45	94.96
Endoscopy	**94.87**	**97.38**	93.87	96.43	93.48	96.23
Fundus	**95.85**	**97.48**	95.47	97.11	94.68	96.36
Microscopy	71.79	76.95	77.27	83.88	**77.80**	**84.38**
Average	82.66	84.31	**84.72**	**86.21**	84.68	85.28

Table 6. Quantitative evaluation of segmentation efficiency in terms of running time (s).

Case ID	Size	Num. Objects	Baseline	w/o Knowledge Distillation	Proposed
3DBox_CT_0566	(287, 512, 512)	6	206.4344	212.4705	**48.5365**
3DBox_CT_0888	(237, 512, 512)	6	55.7089	55.686	**13.6685**
3DBox_CT_0860	(246, 512, 512)	1	7.7789	7.6037	**2.502**
3DBox_MR_0621	(115, 400, 400)	6	101.7202	89.6444	**20.3509**
3DBox_MR_0121	(64, 290, 320)	6	58.291	50.8915	**13.5169**
3DBox_MR_0179	(84, 512, 512)	1	8.1488	7.0312	**1.9713**
3DBox_PET_0001	(264, 200, 200)	1	5.511	3.8106	**1.3485**
2DBox_US_0525	(256, 256, 3)	1	0.4136	0.4332	**0.1382**
2DBox_X-Ray_0053	(320, 640, 3)	34	1.3110	1.3009	**1.271**
2DBox_Dermoscopy_0003	(3024, 4032, 3)	1	0.7331	0.6091	**0.4595**
2DBox_Endoscopy_0086	(480, 560, 3)	1	0.4311	0.4164	**0.1533**
2DBox_Fundus_0003	(2048, 2048, 3)	1	0.4785	0.3656	**0.1998**
2DBox_Microscopy_0008	(1536, 2040, 3)	19	0.9869	0.9626	**0.6367**
2DBox_Microscopy_0016	(1920, 2560, 3)	241	8.7242	8.6334	**8.1791**

4.2 Qualitative Results on Online Validation Set

In this section, we present examples of both good and bad segmentation results to further analyze the performance of our proposed method. Generally, our method performs well with images that exhibit high contrast, simple backgrounds, and regular shapes. However, it encounters challenges with images that contain overlapping textures and irregular shapes and borders.

As illustrated in Fig. 2, in the first row, the brain MR image showcases high contrast against a simple background, while in the second row, the chest X-ray displays the lung in regular shapes, which our model can accurately segment. Conversely, as depicted in Fig. 3, the X-ray image exhibits overlapping textures,

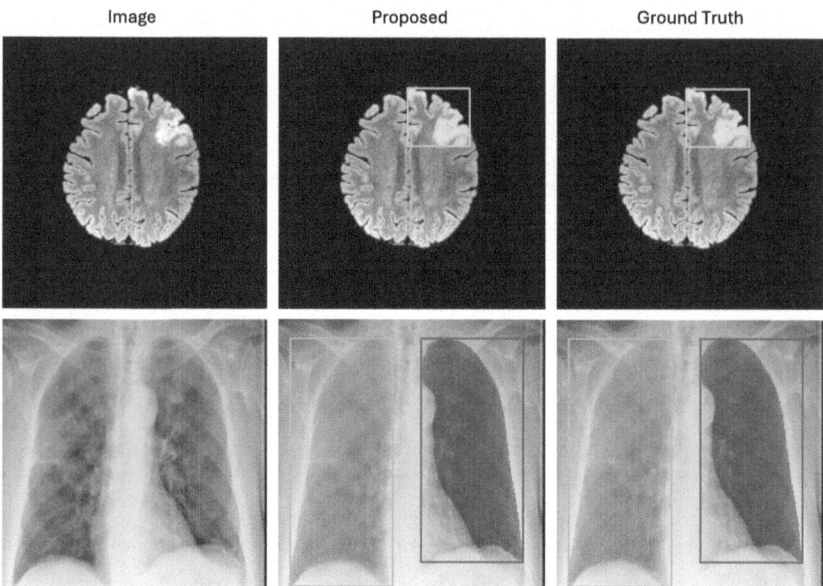

Fig. 2. The examples of good segmentation results.

and the targets within the box are irregularly shaped in both the first and second rows, posing difficulties for accurate segmentation with our method.

4.3 Segmentation Efficiency Results on Online Validation Set

An important challenge for this task is the constraint of the target device, which is equipped with only a CPU and limited memory (8 GB RAM), making segmentation efficiency crucial. We present some challenging cases that require longer processing times in Table 6. Our proposed method consistently demonstrates a significant reduction in running time across almost all cases compared to both the baseline and the LiteMedSAM with Swin-T. This improvement is particularly notable in complex 3D imaging cases. For instance, in the 3DBox_CT_0566 case, the proposed method reduces the running time from over 200 s in the baseline to just 48.54 s. Similarly, in the 3DBox_CT_0888 and 3DBox_CT_0860 cases, the running times decrease from 55.71 and 7.78 s in the baseline to 13.67 and 2.50 s, respectively.

In 2D imaging scenarios, such as 2DBox_US_0525 and 2DBox_X-Ray_0053, the proposed method drastically reduces running times to 0.14 and 1.27 s from 0.41 and 1.31 s in the baseline, respectively. The reductions are even more striking in cases like 2DBox_Dermoscopy_0003 and 2DBox_Endoscopy_0086, where the proposed method achieves running times of 0.46 and 0.15 s, down from 0.73 and 0.43 s in the baseline. These results underscore the effectiveness of our proposed method in enhancing the efficiency of segmentation on devices with limited computational resources.

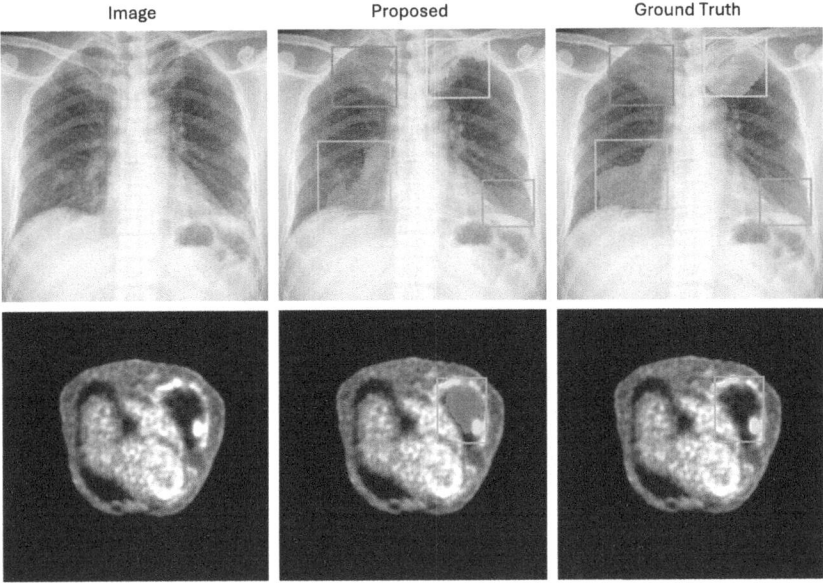

Fig. 3. The examples of bad segmentation results.

4.4 Results on Final Testing Set

The final testing set comprises 9 modalities: CT, MR, Endoscopy, Ultrasound(US), X-Ray, Fundus, Microscopy, PET, and OCT. Our proposed method is evaluated based on two categories of metrics: segmentation accuracy and segmentation efficiency. For accuracy, DSC and NSD are used, while segmentation efficiency is assessed by measuring the running time in seconds. A rank-then-aggregate strategy [65] is utilized for ranking. It includes the following three steps:

- Step 1: Compute the DSC, NSD, and running time for each test case.
- Step 2: Rank the teams for each modality based on each metric.
- Step 3: Calculate the average of all these rankings.

A quantitative comparison of our proposed method with the baseline LiteMedSAM is presented in Table 7. Our method consistently outperforms LiteMedSAM in DSC and NSD across most imaging modalities. Specifically, our method significantly enhances NSD in US and Endoscopy, while markedly improving DSC in X-Ray and Endoscopy modalities. Moreover, our method achieves a reduction in running time for all modalities, thereby increasing both the efficiency and effectiveness of the segmentation.

Overall, our method achieves an average DSC of 79.26% and an average NSD of 81.16%, surpassing the baseline LiteMedSAM of 78.64% and 80.58%. The average running time is also reduced from 14.69 s with LiteMedSAM to 5.66 s, highlighting a substantial enhancement in processing speed.

Furthermore, our method scores an average ranking of 9.22, with a lower score indicating better performance, placing it 5th overall in the final test set.

Table 7. Quantitative evaluation results on final testing set.

Target	LiteMedSAM(Baseline)			Proposed		
	DSC(%)	NSD(%)	RunTime(s)	DSC(%)	NSD(%)	RunTime(s)
CT	55.75	58.48	38.78	**71.04**	**74.64**	**11.33**
MR	64.80	**62.75**	18.57	**67.95**	62.10	**6.45**
PET	76.94	66.98	14.90	**79.26**	**69.09**	**6.30**
US	85.24	89.73	8.96	**87.81**	**92.44**	**4.57**
X-Ray	**85.51**	**94.40**	9.95	75.59	86.61	**4.68**
Endoscopy	**94.41**	**96.95**	7.56	92.32	95.05	**4.12**
Fundus	87.47	89.58	8.77	**89.55**	**91.71**	**4.22**
Microscopy	**84.36**	**86.15**	16.34	69.75	71.45	**4.64**
OCT	73.31	80.20	8.39	**80.06**	**87.38**	**4.64**
Average	78.64	80.58	14.69	**79.26**	**81.16**	**5.66**

4.5 Limitation and Future Work

Although our proposed method has exhibited promising performance and excellent efficiency, it still encounters difficulties with cases characterized by low contrast, irregular shapes, and overlapping textures, as mentioned in Sect. 4.2. These challenges highlight areas for improvement in future work.

One potential avenue for addressing these issues could involve training a more robust teacher model to provide better guidance during knowledge distillation. Additionally, incorporating more diverse and challenging data into the training process could help the model learn to handle such cases more effectively.

5 Conclusion

In this study, we introduced an optimized segmentation framework leveraging knowledge distillation techniques to enhance the efficiency of medical segmentation networks. By integrating knowledge distillation, notable reductions in inference time were achieved while preserving segmentation accuracy, thus demonstrating promising prospects for real-time application in resource-constrained environments. Specifically, our results indicate a significant threefold decrease in processing time compared to the baseline model, along with improvements in quantitative evaluation.

Despite these advancements, challenges remain with low-contrast images, irregular shapes, and overlapping textures. Future work will aim to address these issues, enhancing the robustness and applicability of our proposed framework.

Acknowledgements. We thank all the data owners for making the medical images publicly available and CodaLab [67] for hosting the challenge platform.

Disclosure of Interests. The authors have no competing interests to declare that are relevant to the content of this article.

Appendix

See Table 8 and Table 9.

Table 8. The external public datasets we used for training.

Dataset	Anatomy	Modality
CT Lung & Hearth & Trachea segmentation	Chest	CT
Seg.A. [49]	Aorta	CT
Figshare Brain Tumor Dataset [11]	Brain	MR
Uwaterloo skin cancer [21]	Skin	Dermoscopy
BKAI-IGH NeoPolyp [5]	Abdominal	Endoscopy
CT2USforKidneySeg [59]	Kidney	US
Ultrasound Nerve Segmentation	Neck	US
GlaS@MICCAI'2015: Gland Segmentation [58]	ColonGland	Microscopy
MM-WHS [19]	Heart	CT, MR
MMs-20-21 [10]	Heart	MR
FeTA [51]	Brain	MR
CHAOS [32]	Abdomen	CT, MR
Drive	Eye	Fundus
RAVIR [22,23]	Eye	Fundus
FetoPlac	Fetus	Microscopy
HMC-QU [14]	Heart	US

Table 9. The challenge datasets we used for training.

Dataset	Anatomy	Modality
COVID-19-20 [56]	Chest	CT
AbdomenCT-1K [45]	Abdomen	CT
FDG-PET-CT-Lesions [20]	Whole body	CT
NSCLC Radiogenomics [8]	Chest	CT
NSCLC-Radiomics [1]	Lung	CT
CT Lymph Nodes [55]	Abdomen, Mediastinum	CT
NSCLC-PleuralEffusion [35]	Chest	CT
NSCLC-LungMSD-LUNG [7]	Chest	CT
KiTS23 [24]	Kidney	CT
CT-ORG [54]	whole body	CT
COVID-19-20-CTSEG [43]	Chest	CT
TotalSegmentator [64]	whole body	CT
AMOS [31]	Abdomen	CT, MR
LCTSC [68]	Chest	CT
HCC-TACE-Seg [48]	Liver	CT
Adrenal-ACC-Ki67-Seg [2]	Abdomen	CT
MSD [7]	various	CT, MR
ISLES [25]	Brain	MR
WMH [37]	Brain	MR
BraTS [46]	Head	MR
PROMISE12 [38]	Prostate	MR
MSD-Prostate [57]	Prostate	MR
NCI-ISBI [12]	Prostate	MR
Crossmoda [16]	Brain	MR
QIN-PROSTATE-Repeatability [18]	Prostate	MRI
CC-Tumor Heterogeneity [9]	Cervical Cancer	MR
COVID-19 Radiography Database [53]	Lung	CXR
COVID-QU-Ex [60]	Lung	CXR
Chest Xray Masks and Labels [29]	Chest	CXR
Chest X-Ray Images with Pneumothorax Masks	Chest	CXR
CDD-CESM [33]	Breast	Mammography
Intraretinal Cystoid Fluid [3]	Eye	OCT
ps-fh-aop-2023 [40]	Head	US
hc18 [26]	Fetal Head	US
Breast Ultrasound Images Dataset [4]	Breast	US
ISIC2018 [61]	Skin	Dermoscopy
CholecSeg8k [27]	Abdominal	Endoscopy
Kvasir-SEG [30]	Abdominal	Endoscopy
m2caiSeg	Abdominal	Endoscopy
PAPILA [36]	Eye	Fundus
IDRiD [52]	Eye	Fundus
NeurIPS CellSeg [44]	Cells	Microscopy

References

1. Aerts, H.J., et al.: Decoding tumour phenotype by noninvasive imaging using a quantitative radiomics approach. Nat. Commun. **5**(1), 4006 (2014)
2. Ahmed, A., et al.: Radiomic mapping model for prediction of KI-67 expression in adrenocortical carcinoma. Clin. Radiol. **75**(6), 479–e17 (2020)
3. Ahmed, Z., Panhwar, S.Q., Baqai, A., Umrani, F.A., Ahmed, M., Khan, A.: Deep learning based automated detection of intraretinal cystoid fluid. Int. J. Imaging Syst. Technol. **32**(3), 902–917 (2022)
4. Al-Dhabyani, W., Gomaa, M., Khaled, H., Fahmy, A.: Dataset of breast ultrasound images. Data Brief **28**, 104863 (2020)
5. An, N.S., et al.: Blazeneo: blazing fast polyp segmentation and neoplasm detection. IEEE Access **10**, 43669–43684 (2022). https://doi.org/10.1109/ACCESS.2022.3168693
6. Ansel, J., et al.: Pytorch 2: faster machine learning through dynamic python bytecode transformation and graph compilation. In: Proceedings of the 29th ACM International Conference on Architectural Support for Programming Languages and Operating Systems, vol. 2, pp. 929–947 (2024)
7. Antonelli, M., et al.: The medical segmentation decathlon. Nat. Commun. **13**(1), 4128 (2022)
8. Bakr, S., et al.: A radiogenomic dataset of non-small cell lung cancer. Sci. Data **5**(1), 1–9 (2018)
9. Bowen, S.R., et al.: Tumor radiomic heterogeneity: multiparametric functional imaging to characterize variability and predict response following cervical cancer radiation therapy. J. Magn. Reson. Imaging **47**(5), 1388–1396 (2018)
10. Campello, V.M., et al.: Multi-centre, multi-vendor and multi-disease cardiac segmentation: the m&ms challenge. IEEE Trans. Med. Imaging **40**(12), 3543–3554 (2021). https://doi.org/10.1109/TMI.2021.3090082
11. Cheng, J., et al.: Enhanced performance of brain tumor classification via tumor region augmentation and partition. PLoS ONE **10**(10), e0140381 (2015)
12. Clark, K., et al.: The cancer imaging archive (TCIA): maintaining and operating a public information repository. J. Digit. Imaging **26**, 1045–1057 (2013)
13. De Fauw, J., et al.: Clinically applicable deep learning for diagnosis and referral in retinal disease. Nat. Med. **24**(9), 1342–1350 (2018)
14. Degerli, A., Kiranyaz, S., Hamid, T., Mazhar, R., Gabbouj, M.: Early myocardial infarction detection over multi-view echocardiography. Biomed. Signal Process. Control **87**, 105448 (2024)
15. ONNX Runtime developers: Onnx runtime (2021). https://onnxruntime.ai/. version: x.y.z
16. Dorent, R., et al.: CrossMoDA 2021 challenge: benchmark of cross-modality domain adaptation techniques for vestibular schwannoma and cochlea segmentation. Med. Image Anal. **83**, 102628 (2023)
17. Dosovitskiy, A., et al.: An image is worth 16x16 words: transformers for image recognition at scale. In: ICLR (2021)
18. Fedorov, A., et al.: An annotated test-retest collection of prostate multiparametric MRI. Sci. Data **5**(1), 1–13 (2018)
19. Gao, S., Zhou, H., Gao, Y., Zhuang, X.: BayeSeg: Bayesian modeling for medical image segmentation with interpretable generalizability. Med. Image Anal. **89**, 102889 (2023)

20. Gatidis, S., et al.: A whole-body FDG-PET/CT dataset with manually annotated tumor lesions. Sci. Data **9**(1), 601 (2022)
21. Glaister, J., Wong, A., Clausi, D.A.: Automatic segmentation of skin lesions from dermatological photographs using a joint probabilistic texture distinctiveness approach. IEEE Trans. Biomed. Eng. (2014)
22. Hatamizadeh, A.: An Artificial Intelligence Framework for the Automated Segmentation and Quantitative Analysis of Retinal Vasculature. University of California, Los Angeles (2020)
23. Hatamizadeh, A., et al.: RAVIR: a dataset and methodology for the semantic segmentation and quantitative analysis of retinal arteries and veins in infrared reflectance imaging. IEEE J. Biomed. Health Inform. **26**(7), 3272–3283 (2022)
24. Heller, N., et al.: The state of the art in kidney and kidney tumor segmentation in contrast-enhanced CT imaging: results of the KiTS19 challenge. Med. Image Anal. **67**, 101821 (2021)
25. Hernandez Petzsche, M.R., et al.: ISLES 2022: a multi-center magnetic resonance imaging stroke lesion segmentation dataset. Sci. Data **9**(1), 762 (2022)
26. van den Heuvel, T.L., de Bruijn, D., de Korte, C.L., Ginneken, B.V.: Automated measurement of fetal head circumference using 2D ultrasound images. PloS One **13**(8), e0200412 (2018)
27. Hong, W.Y., Kao, C.L., Kuo, Y.H., Wang, J.R., Chang, W.L., Shih, C.S.: CholecSeg8k: a semantic segmentation dataset for laparoscopic cholecystectomy based on Cholec80. arXiv preprint arXiv:2012.12453 (2020)
28. Howard, A., et al.: Searching for MobileNetV3. In: Proceedings of the IEEE/CVF International Conference on Computer Vision, pp. 1314–1324 (2019)
29. Jaeger, S., et al.: Automatic tuberculosis screening using chest radiographs. IEEE Trans. Med. Imaging **33**(2), 233–245 (2013)
30. Jha, D., et al.: Kvasir-SEG: a segmented polyp dataset. In: Ro, Y.M., et al. (eds.) MMM 2020. LNCS, vol. 11962, pp. 451–462. Springer, Cham (2020). https://doi.org/10.1007/978-3-030-37734-2_37
31. Ji, Y., et al.: AMOS: a large-scale abdominal multi-organ benchmark for versatile medical image segmentation. In: Advances in Neural Information Processing Systems, vol. 35, pp. 36722–36732 (2022)
32. Kavur, A.E., et al.: Chaos challenge-combined (CT-MR) healthy abdominal organ segmentation. Med. Image Anal. **69**, 101950 (2021)
33. Khaled, R., et al.: Categorized contrast enhanced mammography dataset for diagnostic and artificial intelligence research. Sci. Data **9**(1), 122 (2022)
34. Kirillov, A., et al.: Segment anything. In: Proceedings of the International Conference on Computer Vision, pp. 4015–4026 (2023)
35. Kiser, K.J., Barman, A., Stieb, S., Fuller, C.D., Giancardo, L.: Novel autosegmentation spatial similarity metrics capture the time required to correct segmentations better than traditional metrics in a thoracic cavity segmentation workflow. J. Digit. Imaging **34**, 541–553 (2021)
36. Kovalyk, O., Morales-Sánchez, J., Verdú-Monedero, R., Sellés-Navarro, I., Palazón-Cabanes, A., Sancho-Gómez, J.L.: PAPILA: dataset with fundus images and clinical data of both eyes of the same patient for glaucoma assessment. Sci. Data **9**(1), 291 (2022)
37. Kuijf, H.J., et al.: Standardized assessment of automatic segmentation of white matter hyperintensities and results of the WMH segmentation challenge. IEEE Trans. Med. Imaging **38**(11), 2556–2568 (2019)
38. Litjens, G., et al.: Evaluation of prostate segmentation algorithms for MRI: the PROMISE12 challenge. Med. Image Anal. **18**(2), 359–373 (2014)

39. Liu, Z., et al.: Swin transformer: hierarchical vision transformer using shifted windows. In: Proceedings of the IEEE/CVF International Conference on Computer Vision, pp. 10012–10022 (2021)
40. Lu, Y., et al.: The JNU-IFM dataset for segmenting pubic symphysis-fetal head. Data Brief **41**, 107904 (2022)
41. Ma, J., et al.: Loss odyssey in medical image segmentation. Med. Image Anal. **71**, 102035 (2021)
42. Ma, J., He, Y., Li, F., Han, L., You, C., Wang, B.: Segment anything in medical images. Nat. Commun. **15**(1), 654 (2024)
43. Ma, J., et al.: Toward data-efficient learning: a benchmark for covid-19 CT lung and infection segmentation. Med. Phys. **48**(3), 1197–1210 (2021)
44. Ma, J., et al.: The multimodality cell segmentation challenge: toward universal solutions. Nat. Methods, 1–11 (2024)
45. Ma, J., et al.: AbdomenCT-1K: is abdominal organ segmentation a solved problem? IEEE Trans. Pattern Anal. Mach. Intell. **44**(10), 6695–6714 (2021)
46. Menze, B.H., et al.: The multimodal brain tumor image segmentation benchmark (BRATS). IEEE Trans. Med. Imaging **34**(10), 1993–2024 (2014)
47. Minaee, S., Boykov, Y., Porikli, F., Plaza, A., Kehtarnavaz, N., Terzopoulos, D.: Image segmentation using deep learning: a survey. IEEE Trans. Pattern Anal. Mach. Intell. **44**(7), 3523–3542 (2021)
48. Morshid, A., et al.: A machine learning model to predict hepatocellular carcinoma response to transcatheter arterial chemoembolization. Radiol. Artif. Intell. **1**(5), e180021 (2019)
49. Myronenko, A., Yang, D., He, Y., Xu, D.: Aorta segmentation from 3D CT in MICCAI SEG.A. 2023 challenge. In: Pepe, A., Melito, G.M., Egger, J. (eds.) SEGA 2023. LNCS, vol. 14539, pp. 13–18. Springer, Cham (2023). https://doi.org/10.1007/978-3-031-53241-2_2
50. Ouyang, D., et al.: Video-based AI for beat-to-beat assessment of cardiac function. Nature **580**(7802), 252–256 (2020)
51. Payette, K., et al.: An automatic multi-tissue human fetal brain segmentation benchmark using the fetal tissue annotation dataset. Sci. Data **8**(1), 167 (2021)
52. Porwal, P., et al.: Indian diabetic retinopathy image dataset (IDRiD): a database for diabetic retinopathy screening research. Data **3**(3), 25 (2018)
53. Rahman, T., et al.: Exploring the effect of image enhancement techniques on covid-19 detection using chest X-ray images. Comput. Biol. Med. **132**, 104319 (2021)
54. Rister, B., Yi, D., Shivakumar, K., Nobashi, T., Rubin, D.L.: CT-ORG, a new dataset for multiple organ segmentation in computed tomography. Sci. Data **7**(1), 381 (2020)
55. Roth, H.R., et al.: A new 2.5D representation for lymph node detection using random sets of deep convolutional neural network observations. In: Golland, P., Hata, N., Barillot, C., Hornegger, J., Howe, R. (eds.) MICCAI 2014. LNCS, vol. 8673, pp. 520–527. Springer, Cham (2014). https://doi.org/10.1007/978-3-319-10404-1_65
56. Roth, H.R., et al.: Rapid artificial intelligence solutions in a pandemic-the covid-19-20 lung CT lesion segmentation challenge. Med. Image Anal. **82**, 102605 (2022)
57. Simpson, A.L., et al.: A large annotated medical image dataset for the development and evaluation of segmentation algorithms. arXiv preprint arXiv:1902.09063 (2019)
58. Sirinukunwattana, K., et al.: Gland segmentation in colon histology images: the GlaS challenge contest. Med. Image Anal. **35**, 489–502 (2017)

59. Song, Y., Zheng, J., Lei, L., Ni, Z., Zhao, B., Hu, Y.: CT2US: cross-modal transfer learning for kidney segmentation in ultrasound images with synthesized data. Ultrasonics **122**, 106706 (2022). https://doi.org/10.1016/j.ultras.2022.106706. https://www.sciencedirect.com/science/article/pii/S0041624X22000191
60. Tahir, A.M., et al.: Covid-19 infection localization and severity grading from chest X-ray images. Comput. Biol. Med. **139**, 105002 (2021)
61. Tschandl, P., Rosendahl, C., Kittler, H.: The HAM10000 dataset, a large collection of multi-source dermatoscopic images of common pigmented skin lesions. Sci. Data **5**(1), 1–9 (2018)
62. Wang, A., Chen, H., Lin, Z., Pu, H., Ding, G.: RepViT: revisiting mobile CNN from ViT perspective. arXiv preprint arXiv:2307.09283 (2023)
63. Wang, G., et al.: DeepiGeoS: a deep interactive geodesic framework for medical image segmentation. IEEE Trans. Pattern Anal. Mach. Intell. **41**(7), 1559–1572 (2018)
64. Wasserthal, J., et al.: TotalSegmentator: robust segmentation of 104 anatomic structures in CT images. Radiol. Artif. Intell. **5**(5) (2023)
65. Wiesenfarth, M., et al.: Methods and open-source toolkit for analyzing and visualizing challenge results. Sci. Rep. **11**(1), 2369 (2021)
66. Xiong, Y., et al.: EfficientSAM: leveraged masked image pretraining for efficient segment anything. arXiv preprint arXiv:2312.00863 (2023)
67. Xu, Z., et al.: Codabench: flexible, easy-to-use, and reproducible meta-benchmark platform. Patterns **3**(7), 100543 (2022)
68. Yang, J., et al.: Autosegmentation for thoracic radiation treatment planning: a grand challenge at AAPM 2017. Med. Phys. **45**(10), 4568–4581 (2018)
69. Zhang, C., et al.: Faster segment anything: towards lightweight SAM for mobile applications. arXiv preprint arXiv:2306.14289 (2023)
70. Zhang, Z., Cai, H., Han, S.: EfficientViT-SAM: accelerated segment anything model without performance loss. In: CVPR Workshop: Efficient Large Vision Models (2024)
71. Zhou, C., Li, X., Loy, C.C., Dai, B.: EdgeSAM: prompt-in-the-loop distillation for on-device deployment of SAM. arXiv preprint arXiv:2312.06660 (2023)
72. Zou, X., et al.: Segment everything everywhere all at once. In: Advances in Neural Information Processing Systems, vol. 36 (2024)

Taking a Step Back: Revisiting Classical Approaches for Efficient Interactive Segmentation of Medical Images

Zdravko Marinov[1,2](✉)[iD], Alexander Jaus[1,2][iD], Jens Kleesiek[3,4][iD], and Rainer Stiefelhagen[1][iD]

[1] Karlsruhe Institute of Technology, Karlsruhe, Germany
zdravko.marinov@kit.edu
[2] HIDSS4Health - Helmholtz Information and Data Science School for Health, Karlsruhe/Heidelberg, Germany
[3] Institute for AI in Medicine, University Hospital Essen, Essen, Germany
[4] Cancer Research Center Cologne Essen (CCCE), University Medicine Essen, Essen, Germany

Abstract. Interactive segmentation plays a pivotal role in medical image analysis for several reasons. It enables clinicians to precisely delineate regions of interest for accurate diagnosis and treatment planning while also allowing for real-time interaction with rapid annotations without workflow interruptions. While the emergence of MedSAM in 2023 presented a promising solution with its modality-agnostic model, its efficiency is hindered by its large size, resulting in long inference times. In response, we revisited simpler models such as thresholding, k-means clustering, and shape-based slice interpolation for efficient interactive segmentation tailored to specific modalities. Surprisingly, these rudimentary expert models outperformed MedSAM in terms of both segmentation performance and computational efficiency on multiple imaging modalities reaching a Dice score of 85.65 and a Normalized Surface Dice of 86.68 on the validation set. Our findings show the need to compare to older, simpler approaches to unveil the limitations of emerging foundation models. By examining these approaches, we aim to discover why MedSAM fails on certain modalities and enhance its robustness and efficiency leading to a more reliable general model for the segmentation of medical images.

1 Introduction

Background. Advancements in deep learning have propelled the segmentation of anatomical structures and lesions in medical images. However, they often rely on manually annotated datasets [3,7,12,19,33,43]. Additionally, the volumetric nature of some imaging modalities such as CT, MRI, or PET, poses a significant challenge, as annotating each voxel demands extensive time and expertise. To circumvent this hurdle, interactive segmentation methodologies have emerged, utilizing less labor-intensive annotations such as clicks or bounding boxes, rather than dense voxelwise labels [4,9,10,26,31,32,41,42,47]. These interactive models integrate user interactions with the image input to generate predictions, guided by these interactions. Once validated by medical experts, these predictions can serve as new labels [31].

Related Work. Recently, MedSAM [28] released a fine-tuned Segment Anything Model (SAM) [24] on 11 imaging modalities and over 1.5 million image-mask pairs. MedSAM demonstrates great generalizability across various imaging modalities and segmentation tasks [28,31]. However, its large size hinders the real-time interaction between the annotator and the model. There have been multiple light-weight versions of MedSAM such as MobileSam [45] and EfficientViT-SAM [46] that optimize the efficiency of MedSAM while retaining most of its generalization to multiple modalities. To explore this further, Ma et al. [28] hosted the Segment Anything In Medical Images On Laptop Challenge[1] to gather insights on how to design efficient bounding-box-based methods for interactive segmentation. This paper describes our submission to this challenge.

Motivation. We aim to revisit classical methods as they offer a simple and efficient solution to most segmentation tasks. By comparing them to current generalist models such as MedSAM, we aim to gain insights into how such simple models can outperform large pre-trained vision models and delve into the discussion of how to improve MedSAM in future iterations. Our work presents the following contributions:

1. We investigate classical approaches for 11 imaging modalities and investigate if they can outperform MedSAM's lightweight implementation (LiteMedSAM[2]) in terms of segmentation accuracy and efficiency
2. We examine the failure cases and discuss why MedSAM silently fails on certain modalities and propose how to tackle this in future fine-tuning iterations
3. We make all our code and trained models publicly available to the community

2 Method

We go over each of the 11 imaging modalities one-by-one and examine which classical approaches are able to outperform MedSAM and propose techniques to make MedSAM more efficient on modalities on which we could not outperform it. The 11 modalities are: (1) Computed Tomography (CT); (2) Magnetic Resonance Imaging (MRI); (3) Positron Emission Tomography (PET); (4) Ultrasound (US); (5) Dermoscopy; (6) Microscopy; (7) Mammography; (8) X-Ray; (9) Endoscopy; (10) Fundus; and (11) Optical Coherence Tomography (OCT) (Fig. 1).

---

[1] https://www.codabench.org/competitions/1847/.
[2] https://github.com/bowang-lab/MedSAM/tree/LiteMedSAM.

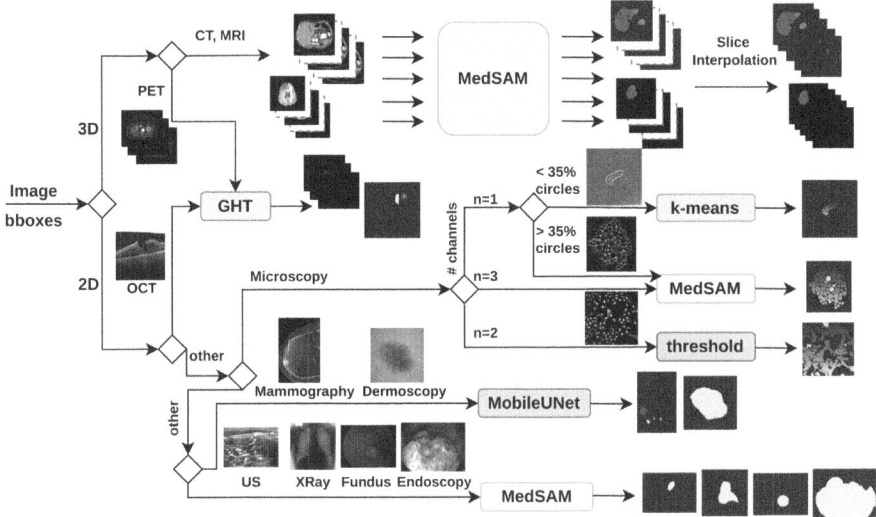

Fig. 1. Overview of our pipeline. We apply a different model for the various imaging modalities. For CT and MRI, we apply MedSAM [28] on a subset of all slices and interpolate the rest with shape-based interpolation [38]. For PET and OCT, we use the generalized histogram threshold (GHT) [5]. For microscopy, we check the number of channels and apply: (1) MedSAM [28] for $n = 3$; (2) a threshold, set to the mean image intensity for $n = 2$; (3) k-means clustering [30] for $n = 1$ if less than 35% of the bounding boxes contain circular objects, otherwise MedSAM. For mammography and dermoscopy, we train a lightweight MobileUNet [20], and for US, XRay, fundus, and endoscopy, we use MedSAM.

Note: We only focus on the segmentation tasks seen in the MedSAM training dataset, e.g., only FDG-PET lesions segmentation and only optic disc segmentation on fundus images. We also always use LiteMedSAM as a lightweight MedSAM implementation and refer to it as MedSAM for brevity.

2.1 CT and MRI

Tasks: The main CT tasks seen in the MedSAM training dataset are extremely diverse as they focus on organs from all regions in the body as well as different diseases such as COVID-19 infections, various tumors, pleural effusion, etc. The same applies to the MRI targets consisting of brain tumors, abdominal organs, prostate cancer, and many other anatomical and pathological targets.

Challenges: The segmentation tasks are highly diverse, making it challenging and time-intensive to manually incorporate expert knowledge for all possible structures. Additionally, both CT and MRI images are 3-dimensional, requiring MedSAM to perform a forward pass for each slice, which results in significant computational overhead. Furthermore, the slice-wise predictions are computed independently, lacking a mechanism to ensure spatial consistency and smoothness across slices.

Classical Approaches: The diversity of potential targets in CT and MRI images necessitates a general model. Therefore, we did not replace MedSAM with a classical segmentation model. Instead, we reduced the number of predictions by applying MedSAM to only a subset of the slices from the volume. The remaining slices are interpolated using shape-based interpolation as proposed in [38]. This interpolation is performed at the prediction level. Specifically, given two binary slice predictions obtained from MedSAM p_i and p_j, with $j > i$, the intermediate slices $k \in \{i+1, ..., j-1\}$ are interpolated as follows:

$$p_k = \texttt{interp}(p_i, p_j, \frac{k-i}{j-i})$$

where $\texttt{interp}(\cdot)$ is defined in [38] and $\frac{k-i}{j-i} \in [0,1]$ is the step size for the interpolation. To decide which slices to predict with MedSAM, we subsample the indices uniformly with a subsampling factor s. For example, $s = 2$ means we predict with MedSAM every second axial slice and interpolate the rest, $s = 3$ means we predict only every 3rd slice, etc. We always predict the first and last axial slice of the bounding box to avoid edge cases.

2.2 PET and OCT

Tasks: The PET data released in the challenge contains samples only from the AutoPET dataset [7] which focuses on the segmentation of whole-body active tumor lesions using Fludeoxyglucose (FDG) as a radioactive tracer. The OCT data also stems from only one dataset [1] and focuses on the segmentation of intraretinal cystoid fluid.

Challenges: There are very few public PET datasets for tumor segmentation [7,8,36] which makes it impossible to train large-scale foundation models on this modality. PET lesions in AutoPET are also with very small contrast to surrounding tissues and there are other healthy anatomical structures that also exhibit a large physiological uptake (heart, brain, bladder, etc.). Additionally, the best results from AutoPET 2023[3] are quite low (Dice Score of 0.36 in the first place) indicating that this task is far from trivial. Regarding OCT, the modality presents images with a high resolution and a very small target size of the retinal fluid voids, leading to a strong class imbalance.

Classical Approaches: Thresholding methods are popular in tumor segmentation from PET scans [17,22,34] and lead to promising results as they are quite simple and intuitive to use. Bounding-box approaches are particularly advantageous because thresholds can be applied within the local context of the box, effectively excluding healthy tissues like the heart and brain that lie outside the defined boundaries, in contrast to previous methods that explicitly remove the

---

[3] https://autopet-ii.grand-challenge.org/leaderboard/.

brain and bladder from the global context of the whole body [7,11,35]. The bounding box also alleviates the class imbalance in OCT images as it constrains the input to only the local context around the object instead of the global high-resolution image.

We compute the Generalized Histogram Threshold (GHT) [5] using the combined PET or OCT values from all bounding boxes. This threshold is then applied to the entire volume to generate a single prediction, with instance indices assigned according to their respective bounding box indices. Additionally, we observe that 99% of the PET tumors occupy between 20% and 88% of their bounding box volume in the training set. To ensure consistency, we apply dilation and erosion to all predictions falling outside this interval until they conform to it. If thresholding results in an empty prediction, we place a foreground voxel within the bounding box and dilate it until it reaches at least 20% of the box volume. For OCT images, we perform the same procedure but do not enforce a target volume between 20% and 88%. For PET images we keep all values above the threshold as tumors are characterized by a high FDG uptake, whereas for OCT we keep all values below the threshold as the cystoid fluids are darker.

2.3 Ultrasound

Tasks: The ultrasound tasks in MedSAM's training data include: (1) breast cancer segmentation; and (2) fetal head segmentation.

Challenges: The ultrasound domain presents several challenges due to weak boundaries and the diversity of tasks (e.g., thyroid, kidney, cardiac structures, fetal head, breast cancer). This necessitates a general model capable of performing well on unseen data, even when the specific task is unknown. MedSAM struggles with fetal head segmentation because the labels are always perfect ellipses, while MedSAM attempts to fit the exact contour present in the image. This label bias can be mitigated by introducing a "prediction bias," where the prediction is also a perfect ellipse. However, this approach requires prior knowledge that the task is fetal head segmentation, which is not available during test time.

Classical Approaches: Although we experimented with ellipse-based template matching, this was not included in the final submission. Additionally, we trained a MobileUNet [20] on ultrasound images from the hc18 [13] and Breast-US [2] datasets. However, the results were suboptimal, as shown in Table 7 so we resorted to using MedSAM in our final submission.

2.4 Dermoscopy

Tasks: The dermoscopy tasks in MedSAM's training data are limited to a single dataset, ISIC 2018 [6], which focuses on skin lesion segmentation.

Challenges: This domain is relatively simpler than others, as skin lesions typically have "blobby" shapes and prominent features. However, the dataset exhibits high variability in annotation styles, as shown in Fig. 2. Some lesions are annotated with detailed boundaries, while others are marked with only a few lines to indicate the lesion boundary.

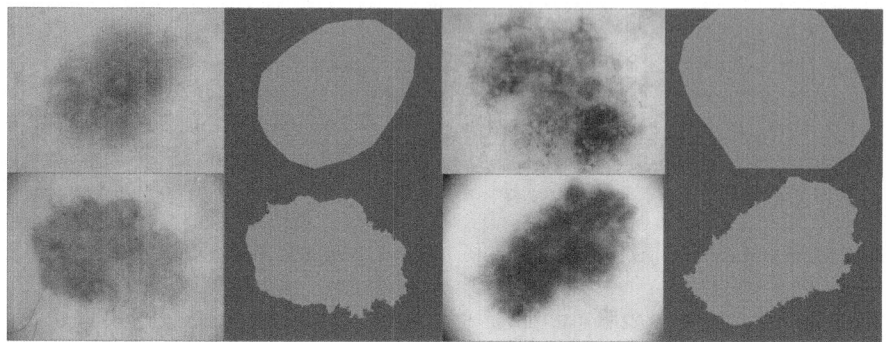

Fig. 2. Difference in annotation styles for skin lesions. Row 1: very coarse annotation with straight lines as boundaries. Row 2: fine-grained annotations with detailed lesion boundaries.

Classical Approaches: Although we did not employ any classical non-deep learning methods, we trained a MobileUNet [20] specifically on the ISIC 2018 dataset [6]. The training details are provided in Sect. 3.2.

2.5 Microscopy

Tasks: MedSAM's microscopy training data is sourced solely from the NeurIPS 2022 CellSeg dataset [29]. However, this dataset presents a wide array of challenges, featuring diverse images captured using different microscope types, including brightfield, fluorescent, phase-contrast (PC), and differential interference contrast (DIC). Moreover, the dataset encompasses various cell types as segmentation targets, adding further complexity to the task.

Challenges: The microscopy imaging modality presents several significant challenges: (1) The number of instances per image can be exceptionally high, exceeding 1000 in some cases, resulting in computational overhead when performing a forward pass for each bounding box. (2) The diversity of microscope types necessitates either a robust generalist model or multiple specialist models to accommodate various imaging characteristics. (3) The high-resolution nature of the images poses a challenge, as details may be lost when resizing to smaller resolutions, as is the case with MedSAM's resizing to 256×256.

Classical Approaches: We adopt different classical methods depending on the number of channels present in the image.

Grayscale: When dealing with grayscale images, we utilize a k-means clustering approach [30] with $k = 2$. To determine which class corresponds to the foreground, we compute the frequency of pixels belonging to each class within a 10 × 10 window at the center of the bounding box. We then select the class with the higher pixel count within this window. As depicted in Fig. 7, MedSAM encounters challenges with grayscale images where the target is dark and the bounding boxes are relatively small compared to the entire image. In contrast, k-means clustering achieves more plausible segmentations for such cases. However, we did not observe this problem with circular cells, so we opted to continue using MedSAM for cases where more than 35% of the bounding boxes contain a circular object. To detect circles, we employed the Hough circle transform [23] with various radii to check for the presence of circle-like objects within each bounding box.

Two-Channel: In the case of images containing only two channels (typically 3 channels in practice, with one filled with zeros, such as in fluorescent microscopy), we simply utilize the mean image intensity as a threshold. This approach is straightforward yet quite effective.

RGB: For RGB images, we opt to use MedSAM directly, as it demonstrates robust performance in such cases.

2.6 Mammography

Tasks: The training set comprises only one publicly available dataset: CDD-CESM [21], which addresses breast abnormalities such as calcifications and benign and malignant tumors.

Challenges: The target structures exhibit considerable variability in size, and the masks are annotated at a coarse level, similar to some labels observed in the ISIC 2018 dataset [6], as illustrated in Fig. 3.

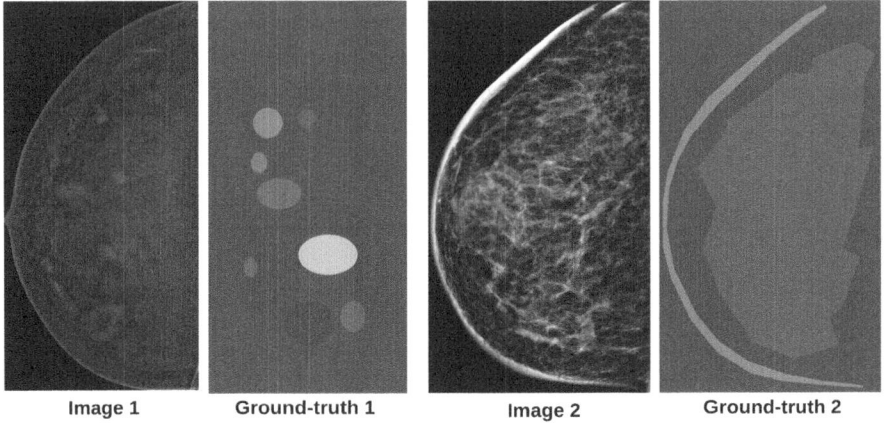

Fig. 3. Examples of images and their ground-truth masks from the training set. The labels are coarse and the targets vary strongly in size.

Classical Approaches: We did not employ any non-deep learning approaches for mammography but we did train a MobileUNet [20] to improve the inference speed.

2.7 X-Ray, Endoscopy, and Fundus

Tasks: The X-Ray, Endoscopy, and Fundus modalities encompass a range of tasks. X-Ray imaging primarily targets anatomical structures like lungs [15] and specific pathologies such as COVID-19 lesions [40]. Endoscopy images are focused on detecting polyps [18] or surgical instruments [14]. In contrast, Fundus images in the training set concentrate solely on optic discs and cups [37]. However, for more intricate structures like vessels in fundus images, the bounding-box interaction signal proves inadequate for highlighting relevant context, and thus was not considered for this challenge.

Challenges: X-Ray images exhibit a strong diversity, featuring various structures. The validation set even includes dental X-Rays requiring teeth segmentation, which requires a model capable of generalizing to such unseen structures. Hence, we employed MedSAM for this modality. In contrast, Fundus and Endoscopy images offer a simpler and less diverse setting than X-Ray. Despite our efforts, we were unable to surpass MedSAM's performance in either of these domains, leading us to utilize it for our final submission for all three modalities.

Classical Approaches: We did not apply any classical approaches to these domains due to time constraints and utilize MedSAM for our submission (Table 1).

Table 1. Summary of our used models for the final submission.

Modality	Used Model
CT and MRI	LiteMedSAM [28] with slice interpolation $s = 3$ [38]
PET and OCT	Generalized Histrogram Threshold [5]
US, X-Ray, Fundus, Endoscopy	LiteMedSAM [28]
Mammography and Dermoscopy	MobileUNet [20]
Microscopy	k-means, thresholding, and LiteMedSAM [28]

2.8 Preprocessing

We re-used the code provided by LiteMedSAM[4] for loading the data and inferring predictions and added more functions to the script for our methods. We

---

[4] https://github.com/bowang-lab/MedSAM/blob/LiteMedSAM/ CVPR24_LiteMedSAM_infer.py.

avoid loading LiteMedSAM's weights for tasks which do not need it and import modules only immediately before they are used. The image loading and preprocessing is done as follows:

LiteMedSAM: The image is resized to a common size of 256×256 and padded to the shorter side to keep the original aspect ratio. Then, the image is min-max normalized and fed to the model. The model performs a forward pass for each bounding box.

MobileUNet: We iterate over each bounding box separately. We first crop the image according to the bounding box and then resize the crop to a common size of 256×256 and pad the shorter side to keep the original aspect ratio. Then, the crop is min-max normalized and fed to the model. The prediction is then resized to the original crop resolution and inserted in the final prediction.

k-Means: When applying k-means clustering, we use the unnormalized values within each bounding box and apply k-means for each bounding box.

Thresholding: Thresholds are always computed using the combination of all image values in the bounding boxes and then applied to the whole unnormalized image. Instance indices are then assigned according to the bounding box indices.

2.9 Post-processing

After each forward pass, we perform two post-processing transformations. For all 2D images, except the ones predicted by MedSAM, we keep the largest connected component and fill all the holes within it. The second transform, which we apply to all images, regardless of the imaging modality or used model, is to filter all the instance predictions that are outside of the bounding box.

3 Experiments

3.1 Dataset and Evaluation Measures

We used only the challenge dataset for model development and validation. The evaluation metrics include two accuracy measures-Dice Similarity Coefficient (DSC) and Normalized Surface Dice (NSD), alongside one efficiency measure: running time. These metrics collectively contribute to the ranking computation.

3.2 Implementation Details

Environment Settings. The development environments and requirements for all our methods (except the training of MobileUNet) are presented in Table 2.

The development environments and requirements for the training of MobileUNet are presented in Table 2.

Table 2. Development environments and requirements for all our methods except MobileUNet training.

System	Ubuntu 22.04.4 LTS
CPU[a]	Intel(R) Core(TM) i7-13700H CPU@5.00GHz
RAM	8×4 GB; 5200MT/s
GPU (number and type)	None
CUDA version	11.8
Programming language	Python 3.10.14
Deep learning framework	torch 2.2.1
Specific dependencies	None
Code	https://github.com/Zrrr1997/medsam_cvhci

[a] https://ark.intel.com/content/www/us/en/ark/products/232128/intel-core-i7-13700h-processor-24m-cache-up-to-5-00-ghz.html.

Table 3. Development environments and requirements for MobileUNet training.

System	Red Hat Enterprise Linux release 8.8 (Ootpa)
CPU	Intel(R) Xeon(R) Platinum 8368 CPU @ 2.40 GHz
RAM	502 GB
GPU NVIDIA A100-SXM4	40 GB
CUDA version	11.8
Programming language	Python 3.10.14
Deep learning framework	torch 2.2.2
Specific dependencies	None
Code	https://github.com/Zrrr1997/medsam_cvhci/

Training Protocols. For MedSAM, we use the provided pre-trained LiteMed-SAM model whose training is described in [28]. For MobileUNet, we trained a model for the dermoscopy and mammography modalities using the ISIC 2018 dataset [6] and the CDD-CESM dataset [21] respectively. In both cases we apply the same training protocol: We train for 500 epochs with a learning rate of 5e−5, and a batch size of 4. We use the Adam optimizer with $\beta_1 = 0.9, \beta_2 = 0.999$ and reduce the learning rate by 10% if the loss has not decreased in the last 5 epochs. As a loss function we use the summation between Dice loss and cross-entropy loss because compound loss functions have been proven to be robust in various medical image segmentation tasks [27]. In each iteration, we sample one random bounding box from each image in the batch and resize it to 256×256 so that all inputs have a uniform resolution. The crops then form the input batch to the model. We do not use any data augmentation and select the checkpoint from the last epoch for both the mammography and dermoscopy models (Table 3).

Table 4. Training protocol for Dermoscopy and Mammography MobileUNet.

Pre-trained Model	None
Batch size	4
Patch size	$256 \times 256 \times 3$
Total epochs	500
Optimizer	Adam ($\beta_1 = 0.9, \beta_2 = 0.999$)
Initial learning rate (lr)	5e−5
Lr decay schedule	ReduceLROnPlateau[a] (factor = 0.9, patience = 5)
Training time	8.4 h (Dermoscopy), 6.8 h (Mammography)
Loss function	Dice Loss + Binary Cross-Entropy Loss (equal weights)
Number of model parameters	41.22M[b]
Number of flops	1.45G[c]
CO_2eq	2.6 KG (Dermoscopy), 1.5 KG (Mammography) Kg[d]

[a] https://pytorch.org/docs/stable/optim.html.
[b] https://github.com/sksq96/pytorch-summary.
[c] https://github.com/facebookresearch/fvcore.
[d] https://github.com/lfwa/carbontracker/.

4 Results and Discussion

We discuss the results of the individual modalities one-by-one as we propose different models for the 11 imaging modalities (Table 4).

4.1 CT and MRI

Efficiency Strategies: The slice interpolation improves the efficiency as it is faster than MedSAM's forward pass. A higher subsampling factor s leads to a better efficiency but it also leads to a drop in performance as high-frequency details are smoothened out and interpolation artifacts may occur (see Fig. 5).

Table 5 shows that for a smaller subsampling factor $s \leq 3$, the performance loss is quite small ($\approx$1% Dice and NSD) but the efficiency boost is quite high (>19 s per sample). However, for larger factors $s > 3$ the performance declines further and this is clearly illustrated by the rough patterns and artifacts in Fig. 5. To balance the performance and efficiency, we opted for $s = 3$ for our final submission.

How to Improve MedSAM on CT and MRI? MedSAM shows a remarkable robustness in these two imaging modalities but exhibits a slow inference as it processes the volumes slice-by-slice. As MedSAM is intended as a foundation model, we believe it should remain in the 2D domain so that it can process other imaging modalities such as OCT, dermoscopy, etc. However, a slice interpolation strategy proves to be quite reliable, especially for smaller subsampling rates, without decreasing MedSAM's performance dramatically. We believe that

Table 5. Results on the validation stage of the challenge for CT and MR images. Our final submission in indicated in **bold**.

Model	Dice	NSD	Time per Image
LiteMedSAM (CT, no subsampling)	92.35	95.09	47.3 s
LiteMedSAM (CT, s = 2)	91.88	94.35	28.1 s
LiteMedSAM (CT, s = 3)	91.59	94.18	21.3 s
LiteMedSAM (CT, s = 6)	90.54	93.14	15.0 s
LiteMedSAM (CT, s = 8)	89.81	92.42	13.0 s
LiteMedSAM (MR, no subsampling)	89.93	94.02	29.8 s
LiteMedSAM (MR, s = 2)	88.96	92.90	18.1 s
LiteMedSAM (MR, s = 3)	88.34	92.57	13.9 s
LiteMedSAM (MR, s = 6)	86.43	90.88	10.2 s
LiteMedSAM (MR, s = 8)	84.99	89.58	9.0 s

exploring such strategies in more detail can be beneficial for MedSAM's efficiency on the CT and MRI domains as well as to impose a smoothness constraint among adjacent slices since its slicewise predictions are independent of each other.

4.2 PET and OCT

Efficiency Strategies: Thresholding eliminates the need for slice-wise forward passes as the threshold is applied directly on the whole volume in a single operation. Table 6 shows that the thresholding outperforms MedSAM on all metrics and is 30x faster on the validation set. For OCT, this effect is less pronounced but still leads to both a better performance and a much higher efficiency on the training dataset as there are no image samples in the validation set.

Table 6. Results on the validation stage of the challenge for PET and on the training dataset for OCT

Model	Dice	NSD	Time per Image
LiteMedSAM (PET)	55.23	29.29	3.33 s
Thresholding (PET)	66.80	49.42	0.14 s
LiteMedSAM (OCT)	79.02	82.33	0.86 s
Thresholding (OCT)	86.34	88.64	0.38 s

How to Improve MedSAM on PET and OCT? The results are concerning as a simple threshold and morphological operators can outperform MedSAM on the PET task. We suppose that the reason is the lack of available data to improve MedSAM so that it can generalize better and extract meaningful features. PET data can also be enhanced with anatomical labels derived from paired CT scans [16,35] which was the winning approach of AutoPET 2023 as it injects expert knowledge regarding the affected anatomical regions as additional information to the model. The OCT domain can also be improved by incorporating additional anatomical labels, e.g., corresponding to the various retinal layers.

4.3 Ultrasound

Efficiency Strategies: We did not improve the efficiency on this task as we use MedSAM in our final submission as our experiments with MobileUNet were unsuccessful as seen in Table 7.

Table 7. Results on the validation stage of the challenge for Ultrasound images

Model	Dice	NSD	Time per Image
LiteMedSAM	94.78	96.81	0.66 s
MobileUNet	79.12	84.55	0.22 s

How to Improve MedSAM on Ultrasound? We observed that the fetal head labels in the training data can be effectively approximated by simple ellipses, as illustrated in Fig. 4, resulting in improved Dice scores and efficiency compared to MedSAM. However, ultrasound imaging is used for various other tasks, such as cardiac structure analysis [25], thyroid cancer detection [48], breast cancer assessment [2], and kidney imaging [39]. Therefore, relying solely on simple ellipses is not viable for all cases. One potential solution is to train a classifier to identify when the ultrasound task involves fetal head segmentation. However, we were unsuccessful in achieving satisfactory results with this approach.

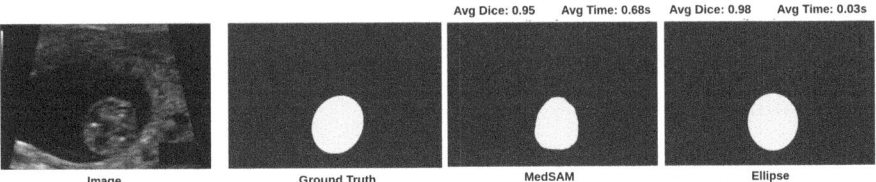

Fig. 4. Prediction for the hc18 dataset [13] with MedSAM and with an ellipse.

4.4 Dermoscopy

Efficiency Strategies: MobileUNet's forward pass is twice as fast as MedSAM's, yet it maintains comparable performance on the validation set, as demonstrated in Table 8.

Table 8. Results on the validation stage of the challenge for Dermoscopy images

Model	Dice	NSD	Time per Image
LiteMedSAM	92.47	93.85	0.71 s
MobileUNet	92.63	94.22	0.31 s

How to Improve MedSAM on Dermoscopy? We cannot make a statement on how to improve MedSAM in this domain as we have not been able to outperform it by a large margin.

4.5 Microscopy

Efficiency Strategies: The k-means clustering and the mean threshold are more than x10 faster than the MedSAM forward pass (Table 9).

Table 9. Results on the validation stage of the challenge for Microscopy images

Model	Dice	NSD	Time per Image
LiteMedSAM	61.70	65.47	13.7 s
k-means OR threshold OR LiteMedSAM	69.96	77.98	2.4 s

How to Improve MedSAM on Microscopy? It seems that MedSAM struggles with miniature bounding boxes, especially since they are resized to 256×256 to fit its input size. We believe that a crop-then-infer approach would be beneficial for MedSAM as it would only resize the crop instead of the whole image. This way, the bounding box would not be miniature and MedSAM can focus on the detail of the cropped local instance. However, we would need to perform a study regarding this in future work to confirm our hypothesis.

4.6 Mammography

Efficiency Strategies: Similarly to dermoscopy, MobileUNet achieves a 2x faster prediction than MedSAM.

Table 10. Results on MedSAM's training dataset for Mammography

Model	Dice	NSD	Time per Image
LiteMedSAM	79.15	82.09	0.86 s
MobileUNet	86.55	88.92	0.38 s

How to Improve MedSAM on Mammography? We cannot make a statement on how to improve MedSAM in this domain as we only evaluate it on the training data. However, it seems that this domain is underrepresented in MedSAM's training data, which leads to a mammography-specialized MobileUNet outperforming MedSAM.

4.7 X-Ray, Endoscopy, and Fundus

Efficiency Strategies: We did not improve the efficiency on this task as we used MedSAM in our final submission.

How to Improve MedSAM on X-Ray, Endoscopy, and Fundus? We have limited expertise in these domains and cannot offer any hypotheses on how to improve MedSAM.

4.8 Quantitative Results on Validation Set

Table 11 shows that our approach outperforms (on average) the baseline (LiteMedSAM). However, we also show in Tables 5–10 that we are able to significantly improve the efficiency of the baseline while sacrificing a negligible amount of performance.

Table 11. Quantitative evaluation results. Baseline: LiteMedSAM. Ablations were done on the subsampling factors for CT and MRI volumes.

Target	Baseline		Ablation $s=2$		Ablation $s=8$		Proposed $s=3$	
	DSC(%)	NSD(%)	DSC(%)	NSD(%)	DSC(%)	NSD(%)	DSC(%)	NSD(%)
CT	92.35	95.09	91.88	94.35	89.81	92.42	91.59	94.18
MR	89.93	94.02	88.99	92.93	84.99	89.58	88.34	92.57
PET	55.23	29.29	66.80	49.42	66.80	49.42	66.80	49.42
US	94.78	96.81	94.78	96.82	94.78	96.82	94.78	96.82
X-Ray	75.83	80.39	75.87	80.44	75.87	80.44	75.87	80.44
Dermoscopy	92.47	93.85	92.63	94.22	92.63	94.22	92.63	94.22
Endoscopy	96.04	98.11	96.04	98.11	96.04	98.11	96.04	98.11
Fundus	94.81	96.41	94.82	96.42	94.82	96.42	94.82	96.42
Microscopy	61.70	65.47	69.96	77.98	69.96	77.98	69.96	77.98
Average	83.68	83.27	85.75	86.74	81.05	83.16	85.65	86.68

4.9 Segmentation Efficiency Results on Validation Set

The efficiency on a few samples from the validation set are listed in Table 12. Our optimization on the CT, MR, PET, microscopy, and dermoscopy modalities contributes to a much more efficient prediction time.

Table 12. Quantitative evaluation of segmentation efficiency in terms of running time (s) on the hardware specified in Table 2. Abl.: Ablation, * Grayscale image

Case ID	Size	#Objects	Baseline	Abl. $s=8$	Ours $s=3$
3DBox_CT_0566	(287, 512, 512)	6	376.4	62.1	109.7
3DBox_CT_0888	(237, 512, 512)	6	100.5	19.0	29.4
3DBox_CT_0860	(246, 512, 512)	1	17.7	4.6	5.8
3DBox_MR_0621	(115, 400, 400)	6	157.1	22.6	42.4
3DBox_MR_0121	(64, 290, 320)	6	99.9	13.6	27.3
3DBox_MR_0179	(84, 512, 512)	1	17.1	4.2	5.6
3DBox_PET_0001	(264, 200, 200)	1	12.1	0.19	0.19
2DBox_US_0525	(256, 256, 3)	1	2.0	2.0	2.0
2DBox_X-Ray_0053	(320, 640, 3)	34	2.9	2.9	2.9
2DBox_Dermoscopy_0003	(3024, 4032, 3)	1	2.2	1.3	1.3
2DBox_Endoscopy_0086	(480, 560, 3)	1	2.0	2.0	2.0
2DBox_Fundus_0003	(2048, 2048, 3)	1	2.0	2.0	2.0
2DBox_Microscope_0008	(1536, 2040, 3)	19	2.6	2.6	2.6
2DBox_Microscope_0016	(1920, 2560, 3)	241	12.9	12.9	12.9
*2DBox_Microscope_0030	(2304, 2304, 3)	137	7.4	1.6	1.6
*2DBox_Microscope_0040	(944, 1266, 3)	56	3.4	0.3	0.3

4.10 Qualitative Results on Validation Set

We show some qualitative image examples for the predictions of our models on various modalities.

3D Slice-Wise Inference. Figure 5 demonstrates the effect of various subsampling rates s on a CT prediction. While the prediction is much more efficient with a higher rate, it also reduces the level of details and even introduces interpolation artifacts. This is one of the reasons that led us to set $s=3$ to a lower value.

Microscopy Classical Approaches. Figure 6 and Fig. 7 demonstrate failure cases of MedSAM in the microscopy domain. It seems that MedSAM struggles with small structures with ambiguous boundaries. In contrast, k-means clustering and mean thresholding perform quite well on these domains, landing a spot into our methodology for our final submission to the challenge.

Microscopy - Failure Cases. Figure 8 depicts examples of predictions on microscopy images. It can be seen that in some instances the k-means clustering and the mean threshold fill up the whole bounding box as the intensity within the local instance is higher than the mean intensity in the global image or the pixels are homogenous. This is an inherent challenge in the microscopy domain.

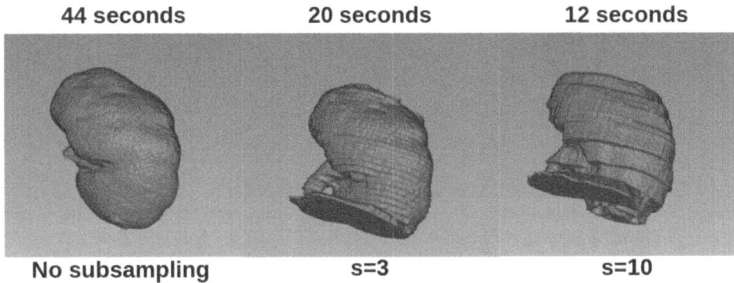

Fig. 5. Example of various subsampling factors s for a kidney from the CT validation set. Higher factors introduce artifacts during the interpolation and smoothen out high-frequency details but improve the efficiency.

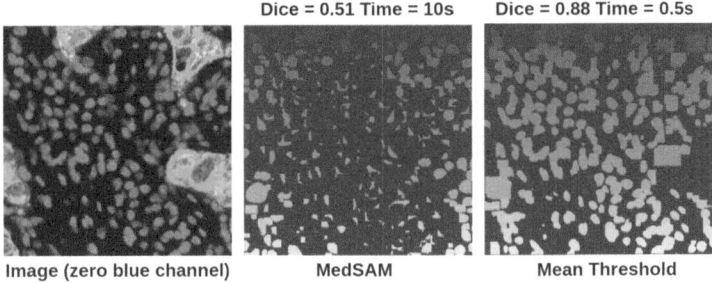

Fig. 6. Examples of predictions for two-channel microscopy images from the training set.

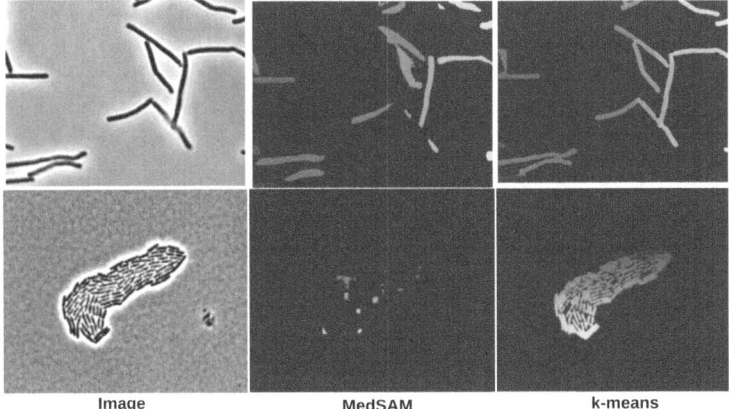

Fig. 7. Examples for grayscale microscopy images from the validation set.

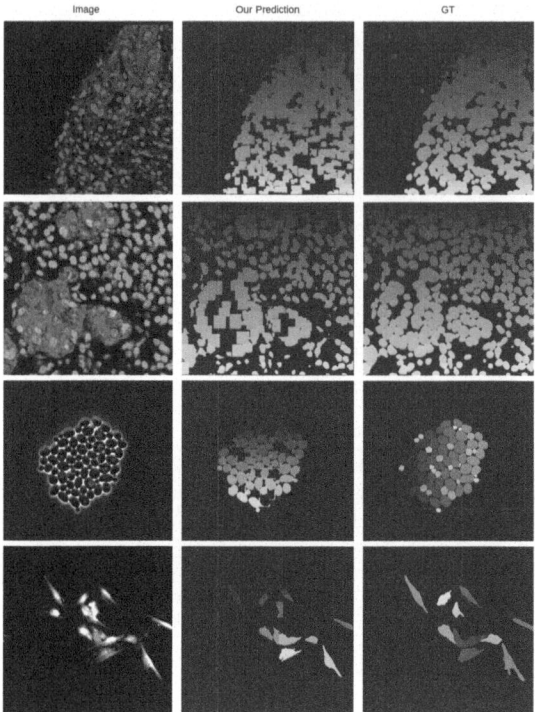

Fig. 8. Examples for failure cases of our microscopy predictions.

Dermoscopy, Endoscopy, Fundus, Mammography. Figure 9 shows examples for predictions on four imaging modalities. The labels are often quite coarse, which may lead to a low reported Dice and NSD although the segmentation mask on its own might be plausible.

PET and OCT Threshold-Based Methods. Figure 10 shows examples of predictions on OCT and PET images. As confirmed in the quantitative results, thresholds produce plausible predictions for both modalities.

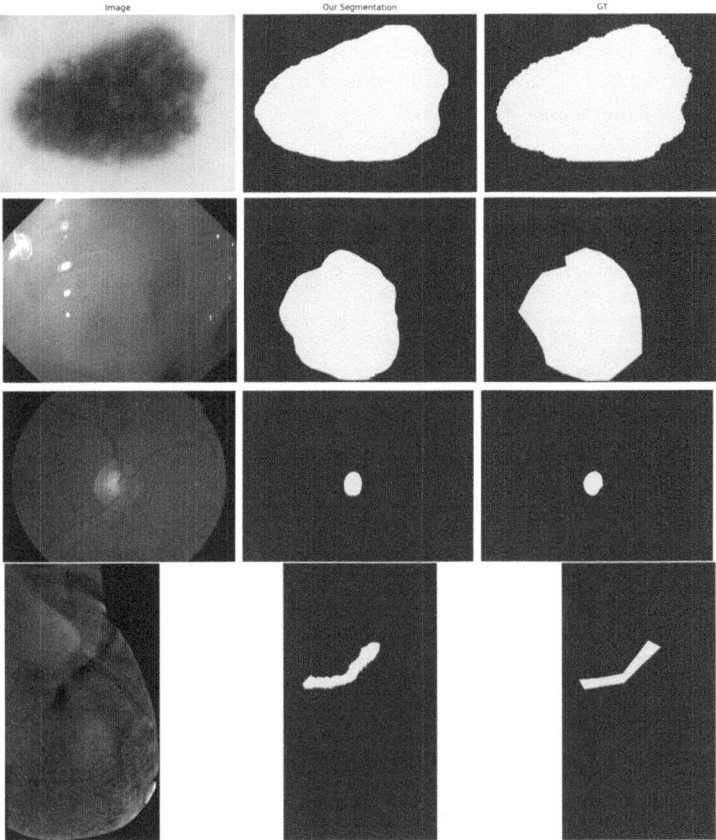

Fig. 9. Examples for Dermoscopy, Endoscopy, Fundus, and Mammography predictions

4.11 Results on Final Testing Set

The results on the final test set are presented in Table 11. Our emphasis on classical methods is reflected in consistently efficient runtimes, consistently placing within the top six methods. However, while threshold-based approaches for OCT and PET demonstrate exceptional efficiency, they suffer from low generalizability. In fact, these methods perform the worst in terms of segmentation quality within the OCT domain. Interestingly, our submission achieved 1st, 2nd, and 4th place in the X-Ray, Endoscopy, and Fundus domains, respectively, in terms of segmentation performance. This success was achieved despite only reusing the baseline model (LiteMedSAM) and incorporating a minor post-processing step, as described in Sect. 2.9-specifically, omitting any predictions outside the bounding box and retaining the largest connected component and filling its holes. This demonstrates that LiteMedSAM already possesses a great generalization ability but could be substantially improved by adding some simple post-transformations. The results for CT and MR are unfortunately one of the worst, perhaps due to the introduced noise from our slice interpolation scheme described in Sect. 4.1. Our method is placed in the 6th place in the final leaderboard out of 23 methods (Table 13).

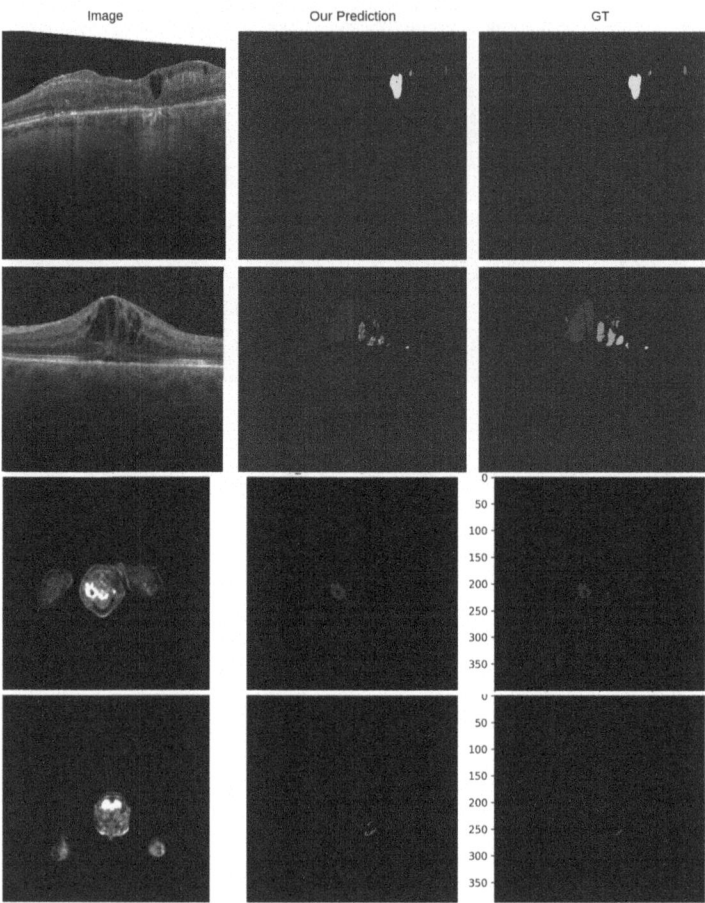

Fig. 10. Examples for OCT and PET predictions.

Table 13. Results on the testing stage of the challenge. Worst rank is 23

Modality	Dice (Rank)	NSD (Rank)	Runtime (Rank)
CT	53.89 (18)	54.27 (19)	20.66 (5)
MR	64.28 (18)	62.61 (15)	9.08 (5)
X-Ray	85.79 (1)	94.06 (1)	5.10 (6)
Endoscopy	94.41 (2)	96.95 (2)	4.58 (6)
Fundus	86.47 (4)	88.54 (4)	4.59 (6)
Microscopy	84.49 (13)	86.30 (14)	5.55 (6)
OCT	65.52 (23)	70.21 (23)	1.11 (1)
PET	74.18 (12)	63.46 (15)	1.07 (1)
US	85.84 (12)	90.13 (12)	6.40 (6)

4.12 Post-challenge Analysis

During the post-challenge phase, we have participated in the **Performance Booster** track without the use of any external datasets. Here, we describe how we have improved our methods.

Changed Methodology. We made only a few adjustments to our methods, focusing on incremental improvements. For 3D-based modalities (CT and MRI, but not PET), we enhanced our implementation by processing bounding boxes in parallel using the `concurrent.futures` Python module, fixing the number of threads to 8. To ensure that the segmentation results matched those of sequential execution, we handled overlapping segmentations by prioritizing larger indices. Specifically, if two bounding boxes overlap in their predictions, the prediction from the last bounding box overwrites the earlier one in areas of conflict. We acknowledge that this is a naive solution to a complex problem, which requires more in-depth analysis. The only other method we changes is the OCT domain, as our original method was the last on the leaderboard. For this, we simply replaced the thresholding method with a trained MobileUNet on the original training data as described in Sect. 3.2.

Results from Post-challenge Analysis. The changes in the code led to an improvement in the runtime for both the CT and MR domains in terms of runtime. For OCT, our method is three times slower than our previous thresholding approach, but it improves the Dice and NSD by over 10% each (Table 14).

Table 14. Post-challenge changes in performance

Modality	Dice	NSD	Runtime
CT	53.89	54.27	19.07
MR	64.28	62.61	8.78
OCT	74.37	81.47	3.35

4.13 Limitation and Future Work

Our methodology has two main limitations: (1) it focuses on individual imaging modalities rather than proposing a unified framework like MedSAM; (2) classical non-deep learning approaches often depend on expert knowledge for optimal performance (e.g., for PET data, we assume that lesions are avid and bright in the image). However, we intentionally adopt this fragmented approach to identify the weaknesses in MedSAM and understand their underlying causes, aiming to improve it in future iterations. Our findings suggest that incorporating explicit assumptions about imaging modalities can serve as a robust signal, sometimes outperforming MedSAM in specific cases.

A promising future direction involves appending a "task adapter" to MedSAM. This would function as a model capable of recognizing the task from the image, such as "fetal head segmentation in ultrasound," and providing this contextual information to MedSAM. This addition would enable MedSAM to produce more accurate and context-specific outputs, such as coarse and ellipsoid-shaped masks. In other words, informing the model about the specific segmentation task should enhance its adaptability and performance. This approach allows the integration of domain knowledge directly into the model, potentially adapting it to specific domains and tasks.

5 Conclusion

Our results indicate that classical approaches can outperform MedSAM on certain imaging modalities, both in segmentation accuracy and efficiency. Several factors contribute to this outcome, including the presence of coarse ground-truth labels in dermoscopy, the scarcity of large public datasets for mammography and PET, and the loss of detail during image resizing in microscopy images. Moreover, our findings highlight that integrating explicit task knowledge is crucial for surpassing MedSAM's performance. We propose that a task adapter, which provides information about the target structure and imaging modality, could enhance MedSAM's effectiveness in these challenging domains. Additionally, our slice interpolation experiments demonstrated that it is possible to improve MedSAM's efficiency without significantly compromising its segmentation performance.

Acknowledgements. We thank all the data owners for making the medical images publicly available and CodaLab [44] for hosting the challenge platform. The present contribution is supported by the Helmholtz Association under the joint research school "HIDSS4Health - Helmholtz Information and Data Science School for Health. Parts of this work were performed on the HoreKa supercomputer funded by the Ministry of Science, Research and the Arts Baden-Württemberg and by the Federal Ministry of Education and Research.

Disclosure of Interests. The authors have no competing interests to declare that are relevant to the content of this article.

References

1. Ahmed, Z., Ahmed, M., Baqai, A., Umrani, F.A.: Intraretinal cystoid fluid (2022). https://doi.org/10.34740/KAGGLE/DS/2277068. https://www.kaggle.com/ds/2277068
2. Al-Dhabyani, W., Gomaa, M., Khaled, H., Fahmy, A.: Dataset of breast ultrasound images. Data Brief **28**, 104863 (2020)
3. Antonelli, M., et al.: The medical segmentation decathlon. Nat. Commun. **13**(1), 4128 (2022)
4. Asad, M., et al.: Adaptive multi-scale online likelihood network for AI-assisted interactive segmentation. In: Greenspan, H., et al. (eds.) MICCAI 2023. LNCS, vol. 14221, pp. 564–574. Springer, Cham (2023). https://doi.org/10.1007/978-3-031-43895-0_53
5. Barron, J.T.: A generalization of Otsu's method and minimum error thresholding. In: Vedaldi, A., Bischof, H., Brox, T., Frahm, J.-M. (eds.) ECCV 2020. LNCS, vol. 12350, pp. 455–470. Springer, Cham (2020). https://doi.org/10.1007/978-3-030-58558-7_27
6. Codella, N., et al.: Skin lesion analysis toward melanoma detection 2018: a challenge hosted by the international skin imaging collaboration (ISIC). arXiv preprint arXiv:1902.03368 (2019)
7. Gatidis, S., et al.: The autoPET challenge: towards fully automated lesion segmentation in oncologic PET/CT imaging (2023)
8. Gatidis, S., et al.: A whole-body FDG-PET/CT dataset with manually annotated tumor lesions. Sci. Data **9**(1), 601 (2022)
9. Hadlich, M., Marinov, Z., Kim, M., Nasca, E., Kleesiek, J., Stiefelhagen, R.: Sliding window FastEdit: a framework for lesion annotation in whole-body pet images. arXiv preprint arXiv:2311.14482 (2023)
10. Hallitschke, V.J., et al.: Multimodal interactive lung lesion segmentation: a framework for annotating PET/CT images based on physiological and anatomical cues. In: 2023 IEEE 20th International Symposium on Biomedical Imaging (ISBI), pp. 1–5. IEEE (2023)
11. Heiliger, L., et al.: AutoPET challenge: combining NN-UNET with Swin UNETR augmented by maximum intensity projection classifier. arXiv preprint arXiv:2209.01112 (2022)
12. Hernandez Petzsche, M.R., et al.: ISLES 2022: a multi-center magnetic resonance imaging stroke lesion segmentation dataset. Sci. Data **9**(1), 762 (2022)
13. van den Heuvel, T.L., de Bruijn, D., de Korte, C.L., Ginneken, B.V.: Automated measurement of fetal head circumference using 2D ultrasound images. PloS One **13**(8), e0200412 (2018)

14. Hong, W.Y., Kao, C.L., Kuo, Y.H., Wang, J.R., Chang, W.L., Shih, C.S.: CholecSeg8k: a semantic segmentation dataset for laparoscopic cholecystectomy based on Cholec80. arXiv preprint arXiv:2012.12453 (2020)
15. Jaeger, S., et al.: Automatic tuberculosis screening using chest radiographs. IEEE Trans. Med. Imaging **33**(2), 233–245 (2013)
16. Jaus, A., et al.: Towards unifying anatomy segmentation: automated generation of a full-body CT dataset via knowledge aggregation and anatomical guidelines. arXiv preprint arXiv:2307.13375 (2023)
17. Jentzen, W., Freudenberg, L., Eising, E.G., Heinze, M., Brandau, W., Bockisch, A.: Segmentation of pet volumes by iterative image thresholding. J. Nucl. Med. **48**(1), 108–114 (2007)
18. Jha, D., et al.: Kvasir-SEG: a segmented polyp dataset. In: Ro, Y.M., et al. (eds.) MMM 2020. LNCS, vol. 11962, pp. 451–462. Springer, Cham (2020). https://doi.org/10.1007/978-3-030-37734-2_37
19. Ji, Y., et al.: AMOS: a large-scale abdominal multi-organ benchmark for versatile medical image segmentation. In: Advances in Neural Information Processing Systems, vol. 35, pp. 36722–36732 (2022)
20. Jing, J., Wang, Z., Rätsch, M., Zhang, H.: Mobile-Unet: an efficient convolutional neural network for fabric defect detection. Text. Res. J. **92**(1–2), 30–42 (2022)
21. Khaled, R., et al.: Categorized contrast enhanced mammography dataset for diagnostic and artificial intelligence research. Sci. Data **9**(1), 122 (2022)
22. Kim, M., et al.: Evaluation of thresholding methods for the quantification of [68Ga] Ga-PSMA-11 pet molecular tumor volume and their effect on survival prediction in patients with advanced prostate cancer undergoing [177Lu] Lu-PSMA-617 radioligand therapy. Eur. J. Nucl. Med. Mol. Imaging **50**(7), 2196–2209 (2023)
23. Kimme, C., Ballard, D., Sklansky, J.: Finding circles by an array of accumulators. Commun. ACM **18**(2), 120–122 (1975)
24. Kirillov, A., et al.: Segment anything. In: Proceedings of the IEEE/CVF International Conference on Computer Vision, pp. 4015–4026 (2023)
25. Leclerc, S., et al.: Deep learning for segmentation using an open large-scale dataset in 2D echocardiography. IEEE Trans. Med. Imaging **38**(9), 2198–2210 (2019)
26. Luo, X., et al.: MIDeepSeg: minimally interactive segmentation of unseen objects from medical images using deep learning. Med. Image Anal. **72**, 102102 (2021)
27. Ma, J., et al.: Loss odyssey in medical image segmentation. Med. Image Anal. **71**, 102035 (2021)
28. Ma, J., He, Y., Li, F., Han, L., You, C., Wang, B.: Segment anything in medical images. Nat. Commun. **15**(1), 654 (2024)
29. Ma, J., et al.: The multi-modality cell segmentation challenge: towards universal solutions. Nat. Methods (2024). https://doi.org/10.1038/s41592-024-02233-6
30. MacQueen, J., et al.: Some methods for classification and analysis of multivariate observations. In: Proceedings of the Fifth Berkeley Symposium on Mathematical Statistics and Probability, Oakland, CA, USA, vol. 1, pp. 281–297 (1967)
31. Marinov, Z., Jäger, P.F., Egger, J., Kleesiek, J., Stiefelhagen, R.: Deep interactive segmentation of medical images: a systematic review and taxonomy. arXiv preprint arXiv:2311.13964 (2023)
32. Marinov, Z., Stiefelhagen, R., Kleesiek, J.: Guiding the guidance: a comparative analysis of user guidance signals for interactive segmentation of volumetric images. In: Greenspan, H., et al. (eds.) MICCAI 2023. LNCS, vol. 14222, pp. 637–647. Springer, Cham (2023). https://doi.org/10.1007/978-3-031-43898-1_61
33. Menze, B.H., et al.: The multimodal brain tumor image segmentation benchmark (BRATS). IEEE Trans. Med. Imaging **34**(10), 1993–2024 (2014)

34. Moussallem, M., Valette, P.J., Traverse-Glehen, A., Houzard, C., Jegou, C., Giammarile, F.: New strategy for automatic tumor segmentation by adaptive thresholding on PET/CT images. J. Appl. Clin. Med. Phys. **13**(5), 236–251 (2012)
35. Murugesan, G.K., et al.: Improving lesion segmentation in FDG-18 whole-body PET/CT scans using multilabel approach: AutoPET II challenge. arXiv preprint arXiv:2311.01574 (2023)
36. Oreiller, V., et al.: Head and neck tumor segmentation in PET/CT: the HECKTOR challenge. Med. Image Anal. **77**, 102336 (2022)
37. Porwal, P., et al.: Indian diabetic retinopathy image dataset (IDRID): a database for diabetic retinopathy screening research. Data **3**(3), 25 (2018)
38. Schenk, A., Prause, G., Peitgen, H.-O.: Efficient semiautomatic segmentation of 3D objects in medical images. In: Delp, S.L., DiGoia, A.M., Jaramaz, B. (eds.) MICCAI 2000. LNCS, vol. 1935, pp. 186–195. Springer, Heidelberg (2000). https://doi.org/10.1007/978-3-540-40899-4_19
39. Song, Y., Zheng, J., Lei, L., Ni, Z., Zhao, B., Hu, Y.: CT2US: cross-modal transfer learning for kidney segmentation in ultrasound images with synthesized data. Ultrasonics **122**, 106706 (2022)
40. Tahir, A.M., et al.: Covid-19 infection localization and severity grading from chest X-ray images. Comput. Biol. Med. **139**, 105002 (2021)
41. Wang, G., et al.: Interactive medical image segmentation using deep learning with image-specific fine tuning. IEEE Trans. Med. Imaging **37**(7), 1562–1573 (2018)
42. Wang, G., et al.: DeepIGeoS: a deep interactive geodesic framework for medical image segmentation. IEEE Trans. Pattern Anal. Mach. Intell. **41**(7), 1559–1572 (2018)
43. Wasserthal, J., et al.: TotalSegmentator: robust segmentation of 104 anatomic structures in CT images. Radiol. Artif. Intell. **5**(5) (2023)
44. Xu, Z., et al.: Codabench: flexible, easy-to-use, and reproducible meta-benchmark platform. Patterns **3**(7), 100543 (2022)
45. Zhang, C., et al.: Faster segment anything: towards lightweight SAM for mobile applications. arXiv preprint arXiv:2306.14289 (2023)
46. Zhang, Z., Cai, H., Han, S.: EfficientViT-SAM: accelerated segment anything model without performance loss. In: CVPR Workshop: Efficient Large Vision Models (2024)
47. Zhao, F., Xie, X.: An overview of interactive medical image segmentation. Ann. BMVA **2013**(7), 1–22 (2013)
48. Zhou, J., et al.: Thyroid nodule segmentation and classification in ultrasound images. In: International Conference on Medical Image Computing and Computer-Assisted Intervention (2020)

ExpertsMedSAM: Faster Medical Image Segment Anything with Mixture-of-Experts

Li Zhi[1], Yaqi Wang[2], and Shuai Wang[1(✉)]

[1] Hangzhou Dianzi University, Hangzhou, China
shuaiwang.tai@gmail.com
[2] Communication University of Zhejiang, Hangzhou, China

Abstract. The Segment Anything Model (SAM) demonstrates remarkable performance in image segmentation but is limited by its large ViT-H encoder, restricting deployment on resource-constrained devices. LiteMedSAM addresses this by incorporating compact encoders like Tiny-ViT, reducing parameters while maintaining performance. However, it underperforms in complex cases such as funduscopic image segmentation using Scribble-Prompt. Scribble-Prompt allows detailed annotations suitable for small or intricate structures but lacks mature optimization strategies in medical image segmentation. To enhance performance in challenging modalities like funduscopic images, we propose ExpertsMedSAM-a multi-expert fusion model integrating Tiny-ViT with a Scribble-Guided Mask Decoder. This approach employs a hybrid multi-expert training strategy and an efficient output fusion method, significantly improving segmentation under Scribble-Prompt conditions while maintaining stability across other modalities. Experimental results show substantial improvements over baseline models. The code is available at https://github.com/RicoLeehdu/ExpertsMedSAM.git..

Keywords: Instance Segment · Segment Anything

1 Introduction

Deep learning-based models have demonstrated significant potential in medical image segmentation due to their ability to learn intricate image features and deliver accurate segmentation results across a diverse range of tasks [3,4], from segmenting specific anatomical structures to identifying pathological regions [6,10,20]. However, a major limitation of many current medical image segmentation models is their task-specific nature [12,15], which hinders their generalizability and presents a substantial challenge to their broader adoption in clinical practice [2,17]. In contrast, recent advances in natural image segmentation have led to the development of foundation models, such as the Segment Anything Model (SAM) [7] and Segment Everything Everywhere with Multi-modal Prompts All at Once [25], which demonstrate exceptional versatility and performance across various segmentation tasks. Similarly, MedSAM [11] has established a foundational segmentation model for medical applications, achieving stable results across multiple modalities. However, the large number of parameters in the image encoder of the SAM architecture restricts the widespread use of MedSAM. As a result, efforts to create lightweight versions of SAM have become a prominent focus. For example, Mobile-SAM [22] replaces the ViT in SAM with Tiny-ViT [19], reducing the parameter count through decoupled distillation operations, while Fast-SAM [24] compresses the model architecture by referencing the YOLO [18] framework.

The Segment Anything Model (SAM) [7] introduced a foundational framework that achieves remarkable performance across various image segmentation tasks. However, the default ViT-H encoder in SAM comprises over 600 million parameters, making it impractical for deployment on resource-constrained devices. To address this limitation, LiteMedSAM have replaced the larger encoder with more compact alternatives, such as Tiny-ViT [19], which incorporates a streamlined ViT architecture. This adjustment effectively reduces the parameter count while maintaining satisfactory segmentation performance. Despite achieving stable results across multiple modalities, LiteMedSAM exhibits suboptimal performance in certain complex cases, particularly in the segmentation of funduscopic images using the Scribble-Prompt.

In the context of current segmentation research, Box-Prompt and Scribble-Prompt are two primary annotation techniques. Box-Prompt offers an intuitive labeling approach, but it is limited in achieving precise segmentation for small lesions or intricate structures. Conversely, Scribble-Prompt allows for more detailed annotations, making it particularly suitable for segmenting smaller or more complex regions [8]. However, research on Scribble-Prompt in medical image segmentation remains relatively underdeveloped, with a lack of mature optimization strategies. Given this background, our study focuses on the Scribble-Prompt approach, aiming to enhance segmentation performance in challenging modalities such as funduscopic images. Our analysis revealed that LiteMedSAM struggles with segmenting funduscopic data under Scribble-Prompt conditions. To address this challenge, we developed a multi-expert fusion fine-tuning strategy that improves performance in this modality with minimal additional training cost, while ensuring stable outcomes across other modalities.

Our main contributions can be summarized as follows:

- We propose a multi-expert fusion segmentation model, ExpertsMedSAM, which integrates Tiny-ViT with a Scribble-Guided Mask Decoder, making it well-suited for deployment on resource-constrained devices and effective in multi-modal medical image segmentation tasks.
- By leveraging a hybrid multi-expert training strategy, our approach enhances segmentation performance in the funduscopic modality under Scribble-Prompt conditions, while maintaining stability and generalizability across other modalities.
- We introduce an efficient output fusion method, which combines the outputs of multiple experts during inference, achieving a balanced trade-off between accuracy and generalization performance.

2 Method

The proposed method is based on the structure of LitedMedSAM. Tiny-ViT is employed as the image encoder to compress inputs from various modalities into a uniform-size image embedding. Unlike the original structure, the method integrates a new decoder with a Scribble-Guided Mask Decoder, inheriting the corresponding weights from pre-trained models. The image embedding, along with annotated scribble prompts, is used as input to the Scribble-Guided Mask Decoder for precise decoding. This approach utilizes a novel training strategy that enhances the model's performance in previously underperforming modalities, such as funduscopic data, while preserving the model's original capabilities and ensuring output stability. As shown in Fig. 1, the distribution of healthy and diseased data during training is different from that during validation and the types of disease distribution are different.

2.1 Preprocessing

All fundusscopic images were segmented by threshold to determine the eyeball area and then remove excess black background. In addition, in the data set g1020, REFUGE related to optic disc and optic cup segmentation, based on the annotation of the optic cup part, We separately segmented the view cup part of the corresponding original image.

2.2 Proposed Method

This study presents a lightweight segmentation model based on SAM, termed ExpertsMedSAM as shown in Fig. 2. The objective is to improve performance in specific modalities while maintaining the model's foundational capabilities, with particular emphasis on segmenting fundus images under Scribble-Prompt conditions.

The architecture of ExpertsMedSAM is derived from the LiteMedSAM framework, utilizing a Tiny-ViT encoder and two decoders, designated as Expert

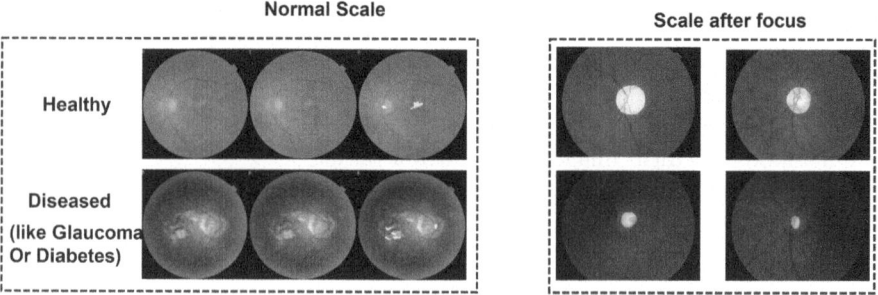

Fig. 1. The different types and scale fundus images.

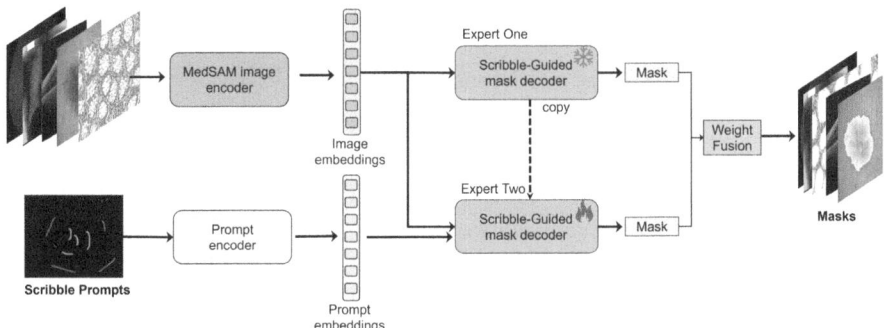

Fig. 2. The input to the network consists of medical images from various modalities. During training, the model keeps Tiny-ViT and the initial Scribble-Guided Mask Decoder (Expert1) frozen, using them only for inference, while training an additional Scribble-Guided Mask Decoder (Expert2). The outputs from both decoders, Mask1 and Mask2, are then weighted and fused to update the model.

One and Expert Two. Expert One retains the original Scribble-Guided Mask Decoder, while Expert Two serves as an additional decoder, fine-tuned on data from new modalities. To reduce training costs, the Tiny-ViT encoder and Expert One remain fixed during training, with updates applied only to Expert Two.

A dynamic weight fusion strategy is employed during training to balance the contributions of the outputs from Expert One (base output) and Expert Two (fine-tuned output). Initially, the base output is assigned a lower weight, and the fine-tuned output receives a higher weight to facilitate thorough training of Expert Two on the new data. As training progresses, the weights are adjusted according to the training loss, gradually balancing the contributions from both outputs. This dynamic adjustment mechanism is designed to preserve essential features during the later stages of training, thereby improving the model's generalization capability.

During inference, the weights are adjusted to emphasize the stability of the base output from Expert One by assigning it a higher weight, while the output from Expert Two is given a lower weight to enhance performance in specific modalities. This approach aims to achieve effective output fusion within the multi-expert framework, ensuring stability and precision throughout the inference phase.

2.3 Post-processing

In the inference phase, ExpertsMedSAM will eventually weight and fuse the output of the two Experts as the final result. Specifically, the output of the Decoder (Expert 1) that was frozen in the training phase during inference accounts for 90% of the final fusion result. And the other ten percent comes from Expert 2. Finally, the two fusion segmentation results are used as the final output.

3 Experiments

3.1 Dataset and Evaluation Measures

For model development, we utilized all the official datasets provided by the competition, supplemented with publicly available fundus image datasets, including G1020 [1], REFUGE [14], DRIVE [16], and RITE [5]. All datasets underwent standardization to ensure consistency in training and evaluation. The inclusion of these additional datasets enables the model to better adapt to the segmentation tasks under Scribble-Prompt conditions, thereby improving its performance on fundus imaging. The details of external fundus modality datasets are shown in Table 1.

The evaluation metrics include two accuracy measures-Dice Similarity Coefficient (DSC) and Normalized Surface Dice (NSD)-alongside one efficiency measure-running time. These metrics collectively contribute to the ranking computation.

Table 1. External fundus dataset details

Dataset	G10200 [1]	REFUGE [14]	DRIVE [16]	RITE [5]
Disease	glaucoma	glaucoma	None	None
Images	1020	1200	40	40
Mask	optic cup, optic disc, and bounding box of disc	optic cup, optic disc	Retinal Vessel/eyeball	Retinal Vessel
info	glaucoma: 296 healthy: 724	glaucoma: 120 healthy: 1080	healthy: 40	healthy: 40
Resolution(pixels)	1944 × 2108 and 2426 × 3007	2124 × 2056	768 × 584	700 × 800

3.2 Implementation Details

Environment Settings. The development environments and requirements are presented in Table 2.

Table 2. Development environments and requirements.

System	Ubuntu 18.04.5 LTS
CPU	AMD EPYC 7002
RAM	48GB
GPU (number and type)	One NVIDIA 4090 24G
CUDA version	12.1
Programming language	Python 3.10
Deep learning framework	torch 2.3.0, torchvision 0.18.0
Code	https://github.com/RicoLeehdu/ExpertsMedSAM/tree/master

Training Protocols. During data preprocessing, we obtained 2300 medical image mask pairs for model development and validation. For internal validation, we randomly split the dataset into 80 and 20: training and validation respectively. The model is initialized using the pre-trained LitedMedSAm model. All trainable parameters in the mask decoder are updated during training. Specifically, the number of trainable parameters of the mask decoder is 8,116,680. Bounding box hints are simulated based on expert annotations with random perturbations of 0–20 pixels. The loss function is the unweighted sum between Dice loss [13] and Cross-entropy loss [23], which has been proven to be robust in various segmentation tasks. The network was optimized by the AdamW optimizer [9] with an initial learning rate of 5e-4 and a weight decay of 0.01. The global batch size is 24 and no data augmentation is used. The model was trained on a 4090 (24G) GPU for 100 epochs, and the one with the best performance on the validation set was selected as the final model. The training protocols are listed in Table 3.

Table 3. Training protocols.

Pre-trained Model	SAM [7] MedSAM [11]
Batch size	2
Patch size	$256 \times 256 \times 3$
number works	14
Total epochs	100
Optimizer	AdamW
Initial learning rate (lr)	0.00005
Lr decay schedule	ReduceLROnPlateau
Training time	8.5 h
Loss function	Dice, BCE
Number of model parameters	41.62M[a]

[a] https://github.com/sksq96/pytorch-summary.

4 Results and Discussion

Because the model is optimized specifically for fundus lens data, the effect on fundus lens segmentation is improved. In the normally captured fundusscopic images, the segmentation results of the optic disc and cup are normal. However, when the eyeball rotation angle is too large, the optic disc position shifts, causing the model to be unable to correctly locate its position. Due to the addition of an additional Decoder, the inference time increases. Therefore, the operating efficiency of the proposed model has actually declined.

4.1 Quantitative Results on Validation Set

The quantitative results are listed in Table 4. Ablation experiment 1 is a fusion of the model training strategy and the final result during training. The original

Table 4. Quantitative evaluation results.

Target	Baseline		Ablation Study 1		Ablation Study 2		Proposed	
	DSC(%)	NSD(%)	DSC(%)	NSD(%)	DSC(%)	NSD(%)	DSC(%)	NSD(%)
CT	80.54	83.38	46.64	49.63	69.94	73.27	80.53	83.37
MR	70.15	76.89	44.42	49.98	54.54	61.28	70.15	76.88
PET	67.15	89.70	58.43	80.42	49.88	72.61	67.16	89.71
US	85.25	88.14	34.17	36.64	37.83	39.73	85.24	88.13
X-Ray	21.82	18.40	37.57	39.17	30.40	28.96	21.82	18.51
Dermotology	89.51	90.84	43.35	41.60	51.42	50.13	89.51	90.84
Endoscopy	94.43	96.65	75.60	78.83	86.71	89.87	94.44	96.66
Fundus	4.64	0.14	8.69	0.14	2.00	0.23	8.368	0.23
Microscopy	11.84	9.44	7.87	5.51	8.01	4.24	11.83	9.44
Average	57.94	61.51	39.64	42.44	43.42	46.70	**58.37**	**61.61**

model segmentation result weight is 0.9, while the new Decoder result weight is 0.1. In the test phase, the original model segmentation result weight is 0.1, while the new Decoder result is 0.9. It can be seen that because the additional Decoder has not been fully trained, the model results cannot output stably and perform poorly on the original example. Ablation experiment 2 is the result after adding additional fundusoscope optic disc segmentation and fundus blood vessel segmentation data training. The model training strategy is the original model 0.1 and the new Decoder 0.9 during training. The output is the original model 0.9 and the new Decoder 0.1. It can be seen that the NSD index has increased in the fundusscopic segmentation results. However, the DSC results did not improve significantly. More experiments need to be done here for verification. The Quantitative evaluation of segmentation efficiency in terms of running time are shwon in Table 5.

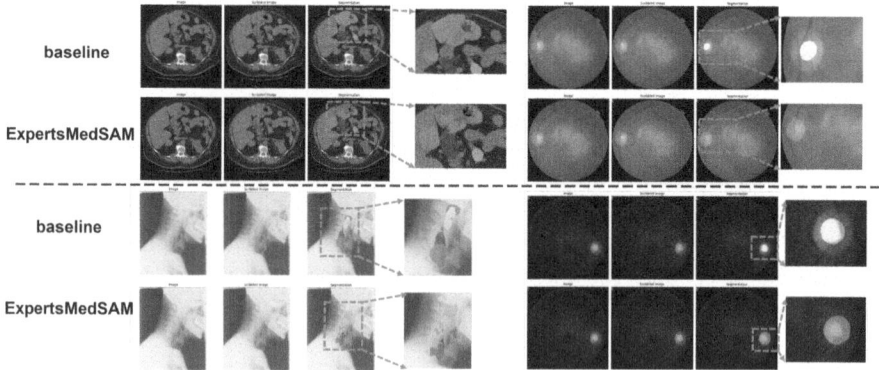

Fig. 3. The segmentation cases between baseline and ExpertsMedSAM.

Table 5. Quantitative evaluation of segmentation efficiency in terms of running time (s).

Case ID	Size	Num. Objects	Baseline	Proposed
3DBox_CT_0566	(287, 512, 512)	6	376.4	380.4
3DBox_CT_0888	(237, 512, 512)	6	100.5	104.5
3DBox_CT_0860	(246, 512, 512)	1	17.7	21.7
3DBox_MR_0621	(115, 400, 400)	6	157.1	161.1
3DBox_MR_0121	(64, 290, 320)	6	99.9	103.9
3DBox_MR_0179	(84, 512, 512)	1	17.1	21.1
3DBox_PET_0001	(264, 200, 200)	1	12.1	16.1
2DBox_US_0525	(256, 256, 3)	1	6.3	9.2
2DBox_X-Ray_0053	(320, 640, 3)	34	7.3	9.6
2DBox_Dermoscopy_0003	(3024, 4032, 3)	1	6.5	9.4
2DBox_Endoscopy_0086	(480, 560, 3)	1	6.1	9.2
2DBox_Fundus_0003	(2048, 2048, 3)	1	6.1	9.2
2DBox_Microscope_0008	(1536, 2040, 3)	19	6.8	13.39
2DBox_Microscope_0016	(1920, 2560, 3)	241	19.1	22.9

4.2 Qualitative Results on Validation Set

Because the model is optimized specifically for fundus lens data, the effect on fundus lens segmentation is improved. In the normally captured fundusscopic images, the segmentation results of the optic disc and cup are normal. However, when the eyeball rotation angle is too large, the optic disc position shifts, causing the model to be unable to correctly locate its position. The segmentation cases between baseline and ExpertsMedSAM are shown in Fig. 3

4.3 Results on Final Testing Set

In the final testing stage, the test results obtained by our method are shown in Table 6. It can be seen that our method still has a lot of room for optimization.

4.4 Limitation and Future Work

Due to limitations of computing resources and time, we mostly followed the structure and weights of LitedMedSAM, and only optimized it for some data sets and scenarios, without verifying the universality of the current model structure on a wider range of data sets. And the weight of the final output fusion of the model was not optimized through more comparative experiments. The next step of work includes innovation of model structure and optimization of Decoder structure based on EfficientViT-SAM.

Table 6. Comparison of NSD, DSC, and Runtime across different modalities for two teams

Modality	ExpertsMedSAM			litemedsamscribble		
	NSD (%)	DSC (%)	Runtime (s)	NSD (%)	DSC (%)	Runtime (s)
CT	61.64	56.50	9.734	74.74	68.55	9.626
MR	43.63	39.52	9.661	54.18	49.66	9.433
X-Ray	34.19	29.81	10.062	63.74	56.30	9.816
Endoscopy	62.32	60.91	9.598	85.80	83.59	9.496
Fundus	59.06	57.80	9.697	81.52	79.56	9.603
Microscopy	35.27	34.83	10.083	54.61	53.68	10.017
OCT	25.55	24.54	9.944	28.37	27.54	9.679
PET	76.73	59.80	9.673	85.77	71.90	9.418
US	23.43	25.49	9.692	61.65	60.97	9.458
Average	46.87	43.24	9.795	**65.60**	**61.31**	**9.616**

5 Conclusion

Just like MoboleSAM, We found that on the basis of ExpertsMedSAM, an additional lightweight Decoder is added, and through the hybrid training method of multi-task experts. The optic disc and blood vessel segmentation tasks have been improved after fine-tuning in the fundusscopic data modality, and performance in other modalities is guaranteed. The fundoscopy results have been slightly improved.

Acknowledgements. We thank all the data owners for making the medical images publicly available and CodaLab [21] for hosting the challenge platform.

Disclosure of Interests. The authors have no competing interests to declare that are relevant to the content of this article.

References

1. Bajwa, M.N., Singh, G.A.P., Neumeier, W., Malik, M.I., Dengel, A., Ahmed, S.: G1020: a benchmark retinal fundus image dataset for computer-aided glaucoma detection. In: 2020 International Joint Conference on Neural Networks (IJCNN), pp. 1–7. IEEE (2020)
2. Chen, X., et al.: Recent advances and clinical applications of deep learning in medical image analysis. Med. Image Anal. **79**, 102444 (2022)
3. Graham, S., et al.: CoNIC challenge: pushing the frontiers of nuclear detection, segmentation, classification and counting. Med. Image Anal. **92**, 103047 (2024)

4. Heller, N., et al.: The state of the art in kidney and kidney tumor segmentation in contrast-enhanced CT imaging: results of the KiTS19 challenge. Med. Image Anal. **67**, 101821 (2021)
5. Hu, Q., Abràmoff, M.D., Garvin, M.K.: Automated separation of binary overlapping trees in low-contrast color retinal images. In: Mori, K., Sakuma, I., Sato, Y., Barillot, C., Navab, N. (eds.) MICCAI 2013. LNCS, vol. 8150, pp. 436–443. Springer, Heidelberg (2013). https://doi.org/10.1007/978-3-642-40763-5_54
6. Isensee, F., Jaeger, P.F., Kohl, S.A., Petersen, J., Maier-Hein, K.H.: nnU-Net: a self-configuring method for deep learning-based biomedical image segmentation. Nat. Methods **18**(2), 203–211 (2021)
7. Kirillov, A., et al.: Segment anything. In: Proceedings of the International Conference on Computer Vision, pp. 4015–4026 (2023)
8. Li, X., et al.: PaintSeg: painting pixels for training-free segmentation. In: Advances in Neural Information Processing Systems, vol. 36 (2024)
9. Loshchilov, I.: Decoupled weight decay regularization. arXiv preprint arXiv:1711.05101 (2017)
10. Luo, X., et al.: MIDeepSeg: minimally interactive segmentation of unseen objects from medical images using deep learning. Med. Image Anal. **72**, 102102 (2021)
11. Ma, J., He, Y., Li, F., Han, L., You, C., Wang, B.: Segment anything in medical images. Nat. Commun. **15**(1), 654 (2024)
12. Ma, J., et al.: Fast and low-GPU-memory abdomen CT organ segmentation: the flare challenge. Med. Image Anal. **82**, 102616 (2022)
13. Milletari, F., Navab, N., Ahmadi, S.A.: V-Net: fully convolutional neural networks for volumetric medical image segmentation. In: 2016 Fourth International Conference on 3D Vision (3DV), pp. 565–571. IEEE (2016)
14. Orlando, J.I., et al.: REFUGE challenge: a unified framework for evaluating automated methods for glaucoma assessment from fundus photographs. Med. Image Anal. **59**, 101570 (2020)
15. Ronneberger, O., Fischer, P., Brox, T.: U-Net: convolutional networks for biomedical image segmentation. In: Navab, N., Hornegger, J., Wells, W.M., Frangi, A.F. (eds.) MICCAI 2015. LNCS, vol. 9351, pp. 234–241. Springer, Cham (2015). https://doi.org/10.1007/978-3-319-24574-4_28
16. Staal, J., Abràmoff, M.D., Niemeijer, M., Viergever, M.A., Van Ginneken, B.: Ridge-based vessel segmentation in color images of the retina. IEEE Trans. Med. Imaging **23**(4), 501–509 (2004)
17. Tajbakhsh, N., Jeyaseelan, L., Li, Q., Chiang, J.N., Wu, Z., Ding, X.: Embracing imperfect datasets: a review of deep learning solutions for medical image segmentation. Med. Image Anal. **63**, 101693 (2020)
18. Talaat, F.M., ZainEldin, H.: An improved fire detection approach based on YOLO-V8 for smart cities. Neural Comput. Appl. **35**(28), 20939–20954 (2023)
19. Wu, K., et al.: TinyViT: fast pretraining distillation for small vision transformers. In: Avidan, S., Brostow, G., Cissé, M., Farinella, G.M., Hassner, T. (eds.) ECCV 2022. LNCS, vol. 13681, pp. 68–85. Springer, Cham(2022). https://doi.org/10.1007/978-3-031-19803-8_5
20. Xie, L., et al.: CNTSeg: a multimodal deep-learning-based network for cranial nerves tract segmentation. Med. Image Anal. **86**, 102766 (2023)
21. Xu, Z., et al.: Codabench: flexible, easy-to-use, and reproducible meta-benchmark platform. Patterns **3**(7), 100543 (2022)
22. Zhang, C., et al.: Faster segment anything: towards lightweight SAM for mobile applications. arXiv preprint arXiv:2306.14289 (2023)

23. Zhang, Z., Sabuncu, M.: Generalized cross entropy loss for training deep neural networks with noisy labels. In: Advances in Neural Information Processing Systems, vol. 31 (2018)
24. Zhao, X., et al.: Fast segment anything. arXiv preprint arXiv:2306.12156 (2023)
25. Zou, X., et al.: Segment everything everywhere all at once. In: Advances in Neural Information Processing Systems, vol. 36 (2024)

Efficient Quantization-Aware Training on Segment Anything Model in Medical Images and Its Deployment

Haisheng Lu⊙, Yujie Fu⊙, Fan Zhang⊙, and Le Zhang(✉)⊙

University of Electronic Science and Technology of China, Chengdu, China
{luhaisheng,fuyujie}@std.uestc.edu.cn, {fan.zhang,lezhang}@uestc.edu.cn

Abstract. Medical image segmentation is a critical component of clinical practice, and the state-of-the-art MedSAM model has significantly advanced this field. Nevertheless, critiques highlight that MedSAM demands substantial computational resources during inference. To address this issue, the CVPR 2024 MedSAM on Laptop Challenge was established to find an optimal balance between accuracy and processing speed. In this paper, we introduce a quantization-aware training pipeline designed to efficiently quantize the Segment Anything Model for medical images and deploy it using the OpenVINO inference engine. This pipeline optimizes both training time and disk storage. Our experimental results confirm that this approach considerably enhances processing speed over the baseline, while still achieving an acceptable accuracy level. The training script, inference script, and quantized model are publicly accessible at https://github.com/AVC2-UESTC/QMedSAM.

Keywords: Quantization-Aware Training · Segment Anything Model

1 Introduction

Drawing inspiration from the remarkable achievements of foundation models in natural language processing, researchers at Meta FAIR introduced a versatile foundation model for image segmentation, termed the Segment Anything Model (SAM) [3]. It is widely recognized that foundation models in any domain often confront challenges stemming from limited data diversity. Despite the considerable scale of the dataset utilized to train SAM (referred to as the SA-1B dataset), comprising over one billion masks, the model's performance fell short in medical image segmentation tasks [10]. This shortfall can be attributed in part to the composition of the SA-1B dataset, which primarily comprises photographs of natural scenes captured by cameras, thus lacking the nuanced features characteristic of medical images. In response to this challenge, Ma et al. curated a diverse and extensive medical image segmentation dataset encompassing 15 modalities, upon which they fine-tuned SAM [10]. Their refined model, dubbed

MedSAM, represents a significant step forward in addressing this discrepancy. However, despite its advancements, MedSAM still grapples with several unresolved challenges. For instance, the training dataset suffers from extreme modality imbalances, the model encounters difficulties in accurately segmenting vessel-like branching structures, and the practicality of text prompts remains limited.

The focus of the CVPR 2024 MedSAM on Laptop Challenge is on enhancing the inference speed of MedSAM. The Segment Anything Model comprises three core components: an image encoder responsible for transforming input images into image embeddings, a prompt encoder that converts prompts into prompt embeddings, and a mask decoder tasked with generating low-resolution masks from image embeddings and prompt embeddings. Notably, in the initial prototype of MedSAM, the image encoder is notably more resource-intensive than the other two components. Consequently, various alternative backbones have been proposed to replace the original image encoder, such as the ViT-Tiny architecture adopted by MobileSAM [15] and EfficientViT in EfficientViT-SAM [17]. The challenge's baseline model (LiteMedSAM) incorporates a distilled ViT-Tiny image encoder, albeit with slight adjustments compared to MobileSAM. A summary of the parameters of the different submodules is provided in Table 1.

Table 1. Parameters of different submodules in LiteMedSAM and MedSAM

Parameters	Image Encoder	Prompt Encoder	Mask Decoder
LiteMedSAM	5.7M	6.2K	4.1M
MedSAM	89.7M		

In addition to optimizing the backbones of SAM, we pursued an alternative approach to expedite inference: quantization. Quantization offers several benefits, including reducing parameter sizes, increasing inference speed, and decreasing power consumption during inference. There are two primary paradigms for quantizing neural networks: post-training quantization (PTQ) [1,8,16] and quantization-aware training (QAT) [2,13]. PTQ involves converting a pre-trained floating-point model directly into a low-precision one by calibrating the model using a batch of calibration data. This method is generally faster since it does not require re-training, and the precision of the quantized model largely depends on the calibration process. On the other hand, QAT integrates quantization and de-quantization nodes into the computational graph, enabling the training of the model while preserving its accuracy after quantization. To ensure prediction accuracy, we chose QAT to quantize SAM.

The attention blocks of transformers serve as the principal components in the backbone of SAM. Several methods have been proposed to enhance the accuracy of quantized transformers. Li et al. introduced an information rectification module and a distribution-guided distillation scheme tailored for fully quantized vision transformers [5]. Liu et al. discovered that incorporating fixed uniform noise into the values being quantized can significantly mitigate quantization errors under provable conditions [6]. In this study, we have chosen to leverage the Xilinx Brevitas framework [11]. This framework offers an excellent workflow, encompassing quantization-aware training through to development on inference engines.

The main contributions of this paper are listed as follows:

1. We propose a quantized LiteMedSAM model with comparable average accuracy, and alleviate the imbalance across different modalities.
2. An optimized online dataset is proposed to replace the offline baseline, yielding a significant reduction in disk storage requirement.
3. Experiments have been proposed to prove that a small subset of the training dataset can maintain the accuracy of the quantized model, making it more efficient in training.
4. The quantized model is deployed on the OpenVINO inference engine, enabling it to compete effectively with other models in the challenge.

2 Method

2.1 Preprocessing

The dataset comprises three types of medical images: grayscale images, RGB images, and 3D images. 3D images are split into individual 2D clips along the z-axis, with each clip treated as a grayscale image. To standardize the grayscale format with the RGB format, grayscale images are duplicated across the red, green, and blue channels. Subsequently, RGB images are resized, padded to dimensions of 256×256, and finally normalized. It's important to note that in the baseline approach, RGB images undergo normalization before padding with zeros. In this case, the padded value is equivalent to the minimum value of the image instead of zero.

We've implemented some optimizations in the dataloader to enhance efficiency during both training and inference. For the training process, in the baseline approach, all compressed 3D npz files are decompressed along the z-axis, which demands approximately 10TB of disk storage. This overhead is significantly disproportionate to the size of the original dataset, which is only around 160 GB. To mitigate this inefficiency, we propose indexing each 3D clip along the z-axis and employing a binary search algorithm to locate the target 2D clip when necessary. By adopting this strategy, we distribute the decompression time across each batch of training data, resulting in substantial savings in disk storage. Additionally, considering that our machine typically processes one batch of data in approximately one second, the computational cost of decompression becomes negligible.

In terms of inference, the baseline method iterates through each 3D prompt box individually. However, when 3D boxes intersect along the z-axis, the baseline recalculates image features. Given that the image encoder constitutes the most computationally intensive aspect of SAM, we propose to preprocess all the 3D boxes into 2D boxes corresponding to 2D clips. This approach ensures that the image embedding of each 2D clip is computed only once, optimizing computational resources. In addition, the challenge has an 8GB limit on the Docker running memory. Experiments show that LiteMedSAM will exceed the memory limit when the number of boxes approaches 100. Since the maximum number of boxes is 255, we propose a block partition algorithm along the batch axis of boxes. This algorithm allows users to specify the maximum running batch size to prevent exceeding the memory limit.

2.2 Proposed Method

We propose to quantize the baseline model LiteMedSAM using QAT. While neural networks consist of various components beyond just matrix multiplications, it's within these operations that the peak of computational complexity resides. Therefore, nearly every QAT method focuses on quantizing inputs and weights during matrix multiplications, such as in linear layers, convolution layers, and attention blocks. In contrast, operations involving biases, activation layers, and normalization layers are typically performed per element. While the quantization of these layers can be selective, in our proposed quantized model, we opt to retain all these layers as floating-point, with only matrix multiplications in the image encoder and the mask decoder being quantized. The reason we choose not to quantize the prompt encoder lies in the fact that its parameter size is over 1000 times smaller than the other two modules, as indicated in Table 1. Some of the most common quantized sub-structures are illustrated in Fig. 1.

Since quantization is non-differentiable, we employ the straight-through estimator (STE) methodology, as demonstrated in previous works [7]. In STE, incoming gradients are directly passed through a threshold operation to become outgoing gradients. For each quantization node, we propose an 8-bit symmetric per-tensor signed integer activations quantizer with a learned floating-point scale factor. This scale factor is initialized from runtime statistics.

2.3 Model Inference and Post-processing

Upon completion of quantization-aware training, Brevitas provides exceptional toolchains for exporting quantized models to diverse backends.

While the standard QuantizeLinear-DeQuantizeLinear (QCQ) representation for quantization in ONNX exists, Brevitas has extended this to QuantizeLinear-Clip-DeQuantizeLinear (QCDQ). With this extension, researchers can confine the range of quantized values. Therefore, we propose exporting the quantized LiteMedSAM to ONNX in the QCDQ representation.

While numerous inference engines support the ONNX format, not all of them are compatible with QCDQ. Given that the challenge mandates CPU inference, we narrow down the options to ONNX Runtime and OpenVINO. An experiment on inference speed between these two inference engines is detailed in Sect. 4.1. Based on the results, we ultimately opt for OpenVINO. Model caching is also supported by OpenVINO. This strategy can reduce the resulting delays

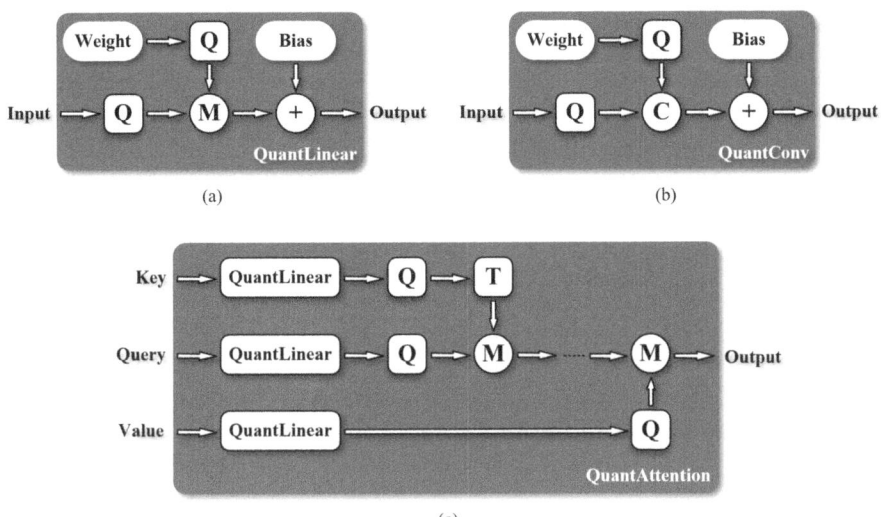

Fig. 1. Common quantized sub-layers. (a) quantized linear layer; (b) quantized convolutional layer; (c) quantized attention block. Circles in the figure represent corresponding calculations: M stands for matrix multiplication, C stands for convolution, and T stands for transpose. Operations involving quantization are represented by round rectangles in the figure. The inputs and output of all the sub-layers depicted in the figure are floating-point tensors.

at application startup, making it considerably suitable for accelerating in this challenge [4,12].

SAM generates a 256 × 256 mask for the provided image and prompt. We binarize the floating-point values to either 0 or 1, crop the padding, and subsequently resize the low-resolution mask to the original dimensions of the input image.

3 Experiments

3.1 Dataset and Sampler

We employed the challenge dataset for training, while the evaluation dataset was obtained by partitioning it at a ratio of one-tenth. The dataset comprises 11 modalities, and their sizes (prior to partitioning into training and evaluation datasets) are summarized in Table 2. An evident issue arises from the significant imbalance in sample numbers across modalities. To address this imbalance and prevent bias or overfitting in the quantized model, as well as to expedite training, we propose randomly sampling N_s 2D clips from each modality in each epoch. Additionally, these samples undergo random horizontal and vertical flips for data augmentation.

Table 2. Samples of modalities in the training dataset (including the additional datasets released in the post-challenge task). 3D modalities are counted with the number of 2D clips on the z-axis.

3D Modalities	CT	MR	PET	
Samples	1218411	236804	89059	
2D Modalities	Endoscopy	X-Ray	Dermoscopy	US
Samples	43443	34893	3694	1646
2D Modalities	OCT	Mammography	Fundus	Microscopy
Samples	1436	1233	1057	1000

3.2 Metrics and Loss Functions

The accuracy of the model is evaluated using the Dice Similarity Coefficient (DSC) and the Normalized Surface Distance (NSD), while efficiency is measured through running time analysis. These metrics are collectively utilized to compute the ranking. In the training phase, we mainly employ a combination of the Dice loss and focal loss. This decision is based on the robustness demonstrated by compound loss functions in various medical image segmentation tasks, as evidenced in prior research [9].

3.3 Training Protocols

The training procedure includes three stages.

In stage one, our goal is to train the quantized image encoder while keeping the floating-point prompt encoder and the mask decoder frozen. Apart from the loss function mentioned in Sect. 3.2, we further distill the image encoder from MedSAM and introduce the distillation loss. This loss is calculated as the product of the mean squared error and the intersection over union ratio across the image embeddings generated from the teacher and student models.

In stage two, we propose to train the quantized mask decoder by concatenating it with the best-trained quantized image encoder from stage one and the floating-point prompt encoder.

In the final stage, the whole model undergoes an end-to-end fine-tuning for further fitting with the dataset.

For each stage, we propose employing linear learning rate warm-up for N_w epochs, commencing at 1% of the initial learning rate. Additional training details are summarized in Table 3. This warm-up period is followed by a cosine annealing scheduler for N_a epochs. The minimum learning rate of the cosine annealing scheduler is set to 0.1% of the initial learning rate, and the half-period of the cosine function is determined as $N_a - 1$. Once the quantization-aware training process is completed, we evaluate the checkpoint of each epoch on the evaluation dataset and select the best-performing one. Additional training details are summarized in Table 3.

Table 3. Training protocols. Values separated by vertical bars in the table correspond to stages 1 ∼ 3.

Pre-trained Model	LiteMedSAM (the baseline)
Batch size	2 | 4 | 2
DDP world size	4
Samples of each modality (N_s)	900
Optimizer	SGD (momentum = 0.9)
Total epochs	14
Initial learning rate	0.01
Warm-up epochs (N_w)	5
Cosine annealing epochs (N_a)	10
Training time	5 | 2.5 | 1 h

3.4 Environment Settings

The development environments and requirements are presented in Table 4.

Table 4. Development environments and requirements.

System	Ubuntu 20.04.3 LTS
CPU	Intel(R) Xeon(R) Gold 5218R CPU@2.10 GHz
RAM	16 × 32 GB
GPU	4× NVIDIA GeForce RTX 3090
CUDA version	12.2
Programming language	Python 3.11
Deep learning framework	PyTorch 2.0.1
Specific dependencies	Brevitas 0.10.3
Code	https://github.com/AVC2-UESTC/QMedSAM

4 Results and Discussion

4.1 Inference Speeds of Different Engines

The challenge evaluates models on an Intel Xeon W-2133 CPU (6c12t@3.8 GHz), while we use an Intel Core i7-8750H CPU (6c12t@4.1 GHz) that offers comparable performance because we do not have an identical environment. We test each variant with a single image and a prompt box. The inference speeds of various methods are detailed in Table 5.

Table 5. Inference speed of different LiteMedSAM variants.

Method	Inference time
LiteMedSAM inferenced on PyTorch	1.180 s
LiteMedSAM exported to ONNX and inferenced on ONNX Runtime	0.787 s
LiteMedSAM exported to ONNX and inferenced on OpenVINO	0.574 s
Quantized LiteMedSAM inferenced on ONNX Runtime	0.769 s
Quantized LiteMedSAM inferenced on OpenVINO	0.585 s

The results indicate that the quantized model does not exhibit the fastest runtime. This is because that our hardware is not optimized for quantized operations, resulting in slower execution compared to standard floating-point operations. For comparison purposes, the inference speeds of both floating-point and quantized versions of MedSAM (which is substantially larger than LiteMedSAM) are provided in Table 6. Interestingly, in this case the quantized model outperforms the floating-point model.

Table 6. Inference speed of different MedSAM variants.

Method	Inference time
MedSAM inferenced on PyTorch	10.181 s
MedSAM exported to ONNX and inferenced on ONNX Runtime	5.707 s
MedSAM exported to ONNX and inferenced on OpenVINO	4.202 s
Quantized MedSAM inferenced on ONNX Runtime	4.531 s
Quantized MedSAM inferenced on OpenVINO	3.558 s

Given the comprehensive advantages of quantization, it is evident that deploying the quantized LiteMedSAM on the OpenVINO inference engine effectively addresses the requirement for medical image segmentation "on laptop".

4.2 Quantitative Results on Validation Set

Table 7 presents the performance of the proposed three stages in comparison with the baseline model on the public validation dataset.

On average, the quantized model scores comparably on DSC and slightly higher on NSD. We highlight the modalities with significant differences in their accuracy. In particular, the quantized model has degraded performance by around 3% and 5% in MR and US, but shows gains of approximately 10% and 9% improvement in PET and Microscope. It is evident that, to a certain extent, the proposed method has effectively addressed the performance imbalance of the baseline model across various modalities, which was caused by the dataset's inherent imbalance.

Table 7. Quantitative evaluation results on the validation dataset.

	Stage 3		Stage 2		Stage 1		Baseline	
	DSC	NSD	DSC	NSD	DSC	NSD	DSC	NSD
CT	89.35%	92.84%	89.73%	93.23%	89.86%	93.27%	90.78%	93.08%
MR	82.41%	87.29%	82.73%	87.76%	82.91%	87.87%	**86.43%**	**90.37%**
PET	**64.80%**	**56.33%**	63.37%	49.52%	63.86%	48.75%	57.64%	43.05%
US	87.87%	92.41%	87.93%	92.50%	87.88%	92.39%	**94.54%**	**96.62%**
X-Ray	78.73%	84.19%	78.14%	83.80%	78.62%	84.31%	79.15%	84.46%
Dermoscopy	91.71%	93.31%	92.15%	93.75%	92.12%	93.70%	91.59%	93.21%
Endoscopy	93.37%	96.61%	93.56%	96.71%	94.08%	97.12%	94.81%	97.70%
Fundus	93.24%	94.66%	93.85%	95.19%	92.97%	94.30%	94.40%	95.77%
Microscope	**70.11%**	**77.35%**	71.77%	79.21%	72.77%	80.18%	60.54%	65.12%
Average	**83.51%**	**86.11%**	83.69%	85.74%	83.90%	85.76%	83.32%	84.38%

A comparison of inference speeds for specific cases between the baseline and the proposed method is presented in Table 8. The results highlight a notable acceleration achieved by the quantization method.

4.3 Qualitative Results on Validation Set

Two sets of successful segmentation results are depicted in Fig. 2. It can be observed that the proposed quantized model performs better in matching the ROI than the floating-point counterpart. Figure 3 illustrates two sets of challenging cases. In these cases, the segmentation results of the proposed quantized model align more closely with the ground truth ROI compared to the baseline. However, since the baseline prediction results were significantly distant from the ground truth, the correction was unsuccessful.

4.4 Ablation Study

Training a Segment **Anything** Model from scratch requires a huge mass of data. However, the proposed quantization-aware training procedure starts with a pre-trained model. Reducing the number of samples N_s from each modality, especially from the larger modalities, certainly benefits in saving training time. However, it still raises questions about its influence on the precision of the quantized model. In this section we propose an ablation study to explore the balance between efficiency and accuracy.

To describe the variation of samples from different modalities clearly, we will use $N_s(m)$ to represent the number of samples from modality m. The total samples of modality m is denoted by $N_m(m)$, and the complete set of modalities is denoted by M. The strategy of the proposed method can be described as

$$N_s(m) = \min_{i \in M} N_m(i).$$

Table 8. Quantitative efficiency in terms of inference running time (seconds). MLE stands for Memory Limit Exceeded.

Case ID	Size	Objects	Baseline	Proposed
3DBox_CT_0566	(287, 512, 512)	6	591.1	142.1
3DBox_CT_0888	(237, 512, 512)	6	168.7	51.0
3DBox_CT_0860	(246, 512, 512)	1	23.4	12.4
3DBox_MR_0621	(115, 400, 400)	6	245.6	51.5
3DBox_MR_0121	(64, 290, 320)	6	168.4	31.4
3DBox_MR_0179	(84, 512, 512)	1	22.5	11.9
3DBox_PET_0001	(264, 200, 200)	1	15.1	7.3
2DBox_US_0525	(256, 256, 3)	1	1.6	0.7
2DBox_X-Ray_0053	(320, 640, 3)	34	9.2	1.8
2DBox_Dermoscopy_0003	(3024, 4032, 3)	1	6.5	1.1
2DBox_Endoscopy_0086	(480, 560, 3)	1	2.3	0.6
2DBox_Fundus_0003	(2048, 2048, 3)	1	3.5	0.7
2DBox_Microscope_0008	(1536, 2040, 3)	19	15.6	1.6
2DBox_Microscope_0016	(1920, 2560, 3)	241	MLE	14.0

The ablation study introduces a strategy that enlarges $N_s(m)$ to one-tenth of $N_m(m)$, in particular,

$$N_s(m) = \max\left\{\frac{N_m(m)}{10}, \min_{i \in M} N_m(i)\right\}.$$

The metrics of the three stage

the ablation study are summarized in Table 9. Compared with Table 7 (we provide the average metrics of the proposed method in

last row of Table 9), the results indicate that increasing N_s does not result in a significant improvement, underscoring the efficiency of the proposed QAT pipeline in terms of training time.

4.5 Results on Final Testing Set

The testing results are summarized in Table 10. The proposed quantized model exhibits a marginal decrease but much more balance in the average accuracy. Additionally, the inference efficiency has been significantly optimized under the same backbone. Compared with Table 7, we can observe that the model's performance on different modalities varies between the validation set and the testing set. However, the trend of balance across modalities remains consistent.

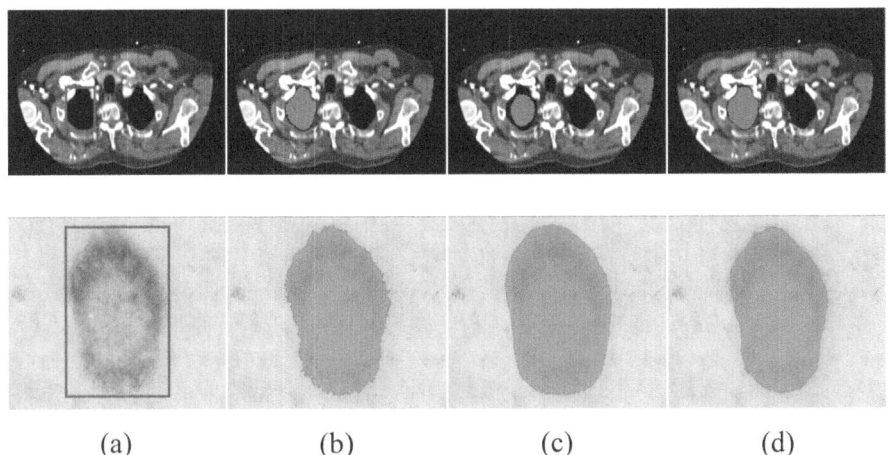

Fig. 2. Good segmentation results. (a) Image and box; (b) Ground truth; (c) Baseline; (d) Proposed method.

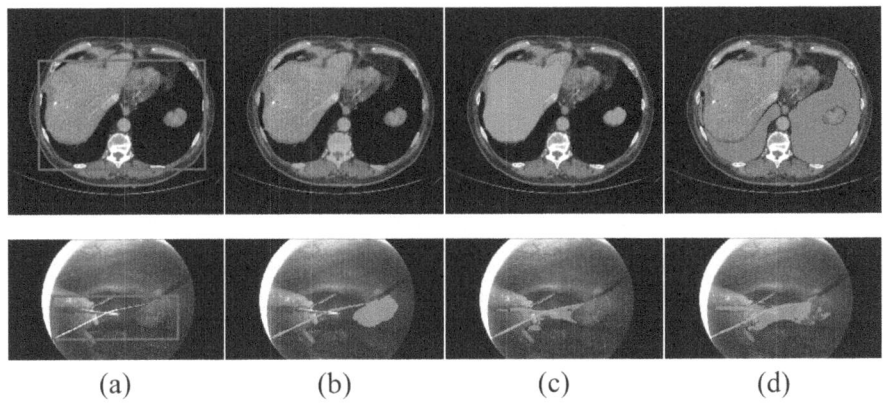

Fig. 3. Bad segmentation results. (a) Image and box; (b) Ground truth; (c) Baseline; (d) Proposed method.

4.6 Limitation and Future Work

Experimental results have shown a significant decrease in performance in certain modalities with larger amounts of data, and the accuracy of the least accurate modalities still lags far behind the average. Hence a more accurate and modality-balanced quantization is expected. On the other hand, the floating-point model runs faster on the OpenVINO inference engine. We did explain a bit about this above, but beyond that, Brevitas also provides an excellent workflow to export the quantized model to FINN for dataflow acceleration on Xilinx FPGAs. Quantized models promise faster and more energy-efficient inference on a customized hardware platform.

Table 9. Evaluation results of the ablation study on the validation dataset.

	Stage 3		Stage 2		Stage 1	
	DSC	NSD	DSC	NSD	DSC	NSD
CT	88.71%	92.37%	87.02%	91.14%	88.81%	92.45%
MR	81.55%	86.48%	80.91%	86.18%	81.61%	86.40%
PET	64.41%	55.09%	64.35%	54.73%	65.21%	52.62%
US	86.93%	91.76%	86.09%	90.87%	87.43%	91.85%
X-Ray	79.07%	84.53%	76.44%	82.13%	76.18%	81.83%
Dermoscopy	91.65%	93.24%	92.63%	94.20%	91.75%	93.34%
Endoscopy	93.42%	96.65%	93.99%	97.09%	92.65%	95.84%
Fundus	93.18%	94.59%	96.05%	97.20%	92.93%	94.33%
Microscope	72.29%	79.64%	71.03%	78.52%	72.94%	80.40%
Average	83.47%	86.04%	83.17%	85.79%	83.28%	85.45%
Proposed	83.51%	86.11%	83.69%	85.74%	83.90%	85.76%

Table 10. Evaluation results on the test dataset.

	Proposed			Baseline		
	DSC	NSD	RunTime	DSC	NSD	RunTime
CT	**69.74%**	**71.91%**	11.78 s	55.75%	58.48%	38.78 s
MR	**69.33%**	**61.77%**	6.20 s	64.80%	62.75%	18.57 s
X-Ray	80.13%	89.56%	2.50 s	**85.51%**	**94.40%**	9.95 s
Endoscopy	89.81%	93.15%	2.18 s	**94.41%**	**96.95%**	7.56 s
Fundus	79.05%	81.28%	2.23 s	**87.47%**	**89.58%**	8.77 s
Microscope	79.68%	81.72%	2.58 s	**84.36%**	**86.15%**	16.34 s
OCT	72.72%	79.50%	2.24 s	73.31%	80.20%	8.39 s
PET	76.53%	67.52%	4.87 s	76.94%	66.98%	14.90 s
US	**87.49%**	**92.09%**	2.75 s	85.24%	89.73%	8.96 s
Average	78.28%	79.83%	4.15 s	78.64%	80.58%	14.69 s

5 Conclusion

In this paper, we present an efficient pipeline for quantizing LiteMedSAM and deploying it on the OpenVINO inference engine. Objective experiments have conclusively shown that our method significantly accelerates the baseline while maintaining an acceptable level of accuracy. Future endeavors will focus on enhancing the speed of the floating-point backbone, further alleviating the imbalance across different modalities, and deploying the quantized model on customized hardware platforms.

Acknowledgements. We express our gratitude to all the data owners for making the medical images publicly available, and to CodaLab [14] for hosting the challenge platform.

Disclosure of Interests. The authors have no competing interests to declare that are relevant to the content of this article.

References

1. Hubara, I., Nahshan, Y., Hanani, Y., Banner, R., Soudry, D.: Accurate post training quantization with small calibration sets. In: International Conference on Machine Learning, pp. 4466–4475. PMLR (2021)
2. Jacob, B., et al.: Quantization and training of neural networks for efficient integer-arithmetic-only inference. CoRR abs/1712.05877 (2017). http://arxiv.org/abs/1712.05877
3. Kirillov, A., et al.: Segment anything. In: Proceedings of the International Conference on Computer Vision, pp. 4015–4026 (2023)
4. Le, B.H., Nguyen-Vu, D.K., Nguyen-Mau, T.H., Nguyen, H.D., Tran, M.T.: MedficientSAM: a robust medical segmentation model with optimized inference pipeline for limited clinical settings. In: Submitted to CVPR 2024: Segment Anything in Medical Images on Laptop (2024). https://openreview.net/forum?id=aa0f77RKI0. Under review
5. Li, Y., Xu, S., Zhang, B., Cao, X., Gao, P., Guo, G.: Q-ViT: accurate and fully quantized low-bit vision transformer. In: Advances in Neural Information Processing Systems, vol. 35, pp. 34451–34463 (2022)
6. Liu, Y., Yang, H., Dong, Z., Keutzer, K., Du, L., Zhang, S.: NoisyQuant: noisy bias-enhanced post-training activation quantization for vision transformers. In: Proceedings of the IEEE/CVF Conference on Computer Vision and Pattern Recognition, pp. 20321–20330 (2023)
7. Liu, Z., Cheng, K.T., Huang, D., Xing, E.P., Shen, Z.: Nonuniform-to-uniform quantization: towards accurate quantization via generalized straight-through estimation. In: Proceedings of the IEEE/CVF Conference on Computer Vision and Pattern Recognition, pp. 4942–4952 (2022)
8. Liu, Z., Wang, Y., Han, K., Zhang, W., Ma, S., Gao, W.: Post-training quantization for vision transformer. In: Advances in Neural Information Processing Systems, vol. 34, pp. 28092–28103 (2021)
9. Ma, J., et al.: Loss odyssey in medical image segmentation. Med. Image Anal. **71**, 102035 (2021)
10. Ma, J., He, Y., Li, F., Han, L., You, C., Wang, B.: Segment anything in medical images. Nat. Commun. **15**(1), 654 (2024)
11. Pappalardo, A.: Xilinx/brevitas. https://doi.org/10.5281/zenodo.3333552
12. Pfefferle, A.T., Purucker, L., Hutter, F.: DAFT: data-aware fine-tuning of foundation models for efficient and effective medical image segmentation. In: Submitted to CVPR 2024: Segment Anything In Medical Images On Laptop (2024). https://openreview.net/forum?id=PObXviy706. Under review
13. Shen, M., et al.: Once quantization-aware training: high performance extremely low-bit architecture search. In: Proceedings of the IEEE/CVF International Conference on Computer Vision, pp. 5340–5349 (2021)

14. Xu, Z., et al.: Codabench: flexible, easy-to-use, and reproducible meta-benchmark platform. Patterns **3**(7), 100543 (2022)
15. Zhang, C., et al.: Faster segment anything: towards lightweight SAM for mobile applications. arXiv preprint arXiv:2306.14289 (2023)
16. Zhang, J., Zhou, Y., Saab, R.: Post-training quantization for neural networks with provable guarantees. CoRR abs/2201.11113 (2022). https://arxiv.org/abs/2201.11113
17. Zhang, Z., Cai, H., Han, S.: EfficientViT-SAM: accelerated segment anything model without performance loss. In: CVPR Workshop: Efficient Large Vision Models (2024)

Lite Class-Prompt Tiny-VIT for Multi-modality Medical Image Segmentation

Haotian Guan, Bingze Dai, and Jiajing Zhang

Department of Electrical and Electronic Engineering, The University of Hong Kong, Hong Kong, China
jiajingz@connect.hku.hk

Abstract. The increasing demand for accurate medical image segmentation is crucial for alleviating the workload of doctors and enhancing diagnostic accuracy, particularly in low-income countries with limited computational resources. This study investigates the application of a novel deep learning model, class-prompt Tiny-VIT, to segment various medical image modalities using a laptop. The primary focus is on the challenges posed by the significant differences across image modalities, which render a unified model ineffective in handling certain modalities like positron emission tomography (PET) with high dice similarity on the segmentation task. Experimental results demonstrate that the class prompt, a simplified yet efficient method, can effectively boost model performance on modalities such as PET and microscopy, achieving improved overall segmentation accuracy. This research holds significant potential for the practical implementation of medical image segmentation in resource-constrained settings. It underlines the importance of developing deep learning algorithms tailored to specific medical imaging modalities.

Keywords: Multi-modality · Medical image segmentation · Class prompt · TinyVIT

1 Introduction

Medical image segmentation plays a crucial role in computer-aided diagnosis, treatment planning, disease progression monitoring, image-guided interventions, and personalized medicine. The accurate delineation of anatomical structures and pathological regions is essential for effective clinical decision-making [1].

Various deep-learning-based semantic segmentation models have been proposed [2,3] while most existing fundamental segmentation models are mainly based on natural images. Various machine learning-based models were proposed to cope with different medical segmentation tasks including brain, liver, tumor, cell, lung, cardiac, vascular, etc. [4–10] with different imaging modalities such as MRI, OCT, ultrasound, X-Ray, ultrasound, etc. and have demonstrated remarkable success in medical image segmentation tasks which helps on various medical tasks including tumor diagnostic [11,12], vessel and tissue characterization and so on [13–16].

However, the diversity of medical imaging modalities, along with the inherent hierarchical complexity of medical image features [17], makes it difficult to design a robust and efficient segmentation model that can perform well in different imaging scenarios [18]. Instead of focusing on specialized models for single tasks, researchers have explored more generalized models that can manage multiple scenarios like SAM [19], this trend also leads to the development of generalized methods for medical image segmentation across different modalities with U-Net architecture [18,20] and models inspired by SAM like MedSAM [21–23] and so on. In the meantime, these methods often require substantial computational resources, which may not be feasible for deployment on resource-constrained devices such as laptops. To enable real-time processing and edge-machine use with such machine learning models, the size and computation complexity need to be reduced. To this end, MobileSAM [24], and EfficientViT-SAM [25], TinyVIT [26] have shown promising results in terms of both accuracy and computational efficiency. These methods employ self-attention mechanisms to capture global and local contextual information to improve performance with comparable small models. However, despite their success, these methods still face limitations in terms of model size, computational complexity, and adaptability to different imaging modalities, particularly when considering the deployment of these methods on resource-constrained devices such as laptops with an 8G CPU without GPU that is commonly used in clinical.

To solve the computation cost and multi-modality generalization challenges mentioned above, inspired by TinyVIT [26] and Vision Transformer (ViT) architecture [27] which have demonstrated great potential in computer vision tasks, here we propose a novel approach Class-prompted TinyVIT network for medical image segmentation across different imaging modalities, with high accuracy and low computation cost that is capable of running on an 8G CPU device in almost real-time. The Class-prompted TinyVIT is inspired by the actual divisions in hospitals where different modalities are assigned to specific doctors instead of letting the same doctor read all modalities images. By this class-prompt method, the model would acquire the modality class information while using the same model with tuned parameters with specific modality while keeping a similar model size.

By adopting this architecture, we aim to provide a compact and efficient solution that can be deployed on devices with limited computational resources. Our primary contribution lies in introducing class prompts to the lite TinyVIT model to cope with the multi-modality medical image segmentation across different imaging modalities effectively as specialized models. The combination of compact model size, high accuracy, and compatibility with resource-constrained CPUs makes our approach a promising solution for real-world medical imaging applications. Furthermore, we conduct experiments on the provided dataset to validate the effectiveness of our approach. The results demonstrate superior segmentation accuracy and computational efficiency, highlighting the potential of our approach in advancing medical image analysis for edge-device applications. In summary, this paper presents a novel class-prompted TinyVIT-based approach for medical image segmentation that addresses the challenges of model size, computational complexity, and adaptability to diverse imaging modalities. Our solution holds the potential to significantly impact the field of medical image analysis, particularly in the context of deployment on resource-constrained devices.

2 Method

We introduce a pioneering class-prompt-based methodology aimed at enhancing segmentation efficacy across a spectrum of medical imaging modalities. Drawing inspiration from the specialized organizational structure of hospitals, where domain experts are assigned to interpret distinct imaging modalities, our objective is to cultivate expert models tailored to each modality. However, the deployment of 11 individual models on a laptop proves unfeasible due to memory constraints. To address this challenge, we propose a prompt-driven approach that effectively communicates the current input modality to the model, thereby transforming it into an adept specialist for the specific modality under consideration. This innovative strategy enables us to uphold a concise and efficient model architecture while attaining superior segmentation performance across diverse medical imaging tasks.

2.1 Preprocessing

The original dataset consists of eleven modalities with unbalanced data samples as illustrated in Fig. 1. Among those, CT holds the biggest portion with 1218411 items. The size of the whole training dataset is about 6TB with 1,000,000+ image-mask pairs, covering 10 medical image modalities and more than 20 cancer types. To deal with such a large and imbalanced dataset, and to avoid redundant and long training time costs, we first sampled the original dataset. Though we can try to train on the whole dataset to get a more comprehensive model, the time and electricity cost for the training process would be very burdensome. As a result, not only to make the model lite, we decided to make the training process also lite so that researchers with a single normal GPU can train it within reasonable time and calculation cost. Here we first sampled the original large dataset less than 1/10 of its original size. As CT images are far more than the number of other modalities, we randomly sampled CT images with 1/50 and randomly sampled other modalities to 1/10 of original numbers as shown in Fig. 1. After sampling, the sampled dataset size drops to less than 300 GB.

Not only the number of each modality is different, but the image and mask size in different modalities are also different which creates a problem in inputting the same model for training. As a result, to fit the training model, we first resize all the input images to 256 * 256 pixels to keep consistency so that we can use the same lite model. Boxes are generated using ground truth. Ground truth is

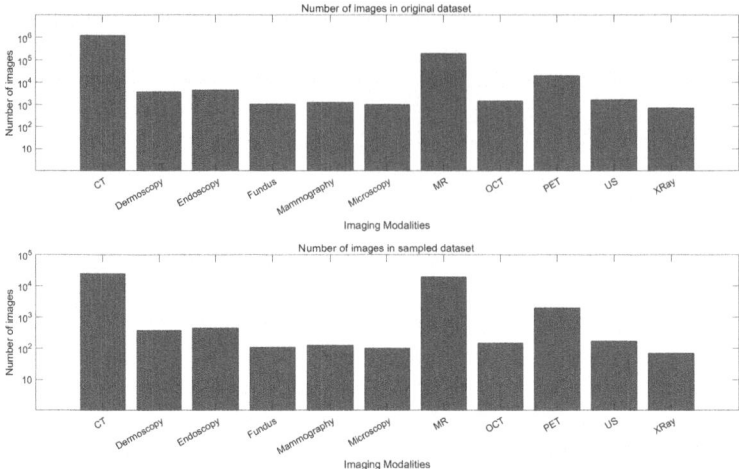

Fig. 1. Number of images of different modalities in the original dataset and sampled dataset for training.

covered completely by the box. In theory, areas outside the box should not be segmented.

2.2 Proposed Method

Class Prompt. Various image classifier models have been explored, including traditional networks, deep learning, transfer learning, self-supervised learning, and more [28–31]. However, most of these models use large architectures, making them unsuitable for tasks with limited computational resources.

In our model, we address this limitation by incorporating a classifier that leverages the TinyVIT encoder. This approach notably diminishes both the model's size and parameter count. To enhance the classifier's efficacy further, we have integrated a three-layer multilayer perceptron (MLP) network as the modality classifier head. This augmentation exploits the insights derived from the encoder structure. As a result, our model showcases outstanding performance.

Specifically, we equipped TinyVIT with a class prediction head, which is implemented as a multilayer perceptron (MLP) that starts with an input dimension of 256. This MLP features a hidden layer dimension of 256 and is designed to classify data into one of 11 distinct categories. The architecture includes three layers, to process and refine the information through successive transformations. The first layer takes the input vector $\mathbf{x}$ of dimension 256 and transforms it to a hidden state $\mathbf{h}_1$ using a linear transformation followed by a non-linear activation function (ReLU). The MLP is represented as:

$$\mathbf{h}_1 = \text{ReLU}(\mathbf{W}_1\mathbf{x} + \mathbf{b}_1) \quad (1)$$
$$\mathbf{h}_2 = \text{ReLU}(\mathbf{W}_2\mathbf{h}_1 + \mathbf{b}_2) \quad (2)$$
$$\mathbf{y} = \mathbf{W}_3\mathbf{h}_2 + \mathbf{b}_3 \quad (3)$$

where $\mathbf{W}_1, \mathbf{W}_2, \mathbf{W}_3$ are the weight matrixes and $\mathbf{b}_1, \mathbf{b}_2, \mathbf{b}_3$ is the bias vectors. This structure allows the classifier to effectively learn and make predictions by capturing complex patterns and relationships in the data, making it a vital component in achieving high accuracy in our classification tasks.

Class-Prompt Tiny-VIT. Class prompt takes the categories from the classification head in the encoder and returns a prompt for the mask decoder. The pretrained encoder makes sure that image modalities can be correctly identified. The small size of the class prompt encoder is specially designed for running inference on a laptop. The prompt is added to the box prompt as the input of the decoder. Our decoder is a transformer with three blocks (Fig. 2).

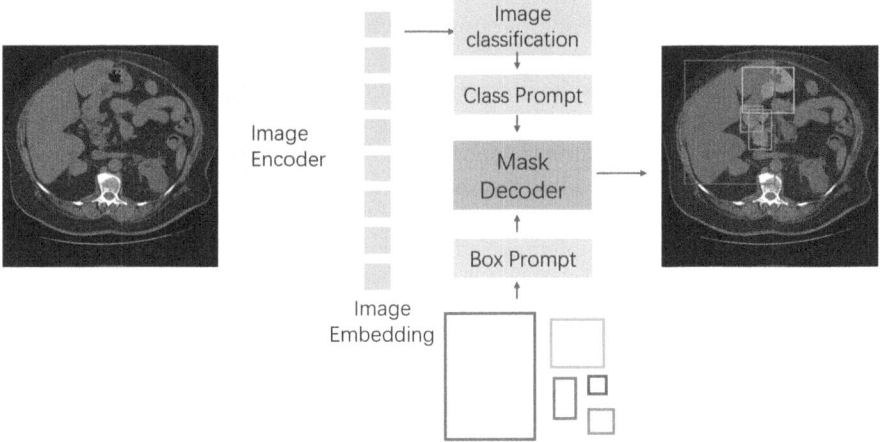

Fig. 2. Class-prompted TinyVIT Network architecture. Class prompt takes the categories from the classification head in the encoder and returns a prompt for the mask decoder.

Loss Function. We use the summation between Dice loss and focal loss because compound loss functions have been proven to be robust in various medical image segmentation tasks [32].

a) Dice loss is a performance metric derived from the Dice coefficient, which is commonly used to gauge the similarity between two samples. Specifically tailored for the field of medical image segmentation, the Dice loss function is particularly effective in handling class imbalance, a frequent challenge where the region of interest occupies a significantly smaller portion of the image compared to the background. The Dice loss is calculated as

$$L_{Dice} = 1 - \frac{2 \times |X \cap Y|}{|X| + |Y|} \quad (4)$$

where X and Y represent the binary prediction and ground truth masks, respectively. This loss function ensures that the model is not only predicting the classes accurately but also aligning closely with the actual contours and boundaries of the regions of interest in the images.

b) Focal loss is an advanced adaptation of the cross-entropy loss, specifically designed to address the prevalent issue of class imbalance by concentrating more on difficult, misclassified examples. This is particularly useful in image segmentation tasks where there is a significant imbalance between different classes. The focal loss function is mathematically represented as:

$$L_{Focal} = -\alpha_t (1 - p_t)^\gamma \log(p_t) \quad (5)$$

Here, p_t is the probability that the model assigns to the ground truth class. The parameter γ is the focusing parameter, which scales how much the function focuses on hard examples. The term $(1-p_t)^\gamma$ decreases the loss contribution from easy examples and increases the importance of correcting misclassified examples. α_t is a balancing factor that can be used to give more focus to rare classes. This formulation helps in fine-tuning the model's predictions, ensuring that it not only achieves high accuracy but also improves performance on the more challenging aspects of the segmentation task.

From the perspective of inference efficiency, our simple MLP structure can be easily implemented on CPU-only machines without complex acceleration strategies.

2.3 Post-processing

The size of the mask outputted from the model is unified to 256 by 256. To obtain the mask for the original medical image, we resize the outputted mask to the original size with bilinear interpolation. The model will produce a prediction for each box with its index. To save the complete result, all boxes and corresponding segmentation are saved as an overlay.

3 Experiments

3.1 Dataset and Evaluation Measures

We used the challenge dataset for model development, including 11 modalities and both 2D and 3D images.

The evaluation metrics include two accuracy measures-Dice Similarity Coefficient (DSC) and Normalized Surface Dice (NSD)-alongside one efficiency measure-running time. The Dice Similarity Coefficient (DSC) is formulated as follows:

$$DSC = \frac{2 \times |P \cap G|}{|P| + |G|} \quad (6)$$

where P represents the set of pixels in the predicted segmentation mask, G represents the set of pixels in the ground truth segmentation mask, $|\cdot|$ denotes the cardinality or size of the set, $\cap$ denotes the intersection of sets.

The formula for Normalized Surface Dice (NSD) is given by:

$$\text{NSD} = 1 - \frac{2 \times \text{Surface}(A \cap B)}{\text{Surface}(A) + \text{Surface}(B)} \quad (7)$$

where A and B are the segmentation mask and ground truth being compared. Surface(A) and Surface(B) represent the surface areas of masks A and B respectively. Surface($A \cap B$) represents the surface area of the intersection of masks A and B. This formula calculates the Dice similarity coefficient between the surfaces of the two masks and normalizes it by the average surface area of the two masks. A higher NSD value indicates a better overlap between the surfaces of the two masks.

3.2 Implementation Details

Environment Settings. The development environments and requirements are presented in Table 1.

Table 1. Development environments and requirements.

System	Ubuntu 18.04.5 LTS
CPU	Intel Xeon W-2225 10C/20T 4.1 Ghz
RAM	32GB DDR4-3200 ECC RDIMM
GPU (number and type)	One NVIDIA GeForce RTX 3090 24G
CUDA version	10.496
Programming language	Python 3.80
Deep learning framework	torch 2.0, torchvision 0.2.2
Specific dependencies	ONNX Runtime
Code	https://github.com/haotian1017/class-prompt-medsam

Table 2. Training protocols.

Pre-trained Model	MedSAM [21]
Batch size	64
Patch size	256 × 256 × 3
Total epochs	20
Optimizer	AdamW [33]
Initial learning rate (lr)	5e−4
Lr decay schedule	ReduceLROnPlateau
Training time	75 h
Loss function	Dice Loss, Cross Entropy Loss, Focal Loss
Number of model parameters	10.99M
Number of flops	2.2G
CO_2eq	15 Kg

Training Protocols. 1. Data augmentation: in the domain of multimodal medical image segmentation, the strategic implementation of data augmentation stands as a pivotal factor in augmenting model generalization and precision. By adhering to a data augmentation rate of 0.5, incorporating stochastic horizontal flips and vertical flips, we enrich the training dataset by introducing nuanced variations within the multimodal input images and their corresponding segmentation maps. These meticulous operations empower the model to discern and delineate anatomical structures resilient to horizontal and vertical transformations, thereby fortifying its resilience and efficacy across a spectrum of modalities. Through these refined data augmentation methodologies, our primary objective is to enhance the model's proficiency in accurately segmenting intricate anatomical entities in multimodal medical images, thereby advancing its efficacy within clinical frameworks (Table 2).

2. Data sampling strategy: during the model training phase, the challenge organizer's publicly available training data was partitioned randomly into training and validation sets in a 7:3 ratio. Specifically, for the 2D image modality, random sampling was directly employed. However, in the case of 3D image modalities such as CT, MRI, and PET, the conventional approach of preprocessing involves segmenting each 3D image into multiple consecutive 2D slices, leading to a proliferation of redundant data due to the significant similarity between adjacent slices. To address this issue, a uniform interval sampling technique was implemented to extract 2D slices from the 3D images, with a fixed spacing of 5 between neighboring samples. This method effectively reduces data redundancy and enhances training efficiency by minimizing the inclusion of highly similar information found in adjacent slices.

3. Optimal model selection criteria: optimal model selection criteria are particularly critical when tasked with segmenting multimodal medical images. In this context, the criteria must be tailored to the nuances of medical image anal-

ysis. Given the complexity and variability of medical data, the selected criteria should prioritize robustness and generalizability across different imaging modalities, such as MRI, CT, and PET scans. Here we used the Dice similarity coefficient, Jaccard index, and Normalized Surface Distance(NSD) to evaluate segmentation performance in medical imaging tasks. Besides, inference time is also included in the selection program, giving the same weight as the segmentation performance.

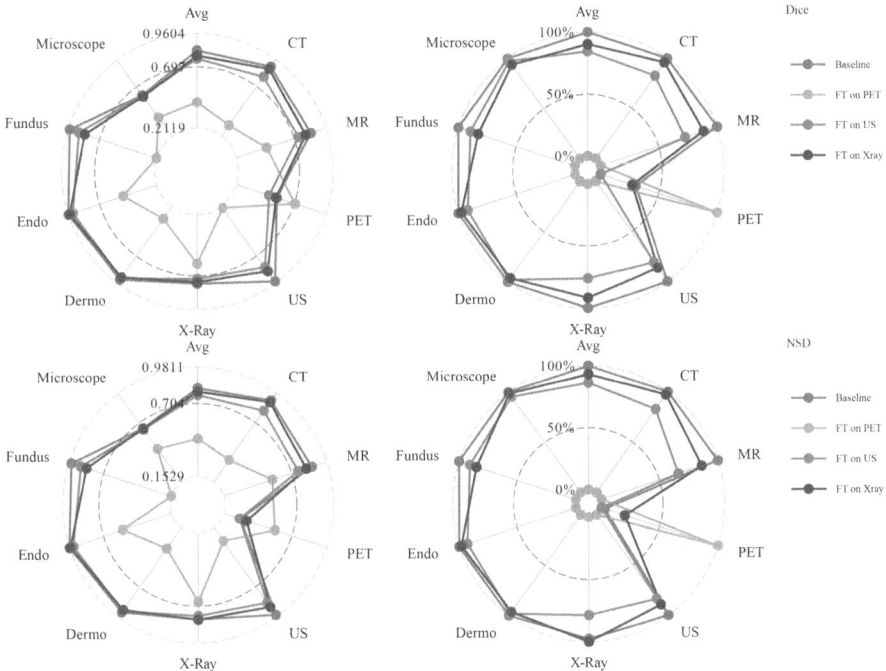

Fig. 3. The Dice result (the first row) and NSD result (the second row) of the baseline model, and baseline model fine-tuned (FT) on PET, Ultrasound, and X-ray datasets, respectively. The left plot shows the raw numerical comparison and the right plot shows the normalized comparison, where the maximum Dice or NSD on each modality is scaled as 1 and the minimum Dice or NSD on each modality is scaled as 0.

4 Results and Discussion

4.1 Quantitative Results on Validation Set

Table 4 explains the efficiency of all models by computing the inference time on 14 representative images across all image modalities. On a laptop with a CPU, 3D images take much longer inference time since the model deals with segmentation frame by frame. The bottleneck is also on resizing large images to

Table 3. Quantitative evaluation results on the validation set.

Modality	Baseline		Ablation Study		Proposed	
	DSC(%)	NSD(%)	DSC(%)	NSD(%)	DSC(%)	NSD(%)
CT	89.1	91.03	89.69	91.29	92.26	94.90
MR	83.28	86.1	81.39	83.42	89.63	93.37
PET	55.1	29.12	63.19	46.04	70.28	56.88
US	94.78	96.81	92.92	96.3	94.77	96.81
X-Ray	75.83	80.39	76.7	82.53	76.74	82.53
Dermatology	92.47	93.85	92.45	94.01	93.73	94.01
Endoscopy	96.04	98.11	95.41	97.56	96.04	98.11
Fundus	94.8	96.41	94.56	96.2	94.81	96.41
Microscopy	61.63	65.39	73.76	79.34	73.76	79.34
Average	82.56	81.91	84.45	85.18	86.89	88.04

regular input size 256 by 256. Overall, the baseline model runs fastest and the ablation study is comparable in running time. Our proposed method runs 1.3% to 16.7% slower than the baseline model.

The results of our quantitative experiments are shown in Table 3, which presents a comprehensive evaluation of three models: baseline, ablation model, and our class-prompt Tiny-VIT. Each model's performance is assessed based on Dice Similarity Coefficient (DSC) and Normalized Surface Dice (NSD) metrics across various imaging modalities including CT, MR, PET, US, X-ray, dermatology, endoscopy, fundus, and microscopy. The ablation study shows the model performance without class prompts. The model can outperform the baseline model by combining focal loss and dice loss.

The quantitative results show that our class-prompt Tiny-VIT consistently outperforms both the baseline and ablation model across most modalities. Specifically, compared with the baseline, our class-prompt Tiny-VIT demonstrates superior DSC of 3.54%, 7.62%, 27.55%, 1.20%, 1.36%, and 19.68% for CT, MR, PET, X-ray, dermatology, and microscopy, respectively. Compared with the baseline, our class-prompt Tiny-VIT demonstrates superior NSD of 4.25%, 8.44%, 95.32%, 2.66%, 0.17%, and 21.33% for CT, MR, PET, X-ray, dermatology, and microscopy, respectively. The improvement indicates our efficacy in accurately segmenting, especially for PET and microscopy images, as evidenced by the normalized radargram. As for ultrasound, endoscopy, and fundus images, our class-prompt Tiny-VIT can reach segmentation performance in line with the baseline, thus demonstrating that our improvement in the majority of modalities does not compromise the segmentation performance of the minority modalities. Notably, our class-prompt Tiny-VIT achieves the highest average DSC and NSD values of 86.89% and 88.04% respectively, showcasing its overall effectiveness in comparison to the baseline and ablation modal.

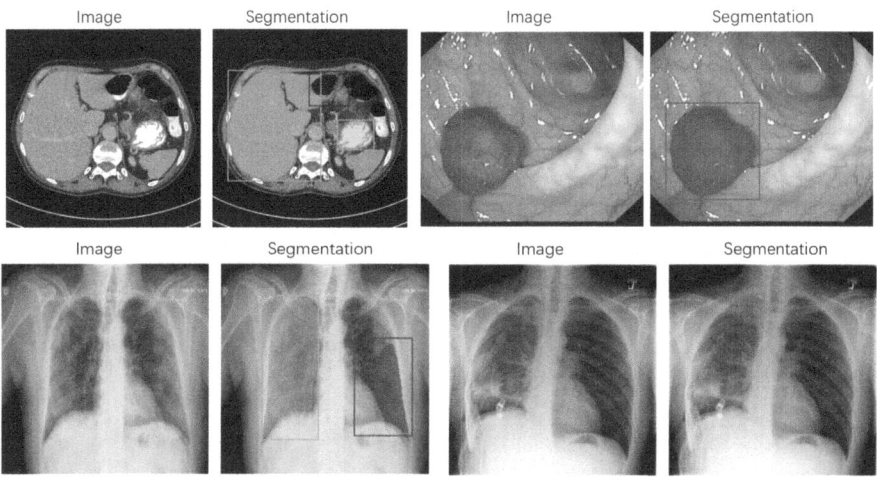

Fig. 4. Examples with good segmentation results

To further demonstrate the role of class prompts, we conducted three fine-tuning experiments. We fine-tuned the baseline on PET, ultrasound, and X-ray datasets separately to simulate the effect when the model focuses only on a certain class of modes. The DSC and NSD radargrams of the fine-tuning results are shown in Fig. 3. The results show that continual fine-tuning on the ultrasound and X-ray datasets alone does not improve the model performance, but rather leads to a degradation of it. Therefore, it is not feasible to simply fine-tune on each class and then integrate the fine-tuned models of each class. However, the original baseline performs poorly on certain modalities (e.g., PET), and further fine-tuning on these modalities can significantly boost the segmentation performance on that modality, which is not achievable with multimodal mixed training. Therefore, it is worthwhile to enable the model to have an independent perception of each class and to make class-specific processing.

4.2 Qualitative Results on Validation Set

Here we show some examples with good segmentation results and two examples with bad segmentation results. The good cases can almost perfectly segment the region of interest with high DSC and NSD. Figure 4 shows the examples with good segmentation results. Figure 5 shows the examples with bad segmentation results. In bad performance cases, some of the segmentation masks cannot fully cover the correct area, and others cover more than the region of interest.

4.3 Segmentation Efficiency Results on Validation Set

Here we compare the segmentation efficiency based on the time cost on the Codabench platform. On the validation set, the proposed method costs 03:08 min

Table 4. Quantitative evaluation of segmentation efficiency in terms of running time (s).

Case ID	Size	Num. Objects	Baseline	Ablation	Proposed
3DBox_CT_0566	(287, 512, 512)	6	373.6	373.5	381.2
3DBox_CT_0888	(237, 512, 512)	6	92.4	92.3	95.1
3DBox_CT_0860	(246, 512, 512)	1	10.3	10.1	12.7
3DBox_MR_0621	(115, 400, 400)	6	143.6	143.2	150.5
3DBox_MR_0121	(64, 290, 320)	6	91.3	91.5	95.3
3DBox_MR_0179	(84, 512, 512)	1	10.5	10.7	12.2
3DBox_PET_0001	(264, 200, 200)	1	5.8	5.9	7.4
2DBox_US_0525	(256, 256, 3)	1	0.6	0.6	0.7
2DBox_X-Ray_0053	(320, 640, 3)	34	1.9	2.0	2.1
2DBox_Dermoscopy_0003	(3024, 4032, 3)	1	0.8	0.9	1.1
2DBox_Endoscopy_0086	(480, 560, 3)	1	0.6	0.6	0.7
2DBox_Fundus_0003	(2048, 2048, 3)	1	0.8	0.8	0.8
2DBox_Microscope_0008	(1536, 2040, 3)	19	1.7	1.6	1.8
2DBox_Microscope_0016	(1920, 2560, 3)	241	12.9	13.5	14.1

to segment all images and the baseline model costs 03:35 min. For single cases, please refer to Table 4. We further investigated the effect of ONNX (Open Neural Network Exchange) after the challenge. On average, our model is 30% faster when it's exported to ONNX.

4.4 Results on Final Testing Set

The final testing set encompasses nine imaging modalities: CT, MR, endoscopy, ultrasound (US), X-ray, fundus imaging, microscopy, PET, and OCT. Our proposed method is evaluated through accuracy metrics, including the Dice Similarity Coefficient (DSC) and Normalized Surface Dice (NSD), along with efficiency assessed by runtime in seconds. The quantitative results of the testing set are shown in Table 5. The quantitative results on the testing set are presented in Table 5, where our model demonstrates superior performance in the endoscopy, X-ray, fundus imaging, and PET modalities, achieving Dice rankings of 6th, 2nd, 6th, and 7th, respectively, and NSD rankings of 6th, 2nd, 6th, and 6th.

As we adopt a class-prompt strategy, and modalities are using the same model, for the submitted model, there's a glitch that we were referencing a wrong fine-tuned model which caused the worse performance in the final testing set for several modalities such as CT and Microscopy.

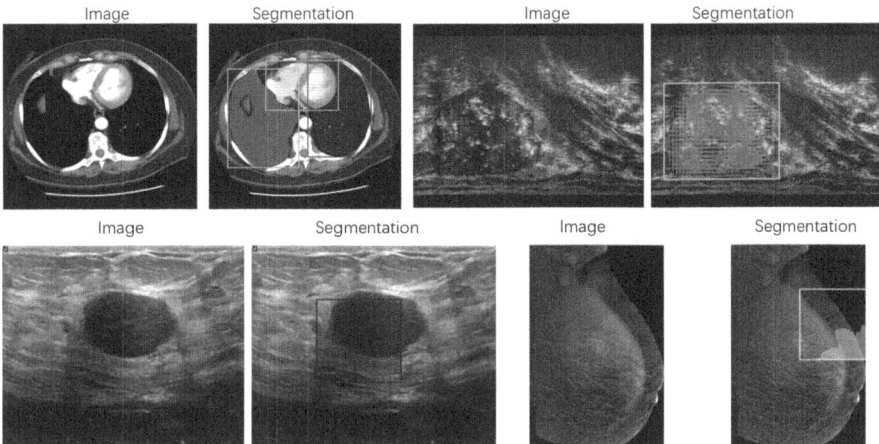

Fig. 5. Examples with bad segmentation results

Table 5. Quantitative evaluation results on the testing set.

Modality	DSC (%)	NSD (%)	Running Time (s)
CT	51.24	50.33	34.58
MR	59.17	53.49	17.22
PET	61.35	57.70	81.05
US	85.60	89.95	9.13
X-Ray	85.74	94.03	6.87
Dermatology	92.47	93.85	92.45
Endoscopy	94.41	96.95	6.84
Fundus	86.33	88.40	6.75
Microscopy	54.30	55.77	6.99
OCT	67.27	73.35	6.65
Average	71.71	73.33	19.57

4.5 Limitation and Future Work

In this work, we demonstrate that class prompts can enhance the segmentation performance in medical images. Unlike natural images, medical images are obtained based on physics. A universal model that understands how all modalities work is difficult to achieve. Prompts such as image modality are crucial as patients need to be divided into different departments in a hospital. The class prompt is now built with a 3-layer MLP module. We will design more complicated and reasonable prompt that better suits medical images. Currently, the proposed class-prompt TinyVIT is a structure based on TinyVIT. The transformer architecture is still a heavy burden for segmenting medical images on a laptop. A smaller model with the same or better precision is highly demanded.

In the future, we will explore the potential generalization of our approach to other medical imaging tasks like detection or classification to emphasize the versatility and applicability of our method. We suspect that the class prompt cannot provide sufficient features for distinguishing modalities and anatomies. In the future, we plan to encode more modality-level and anatomy-level features to further improve performance. For inference speed, we will further investigate the effect of quantization. It will be ideal to quantize to int8 or even int4 while maintaining the same level of accuracy.

5 Conclusion

Segmenting medical images using a laptop is indispensable for alleviating the workload of doctors and improving diagnosing accuracy, especially in low-income countries. The main findings and results show that differences across image modalities are huge and a unified model cannot handle modalities such as PET with high dice similarity on segmentation tasks. Class prompt, as a simple network, can efficiently boost model performance on PET thus leading to better accuracy overall.

Acknowledgements. We thank all the data owners for making the medical images publicly available and CodaLab [34] for hosting the challenge platform. This work was supported in part by Hong Kong Health and Medical Research Fund (08192616) and in part by Healthy Longevity Catalyst Awards (HCLA/706/22).

Disclosure of Interests. The authors have no competing interests to declare that are relevant to the content of this article.

References

1. Litjens, G., et al.: A survey on deep learning in medical image analysis. Med. Image Anal. **42**, 60–88 (2017). https://doi.org/10.1016/j.media.2017.07.005
2. Kirillov, A., et al.: Segment anything. In: Proceedings of the International Conference on Computer Vision, pp. 4015–4026 (2023)
3. Mo, Y., Wu, Y., Yang, X., Liu, F., Liao, Y.: Review the state-of-the-art technologies of semantic segmentation based on deep learning. Neurocomputing **493**, 626–646 (2022). https://www.sciencedirect.com/science/article/pii/S0925231222000054
4. Vivanti, R., Ephrat, A., Joskowicz, L., Karaaslan, O., Lev-Cohain, N., Sosna, J.: Automatic liver tumor segmentation in follow-up CT studies using convolutional neural networks. In: Proceedings Patch-Based Methods in Medical Image Processing Workshop, vol. 2, p. 2 (2015)
5. Zhang, J., Gu, L., Han, G., Liu, X.: AttR2U-Net: a fully automated model for MRI nasopharyngeal carcinoma segmentation based on spatial attention and residual recurrent convolution. Front. Oncol. **11**, 816672 (2022)
6. Wu, F., Zhuang, X.: CF distance: a new domain discrepancy metric and application to explicit domain adaptation for cross-modality cardiac image segmentation. IEEE Trans. Med. Imaging **39**(12), 4274–4285 (2020)

7. Onishi, Y., et al.: Multiplanar analysis for pulmonary nodule classification in CT images using deep convolutional neural network and generative adversarial networks. Int. J. Comput. Assist. Radiol. Surg. **15**, 173–178 (2020)
8. Song, T.-H., Sanchez, V., ElDaly, H., Rajpoot, N.M.: Dual-channel active contour model for megakaryocytic cell segmentation in bone marrow trephine histology images. IEEE Trans. Biomed. Eng. **64**(12), 2913–2923 (2017)
9. Cherukuri, V., Ssenyonga, P., Warf, B.C., Kulkarni, A.V., Monga, V., Schiff, S.J.: Learning based segmentation of CT brain images: application to postoperative hydrocephalic scans. IEEE Trans. Biomed. Eng. **65**(8), 1871–1884 (2017)
10. Farshad, A., Yeganeh, Y., Gehlbach, P., Navab, N.: Y-Net: a spatiospectral dual-encoder network for medical image segmentation. In: Wang, L., Dou, Q., Fletcher, P.T., Speidel, S., Li, S. (eds.) MICCAI 2022. LNCS, vol. 13432, pp. 582–592. Springer, Cham (2022). https://doi.org/10.1007/978-3-031-16434-7_56
11. Menze, B.H., et al.: The multimodal brain tumor image segmentation benchmark (BRATS). IEEE Trans. Med. Imaging **34**(10), 1993–2024 (2014)
12. Pereira, S., Pinto, A., Alves, V., Silva, C.A.: Brain tumor segmentation using convolutional neural networks in MRI images. IEEE Trans. Med. Imaging **35**(5), 1240–1251 (2016)
13. Gibson, E., et al.: Automatic multi-organ segmentation on abdominal CT with dense V-networks. IEEE Trans. Med. Imaging **37**(8), 1822–1834 (2018)
14. Çiçek, Ö., Abdulkadir, A., Lienkamp, S.S., Brox, T., Ronneberger, O.: 3D U-Net: learning dense volumetric segmentation from sparse annotation. In: Ourselin, S., Joskowicz, L., Sabuncu, M.R., Unal, G., Wells, W. (eds.) MICCAI 2016. LNCS, vol. 9901, pp. 424–432. Springer, Cham (2016). https://doi.org/10.1007/978-3-319-46723-8_49
15. Zhang, J., et al.: Automatic centroid angle measurement from CT image for preoperative rod design of robotic-assisted screw-rod system implantation. IEEE Trans. Med. Rob. Bionics (2024)
16. Dai, B.: Power doppler ultrasound for peripheral perfusion imaging. Ph.D. dissertation, University of Illinois at Urbana-Champaign (2023)
17. Gao, Z., Guo, Y., Zhang, J., Zeng, T., Yang, G.: Hierarchical perception adversarial learning framework for compressed sensing MRI. IEEE Trans. Med. Imaging **42**(6), 1859–1874 (2023)
18. Ronneberger, O., Fischer, P., Brox, T.: U-Net: convolutional networks for biomedical image segmentation. In: Navab, N., Hornegger, J., Wells, W.M., Frangi, A.F. (eds.) MICCAI 2015. LNCS, vol. 9351, pp. 234–241. Springer, Cham (2015). https://doi.org/10.1007/978-3-319-24574-4_28
19. Kirillov, A., et al.: Segment anything (2023)
20. Azad, R., et al.: Medical image segmentation review: the success of U-Net (2022)
21. Ma, J., He, Y., Li, F., Han, L., You, C., Wang, B.: Segment anything in medical images. Nat. Commun. **15**(1), 654 (2024)
22. Mazurowski, M.A., Dong, H., Gu, H., Yang, J., Konz, N., Zhang, Y.: Segment anything model for medical image analysis: an experimental study. Med. Image Anal. **89**, 102918 (2023)
23. Wu, J., et al.: Medical SAM adapter: adapting segment anything model for medical image segmentation (2023)
24. Zhang, C., et al.: Faster segment anything: towards lightweight SAM for mobile applications. arXiv preprint arXiv:2306.14289 (2023)
25. Zhang, Z., Cai, H., Han, S.: EfficientViT-SAM: accelerated segment anything model without performance loss. In: CVPR Workshop: Efficient Large Vision Models (2024)

26. Wu, K., et al.: TinyViT: fast pretraining distillation for small vision transformers (2022)
27. Dosovitskiy, A., et al.: An image is worth 16x16 words: transformers for image recognition at scale (2021)
28. Cai, L., Gao, J., Zhao, D.: A review of the application of deep learning in medical image classification and segmentation. Ann. Transl. Med. **8**(11) (2020)
29. Dai, B., Qiu, T., Ye, K.: Foliar disease classification (2020)
30. Azizi, S., et al.: Big self-supervised models advance medical image classification. In: Proceedings of the IEEE/CVF International Conference on Computer Vision, pp. 3478–3488 (2021)
31. Kim, H.E., Cosa-Linan, A., Santhanam, N., Jannesari, M., Maros, M.E., Ganslandt, T.: Transfer learning for medical image classification: a literature review. BMC Med. Imaging **22**(1), 69 (2022)
32. Ma, J., et al.: Loss odyssey in medical image segmentation. Med. Image Anal. **71**, 102035 (2021)
33. Loshchilov, I., Hutter, F.: Decoupled weight decay regularization. arXiv preprint arXiv:1711.05101 (2017)
34. Xu, Z., et al.: Codabench: flexible, easy-to-use, and reproducible meta-benchmark platform. Patterns **3**(7), 100543 (2022)

Segment Anything in Medical Images with nnUNet

Raphael Stock[1,2], Yannick Kirchhoff[1,2,3,4(✉)], Maximilian R. Rokuss[1,2], Ashis Ravindran[1], and Klaus Maier-Hein[1,5]

[1] Division of Medical Image Computing, German Cancer Research Center (DKFZ), Heidelberg, Germany
{raphael.stock,yannick.kirchhoff,maximilian.rokuss}@dkfz-heidelberg.de
[2] Faculty of Mathematics and Computer Science, Heidelberg University, Heidelberg, Germany
[3] HIDSS4Health - Helmholtz Information and Data Science School for Health, Karlsruhe, Germany
[4] HIDSS4Health - Helmholtz Information and Data Science School for Health, Heidelberg, Germany
[5] Pattern Analysis and Learning Group, Department of Radiation Oncology, Heidelberg University Hospital, Heidelberg, Germany

Abstract. In this paper, we present an enhanced medical image segmentation approach leveraging the nnUNet framework, specifically tailored to integrate bounding box prompts for improved segmentation accuracy in resource-constrained environments. By incorporating these prompts as binary masks in an additional input channel, we enable more precise and context-aware segmentation. Our methodology employs a 2D slice-wise approach optimized for CPU-based inference through just-in-time (JIT) compiled functions, ensuring efficient processing on standard clinical equipment. Our solution demonstrates robust performance, achieving an average Dice Similarity Coefficient (DSC) of 80.98% and a Normalized Surface Dice (NSD) of 83.23% across multiple modalities in the validation set. This indicates its practical applicability and effectiveness in real-world clinical settings, where computational resources may be limited. By focusing on both accuracy and efficiency, our approach makes advanced segmentation technology accessible to a broader range of healthcare providers, facilitating enhanced clinical decision-making and patient care.

Keywords: Medical Image Segmentation · nnUNet · Bounding Box Prompts · CPU Inference

---

R. Stock, Y. Kirchhoff and M. R. Rokuss—Contributed equally. Each co-first author may list themselves as lead author on their CV.

1 Introduction

1.1 Background and Difficulty of the Challenge

Medical image segmentation is a crucial process in clinical practice, enabling precise quantification of anatomical structures and identification of pathological regions. With the advancement of technology, there is a significant transition in this field from the use of specialized models tailored to specific tasks to the adoption of foundation models that can handle diverse segmentation scenarios. However, this shift is fraught with challenges, particularly due to the variability across different medical domains and the resource limitations faced during inference.

The primary difficulty lies in developing models that can generalize across a wide range of medical image modalities and pathological conditions. Each medical domain, such as radiology, histopathology, and oncology, presents unique imaging characteristics and diagnostic requirements, necessitating highly adaptable models. Furthermore, the computational resources required for inference with state-of-the-art models often exceed the capabilities of standard clinical equipment, particularly in settings where high-end GPUs are not available. This creates a significant barrier to the practical implementation of advanced segmentation tools in many healthcare facilities, thereby limiting their accessibility and utility.

The Segment Anything on Laptop 2024 Challenge is therefore launched to advance the current state of segmentation technologies, aiming to develop truly universal and resource-efficient medical image segmentation models. Recognizing the limitations of existing approaches, the objective of this challenge is to inspire innovations that will result in models deployable on standard clinical equipment, such as laptops or edge devices, without the necessity for GPUs.

To facilitate this, this challenge provides an extensive training dataset comprising over 1,000,000 image-mask pairs, encompassing 10 different medical image modalities and more than 20 types of cancer. This dataset is designed to support the development of models that can generalize across a broad spectrum of medical imaging scenarios. By focusing on lightweight, bounding box-based segmentation techniques, the organizers aim to encourage solutions that not only achieve high accuracy but also maintain efficiency in resource-constrained environments.

The challenge shall drive methodological advancements in the field of medical image segmentation, leading to the creation of universal models with broad applicability. Additionally, by emphasizing ease of interaction and deployment, it is envisioned that sophisticated segmentation tools are more accessible to a wider range of healthcare providers, ultimately enhancing clinical decision-making and patient care.

1.2 Related Work and State-of-the-Art Methods

Recent advancements in segmentation models have shown promise in addressing some of the above-mentioned challenges. Models like SAM (Segment

Anything Model) [3,5] and its variants, including MedSAM [4], MobileSAM [7], and EfficientViT-SAM [8], represent the state-of-the-art in segmentation technology. SAM and its derivatives have demonstrated remarkable performance in natural image segmentation, leveraging large-scale datasets and powerful computational frameworks.

MedSAM, an adaptation of SAM for medical imaging, has improved performance in medical domains but still requires significant computational resources. MobileSAM and EfficientViT-SAM have attempted to address the resource constraints by optimizing for mobile and edge devices, yet their effectiveness across the wide variety of medical imaging modalities and conditions remains a subject of ongoing research. These models provide a strong foundation but highlight the need for further advancements to achieve the goal of universal, resource-efficient medical image segmentation.

1.3 Motivation and Contribution

In approaching this task, we leverage the well-established nnUNet framework [1], renowned for its state-of-the-art performance across various medical imaging tasks and domains. nnUNet's robust out-of-the-box capabilities on new datasets make it a baseline for numerous model developments. However, nnUNet is inherently designed for automatic semantic segmentation of target structures it is trained on, without the flexibility to accept prompts.

Our contribution addresses this limitation by integrating a straightforward, yet effective, method for incorporating bounding box prompts into the nnUNet framework. This enhancement allows nnUNet to adapt to the challenge's requirements for prompt-based segmentation. Additionally, nnUNet's use of a lightweight CNN-based UNet architecture, as opposed to more computationally demanding transformer-based models, ensures excellent computational efficiency.

Our approach introduces a patch-based processing methodology, which contrasts with conventional methods that process entire images at once. While this patch-based strategy can introduce computational overhead, we mitigate this by optimizing our model for rapid CPU-based inference. We employ just-in-time (JIT) compiled functions to accelerate prediction speed, ensuring our model remains efficient even on resource-constrained devices like laptops and edge devices.

2 Method

2.1 Using nnUNet as Base Model

For this challenge, we employ nnUNet as our base model due to its proven track record of achieving state-of-the-art performance across various medical imaging tasks. nnUNet's inherent flexibility and robust architecture provide a solid foundation for our modifications, ensuring reliable and high-quality segmentation results. Furthermore, we use the residual encoder blocks (ResEnc) as introduced in [2] for nnUNet.

2.2 Incorporating Prompts as an Additional Input Channel

To adapt nnUNet for prompt-based segmentation, we introduce a method of incorporating prompts using channel masks. Specifically, we integrate bounding box prompts as additional input channels, allowing the model to focus on specific regions of interest within the medical images (cf. Fig. 1). This approach effectively guides the segmentation process, enhancing the model's ability to accurately delineate target structures based on the provided prompts.

2.3 Fully Slice Wise 2D Approach

Given the computational constraints and the need for efficient processing on edge devices, we opt for a full 2D approach. By processing images slice-by-slice rather than in a 3D context, we significantly reduce the computational burden. Although a 2D approach typically sacrifices some performance compared to a 3D setting, it allows us to use a single model across all input image modalities. This unified approach eliminates the need to develop and maintain separate 2D and 3D models, streamlining our contribution and ensuring consistency across different types of medical images. This strategy not only aligns with our goal of achieving resource-efficient segmentation but also simplifies the integration of bounding box prompts into the nnUNet framework.

2.4 Training vs. Inference

Our training and inference pipelines are designed to maximize efficiency and performance. For training, all images were preprocessed with z-score normalization of the standard nnUNet framework. During training, we focus on optimizing the model's ability to handle various types of bounding box prompts, using a diverse set of training samples from the provided dataset. A random component of one of the foreground classes of each image is sampled and used for the ground truth mask, as well as to extract a bounding box prompt. This bounding box is augmented by random dilations and concatenated to the input image for training. We employ data augmentation techniques to ensure the model generalizes well across different medical imaging modalities and conditions (see [1] for details on the pipeline).

For inference, we streamline the process to ensure rapid and accurate segmentation on CPU-based systems. We only predict on a patch, which extends by half the patch-size around the bounding box prompt. Furthermore, just-in-time (JIT) compiling the model architecture minimizes latency and maximizes throughput, ensuring that our approach is viable for real-time clinical applications.

2.5 Postprocessing

To enhance the accuracy and usability of the segmentation results, we incorporate a postprocessing step that involves removing all predictions that do not lie in the region specified by the bounding box prompts. This step refines the segmentation output, removing any extraneous areas outside the region of interest, and ensures that the final results are focused and relevant for clinical interpretation.

2.6 Compiling Using OpenVINO

To further optimize our model for deployment on edge devices, we compile it using OpenVINO[1]. OpenVINO is an open-source toolkit for optimizing and deploying deep learning models from cloud to edge. This optimization toolchain converts our trained model into an optimized intermediate representation, enabling efficient execution on Intel CPUs and other compatible hardware. By leveraging OpenVINO, we achieve significant improvements in inference speed and resource utilization (cf. Table 4), making our solution practical for use in real-world clinical settings where computational resources are limited.

In summary, our method combines the strengths of nnUNet with innovative prompt integration, a 2D processing approach, efficient training and inference pipelines, targeted postprocessing, and deployment optimization using Open-VINO. This comprehensive strategy ensures that our model meets the challenge's requirements for universal, resource-efficient medical image segmentation.

3 Experiments

3.1 Dataset and Evaluation Measures

We exclusively utilized the challenge dataset for model development. The evaluation metrics include two accuracy measures—Dice Similarity Coefficient (DSC) and Normalized Surface Dice (NSD)—alongside one efficiency measure—running time. These metrics collectively contribute to the ranking computation. For model selection we opted for the model showing superior performance across all modalities based on average ranking. We explored the potential of modality-specific models to enhance results for particular modalities. However, we abandoned this "specialist" approach for two reasons. Firstly, selecting the appropriate specialist model would either rely solely on the file name of the case or require an additional modality classification method, which again would increase latency. Secondly, in a real-world setting, switching model weights between predicting

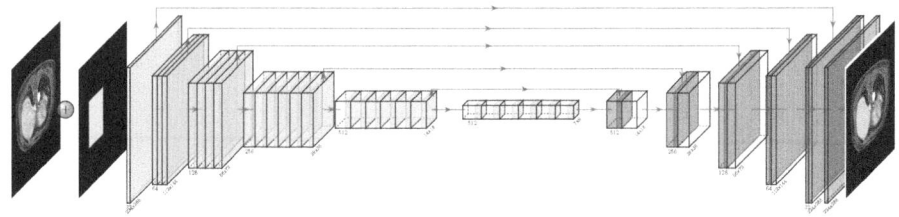

Fig. 1. Network architecture: We use nnUNet [1] with residual encoder (ResEnc) blocks [2], which here are illustrated by the orange blocks. The input image is concatenated with the bounding box represented as binary mask and then fed into the network. The patch size of the model is 224×288.

---

[1] https://github.com/openvinotoolkit/openvino and https://docs.openvino.ai/.

images of different modalities would increase latency. We recognize that this switching of model weights is not penalized in the challenge's runtime evaluation, as the docker container is run for each case individually.

3.2 Implementation Details

Environment Settings. The development environments and requirements are presented in Table 1.

Table 1. Development environments and requirements.

System	Ubuntu 20.04
CPU	AMD Ryzen 9 3900X processor
RAM	64GB DDR4-3600 RAM; 256 GB per socket
GPU (number and type)	One NVIDIA RTX3090 GPU with 24 GB
CUDA version	12.1
Programming language	Python 3.12.2
Deep learning framework	torch 2.2.1
Specific dependencies	-
Code	-

Table 2. Training protocols.

Pre-trained Model	Not applicable
Batch size	51
Patch size	224 × 288 × 3
Total epochs	1000
Optimizer	SGD with nesterov momentum ($\mu = 0.99$)
Initial learning rate (lr)	0.01
Lr decay schedule	linear LR decay
Training time	72.5 h
Loss function	Soft Dice loss + Cross Entropy loss
Number of model parameters	71.81M
Number of flops	-
CO_2eq	-

4 Results and Discussion

Our proposed method demonstrates robust performance in various medical imaging scenarios, particularly excelling when clear, well-defined anatomical structures are present within the bounded regions. The integration of bounding box prompts effectively guides the segmentation model, allowing it to focus on specific areas of interest and thereby improving accuracy. This method is notably beneficial in common modalities such as MRI and CT, where the target structures often have distinct and recognizable boundaries. In clinical settings, the method proves effective in tasks such as segmenting organs and tissues in high-contrast images, delineating target structures in MRI images, and segmenting regions of interest in X-Ray images with minimal noise or artifacts (Table 2).

The method works exceptionally well in scenarios involving the segmentation of organs and tissues in high-contrast images, such as liver and kidney segmentation in CT scans, as well as the delineation of structures such as single teeth or bones in X-Ray images. It is also successful in ultrasound images where the region of interest is well-isolated and less affected by noise or artifacts. In these cases, the bounding box prompts provide a significant advantage by narrowing the focus of the segmentation model, leading to precise and reliable outcomes.

Despite its strengths, the proposed method encounters challenges in certain situations. Primary reasons for failed cases include poor image quality, such as low resolution, significant noise, or artifacts, which can hinder the model's ability to accurately segment target structures. Ambiguous boundaries, particularly in the presence of diffuse pathological regions or overlapping anatomical features, also pose difficulties, as the model may struggle to produce accurate segmentations. Additionally, extreme variability in the appearance of target structures across different patients or imaging conditions can lead to poor generalization by the model.

Table 3. Quantitative evaluation results comparing the performance of the nnUNet architecture under different training conditions. Ablation study 1 involves training exclusively on 1% of the SAM dataset, while ablation study 2 entails pre-training on 1% of the SAM dataset followed by fine-tuning on the challenge dataset. Our proposed and submitted solution was trained solely on the provided challenge dataset from scratch.

Target	Baseline (LiteMedSAM)		Ablation Study 1		Ablation Study 2		Proposed	
	DSC(%)	NSD(%)	DSC(%)	NSD(%)	DSC(%)	NSD (%)	DSC(%)	NSD (%)
CT	92.26	94.90	67.64	69.14	90.60	93.37	90.05	92.84
MR	89.63	93.37	43.84	44.24	81.31	85.89	82.22	86.61
PET	51.58	25.17	30.69	23.36	34.33	24.84	45.84	32.82
US	94.77	96.81	64.17	68.60	80.03	86.45	80.85	87.00
X-Ray	75.82	80.38	16.24	15.34	78.79	84.94	79.54	85.73
Dermatology	92.47	93.86	52.95	54.28	90.29	91.84	89.75	91.36
Endoscopy	96.04	98.11	2.41	1.55	95.07	97.31	95.75	98.06
Fundus	94.81	96.42	3.03	0.00	89.66	91.42	88.70	90.49
Microscopy	61.63	65.39	2.26	0.43	76.06	84.38	76.11	84.13
Average	83.23	82.71	31.47	30.77	79.57	82.27	80.98	83.23

4.1 Quantitative Results on Validation Set

The quantitative results are summarized in Table 3. In addition to presenting the final submitted solution, we conducted ablation experiments to assess the impact of varying training sets on the model's downstream performance. Ablation study 1 involved training our nnUNet architecture solely on 1% of the SAM data, while ablation study 2 employed pre-training on the same 1% subset of SAM followed by training on the provided challenge dataset. Results indicate that utilizing the non-medical dataset of SAM in ablation study 1 yields unsatisfactory outcomes, underscoring the disparity between natural and medical images. Of note, training solely on the provided challenge data appears, on average, to outperform using the pre-trained checkpoint (ablation study 2). However, pre-training showed slight improvements in certain modalities (CT, Dermatology, Fundus). Furthermore, we observed marginal enhancements when pre-training on the entire challenge dataset and subsequently fine-tuning modality-wise on the corresponding subset of the challenge dataset. Nevertheless, we opted against training modality-specific models due to the aforementioned reasons (cf. Sect. 3.1).

4.2 Qualitative Results on Validation Set

In Figs. 2 and 3 qualitative results across 10 modalities are shown. While in Fig. 2 samples are shown where nnUNet is likely outperformed by LiteMedSAM, Fig. 3 shows examples where nnUNet performs well.

4.3 Segmentation Efficiency Results on Validation Set

Our approach prioritizes efficiency, making it suitable for deployment on edge devices and in resource-constrained environments. By adopting a 2D processing methodology and utilizing just-in-time (JIT) compiled functions, we achieve significant reductions in computational load and inference time, as demonstrated in Table 4. Notably, for CT, MR, Endoscopy, and PET modalities, our method achieves significantly reduced inference times compared to the MedSAM baseline, with the improvement being especially pronounced in ultrasound (US) images.

However, for large 2D images, such as those in Dermoscopy and Microscope imaging, our model experiences a notable increase in inference time over the baseline. This increase is due to our patch-based approach, which necessitates multiple forward passes for large images, resulting in slower inference speeds. This represents one of the major limitations of our method.

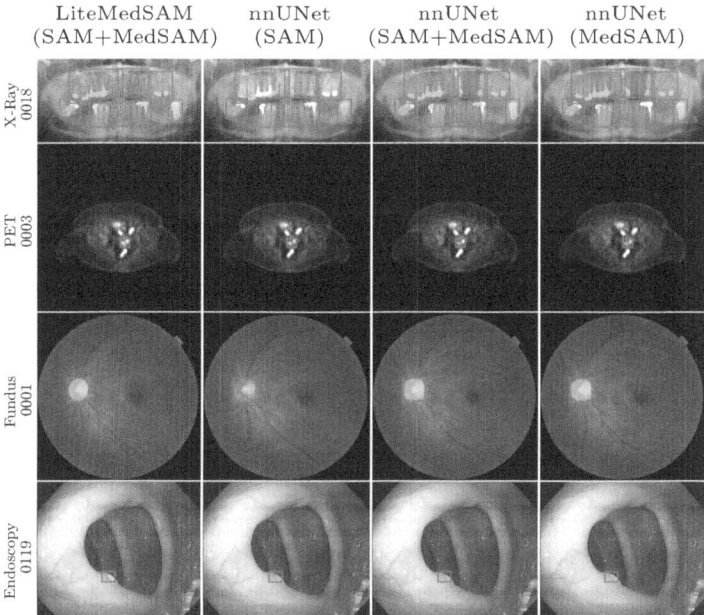

Fig. 2. Qualitative results. Within each column the same model was used for prediction. In parenthesis, the training data is indicated, where SAM is the SegmentAnything dataset from Meta and MedSAM the provided challenge dataset. For nnUNet only 1% of the actual SAM dataset was used. The right most model was submitted as final solution. In the first row, nnUNet struggles to understand the box prompt correctly as the dental field is continuously segmented instead of the single teeth within the bounding box. Here, LiteMedSAM correctly understands the intention of the prompt. Despite the different model, this could be due to the larger pre-training on the whole SAM dataset, which could help the model understand the intention of the prompt. The other rows likely also show worse performances of nnUNet compared to LiteMedSAM.

Despite this, our model generally demonstrates reduced inference time and lower resource usage, making it capable of running effectively on standard laptops and edge devices without the need for high-end GPUs. This broadens its accessibility and potential impact, allowing advanced medical image segmentation to be more widely adopted in various clinical settings.

4.4 Results on Final Testing Set

Table 5 shows average DSC, NSD and runtime on the different modalities of the hidden test set.

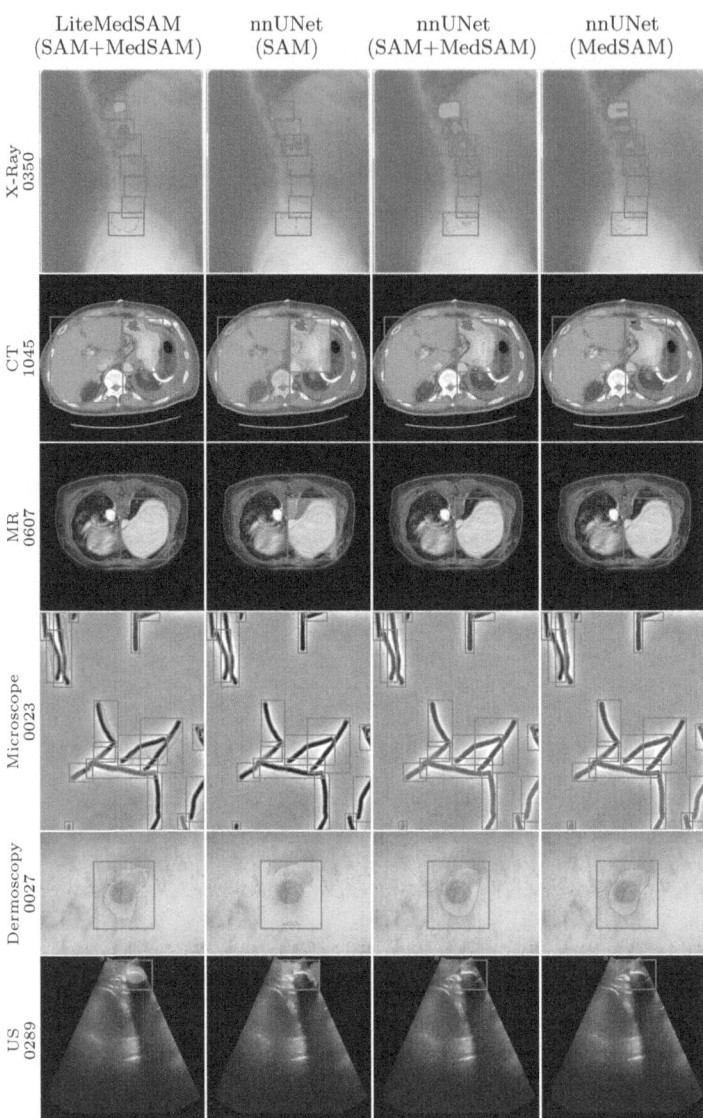

Fig. 3. Qualitative results. While under-performing for teeth in the X-Ray modality, nnUNet does a better job at segmenting the vertebrae in X-Rays compared to LiteMed-SAM. Furthermore, nnUNet provides seemingly better segmentations for the depicted microscopy image.

4.5 Limitation and Future Work

Looking forward, several avenues for further enhancement and exploration are evident. Improving the model's robustness to handle a wider range of image qualities and boundary ambiguities will be a key focus, with techniques such as

Table 4. Quantitative evaluation of segmentation efficiency measured in terms of running time (seconds). The baseline is the LiteMedSAM method developed by the challenge organizers. Ablation study presents our proposed solution without OpenVINO optimization, while Proposed refers to the same method post-runtime optimization using OpenVINO. Note: Our reported times for "Ablation Study" and "Proposed" reflect only the time for inference without the model loading and initialization overhead. These times were measured on the machine specified in Table 4.

Case ID	Size	Num. Objects	Baseline	Ablation Study	Proposed
3DBox_CT_0566	(287, 512, 512)	6	376.4	466.70	159.03
3DBox_CT_0888	(237, 512, 512)	6	100.5	97.27	35.88
3DBox_CT_0860	(246, 512, 512)	1	17.7	20.70	7.65
3DBox_MR_0621	(115, 400, 400)	6	157.1	130.39	51.48
3DBox_MR_0121	(64, 290, 320)	6	99.9	83.72	31.78
3DBox_MR_0179	(84, 512, 512)	1	17.1	10.85	4.87
3DBox_PET_0001	(264, 200, 200)	1	12.1	6.93	2.75
2DBox_US_0525	(256, 256, 3)	1	6.3	1.04	0.45
2DBox_X-Ray_0053	(320, 640, 3)	34	7.3	20.52	8.28
2DBox_Dermoscopy_0003	(3024, 4032, 3)	1	6.5	192.03	49.10
2DBox_Endoscopy_0086	(480, 560, 3)	1	6.1	2.99	0.89
2DBox_Fundus_0003	(2048, 2048, 3)	1	6.1	6.15	1.87
2DBox_Microscope_0008	(1536, 2040, 3)	19	6.8	47.41	13.97
2DBox_Microscope_0016	(1920, 2560, 3)	241	19.1	506.83	153.71
Total		325	839	1593.53	521.71

advanced data augmentation and semi-supervised learning potentially enhancing generalization. While our current approach is 2D-based, integrating 3D context in a hybrid model could combine the strengths of both approaches, offering better performance for complex cases without sacrificing efficiency. Furthermore, addressing the main limitation of increased inference time for large-sized images is a key aspect of future investigation. Potential solutions include optimizing the patch-based system or eliminating the need for patches altogether. Extending the model to handle additional medical imaging modalities and pathologies, including more rare and complex conditions, will further demonstrate its versatility and utility in diverse clinical scenarios.

Table 5. Final test set results of our proposed method. Shown are average DSC, NSD and runtime on the different modalities.

Target	DSC(%)	NSD(%)	runtime (s)
CT	70.44	72.32	44.82
MR	70.2	69.11	13.98
PET	63.96	61.53	39.22
US	82.86	88.38	50.23
X-Ray	69.1	79.31	10.42
OCT	79.03	86.37	8.03
Endoscopy	91.32	94.21	8.25
Fundus	86.27	88.36	8.98
Microscopy	82.51	86.28	18.34
Average	77.3	80.65	22.47

5 Conclusion

In conclusion, while the proposed method shows promise in many areas of medical image segmentation, ongoing refinement and adaptation will be essential to fully realize its potential and address the remaining challenges. The focus on efficiency and universal applicability positions our approach as a valuable tool in advancing medical imaging technologies and improving patient care outcomes.

Acknowledgements. We thank all the data owners for making the medical images publicly available and CodaLab [6] for hosting the challenge platform. This work was supported by the Helmholtz Association's Initiative and Networking Fund on the HAICORE@FZJ partition. The present contribution is supported by the Helmholtz Association under the joint research school "HIDSS4Health – Helmholtz Information and Data Science School for Health".

Disclosure of Interests. The authors have no competing interests to declare that are relevant to the content of this article.

References

1. Isensee, F., Jaeger, P.F., Kohl, S.A., Petersen, J., Maier-Hein, K.H.: nnU-Net: a self-configuring method for deep learning-based biomedical image segmentation. Nat. Methods **18**(2), 203–211 (2021)
2. Isensee, F., Ulrich, C., Wald, T., Maier-Hein, K.H.: Extending nnU-Net is all you need. In: Deserno, T.M., Handels, H., Maier, A., Maier-Hein, K., Palm, C., Tolxdorff, T. (eds.) BVM 2023. Informatik aktuell, pp. 12–17. Springer, Wiesbaden (2023). https://doi.org/10.1007/978-3-658-41657-7_7
3. Kirillov, A., et al.: Segment anything. In: Proceedings of the International Conference on Computer Vision, pp. 4015–4026 (2023)

4. Ma, J., He, Y., Li, F., Han, L., You, C., Wang, B.: Segment anything in medical images. Nat. Commun. **15**(1), 654 (2024)
5. Wald, T., et al.: SAM.MD: zero-shot medical image segmentation capabilities of the segment anything model. In: Medical Imaging with Deep Learning, Short Paper Track (2023)
6. Xu, Z., et al.: Codabench: flexible, easy-to-use, and reproducible meta-benchmark platform. Patterns **3**(7), 100543 (2022)
7. Zhang, C., et al.: Faster segment anything: towards lightweight SAM for mobile applications. arXiv preprint arXiv:2306.14289 (2023)
8. Zhang, Z., Cai, H., Han, S.: EfficientViT-SAM: accelerated segment anything model without performance loss. In: CVPR Workshop: Efficient Large Vision Models (2024)

SwiftMedSAM: An Ultra-lightweight Prompt-Based Universal Medical Image Segmentation Model for Highly Constrained Environments

Youngbin Kong[1,2], Kwangtai Kim[2,6], Seoi Jeong[2,5], Kyu Eun Lee[3,5], and Hyoun-Joong Kong[2,4,5(✉)]

[1] Interdisciplinary Program in Bioengineering, Graduate School, Seoul National University, Seoul, Republic of Korea
[2] Department of Transdisciplinary Medicine, Seoul National University Hospital, Seoul, Republic of Korea
gongcop7@snu.ac.kr
[3] Department of Surgery, Seoul National University Hospital and College of Medicine, Seoul, Republic of Korea
[4] Department of Medicine, Seoul National University College of Medicine, Seoul, Republic of Korea
[5] Innovative Medical Technology Research Institute, Seoul National University Hospital, Seoul, Republic of Korea
[6] Interdisciplinary Program of Medical Informatics, Seoul National University College of Medicine, Seoul, Republic of Korea

Abstract. Medical image segmentation is a crucial step for accurate diagnosis and treatment planning, as it provides quantitative information about anatomical structures and pathological lesions in various clinical scenarios. However, the existing methodologies have limitations in terms of their generalizability and computational efficiency. In this study, we propose SwiftMedSAM, an ultra-lightweight prompt-based general model, to enable efficient medical image segmentation even in resource-constrained environments. Based on LiteMedSAM, we significantly reduced the model size and computational complexity through the hyperparameter optimization of the image encoder and mask decoder components. SwiftMedSAM showed remarkable performance across various imaging modalities enabling real-time inference in resource-limited computing environments. It achieved a validation score of 0.75 demonstrating that SwiftMedSAM outperformed the existing methodologies in terms of the trade-off between accuracy and efficiency. Owing to its unprecedented generalizability and low computational cost, SwiftMedSAM is expected to enable high-quality medical image analysis in resource-constrained settings, thereby contributing to advancements in precision medicine and telemedicine.

Keywords: Medical Imaging Segmentation · Segment Anything · Deep Learning

1 Introduction

Medical image segmentation is a critical step in accurate diagnosis and treatment planning. It provides quantitative information about anatomical structures and pathological lesions in various clinical scenarios such as computer-aided diagnosis, surgical guidance, treatment monitoring, and patient follow-up. For example, accurate identification of the location, size, and boundaries of a tumor is essential for determining cancer staging, surgical planning, and radiation therapy. However, such segmentation tasks are highly complex and time-consuming, necessitating the development of automated high-performance segmentation models [34].

Driven by advancements in deep learning techniques, innovative achievements have been made in the field of medical image analysis in recent years, with significant progress in segmentation problems. Initially, transfer-learned CNN-based models such as U-Net [49] and V-Net [43] were predominant, and subsequently, the introduction of cutting-edge models such as Vision Transformer [15] and Swin Transformer [36] led to substantial accuracy improvements. However, most existing studies have been limited by a lack of generalizability as they employ architectures and training methods tailored to specific clinical tasks or datasets [17].

Active research has been conducted in the field of segmentation foundation models for prompt-based universal image segmentation. A representative model, the Segment Anything Model (SAM), has demonstrated the ability to effectively perform various general image segmentation tasks using a single model through prompt engineering. However, SAM is a heavy model, making it impractical for use in resource-constrained environments or edge devices. To address this issue, lightweight models such as MobileSAM [61] and EfficientViT-SAM [62] have been proposed; however, they are specialized for natural image datasets rather than medical images, which presents a limitation.

In response, MedSAM was introduced, fine-tuning the existing SAM model on an unprecedented large-scale dataset comprising over one million medical image-mask pairs, achieving remarkable performance in medical image segmentation. MedSAM underwent comprehensive experimental evaluation on 86 internal and 60 external validation tasks, encompassing various anatomical structures, pathological conditions, and medical imaging modalities. The results showed that MedSAM consistently outperformed the previous SOTA segmentation model, SAM, and exhibited performance on par with or superior to specialized models [25] trained on the same imaging modality.

However, MedSAM, with 93M parameters, is an extremely large model that requires significant computational resources, making it difficult to utilize in resource-constrained computing environments. To address this limitation, LiteMedSAM, a lightweight version of the original MedSAM, was proposed. It was trained in two stages: distilling a lightweight encoder from MedSAM's large image encoder and then fine-tuning the entire pipeline with the distilled encoder. Through this process, LiteMedSAM achieved a significant reduction in model size and computational complexity compared to MedSAM, enabling faster inference in resource-constrained settings.

CVPR 2024: SEGMENT ANYTHING IN MEDICAL IMAGES ON LAPTOP Challenge focuses on developing a prompt-based general model for medical image segmentation. This challenge provides a large-scale dataset comprising over 1,000,000 image-mask pairs, including 11 medical imaging modalities and more than 20 types of cancer. The goal is to develop a prompt-based universal segmentation model that can handle various medical image segmentation tasks while being computationally lightweight enough to run on edge devices such as laptops.

In this study, we used LiteMedSAM as the baseline model and optimized the hyperparameters of the image encoder and mask decoder components to develop a more lightweight SwiftMedSAM. While leveraging the large-scale dataset provided, we further reduced the model size and computational complexity to enable real-time inference, even in resource-constrained computing environments.

The developed SwiftMedSAM model is expected to have a significantly reduced model size and computational cost compared to LiteMedSAM, enabling real-time inference in even more constrained environments. Through this research, we aim to further mitigate the generalizability-efficiency trade-off of existing methods and achieve high-quality medical image segmentation under highly limited computing resources (Fig. 1).

2 Method

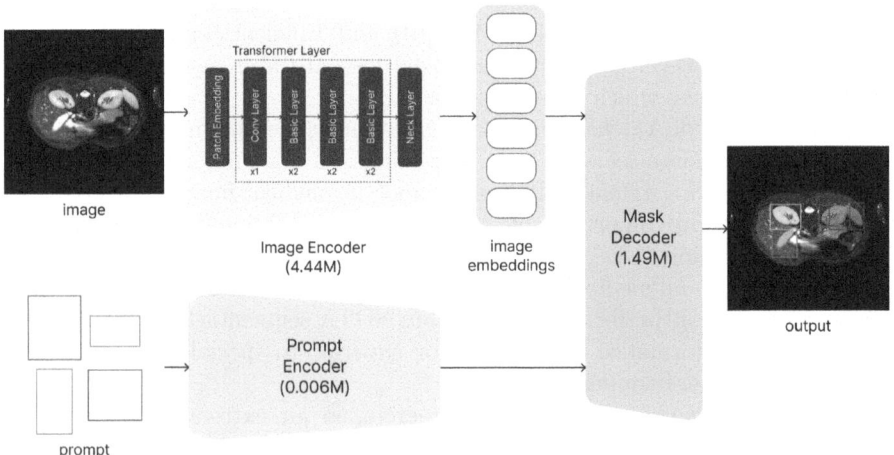

Fig. 1. Overall framework of the proposed method. The image and bounding box prompts serve as inputs to the model, passing through their respective encoders. The resulting outputs are then passed through the mask decoder to produce the segmentation results.

2.1 Preprocessing

The preprocessing strategy was inspired by MedSAM. We utilized a large-scale dataset with over one million image-mask pairs based on publicly available datasets that were used for MedSAM training. This dataset includes 11 imaging modalities (CT, MRI, endoscopy, ultrasound, etc.) and more than 30 types of cancers. The original 3D CT and MRI data, as well as grayscale images (X-ray, ultrasound, etc.) and RGB images (endoscopy, fundus, etc.), were converted to npz format for use. To structure the dataset and enable efficient management, the ground-truth masks and additional information, such as spacing, for both 2D and 3D images were stored together in a single file.

2.2 Proposed Method

The proposed SwiftMedSAM model builds upon the architecture of LiteMedSAM, with a focus on hyperparameter optimization and structural modifications to achieve ultra-lightweight performance. Our approach targets both the image encoder and mask decoder components, aiming to reduce computational load while maintaining high segmentation accuracy. The backbone of the existing LiteMedSAM was maintained, with the primary focus on hyperparameter optimization to achieve a balance between model efficiency and performance.

In the image encoder component, we made adjustments to the block depths to reduce the computational load. As the block depth increases, both the model capacity and computational complexity increase. Therefore, we employed a strategy of gradually decreasing the depths. In SwiftMedSAMv1, we applied block depths of [2, 2, 4, 2], whereas in SwiftMedSAMv2, we further reduced this to [1, 2, 2, 2]. This adjustment resulted in a lighter model while still preserving essential feature extraction capabilities.

For the mask decoder, we implemented several key modifications, primarily in the transformer and IoU head components. First, we reduced the transformer depth from 2 to 1, significantly decreasing the computational cost. Additionally, we made substantial reductions to the transformer's MLP dimensions, lowering them from the original 2048 to 1024, and further to 256. Larger MLP dimensions increase both model capacity and computational load, so reducing them contributes significantly to the lightening effect we aimed to achieve.

We also decreased the number of multi-head attention units in the transformer, reducing them from 8 to 4. While a higher number of attention heads allows for feature extraction from diverse perspectives, an excessive number risks overfitting and increases computational complexity. Therefore, we made an appropriate reduction to optimize both model capacity and computational load.

Lastly, we lowered the depth of the IoU head from 3 to 2, further reducing computations in this component. Although the IoU head, which is related to mask prediction, does not constitute a large portion of the overall computational load, we considered this adjustment valuable for our lightening purposes.

As a result of these optimizations, SwiftMedSAM has approximately 5.9M parameters, which represents a reduction of about 40% compared to the original 9.8M parameters of LiteMedSAM. This significant reduction in model size contributes to improved inference speed and reduced memory requirements, making SwiftMedSAM more suitable for deployment in resource-constrained environments.

To address the challenge of dataset imbalance, particularly the substantially lower number of PET modality images in the provided training dataset, we incorporated an additional dataset known as autoPETIII. This supplementary data was used to construct the final training dataset, helping to improve the model's performance across various imaging modalities, especially for PET images. The inclusion of this additional data helped to mitigate potential biases and enhance the model's generalization capabilities.

Through the combination of these structural lightening strategies and careful dataset curation, SwiftMedSAM achieves real-time performance and efficiency while maintaining high segmentation accuracy. The decrease in segmentation accuracy compared to the original model was not substantial, thanks to the pre-training on large-scale medical image data. This approach allows SwiftMedSAM to offer a compelling solution for medical image segmentation tasks in scenarios where computational resources are limited, without significantly compromising on the quality of the segmentation results (Table 1).

Table 1. SwiftMedSAM Hyperparameters.

Component	HyperParameters	Lite MedSAM	Swift MedSAMv1	Swift MedSAMv2
Image Encoder	Block Depths	[2, 2, 6, 2]	[2, 2, 4, 2]	[1, 2, 2, 2]
Mask Decoder	Transformer Depth	2	1	1
Mask Decoder	Transformer MLP Dim	2048	1024	256
Mask Decoder	Transformer Num Heads	8	8	4
Mask Decoder	IOU Head Depth	3	2	2

2.3 Post-processing

The Swift MedSAM model proposed in this study includes a post-processing stage that converts the predicted mask to the original image size through a series of steps. This post-processing stage ensures that the mask output by the model is aligned with the original image size, thereby providing an accurate segmentation result. The post-processing stage consists of the following steps:

1. Cropping
   The predicted mask is resized to the size of the input image (256×256) for the model, the mask undergoes a cropping process to eliminate unnecessary padding areas.

2. Resizing
   The cropped mask is resized to the original size of the image. This is achieved through bilinear interpolation, upsampling the mask to the same size as the original image.
3. Sigmoid Activation Function
   A sigmoid activation function is applied to the upsampled mask, normalizing the values of each pixel between 0 and 1. This step ensures that each pixel in the mask represents the probability of belonging to the target region.
4. Binarization
   The mask that undergoes the sigmoid activation function is binarized using a threshold of 0.5. In other words, values greater than or equal to 0.5 are converted to 1, and values below 0.5 are converted to 0, generating the final mask. This process ensures that the predicted mask has a clear binary form.

3 Experiments

3.1 Dataset and Evaluation Measures

In the CVPR 2024: SEGMENT ANYTHING IN MEDICAL IMAGES ON LAPTOP challenge, participants could use the training and validation datasets provided by the organizers and external publicly available datasets. The datasets used in developing SwiftMedSAM are as follows: COVID-19-20 [51], AbdomenCT-1K [40], FDG-PET-CT-Lesions [18], NSCLC Radiogenomics [6], NSCLC-Radiomics [18], CT Lymph Nodes [50], NSCLC-PleuralEffusion [31], NSCLC-Lung MSD-LUNG [4,38,52], KiTS23 [20], CT-ORG [4], COVID-19-20-CTSEG [38], TotalSegmentator [58], AMOS [28], LCTSC [60], HCC-TACE-Seg [45], Adrenal-ACC-Ki67-Seg [44], MSD [4,53], ISLES [21], WMH [33], BraTS [5,42], PROMISE12 [35], MSD-Prostate [4,53], NCI-ISBI [7], Crossmoda [14], QIN-PROSTATE-Repeatability [16], CC-Tumor Heterogeneity [8], COVID-19 Radiography Database [10,48], COVID-QU-Ex [10,13,48,55], Chest Xray Masks and Labels [9,26], Chest X-Ray Images with Pneumothorax Masks, CDD-CESM [29,30], Intraretinal Cystoid Fluid [2], ps-fh-aop-2023 [37], hc18 [22,23], Breast Ultrasound Images Dataset [3], ISIC2018 [11,12,56], CholecSeg8k [24,57], Kvasir-SEG [27,46], m2caiSeg [41], PAPILA [32], IDRiD [47], NeurIPS CellSeg [39], autoPETIII.

The training dataset includes 11 imaging modalities: Computed Tomography (CT), Magnetic Resonance Imaging (MRI), Positron Emission Tomography (PET), X-ray, ultrasound, mammography, Optical Coherence Tomography (OCT), endoscopy, fundus, dermoscopy, and microscopy. A total of 1,490,576 medical image-mask pairs were used to train our model. The validation dataset contains 9 modalities and is a subset of the testing set used in this challenge.

The evaluation metrics for this challenge were divided into accuracy and efficiency. The accuracy metrics are Dice Similarity Coefficient (DSC), which measures the overlap between the ground truth and predictions, and Normalized Surface Dice (NSD), which measures the similarity between the ground truth boundary and predictions. The efficiency metric is runtime, measured using only the CPU without GPU assistance.

3.2 Implementation Details

Environment Settings The development environments and requirements are presented in Table 2.

Table 2. Development environments and requirements.

System	Ubuntu 20.04.6 LTS
CPU	AMD EPYC™ 7402X CPU@2.8 GHz
RAM	8 × 64 GB; 3200MT/s
GPU (number and type)	Four NVIDIA A100 80G
CUDA version	11.8
Programming language	Python 3.10.13
Deep learning framework	torch 2.1.0, torchvision 0.16.0

Training Protocols. The training protocols of SwiftMedSAM is listed in Table 3.

Table 3. Training protocols.

Pre-trained Model	LiteMedSAM
Batch size	32
Patch size	256 × 256 × 3
Total epochs	26
Optimizer	AdamW ($\beta_1 = 0.9$, $\beta_2 = 0.999$)
Initial learning rate (lr)	0.005
Lr decay schedule	ReduceLROnPlateau
Training time	93.5 h
Loss function	Dice Loss, Binary Cross Entropy Loss
Number of model parameters	5.94M[a]
Number of flops	30.04G[b]
CO_2eq	16.16 Kg[c]

[a] https://github.com/sksq96/pytorch-summary
[b] https://github.com/facebookresearch/fvcore
[c] https://github.com/lfwa/carbontracker/

4 Results and Discussion

4.1 Quantitative Results on Validation Set

In this study, we conducted experiments to evaluate the performance of SwiftMedSAM. The accuracy was measured based on the 3,076 validation data images provided and compared with the baseline model, LiteMedSAM. The results are presented in Table 4. Compared to the baseline, SwiftMedSAMv1 exhibited a 0.05% average decrease in DSC, but a 2.00% improvement in NSD. Compared to SwiftMedSAMv1, SwiftMedSAMv2 showed a 0.63% improvement in DSC and 0.73% improvement in NSD.

In particular, when examining each imaging modality, for CT images, SwiftMedSAMv1 achieved a 2.38% improvement in DSC and a 3.39% improvement in NSD compared to the baseline. For MR images, DSC improved by 3.42% and NSD improved by 4.45%. For PET images, there was a significant improvement, with DSC increasing by 13.77% and NSD by 21.79%. However, for US images, DSC decreased by 15.61% and NSD decreased by 11.69%. For X-ray images, DSC decreased by 11.34% and NSD decreased by 9.55%.

Comparing SwiftMedSAMv2 and SwiftMedSAMv1, for CT images, DSC decreased by 0.33%, whereas NSD decreased by 0.27%. For MR images, DSC decreased by 0.78% and NSD decreased by 0.56%. For PET images, DSC decreased by 5.49% and NSD decreased by 0.93%. For US images, DSC improved by 1.72%, and NSD improved by 2.14%. For X-ray images, DSC improved by 6.24%, and NSD improved by 5.88%.

Table 4. Quantitative evaluation results on validation set.

Target	Baseline		Swift MedSAMv1		Swift MedSAMv2	
	DSC (%)	NSD (%)	DSC (%)	NSD (%)	DSC (%)	NSD (%)
CT	40.71	40.27	43.09	43.66	42.76	43.39
MR	61.17	62.40	64.59	66.85	63.81	66.29
PET	55.10	29.17	68.87	50.96	63.38	50.03
US	94.77	96.81	79.16	85.12	80.88	87.26
X-Ray	75.82	80.38	64.48	70.83	70.72	76.71
Dermotology	92.47	93.85	93.88	95.30	93.43	94.80
Endoscopy	96.04	98.11	94.57	97.22	95.58	98.02
Fundus	94.81	96.41	94.10	95.79	96.13	97.69
Microscopy	61.63	65.39	69.41	75.05	66.13	73.13
Average	74.73	73.64	74.68	75.64	75.31	76.37

4.2 Qualitative Results on Validation Set

For the comparison of qualitative results, we used publicly available datasets with ground truth annotations: CT2USforKidneySeg [54], HipXRay [19], and NSCLC-Radiomics [1], which contain ultrasound, X-ray, and CT modalities, respectively. Examples of SwiftMedSAMv2's segmentation results for these datasets are shown in Fig 2. While SwiftMedSAMv2 demonstrated refined segmentation performance on the CT2USforKidneySeg and NSCLC-Radiomics datasets, it yielded suboptimal results for some images from the HipXRay dataset with low-contrast or unclear boundaries.

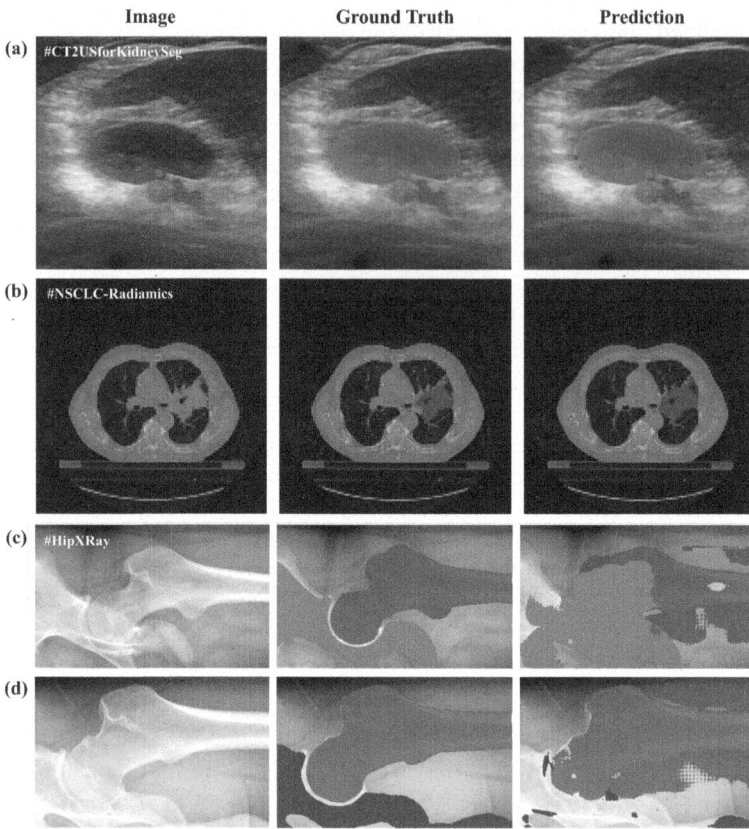

Fig. 2. Qualitative results of our SwiftMedSAMv2. (a–b) Good segmentation cases from CT2USforKidneySeg dataset and NSCLC-Radiomics dataset, respectively. Our method accurately delineates the kidney boundaries in the CT image (a) and captures the tumor region in the lung CT image (b). (c–d) Bad segmentation cases from the HipXRay dataset, where our method struggles to segment the femoral head and acetabulum regions precisely due to low contrast and complex anatomical structures.

4.3 Segmentation Efficiency Results on Validation Set

The efficiency experiments for the final model were performed on a CPU: AMD EPYC^{TM}7402X CPU@2.8 GHz, RAM: 8×64 GB; 3200 MT/s. The specific inference time measurements for some cases are listed in Table 5. Consequently, the SwiftMedSAMv1 and SwiftMedSAMv2 models showed reduced execution times compared to the baseline model in most cases. Particularly, for the 3DBox_MR_0621 case, while the baseline model's execution time was 630.2 s, SwiftMedSAMv1 and SwiftMedSAMv2 took 166.8 s and 145.0 s, respectively, showing a significant reduction. Compared to SwiftMedSAMv1, SwiftMedSAMv2 exhibited better performance in some cases, and an overall slight improvement was observed. For instance, in the 3DBox_CT_0566 case,

SwiftMedSAMv1 recorded 343.2 s, while SwiftMedSAMv2 took 331.9 s, demonstrating a faster execution time.

Table 5. Quantitative evaluation of efficiency in terms of running time (s).

Case ID	Size	Num. Objects	Baseline	Swift MedSAMv1	Swift MedSAMv2
3DBox_CT_0566	(287, 512, 512)	6	499.2	343.2	331.9
3DBox_CT_0888	(237, 512, 512)	6	114.1	97.4	94.1
3DBox_CT_0860	(246, 512, 512)	1	17.7	15.9	14.2
3DBox_MR_0621	(115, 400, 400)	6	630.2	166.8	145.0
3DBox_MR_0121	(64, 290, 320)	6	119.4	94.7	90.7
3DBox_MR_0179	(84, 512, 512)	1	17.7	14.7	13.3
3DBox_PET_0001	(264, 200, 200)	1	31.9	9.9	8.6
2DBox_US_0525	(256, 256, 3)	1	1.8	1.7	1.6
2DBox_X-Ray_0053	(320, 640, 3)	34	9.8	9.3	9.8
2DBox_Dermoscopy_0003	(3024, 4032, 3)	1	7.9	8.4	7.9
2DBox_Endoscopy_0086	(480, 560, 3)	1	6.1	2.7	2.6
2DBox_Fundus_0003	(2048, 2048, 3)	1	2.6	4.2	4.0
2DBox_Microscope_0008	(1536, 2040, 3)	19	19.5	18.1	18.0
2DBox_Microscope_0016	(1920, 2560, 3)	241	257.5	253.1	267.1

4.4 Results on Final Testing Set

The SwiftMedSAM was evaluated on the final testing set across various medical imaging modalities. In terms of segmentation accuracy metrics, endoscopy achieved the highest DSC of 91.55% and NSD of 94.44%. The average DSC and NSD across all modalities were 75.50% and 78.95%, respectively. Regarding efficiency, the mean runtime was 12.86 s, with endoscopy being the fastest at 7.37 s and CT the slowest at 30.89 s. Detailed results are presented in Table 6.

Table 6. Testing results on final testing set

Target	SwiftMedSAM		
	DSC (%)	NSD (%)	Runtime (s)
CT	61.03	65.56	30.89
MR	66.73	68.62	14.51
X-Ray	64.55	77.04	9.25
Endoscopy	91.55	94.44	7.37
Fundus	85.96	88.15	8.96
Microscopy	81.00	83.00	15.73
OCT	71.09	78.47	7.84
PET	79.30	70.65	12.09
US	78.28	84.63	9.10
Average	75.50	78.95	12.86

4.5 Limitation and Future Work

SwiftMedSAM exhibited versatility in medical image segmentation despite its remarkably small model size and low computational complexity. However, there are still limitations in which segmentation errors occur when the boundaries of the structures/lesions are ambiguous. We expect that these issues can be resolved with higher-quality data and more powerful training strategies in the future. Currently, the performance is maintained at the level of the baseline model, but we aim to achieve a fast inference speed and improve the performance in the future.

5 Conclusion

In this study, we proposed SwiftMedSAM, an ultra-lightweight prompt-based model that enables real-time high-performance medical image segmentation even in highly constrained computing environments. While maintaining the backbone of the existing SOTA model MedSAM, we introduced the lightweight LiteMedSAM as the baseline and performed a process of hyperparameter tuning to drastically reduce the model size and computational complexity. Through experiments, we verified the comparable segmentation performance and fast inference speed of SwiftMedSAM.

The proposed SwiftMedSAM demonstrates the potential for a universal prompt-based medical image segmentation model while simultaneously pursuing efficiency and generalizability. This will enable high-quality medical image analysis, even in resource-constrained environments, contributing to advancements in precision medicine and telemedicine.

Acknowledgements. We thank all the data owners for making the medical images publicly available and CodaLab [59] for hosting the challenge platform.

This research was supported by a grant of 'Korea Government Grant Program for Education and Research in Medical AI' through the Korea Health Industry Development Institute (KHIDI), funded by the Korea government(MOE, MOHW), the NAVER Digital Bio Innovation Research Fund, funded by NAVER Corporation (Grant No. [3720230030]) and the Institute of Information & Communications Technology Planning & Evaluation(IITP)-Global Data-X Leader HRD program grant funded by the Korea government (MSIT) (IITP-2024-RS-2024-00441407).

Disclosure of Interests. The authors have no competing interests to declare that are relevant to the content of this article.

References

1. Aerts, H.J.W.L., et al.: Data from NSCLC-radiomics (version 4) [data set]. Cancer Imaging Arch. (2014). https://doi.org/10.7937/K9/TCIA.2015.PF0M9REI
2. Ahmed, Z., Panhwar, S.Q., Baqai, A., Umrani, F.A., Ahmed, M., Khan, A.: Deep learning based automated detection of intraretinal cystoid fluid. Int. J. Imaging Syst. Technol. **32**(3), 902–917 (2022). https://doi.org/10.1002/ima.22662, https://onlinelibrary.wiley.com/doi/abs/10.1002/ima.22662

3. Al-Dhabyani, W., Gomaa, M., Khaled, H., Fahmy, A.: Dataset of breast ultrasound images. Data Brief **28**, 104863 (2020). https://doi.org/10.1016/j.dib.2019.104863
4. Antonelli, M., Reinke, A., Bakas, S., et al.: The medical segmentation decathlon. Nat. Commun. **13**, 4128 (2022). https://doi.org/10.1038/s41467-022-30695-9
5. Bakas, S., et al.: Identifying the best machine learning algorithms for brain tumor segmentation, progression assessment, and overall survival prediction in the BRATS challenge. CoRR abs/1811.02629 (2018). http://arxiv.org/abs/1811.02629
6. Bakr, S., Gevaert, O., Echegaray, S., et al.: A radiogenomic dataset of non-small cell lung cancer. Sci. Data **5**, 180202 (2018). https://doi.org/10.1038/sdata.2018.202
7. Bloch, N., et al.: NCI-ISBI 2013 challenge: automated segmentation of prostate structures. Cancer Imaging Arch. (2015). https://doi.org/10.7937/K9/TCIA.2015.zF0vlOPv
8. Bowen, S.R., et al.: Tumor radiomic heterogeneity: multiparametric functional imaging to characterize variability and predict response following cervical cancer radiation therapy. J. Magn. Resonan. Imaging **47**(5), 1388–1396 (2018). https://doi.org/10.1002/jmri.25874, https://onlinelibrary.wiley.com/doi/abs/10.1002/jmri.25874
9. Candemir, S., et al.: Lung segmentation in chest radiographs using anatomical atlases with nonrigid registration. IEEE Trans. Med. Imaging **33**(2), 577–590 (2014). https://doi.org/10.1109/TMI.2013.2290491
10. Chowdhury, M.E.H., et al.: Can AI help in screening viral and COVID-19 pneumonia? IEEE Access **8**, 132665–132676 (2020). https://doi.org/10.1109/ACCESS.2020.3010287
11. Codella, N.C.F., et al.: Skin lesion analysis toward melanoma detection: a challenge at the 2017 international symposium on biomedical imaging (ISBI), hosted by the international skin imaging collaboration (ISIC). CoRR abs/1710.05006 (2017). http://arxiv.org/abs/1710.05006
12. Codella, N.C.F., et al.: Skin lesion analysis toward melanoma detection 2018: a challenge hosted by the international skin imaging collaboration (ISIC). CoRR abs/1902.03368 (2019). http://arxiv.org/abs/1902.03368
13. Degerli, A., Ahishali, M., Yamac, M., et al.: COVID-19 infection map generation and detection from chest x-ray images. Health Inf. Sci. Syst. **9**, 15 (2021). https://doi.org/10.1007/s13755-021-00146-8
14. Dorent, R., et al.: Crossmoda 2021 challenge: benchmark of cross-modality domain adaptation techniques for vestibular schwannoma and cochlea segmentation. Med. Image Anal. **83**, 102628 (2023). https://doi.org/10.1016/j.media.2022.102628, https://www.sciencedirect.com/science/article/pii/S1361841522002560
15. Dosovitskiy, A., et al.: An image is worth 16x16 words: transformers for image recognition at scale. arXiv abs/2010.11929 (2020). https://api.semanticscholar.org/CorpusID:225039882
16. Fedorov, A., Schwier, M., Clunie, D., et al.: An annotated test-retest collection of prostate multiparametric MRI. Sci. Data **5**, 180281 (2018). https://doi.org/10.1038/sdata.2018.281, https://doi.org/10.1038/sdata.2018.281
17. Fidon, L.: Trustworthy deep learning for medical image segmentation (2023).https://doi.org/10.48550/arXiv.2305.17456
18. Gatidis, S., Hepp, T., Früh, M., et al.: A whole-body FDG-PET/CT dataset with manually annotated tumor lesions. Sci. Data **9**, 601 (2022). https://doi.org/10.1038/s41597-022-01718-3
19. Gut, D.: X-ray images of the hip joints. Mendeley Data, V1 (2021). https://doi.org/10.17632/zm6bxzhmfz.1

20. Heller, N., et al.: The state of the art in kidney and kidney tumor segmentation in contrast-enhanced CT imaging: Results of the kits19 challenge. Med. Image Anal. **67**, 101821 (2021). https://doi.org/10.1016/j.media.2020.101821, https://www.sciencedirect.com/science/article/pii/S1361841520301857
21. Hernandez Petzsche, M.R., de la Rosa, E., Hanning, U., et al.: Isles 2022: a multicenter magnetic resonance imaging stroke lesion segmentation dataset. Sci. Data **9**, 762 (2022). https://doi.org/10.1038/s41597-022-01875-5
22. van den Heuvel, T.L., de Bruijn, D., de Korte, C.L., van Ginneken, B.: Automated measurement of fetal head circumference using 2D ultrasound images. PloS ONE **13**(8), e0200412 (2018)
23. van den Heuvel, T., de Bruijn, D., de Korte, C.L., van Ginneken, B.: Automated measurement of fetal head circumference (2018). https://doi.org/10.5281/zenodo.xxxxxxx
24. Hong, W., Kao, C., Kuo, Y., Wang, J., Chang, W., Shih, C.: Cholecseg8k: a semantic segmentation dataset for laparoscopic cholecystectomy based on cholec80. CoRR abs/2012.12453 (2020). https://arxiv.org/abs/2012.12453
25. Isensee, F., Jaeger, P.F., Kohl, S.A., Petersen, J., Maier-Hein, K.H.: NNU-net: a self-configuring method for deep learning-based biomedical image segmentation. Nat. Methods **18**(2), 203–211 (2021)
26. Jaeger, S., et al.: Automatic tuberculosis screening using chest radiographs. IEEE Trans. Med. Imaging **33**(2), 233–245 (2014). https://doi.org/10.1109/TMI.2013.2284099
27. Jha, D., et al.: Kvasir-SEG: a segmented polyp dataset. In: Ro, Y.M., et al. (eds.) MMM 2020. LNCS, vol. 11962, pp. 451–462. Springer, Cham (2020). https://doi.org/10.1007/978-3-030-37734-2_37
28. Ji, Y., et al.: Amos: a large-scale abdominal multi-organ benchmark for versatile medical image segmentation. In: Advances in Neural Information Processing Systems, vol. 35, pp. 36722–36732 (2022)
29. Khaled, R., et al.: Categorized digital database for low energy and subtracted contrast enhanced spectral mammography images (2021). https://doi.org/10.7937/29kw-ae92
30. Khaled, R., Helal, M., Alfarghaly, O., et al.: Categorized contrast enhanced mammography dataset for diagnostic and artificial intelligence research. Sci. Data **9**, 122 (2022). https://doi.org/10.1038/s41597-022-01238-0
31. Kiser, K.J., Barman, A., Stieb, S., et al.: Novel autosegmentation spatial similarity metrics capture the time required to correct segmentations better than traditional metrics in a thoracic cavity segmentation workflow. J. Digit. Imaging **34**, 541–553 (2021). https://doi.org/10.1007/s10278-021-00460-3
32. Kovalyk, O., Morales-Sánchez, J., Verdú-Monedero, R., et al.: Papila: dataset with fundus images and clinical data of both eyes of the same patient for glaucoma assessment. Sci. Data **9**, 291 (2022). https://doi.org/10.1038/s41597-022-01388-1
33. Kuijf, H.J., et al.: Standardized assessment of automatic segmentation of white matter hyperintensities and results of the WMH segmentation challenge. IEEE Trans. Med Imaging **38**(11), 2556–2568 (2019). https://doi.org/10.1109/TMI.2019.2905770
34. Lei, T., Nandi, A.: Image Segmentation for Medical Analysis, pp. 199–227 (2022). https://doi.org/10.1002/9781119859048.ch9
35. Litjens, G., et al.: Promise12: data from the MICCAI grand challenge: prostate MR image segmentation 2012. Med. Image Anal. **18**(2), 359–373 (2023). https://doi.org/10.5281/zenodo.8026660

36. Liu, Z., et al.: Swin transformer: hierarchical vision transformer using shifted windows. In: Proceedings of the IEEE/CVF International Conference on Computer Vision, pp. 10012–10022 (2021)
37. Lu, Y., et al.: The JNU-IFM dataset for segmenting pubic symphysis-fetal head. Data Brief **41**, 107904 (2022). https://doi.org/10.1016/j.dib.2022.107904, https://www.sciencedirect.com/science/article/pii/S2352340922001160
38. Ma, J., et al.: Toward data-efficient learning: a benchmark for COVID-19 CT lung and infection segmentation. Med. Phys. **48**(3), 1197–1210 (2021)
39. Ma, J., et al.: The multimodality cell segmentation challenge: toward universal solutions. Nat. Methods (2024). https://doi.org/10.1038/s41592-024-02233-6
40. Ma, J., et al.: Abdomenct-1k: is abdominal organ segmentation a solved problem? IEEE Trans. Pattern Anal. Mach. Intell. **44**(10), 6695–6714 (2022)
41. Maqbool, S., Riaz, A., Sajid, H., Hasan, O.: m2caiSeg: semantic segmentation of laparoscopic images using convolutional neural networks (2020). https://doi.org/10.48550/arXiv.2008.10134
42. Menze, B.H., et al.: The multimodal brain tumor image segmentation benchmark (brats). IEEE Trans. Med. Imaging **34**(10), 1993–2024 (2015). https://doi.org/10.1109/TMI.2014.2377694
43. Milletari, F., Navab, N., Ahmadi, S.A.: V-net: fully convolutional neural networks for volumetric medical image segmentation. In: 2016 Fourth International Conference on 3D Vision (3DV), pp. 565–571. IEEE (2016)
44. Moawad, A.W., et al.: Voxel-level segmentation of pathologically-proven adrenocortical carcinoma with ki-67 expression (adrenal-acc-ki67-seg). Data Set (2023). https://doi.org/10.7937/1FPG-VM46
45. Morshid, A., et al.: A machine learning model to predict hepatocellular carcinoma response to transcatheter arterial chemoembolization. Radiol. Artif. Intell. **1**(5), e180021 (2019). https://doi.org/10.1148/ryai.2019180021, pMID: 31858078
46. Pogorelov, K., et al.: KVASIR: a multi-class image dataset for computer aided gastrointestinal disease detection (2017). https://doi.org/10.1145/3193289
47. Porwal, P., et al.: Indian diabetic retinopathy image dataset (IDRID): a database for diabetic retinopathy screening research. Data **3**(3), 25 (2018). https://doi.org/10.3390/data3030025
48. Rahman, T., et al.: Exploring the effect of image enhancement techniques on COVID-19 detection using chest x-ray images. Comput. Biol. Med. **132**, 104319 (2021). https://doi.org/10.1016/j.compbiomed.2021.104319, https://www.sciencedirect.com/science/article/pii/S001048252100113X
49. Ronneberger, O., Fischer, P., Brox, T.: U-net: convolutional networks for biomedical image segmentation. In: International Conference on Medical Image Computing and Computer-Assisted Intervention, pp. 234–241 (2015)
50. Roth, H.R., et al.: A new 2.5D representation for lymph node detection using random sets of deep convolutional neural network observations. In: Golland, P., Hata, N., Barillot, C., Hornegger, J., Howe, R. (eds.) MICCAI 2014. LNCS, vol. 8673, pp. 520–527. Springer, Cham (2014). https://doi.org/10.1007/978-3-319-10404-1_65
51. Roth, H.R., et al.: Rapid artificial intelligence solutions in a pandemic-the COVID-19-20 lung CT lesion segmentation challenge. Med. Image Anal. **82**, 102605 (2022). https://doi.org/10.1016/j.media.2022.102605, https://www.sciencedirect.com/science/article/pii/S1361841522002353
52. Simpson, A.L., et al.: A large annotated medical image dataset for the development and evaluation of segmentation algorithms. CoRR abs/1902.09063 (2019). http://arxiv.org/abs/1902.09063

53. Simpson, A.L., et al.: A large annotated medical image dataset for the development and evaluation of segmentation algorithms. arXiv abs/1902.09063 (2019). https://api.semanticscholar.org/CorpusID:67855790
54. Song, Y., Zheng, J., Lei, L., Ni, Z., Zhao, B., Hu, Y.: Ct2us: Cross-modal transfer learning for kidney segmentation in ultrasound images with synthesized data. Ultrasonics **122**, 106706 (2022)
55. Tahir, A.M., et al.: COVID-19 infection localization and severity grading from chest x-ray images. Comput. Biol. Med. **139**, 105002 (2021). https://doi.org/10.1016/j.compbiomed.2021.105002, https://www.sciencedirect.com/science/article/pii/S0010482521007964
56. Tschandl, P., Rosendahl, C., Kittler, H.: The ham10000 dataset, a large collection of multi-source dermatoscopic images of common pigmented skin lesions. Sci. Data **5**, 180161 (2018). https://doi.org/10.1038/sdata.2018.161
57. Twinanda, A.P., Shehata, S., Mutter, D., Marescaux, J., de Mathelin, M., Padoy, N.: Endonet: a deep architecture for recognition tasks on laparoscopic videos. CoRR abs/1602.03012 (2016). http://arxiv.org/abs/1602.03012
58. Wasserthal, J., et al.: Totalsegmentator: robust segmentation of 104 anatomic structures in CT images. Radiol. Artif. Intelli. **5**(5), e230024 (2023). https://doi.org/10.1148/ryai.230024
59. Xu, Z., et al.: Codabench: flexible, easy-to-use, and reproducible meta-benchmark platform. Patterns **3**(7), 100543 (2022)
60. Yang, J., et al.: Autosegmentation for thoracic radiation treatment planning: a grand challenge at AAPM 2017. Med. Phys. **45**(10), 4568–4581 (2018). https://doi.org/10.1002/mp.13141, https://aapm.onlinelibrary.wiley.com/doi/abs/10.1002/mp.13141
61. Zhang, C., et al.: Faster segment anything: towards lightweight SAM for mobile applications (2023). https://doi.org/10.48550/arXiv.2306.14289
62. Zhang, Z., Cai, H., Han, S.: EfficientViT-SAM: accelerated segment anything model without performance loss. In: CVPR Workshop: Efficient Large Vision Models (2024)

RepViT-MedSAM: Efficient Segment Anything in the Medical Images

Qasim Ali[✉][iD], Yuhao Chen[iD], and Alex Wong[iD]

University of Waterloo, Waterloo, ON, Canada
{m45ali,yuhao.chen1,alexander.wong}@uwaterloo.ca

Abstract. Segmenting medical images to identify lesions, organs and other areas of interest is crucial for diagnosis and treatment decisions. Traditionally, segmentation is accomplished through manual tools or using automated task-specific neural network models. A promising alternative solution to this problem is to create general-purpose models for segment anything in medical images, such as MedSAM [8]. These foundation models can segment regions across a multitude of modalities, at levels comparable to task-specific models. However, these models are often large and computationally expensive, preventing them from being used in clinical settings where they lack dedicated GPUs. We propose an efficient model for the segment anything in medical images problem, RepViT-MedSAM, created from a two step training process. First, the image encoder of MedSAM is distilled into a more efficient RepViT feature detector using aggressively augmented medical images. Then the entire end-to-end model, with the prompt encoder and mask decoder, is fine-tuned using ground truth masks and MedSAM's predictions. On the test set, RepViT-MedSAM surpasses the performance of baseline MedSAM in performance and efficiency, achieving an average Dice Similarity Coefficient (DSC) of 0.8528, an average Normalized Surface Distance (NSD) of 0.8666, taking a total execution time of 195 s, and ranking 12/23 among other contestants. RepViT-SAM offers a promising solution for real-world medical image segmentation with its efficiency and accuracy. The code for this project is available at https://github.com/icecap360/TurboMedSAM.

Keywords: Segment Anything · SAM · Medical Image Segmentation · Image Segmentation · Efficient Neural Networks · CNN · SAM · RepViT

1 Introduction

Medical imaging empowers physicians when making diagnostic and treatment decisions, giving them valuable insights into specific regions. Segmentation is a core component of medical imaging analysis, used to delineate regions of interest (ROI) a professional may deem useful [7]. Manual image segmentation is a labour-intensive and time-consuming process often requiring professional expertise. Many semi- or fully automatic segmentation algorithms are designed to operate in particular image modalities or delineate particular anatomical structures and pathological regions [7]. These limitations indicate the need for a Foundation Model [2] for medical image segmentation, that can generalize to a wide variety of modalities and regions of interest.

Foundation Models, deep neural networks trained on broad data at scale, have been shown to generalize to a wide range of downstream tasks [2]. SAM [6] is a image segmentation foundation model used to delineate regions in natural images. However, SAM is a heavy transformer model with substantial computational requirements, preventing it from being used in resource-constrained environments. Mobile-SAM [16] creates a lightweight SAM for mobile hardware. They distill the image-encoder of SAM into a lightweight TinyViT, retaining the prompt encoder and mask decoder architecture. They train their model on a 1% of the SA-1B dataset [6]. Similarly, RepViT-SAM [11] follows an identical design to MobileSAM but use an efficient CNN (RepViT [10]) architecture for their image encoder. Efficient-ViT SAM [17] distills the image-encoder of SAM into an Efficient-ViT, retaining the prompt encoder and mask decoder. They train the image encoder on the whole SA-1B dataset [6].

MedSAM [8] is a recent foundation model for medical segmentation on a multitude of different modalities and regions of interest. It exhibits better accuracy and robustness than modality-wise specialist models. MedSAM is however a large model, with over 90 Million parameters, preventing it from being used in resource-constrained settings. This prevents MedSAM from being used in many clinical settings, where PCs often lack dedicated GPU hardware. The original authors released an efficient MedSAM, LiteMedSAM [1]. LiteMedSAM distills the ViT-B [4] image encoder of MedSAM into a TinyViT [13]. However, LiteMedSAM results in a significant decrease in performance relative to MedSAM.

This paper describes a solution of the "waterlooviplab" team to the "CVPR2024 Segment Anything in Medical Images on Laptop" challenge. The challenge involves training an efficient segment anything foundation model for medical imaging. A key constraint is that the evaluation platform consists of a 3.6 GHz Intel Xeon CPU, 8G of RAM, and no GPUs. Another difficulty is the scale of the dataset, consisting of over 1.5 million training samples across 11 image modalities, which is large relative to the compute available to the team.

Building upon RepViT-SAM [11] architecture, our solution uses the RepViT [10] architecture as the image encoder instead of the heavy vision transformer (ViT-B) [4]. The first stage of training consists of distilling the MedSAM encoder into a RepViT backbone using aggressively augmented images. Afterwards, we fine-tune the full MedSAM model, with the prompt encoder and mask decoder using labeled ground truth (GT) masks and MedSAM [8] predictions. The final trained model surpasses MedSAM in performance and efficiency. On the test set, RepViT-MedSAM achieves an average Dice Similarity Coefficient (DSC) of 0.8528, an average Normalized Surface Distance (NSD) of 0.8666, a total execution time of 195 s, and ranking 12/23 among other contestants.

2 Method

Our proposed architecture follows the design described in SAM, but we replace the image encoder with the efficient feature detector RepViT. Our two step training procedure, distillation and fine-tuning, are illustrated in Fig. 1. The usage of two phases helps to stabilize training between the encoder and decoder.

2.1 Preprocessing

We maintain the file format provided, saving each image-mask pair in the same npz file. We split 3D voxel grids into 2D slices. In the interest of simplicity, we use a PyTorch dataloader that loads image-mask pairs from the npz files. The bounding box prompts of the training set were computed on the fly using randomly perturbed ground truth masks. To preserve fine image details crucial for accurate analysis, bounding boxes, masks, and images are resized to 1024×1024. The input image is also normalized to a mean of 0 and standard deviation of 1. The mean and standard deviation were calculated from images on the training set.

2.2 Architecture

The architecture was chosen to be similar to the original MedSAM, but with a RepViT as the image encoder. The prompt encoder and mask decoder remain the same.

RepViT [10] is a MobileNetV3 [5] based CNN that incorporates architectural design efficiencies of modern lightweight ViTs. It outperformed existing state of the art lightweight ViTs of similar size, while exhibiting favourable latency on mobile devices such as the iPhone12. We choose the RepViT-M1.1 variant, as its speed on CPU was significantly less than that of the contest baseline which used a TinyViT [13] backbone. Following [13], we set the stride of the last downsampling depth-wise convolution to 1 (instead of 2) to make the output resolution compatible with the mask decoder in the original MedSAM.

Our main strategy for improving inference on CPU was to choose a CNN, RepViT, as our image encoder. The logic being that because CNNs contain many local operations and lack expensive global operators (such as self-attention) they would be more efficient on CPUs.

2.3 Training Pipeline

In the distillation phase of training Fig. 1a, the ViT-B image encoder of the MedSAM model is distilled into a smaller RepViT. Each image is augmented with random crop, random horizontal flip, and random vertical flip. Prior work showed that a student model can outperform its teacher provided that it has a sufficiently large model capacity and aggressive data augmentation is applied [3]. An aggressive augmentation can be described as one that reduces the covariance

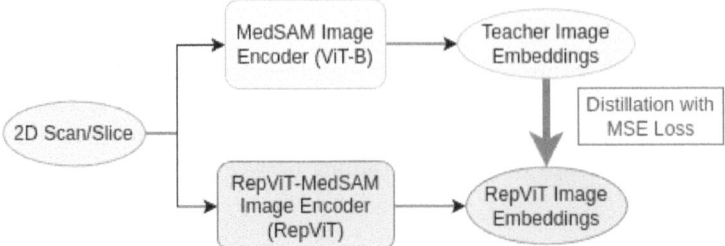

(a) Distillation process, MedSAM's image encoder is distilled using mean square error.

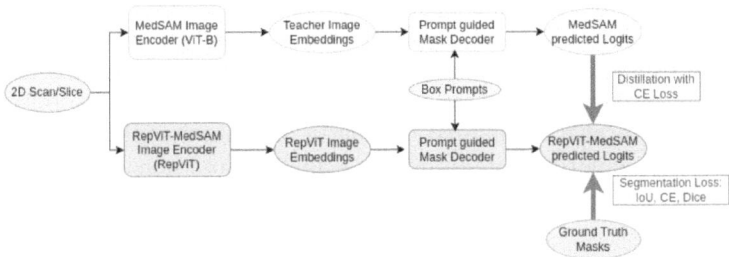

(b) Fine-tuning process, the loss is composed of two components, segmentation loss from the ground truth segmentations and distillation loss from MedSAM's image encoder.

Fig. 1. Illustrations of the two phases of training, Distillation and Fine-tuning. Blue ovals indicate data and rounded rectangles indicate models. Gray rectangles and their corresponding red arrows indicate losses. (Color figure online)

of the teacher-student cross-entropy [12]. Given these findings, we choose to randomly apply one of the following three augmentations on a given batch - CutMix [15], MixPatch [3], or no augmentation. The loss function is simply the mean-square error (MSE) loss between the student feature map and the teacher feature map.

During the second phase of training, fine-tuning 1b, we train end to end with the prompt encoder and mask decoder. The prompt encoder and mask decoder are initialized with the MedSAM weights. Each image is augmented with basic transformations; random horizontal flip and random vertical flip. The loss during this stage contains two components, segmentation loss with the ground truth masks, and distillation loss where the teacher targets are the MedSAM predicted logits. The segmentation loss is designed to be well-suited for diverse medical image applications, composed of intersection over union (IoU) loss, cross-entropy (CE) loss, and dice loss [9]. The distillation loss is the cross-entropy between the predicted logits and MedSAM logits.

2.4 Post-processing

The final masks are computed by resizing the predicted logits to the original image size, followed by a sigmoid activation function.

3 Experiments

3.1 Dataset and Evaluation Measures

The dataset consisted of 1,516,396 image mask pairs from 11 image modalities, containing both 3D and 2D data. The dataset was significantly imbalanced, with CT scans and MR scans accounting for 78% and 12% of the data respectively. The CT and MR scans contain many more data samples primarily because the preprocessing decided to split the 3D voxels into 2D slices. The 2D image modalities exhibited a imbalance in their distribution, as the PET, Endoscopy, and X-Ray datasets take approximately 43%, 29%, and 22% respectively. We do not use any external public datasets for model development.

The evaluation metrics mirrored the ranking metrics used by the CVPR 2024 MedSAM on Laptop Contest. They included two accuracy measures-Dice Similarity Coefficient (DSC) and Normalized Surface Dice (NSD)-alongside one efficiency measure-running time.

3.2 Implementation Details

Environment Settings. The development environments and requirements are presented in Table 1.

Table 1. Development environments and requirements. (mandatory table)

System	Ubuntu 18.04.5 LTS
CPU	AMD Ryzen Threadripper PRO 5955WX 16-Cores 1800 MHz
RAM	264 GB
GPU (number and type)	3 NVIDIA RTX A6000 49G
CUDA version	12.0
Programming language	Python 3.11
Deep learning framework	torch 2.4.0, torchvision 0.19.0, timm 0.9.16
Specific dependencies	
Code	https://github.com/icecap360/TurboMedSAM

Training Protocols. In the distillation phase of training, aggressive augmentation is used. Each image is augmented with random crop, random horizontal flip, and random vertical flip. Furthermore, we randomly apply one of the following three augmentations on all batches - CutMix [15], MixPatch [3], or no augmentation. During fine-tuning, we apply minimal data augmentation using just random horizontal flip and random vertical flip. We found that this prevented the corruption of the masks and improved training stability.

A class-balanced sampler was used, ensuring that the model performs equally well on all modalities regardless of the number of training images for each modality.

Three metrics are used to assess the performance of a model; Dice Similarity Coefficient (DSC), Normalized Surface Dice (NSD), and running time (sec). A model is better than another model if its performance on two of the three metrics is superior.

The training protocols during distillation are presented in Table 3 and protocols during fine-tuning are presented in Table 2.

4 Results and Discussion

4.1 Quantitative Results on Validation Set

The results of the proposed method on the validation set are displayed in Table 4. Our model outperforms MedSAM on both accuracy metrics, achieving an Average Dice Similarity Coefficient (DSC) of 0.8626 and Average Normalized Surface Distance (NSD) of 0.8828. This represents a significant improvement over MedSAM's 0.8528 DSC and 0.8666 NSD. As per the validation rankings it placed 6th in average DSC and 4th in average NSD, where its performance relative to the 5 higher ranked (as per DSC) teams lagged most severely in Ultrasound and X-Ray imagery.

The model performed best on Dermoscopy and Endoscopy based on average DSC and average NSD scores respectively. It performed most poorly on the PET and X-Ray modalities based on DSC. The results on the different modalities are expected, as Dermoscopy and Endoscopy are RGB images where the target is often large, clearly delineated and isolated in the frame.

Table 2. Training protocols during fine-tuning.

Teacher Model	MedSAM [8]
Initial decoder and prompt encoder weights	MedSAM [8]
Batch size	10
Image size	$1024 \times 1024 \times 3$
Patch size	16×16
Total epochs	9
Optimizer	AdamW
Initial learning rate (lr)	$1e-3 \times 10 \times \times 3/256$
Lr decay schedule	Decay 0.1 after 2 epochs
Warmup	Learning rate $1e-4$ for first epoch
Training time	96 h
Loss function	Dice loss with GT+ IoU with GT + CE with GT + CE with teacher
Number of model parameters	12.56M
Number of flops	86.15 GLOPs
CO_2eq	45.395 kg

Table 3. Training protocols during distillation

Teacher Model	MedSAM [8]
Batch size	10
Image size	$1024 \times 1024 \times 3$
Patch size	16×16
Total epochs	9
Optimizer	AdamW
Initial learning rate (lr)	5e−4
Lr decay schedule	None
Training time	48 h
Loss function	MSE
Number of model parameters	8.5M
Number of flops	82.6 GLOPs
CO_2eq	6.47 kg

Table 4. Quantitative evaluation results on the validation set. Baseline corresponds to the performance of MedSAM [8], Ablation 1 corresponds to not using distillation during finetuning and Ablation 2 corresponds to not using aggressive augmentation during distillation. All results are in percentage (%)

Target	Baseline		Ablation 1		Ablation 2		Proposed Ep4		Proposed Ep9	
	DSC	NSD	DSC	NSD	DSC	NSD	DSC	NSD	DSC	NSD
CT	0.9266	0.9532	0.9083	0.9387	0.9106	0.9407	0.9215	0.9523	0.9239	0.9541
MR	0.9041	0.9395	0.8605	0.9072	0.852	0.9008	0.8727	0.9168	0.8769	0.9208
PET	0.6312	0.4818	0.7255	0.5638	0.7263	0.61	0.6934	0.5272	0.7381	0.6172
US	0.9192	0.9555	0.7831	0.8289	0.8109	0.8584	0.8086	0.8556	0.8015	0.8478
X-Ray	0.7828	0.8401	0.3785	0.3637	0.7052	0.7679	0.7563	0.8162	0.759	0.8184
Dermotology	0.9137	0.9281	0.8961	0.9116	0.9344	0.9498	0.941	0.9563	0.9441	0.9592
Endoscopy	0.9683	0.9886	0.9282	0.9583	0.9175	0.9496	0.9204	0.9488	0.9313	0.9615
Fundus	0.9501	0.9664	0.9367	0.9534	0.9178	0.9359	0.9255	0.9435	0.9214	0.9395
Microscopy	0.679	0.7465	0.8271	0.8845	0.8383	0.9016	0.8648	0.9255	0.867	0.927
Average	0.8528	0.8666	0.8049	0.8122	0.8459	0.8683	0.856	0.8714	0.8626	0.8828

We also perform two ablations, using the same training protocols in Tables 3, 2 but in the interest of training time we report results Table 4 after only 4 epochs of fine-tuning instead of 9. Ablation 1 corresponds to not adding distillation loss (calculated from MedSAMs predicted logits) during the fine-tuning stage. Ablation 2 corresponds to not using aggressive data augmentations during the distillation phase. As can be seen from the results, neither ablation performs as well as the proposed method after 4 epochs of training.

4.2 Qualitative Results on Validation Set

Figure 2 displays some results on the validation set, for which ground truth was unavailable. Figure 2a shows multiple successful segmentations, showcasing that given a prompt the model can successfully recognize the correct object. However several issues persist. Firstly segmentations often fail to correctly delineate precise boundaries of the lesion or organ. Figure 2b showcases undersegmentation, where the model fails to delineate regions close to the edges of the organ. In Fig. 2c the segmentation leaks beyond the intended lesion. The model also fails to delineate fine details, as seen in the delineation of teeth of Fig. 2d. Secondly the shape of the segmentations are sometimes incoherent, with non-smooth boundaries, disjoint elements and holes. For example, the segmentation associated with the dark green prompt in Fig. 2d features a non-smooth boundary, contains disjoint components and internal gaps.

4.3 Segmentation Efficiency Results on Validation Set

The running time of several test cases are shown in Table 5. The measurements were taken on an Intel Core i9-9920X 3.50 GHz CPU. The average segmentation time of the proposed method and baseline (LiteMedSAM) was 2.53 s and 3.184 s respectively.

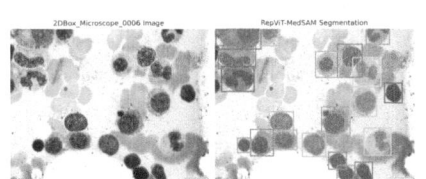

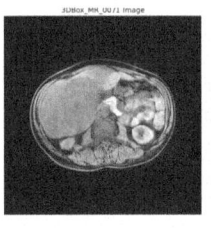

(a) Successful segmentation

(b) Failure to delineate the boundary of large isolated object.

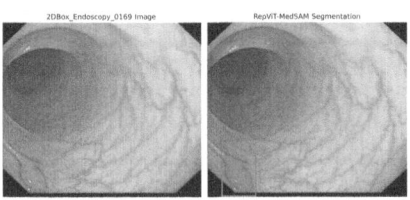

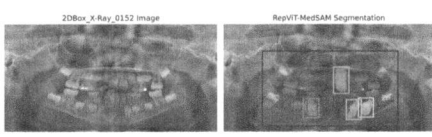

(c) Leakage of segmentation boundary.

(d) Inability to delineate shape of small teeth, and incoherent segmentation of dark green prompt.

Fig. 2. Sample predictions of the proposed method. (Color figure online)

Table 5. Quantitative evaluation of segmentation efficiency in terms of running time (sec).

Case ID	Size	Num. Objects	Baseline	Proposed
3DBox_CT_0566	(287, 512, 512)	6	197.977	161.506
3DBox_CT_0888	(237, 512, 512)	6	53.563	41.840
3DBox_CT_0860	(246, 512, 512)	1	7.6142	6.0781
3DBox_MR_0621	(115, 400, 400)	6	91.684	65.990
3DBox_MR_0121	(64, 290, 320)	6	53.810	43.988
3DBox_MR_0179	(84, 512, 512)	1	7.0516	5.8353
3DBox_PET_0001	(264, 200, 200)	1	4.5094	3.5300
2DBox_US_0525	(256, 256, 3)	1	0.3707	0.3072
2DBox_X-Ray_0053	(320, 640, 3)	34	0.9485	0.9216
2DBox_Dermoscopy_0003	(3024, 4032, 3)	1	0.6430	0.5223
2DBox_Endoscopy_0086	(480, 560, 3)	1	0.3644	0.3148
2DBox_Fundus_0003	(2048, 2048, 3)	1	0.4358	0.3652
2DBox_Microscope_0008	(1536, 2040, 3)	19	0.8528	0.7943
2DBox_Microscope_0016	(1920, 2560, 3)	241	6.2376	6.2868

4.4 Results on Final Testing Set

The results of the testing set of the contest are shown in Table 6. The total execution time was 194.73 s, measured on an Intel Xeon W-2133 3.60 GHz CPU. The average DSC was 0.8528 and the average NSD was 0.8666. The submission ranked 12/23 submissions according to rank-then-aggregate strategy (i.e. average of rank across nine modalities and three metrics).

Table 6. Quantitative evaluation results on the test set. All results are in percentage (%)

Target	DSC (%)	NSD (%)	Runtime (s)
CT	0.730759	0.786019	38.66128
MR	0.733583	0.693984	17.5917
PET	0.606909	0.544005	74.11131
US	0.887694	0.934459	9.666569
X-Ray	0.752008	0.855376	7.075892
Endoscopy	0.943635	0.970323	7.096959
Fundus	0.865523	0.885222	7.124286
Microscopy	0.881099	0.899042	7.176372
OCT	0.759746	0.823903	6.761073
Average	0.8528	0.8666	19.4739

4.5 Limitation and Future Work

While the proposed method is able to identify regions of various sizes, it struggles to form coherent segmentations and delineate accurate boundaries. The issues are particularly pronounced on objects with intricate shapes and objects in cluttered settings. A possible reason for these shortcomings is the reliance solely on high level feature maps. Incorporating low level feature maps that capture finer and more detailed semantics would help to alleviate this issue.

Further potential improvements include incorporating the 3D structure of voxel grids for 3D images, as treating each slice independently ignores the 3D relationships among the slices. Another potential improvement can be made to the final inference model, where pruning and quantization can be applied to improve inference speed.

5 Conclusion

In this paper we detailed the design of RepViT-MedSAM, an efficient model for the segment anything in medical images problem. We replace the image encoder of the MedSAM baseline with a RepViT variant. Our novel distillation pipeline consists of first aggressively distilling the image encoder features into RepViT, and then fine-tuning the end to end model using ground truth masks and MedSAM's predicted logits. The model achieved an impressive average DSC of 0.8626 and average NSD of 0.8828. However key limitations remain, including the ability to delineate intricate boundaries and form well-defined segmentations.

Acknowledgements. We thank all the data owners for making the medical images publicly available and CodaLab [14] for hosting the challenge platform.

Disclosure of Interests. The authors have no competing interests to declare that are relevant to the content of this article.

References

1. Bo Wang, J.M.: Litemedsam (2024). https://github.com/bowang-lab/MedSAM/tree/LiteMedSAM
2. Bommasani, R., et al.: On the opportunities and risks of foundation models (2022)
3. Deng, X., Zheng, J., Zhang, Z.: Personalized education: blind knowledge distillation (2022)
4. Dosovitskiy, A., et al.: An image is worth 16x16 words: transformers for image recognition at scale (2021)
5. Howard, A., et al.: Searching for mobilenetv3 (2019)
6. Kirillov, A., et al.: Segment anything. In: Proceedings of the International Conference on Computer Vision, pp. 4015–4026 (2023)
7. Liu, X., Song, L., Liu, S., Zhang, Y.: A review of deep-learning-based medical image segmentation methods. Sustainability **13**(3) (2021). https://doi.org/10.3390/su13031224, https://www.mdpi.com/2071-1050/13/3/1224

8. Ma, J., He, Y., Li, F., Han, L., You, C., Wang, B.: Segment anything in medical images. Nat. Commun. **15**(1), 654 (2024)
9. Sudre, C.H., Li, W., Vercauteren, T., Ourselin, S., Jorge Cardoso, M.: Generalised dice overlap as a deep learning loss function for highly unbalanced segmentations. In: Cardoso, M.J., et al. (eds.) DLMIA/ML-CDS -2017. LNCS, vol. 10553, pp. 240–248. Springer, Cham (2017). https://doi.org/10.1007/978-3-319-67558-9_28
10. Wang, A., Chen, H., Lin, Z., Han, J., Ding, G.: RepViT: revisiting mobile CNN from ViT perspective (2024)
11. Wang, A., Chen, H., Lin, Z., Han, J., Ding, G.: RepViT-SAM: towards real-time segmenting anything (2024)
12. Wang, H., Lohit, S., Jones, M., Fu, Y.: What makes a "good" data augmentation in knowledge distillation – a statistical perspective (2023)
13. Wu, K., et al.: TinyViT: fast pretraining distillation for small vision transformers (2022)
14. Xu, Z., et al.: Codabench: flexible, easy-to-use, and reproducible meta-benchmark platform. Patterns **3**(7), 100543 (2022)
15. Yun, S., Han, D., Oh, S.J., Chun, S., Choe, J., Yoo, Y.: Cutmix: regularization strategy to train strong classifiers with localizable features (2019)
16. Zhang, C., et al.: Faster segment anything: towards lightweight SAM for mobile applications. arXiv preprint arXiv:2306.14289 (2023)
17. Zhang, Z., Cai, H., Han, S.: EfficientViT-SAM: accelerated segment anything model without performance loss. In: CVPR Workshop: Efficient Large Vision Models (2024)

U-MedSAM: Uncertainty-Aware MedSAM for Medical Image Segmentation

Xin Wang[1]($\boxtimes$) , Xiaoyu Liu[2], Peng Huang[3], Pu Huang[2], Shu Hu[4], and Hongtu Zhu[5]

[1] College of Integrated Health Sciences and the AI Plus Institute, University at Albany, State University of New York (SUNY), Albany, USA
xwang56@albany.edu
[2] School of Physics and Electronics, Shandong Normal University, Jinan, China
huangpu@sdnu.edu.cn
[3] School of Computing and Artificial Intelligence, Southwest Jiaotong University, Chengdu, China
huangpeng@my.swjtu.edu.cn
[4] Department of Computer and Information Technology, Purdue University, West Lafayette, USA
hu968@purdue.edu
[5] University of North Carolina at Chapel Hill, Chapel Hill, USA
htzhu@email.unc.edu

Abstract. Medical Image Foundation Models have proven to be powerful tools for mask prediction across various datasets. However, accurately assessing the uncertainty of their predictions remains a significant challenge. To address this, we propose a new model, U-MedSAM, which integrates the MedSAM model with an uncertainty-aware loss function and the Sharpness-Aware Minimization (SharpMin) optimizer. The uncertainty-aware loss function automatically combines region-based, distribution-based, and pixel-based loss designs to enhance segmentation accuracy and robustness. SharpMin improves generalization by finding flat minima in the loss landscape, thereby reducing overfitting. Our method was evaluated in the CVPR24 MedSAM on Laptop challenge, where U-MedSAM demonstrated promising performance.

Keywords: Medical Image Segmentation · Segment Anything Model · Uncertainty-aware Learning · Sharpness-Aware Minimization

1 Introduction

Medical image segmentation is vital in clinical practice, enabling precise medicine [23,24], assessing therapeutic outcomes, and disease diagnosis by delineating organ boundaries and pathological regions, enhancing anatomical understanding, and abnormality detection [6]. Early segmentation models for medical images are typically designed for specific tasks with limited data. They might not handle the complex patterns and minute variations in medical images, which are often critical for clinical diagnosis and health science study [14].

Recently, foundation models, such as MedSAM [17] have been developed for medical image segmentation [10,26,27] (See Fig. 1), which are more strong, efficient, and applicable to different data modalities and situations. However, the uncertainty of the learning process associated with MedSAM on the diverse dataset has not been thoroughly investigated. By understanding this uncertainty, we can improve the robustness of MedSAM, making it more trustworthy for practical applications [21].

In this paper, we address the above challenge by proposing the U-MedSAM model, an extension of the MedSAM model [17], and improve its training by incorporating a **novel uncertainty-aware hidden task learning**. The uncertainty-aware framework enables the model to balance different aspects of the segmentation sub-tasks (e.g., boundary, pixel, region) adaptively, improving overall performance and robustness,

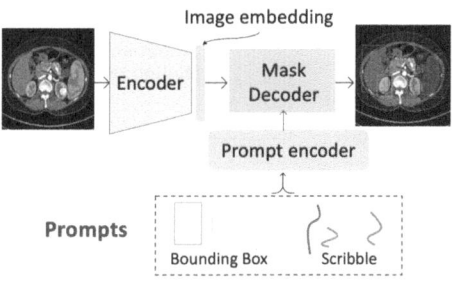

Fig. 1. Overview of the MedSAM [17].

and addressing issues like class imbalance [2]. Specifically, our newly introduced uncertainty-aware loss function integrates three components [8]: (1) *Pixel-based loss*: Measures differences at the pixel level (*e.g.*, Mean Squared Error loss) [16]. (2) *Region-based loss*: Used for regions segmentation (*e.g.*, Dice coefficient loss). (3) *Distribution-based loss*: Compares predicted and ground truth distributions (*e.g.*, Cross-entropy loss and Shape-Distance loss). Finally, we utilize the **Sharpness-Aware Minimization (SharpMin) optimizer** [3,11–14] to improve the generalization of our U-MedSAM. We evaluate and compare our method against state-of-the-art MedSAM models, demonstrating superior performance. Our approach achieves optimal results by promoting sharper and more precise segmentation boundaries, thereby enhancing the accuracy and robustness.

In summary, we make the following key contributions:

- We introduce an uncertainty-aware learning loss combining pixel-based loss (*e.g.*, Mean Squared Error loss), region-based loss (*e.g.*, Dice coefficient loss), and distribution-based loss (*e.g.*, Cross-entropy loss and Shape-Distance loss). This design enables the model to conveniently incorporate any loss function for training the model jointly.
- By employing **auto-learnable weights** [9] rather than fixed weights, our model can dynamically adjust the contribution of each loss component based on the uncertainty associated with each prediction. This approach allows the model to prioritize confident predictions and reduce the impact of ambiguous or noisy data.
- By using the Sharpness-Aware Minimization (ShapMin) optimizer, our U-MedSAM finds parameter values that result in flat minima in the loss

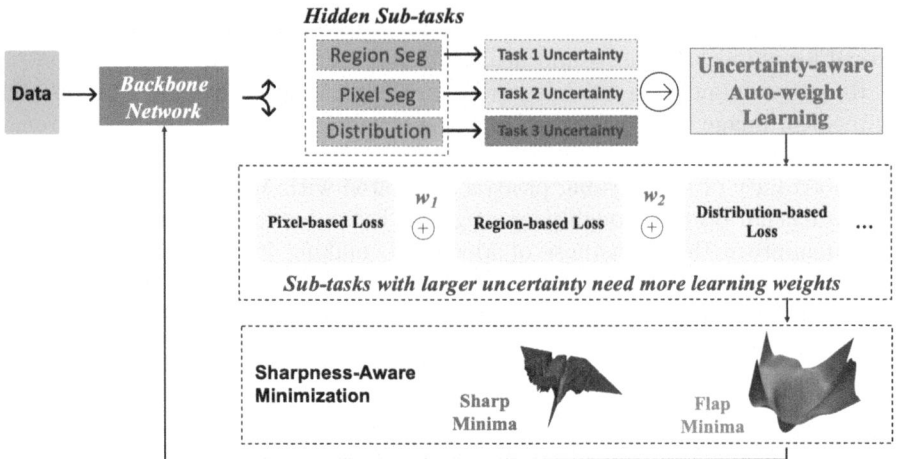

Fig. 2. Overview of our proposed **U-MedSAM model**: Building on the MedSAM architecture, we encode input images and introduce a novel uncertainty-aware learning method for automatic weight learning across multiple loss functions. The Sharpness-Aware Minimization (SharpMin) optimizer is employed, operating within a flattened loss landscape to enhance the generalization.

landscape. This technique improves the model's ability to generalize and mitigates overfitting, a common issue in deep learning applications for medical imaging [18].

2 Method

This section will describe the entire workflow and implementation details. Figure 2 shows an overview of our proposed method.

2.1 Preprocessing

We follow the preprocessing in LiteMedSAM implementation (baeline) [17].

2.2 Proposed Method

Knowledge Distillation. In the LiteMedSAM model, both the prompt encoder and mask decoder are lightweight models, and the image encoder compresses the model through TinyViT. However, TinyViT uses Softmax-based self-attention mechanism, and the computational complexity is still high. So, in order to reduce the computational complexity of the model, we use EfficientViT to replace TinyViT. EfficientViT reduces the computational complexity from quadratic to linear by lightweight ReLU linear attention. During the initialisation process, we use TinyViT as a teacher model for knowledge distillation, efficiently migrated to EfficientViT. Prompt encoder and mask decoder are already very lightweight models and no other changes were made. The knowledge distillation process was supervised using the L2 loss function.

Uncertainty-Aware Auto-learning. Uncertainty-aware learning enables the model to adapt its learning process based on detected uncertainties, enhancing resilience and precision by focusing on confident predictions and minimizing the influence of ambiguous ones [8]. This optimization of the training process across various datasets results in improved overall performance [28,29].

By incorporating uncertainty into the loss computation, the model can dynamically assign weights to each loss component [5]. This strategy effectively balances global and local accuracy while mitigating the impact of class imbalance. This approach allows the model to prioritize learning from reliable instances and reduce the impact of potentially erroneous or ambiguous data. Consequently, the model becomes more resilient to noisy or ambiguous data, leading to significantly improved segmentation performance [4,19,22].

The uncertainty-aware loss $\mathcal{L}$ if formulated as following:

$$\mathcal{L} = \sum_{m=1}^{M} \left(\frac{1}{2\sigma_m^2} \mathcal{L}_m + \log(1 + \sigma_m^2) \right) \tag{1}$$

where M is the number of individual loss components, $\mathcal{L}_m$ represents each individual loss component (such as DC, CE, MSE, and Shape-Distance loss), and σ_m are learnable noise parameters. Larger noise levels indicate that the talk is not properly understood, necessitating greater learning weights. These learnable parameters are optimized during the training process to minimize the overall loss. The last term can constrain the noise to be increased too much [20]. Specifically, we incorporate the following loss functions, see the survey [7] to find more losses.

1. **Mean Squared Error (MSE) loss**: This pixel-based loss ensures accurate classification of individual pixels by calculating the squared difference between each pixel's predicted value and the true label to quantify the model's prediction accuracy [7].
2. **Dice Coefficient (DC) loss**: This region-based metric emphasizes the overlap between predicted and ground truth areas, preserving the accuracy of the shape and boundaries of segmented regions [7].
3. **Cross-Entropy (CE) loss**: This distribution-based loss ensures accurate categorization of individual pixels, improving classification precision [7].
4. **Shape-Distance (SD) loss**: This distribution-based loss enhances shape features in image segmentation, strengthens boundary alignment, and ensures that the model pays closer attention to the geometric and structural information of the targets during the training process [1].

Sharpness-Aware Minimization. Our approach employs Sharpness aware Minimization (SharpMin) optimization [3,11,12,14,15,21] to enhance the generalization ability of U-MedSAM. By flattening the loss landscape, Sharpness-Aware optimization improves the model's generalization potential. Traditional optimization techniques target the lowest points in the loss landscape, which can be steep and result in poor generalization on new data. In contrast, Sharpness-Aware Minimization identifies smoother minima, regions in the parameter space where the model's performance remains consistent and less susceptible to disturbances.

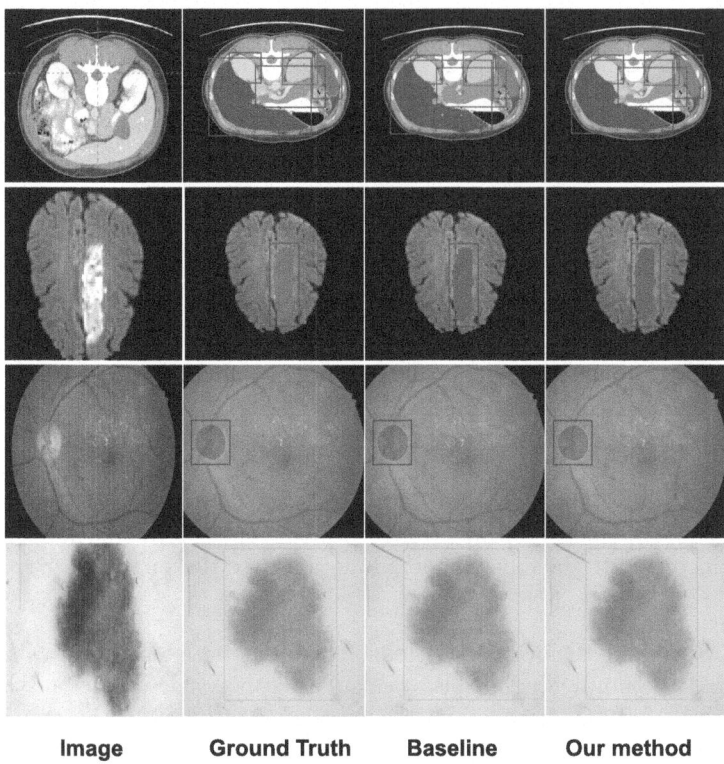

Fig. 3. Qualitative results of well-segmented from various modalities.

2.3 Post-processing

No post-processing techniques were applied, and no strategies were implemented to enhance inference speed.

3 Experiments

3.1 Dataset and Evaluation Measures

We only used the challenge dataset for model development.

The evaluation metrics consist of two accuracy measures: the Dice Similarity Coefficient (DSC) and Normalized Surface Dice (NSD), along with an efficiency

U-MedSAM: Uncertainty-Aware MedSAM for Medical Image Segmentation 211

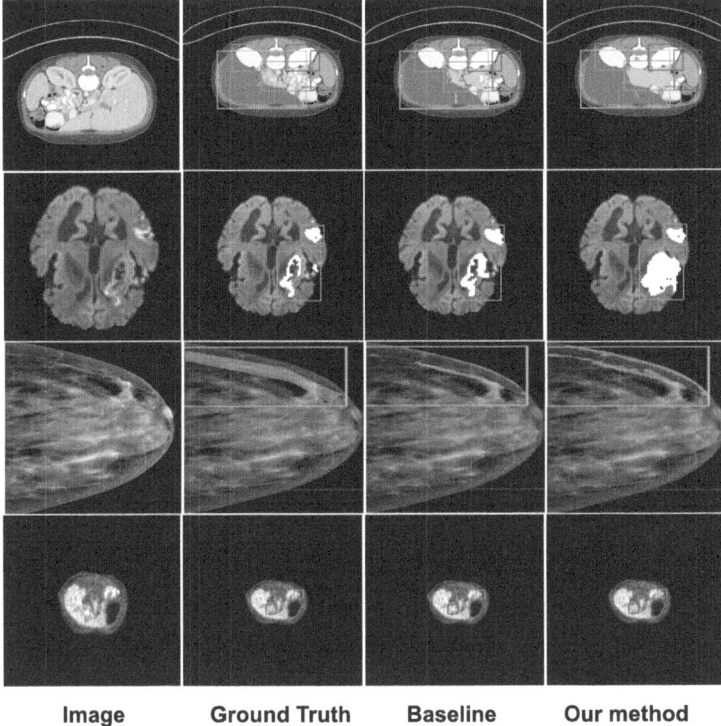

Fig. 4. Qualitative results of challenging examples from various modalities.

measure of running time. DSC is used to measure the degree of overlap between the segmentation result and the ground truth. And NSD is a surface-based distance metric for measuring the difference between segmentation boundaries, which takes into account the distance between the boundary of the segmentation result and the label boundary. They are calculated as follows in Eqs. 2 and 3:

$$\text{DSC} = \frac{2 \times |y \cap \hat{y}|}{|y| + |\hat{y}|} \tag{2}$$

$$\text{NSD} = \frac{|\{x \in y : d(x, \hat{y}) \leq T\}| + |\{x \in \hat{y} : d(x, y) \leq T\}|}{|y| + |\hat{y}|} \tag{3}$$

where, y and $\hat{y}$ represent the segmentation result and the ground truth, respectively. $d(x, A)$ denotes the shortest distance from point x to the surface of set A, and T is the tolerance distance threshold. Both DSC and NSD are closer to 1, indicating better segmentation performance, which implies a higher degree of overlap and boundary similarity between the predicted segmentation and the ground truth annotation. Together, these metrics contribute to the overall ranking computation.

Table 1. Development environments and requirements.

System	Ubuntu 20.04.1 LTS
CPU	Intel(R) Xeon(R) CPU E5-2690 v4 @ 2.60 GHz
RAM	125 GB; 1.03 MT/s
GPU (number and type)	Four NVIDIA Titan Xp
CUDA version	11.4
Programming language	Python 3.10.14
Deep learning framework	torch 2.1.2, torchvision 0.16.2

Table 2. Training protocols.

Pre-trained Model	SAM [10] MedSAM [17]
Batch size	2
Patch size	$256 \times 256 \times 3$
Total epochs	135
Optimizer	AdamW
Initial learning rate (lr)	0.00005
Lr decay schedule	ReduceLROnPlateau (mode = min, factor = 0.9, patience = 5, cooldown = 0)
Training time	370 h
Loss function	Dice loss, BCE loss, SD loss and IoU loss
Number of model parameters	N/A - not tracked
Number of flops	N/A - not tracked

3.2 Implementation Details

Environment Settings. The development environments and requirements are presented in Table 1 (Table 2).

Stage 1. Code and models are available at: https://github.com/liangzw599/Co-developed-by-LiteMedSAM.

Stage 2 (Post challenge analysis). Code and models are available at: https://github.com/liangzw599/Co-developed-by-LiteMedSAM.

Training Protocols. We follow the training protocols in LiteMedSAM implementation (baseline) [17].

4 Results and Discussion

4.1 Quantitative Results on Validation Set

Table 3 summarizes these results. The results demonstrate that incorporating uncertainty-aware loss and the SharpMin optimization indeed improves segmentation accuracy.

Training using only the SD loss yields 83.86% DSC. In comparison, training using the uncertainty-aware loss (which incorporates the DC loss, CE loss, and

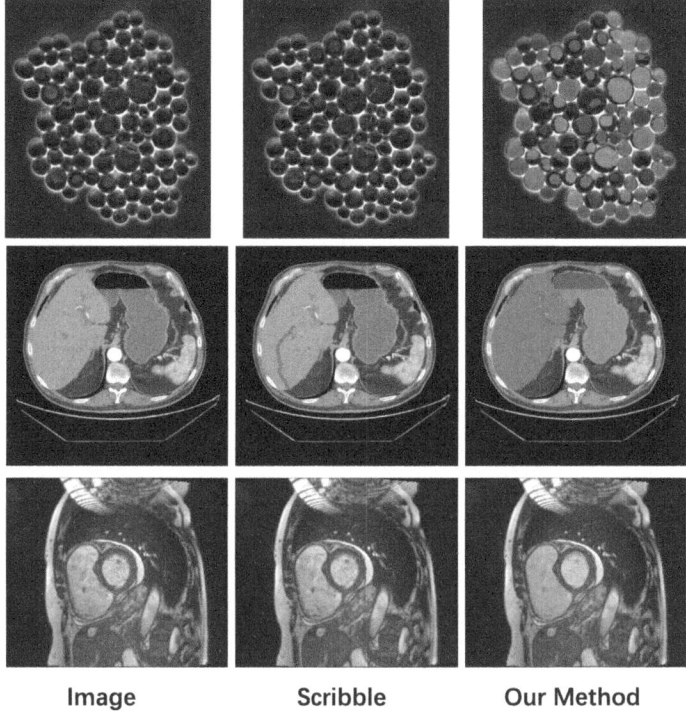

Fig. 5. Scribble-based cases with good results for various modality segmentations.

focused loss), enhances DSC to 85.48%. This result shows the capability of the uncertainty-aware loss to increase the robustness and accuracy of models by prioritizing confident predictions and minimizing the impact of uncertain ones. It effectively addresses the limitations of using a single loss function by balancing various aspects of the segmentation task.

Incorporating the SharpMin optimization into the uncertainty-aware loss yields 86.10% DSC, the highest among the examined approaches. SharpMin improves segmentation accuracy by generating clearer and more accurate borders, guiding the optimization process toward flat minima in the loss landscape. This leads to better generalization across diverse data samples. The increase in DSC from 85.48% to 86.10% highlights the effectiveness of SharpMin in enhancing segmentation results and more precisely identifying heart components.

4.2 Qualitative Results on Validation Set

We show some examples with good segmentation results in Fig. 3 and examples with bad segmentation results in Fig. 4. Figure 5 and Fig. 6 show the results of good and poor visualisation of scribble-based segmentation, respectively.

Table 3. Quantitative evaluation results.

Target	LiteMedSAM DSC (%)	LiteMedSAM NSD (%)	Only SD-loss DSC (%)	Only SD-loss NSD (%)	No SharpMin DSC (%)	No SharpMin NSD (%)	U-MedSAM DSC (%)	U-MedSAM NSD (%)
CT	89.10	91.03	87.20	89.63	89.61	91.66	**89.89**	**91.69**
MR	**83.28**	**86.10**	79.27	82.01	81.68	83.81	82.79	84.61
PET	55.10	29.12	65.23	47.23	66.34	**50.17**	**66.63**	48.71
US	**94.77**	**96.81**	83.40	88.63	84.30	89.27	85.23	90.38
X-Ray	75.83	80.39	78.59	84.31	83.22	88.94	**85.28**	**90.14**
Dermotology	92.47	93.85	93.83	95.32	93.89	95.34	**94.10**	**95.58**
Endoscopy	96.04	98.11	93.60	96.24	95.65	97.93	**96.24**	**98.33**
Fundus	94.81	96.41	95.45	97.05	94.87	96.50	**95.66**	**97.26**
Microscopy	61.63	65.38	78.20	84.59	**79.92**	**86.64**	79.05	85.33
Average	82.56	81.91	83.86	85.00	85.48	86.64	**86.10**	**86.89**

Table 4. Quantitative evaluation of segmentation efficiency in terms of running time (s). Note: The inference process cannot use GPU.

Case ID	Size	Num. Objects	Baseline	Proposed
3DBox_CT_0566	(287, 512, 512)	6	376.4	286.3
3DBox_CT_0888	(237, 512, 512)	6	100.5	88.7
3DBox_CT_0860	(246, 512, 512)	1	17.7	18.5
3DBox_MR_0621	(115, 400, 400)	6	157.1	146.7
3DBox_MR_0121	(64, 290, 320)	6	99.9	73.5
3DBox_MR_0179	(84, 512, 512)	1	17.1	9.8
3DBox_PET_0001	(264, 200, 200)	1	12.1	13.2
2DBox_US_0525	(256, 256, 3)	1	6.3	5.4
2DBox_X-Ray_0053	(320, 640, 3)	34	7.3	6.5
2DBox_Dermoscopy_0003	(3024, 4032, 3)	1	6.5	3.2
2DBox_Endoscopy_0086	(480, 560, 3)	1	6.1	7.3
2DBox_Fundus_0003	(2048, 2048, 3)	1	6.1	7.5
2DBox_Microscope_0008	(1536, 2040, 3)	19	6.8	6.4
2DBox_Microscope_0016	(1920, 2560, 3)	241	19.1	15.9

4.3 Segmentation Efficiency Results on Validation Set

As shown in Table 4, we compared the running speed of the proposed method to the LiteMedSAM (baseline) [17].

4.4 Results on Final Testing Set

This is a placeholder. We will announce the testing results for Post-challenge analysis.

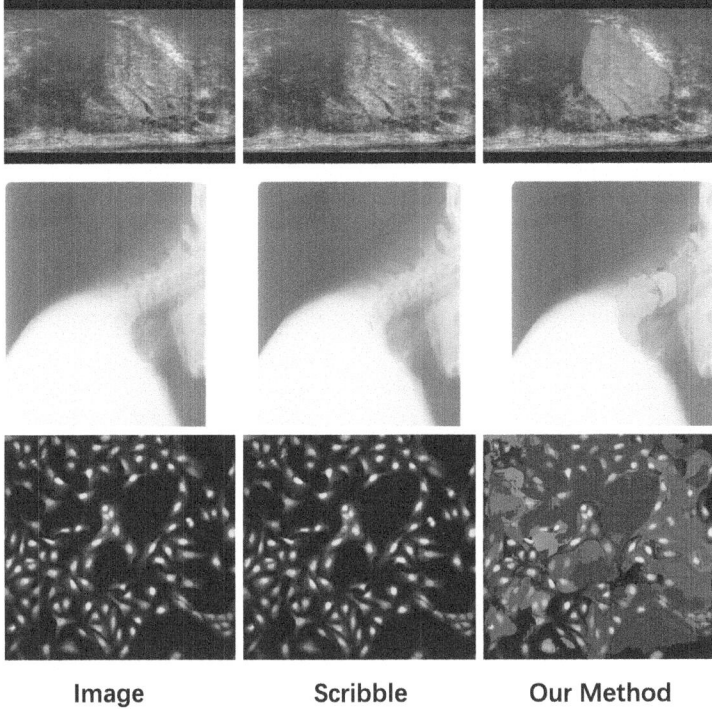

Fig. 6. Scribble-based cases with bad results for various modality segmentations.

4.5 Limitation and Future Work

Despite achieving promising dice scores, we did not optimize the model's speed, encountering limitations in this area.

In future work, we will explore various model compression techniques to address these speed constraints. Techniques such as quantization and tensor compression will be investigated to enhance the model's efficiency. Additionally, we will examine other advanced methods and approaches to further improve the performance and speed of the model. Our goal is to balance high accuracy with faster processing times, ensuring the model's effectiveness and efficiency for practical applications. By integrating these enhancements, we aim to develop a more robust and versatile model capable of handling real-world scenarios with greater ease and reliability.

5 Conclusion

We present U-MedSAM, an innovative model engineered for robust medical image segmentation. This model combines the MedSAM architecture with an uncertainty-aware learning framework to dynamically adjust the contribution of multiple loss functions. By employing the SharpMin optimizer, U-MedSAM is steered towards flat minima in the loss landscape, enhancing its resilience and improving generalization. Comparative analysis with top-performing models highlights U-MedSAM's superior accuracy and robustness in segmentation performance.

Acknowledgements. We thank all the data owners for making the medical images publicly available and CodaLab [25] for hosting the challenge platform. Xin Wang is supported by the University at Albany Start-up Grant.

Disclosure of Interests. The authors have no competing interests to declare that are relevant to the content of this article.

References

1. Chalcroft, L., et al.: Large-kernel attention for efficient and robust brain lesion segmentation. arXiv preprint arXiv:2308.07251 (2023)
2. Cho, M.S., Nguyen, T.: Improving segmentation with advanced loss functions. J. Comput. Diagnos. (2022)
3. Harper, J., Stone, M.: SAM optimizer: advancing model generalization. J. Mach. Learn. Res. (2022)
4. Hu, J., Fan, Q., Hu, S., Lyu, S., Wu, X., Wang, X.: UMedNeRF: uncertainty-aware single view volumetric rendering for medical neural radiance fields. In: IEEE International Symposium on Biomedical Imaging (2024)
5. Hu, S., Wang, X., Lyu, S.: Rank-based decomposable losses in machine learning: a survey. IEEE Trans. Pattern Anal. Mach. Intell. (2023)
6. Huang, P., Hu, S., Peng, B., Zhang, J., Wu, X., Wang, X.: Robustly optimized deep feature decoupling network for fatty liver diseases detection. In: Linguraru, M.G., et al. (eds.) MICCAI 2024. LNCS, vol. 15001, pp. 68–78. Springer, Cham (2024). https://doi.org/10.1007/978-3-031-72378-0_7
7. Jadon, S.: A survey of loss functions for semantic segmentation. In: 2020 IEEE Conference on Computational Intelligence in Bioinformatics and Computational Biology (CIBCB), pp. 1–7. IEEE (2020)
8. Kendall, A., Gal, Y., Cipolla, R.: Multi-task learning using uncertainty to weigh losses for scene geometry and semantics. In: Proceedings of the IEEE Conference on Computer Vision and Pattern Recognition, pp. 7482–7491 (2018)
9. Kim, J., Park, S.H.: Multiloss strategy for medical image segmentation. Comput. Med. (2023)
10. Kirillov, A., et al.: Segment anything. In: Proceedings of the International Conference on Computer Vision, pp. 4015–4026 (2023)
11. Lin, L., Amerini, I., Wang, X., Hu, S., et al.: Robust CLIP-based detector for exposing diffusion model-generated images. arXiv preprint arXiv:2404.12908 (2024)
12. Lin, L., He, X., Ju, Y., Wang, X., Ding, F., Hu, S.: Preserving fairness generalization in deepfake detection. In: CVPR (2024)
13. Lin, L., Krubha, Y.S., Yang, Z., Ren, C., Wang, X., Hu, S.: Robust COVID-19 detection in CT images with CLIP. In: MIPR (2024)
14. Lin, L., Papabathini, S., Wang, X., Hu, S.: Robust light-weight facial affective behavior recognition with CLIP. In: MIPR (2024)

15. Lin, L., Wang, X., Hu, S., et al.: AI-face: a million-scale demographically annotated AI-generated face dataset and fairness benchmark. arXiv preprint arXiv:2406.00783 (2024)
16. Ma, J., et al.: Loss odyssey in medical image segmentation. Med. Image Anal. **71**, 102035 (2021)
17. Ma, J., He, Y., Li, F., Han, L., You, C., Wang, B.: Segment anything in medical images. Nat. Commun. **15**(1), 654 (2024)
18. Murray, A., et al.: Deep learning in medical imaging: Overfitting issues. Med. Image Anal. (2022)
19. Peng, Y., et al.: Uncertainty-aware explainable recommendation with large language models. In: IJCNN (2024)
20. Tsai, T.Y., et al.: UU-Mamba: uncertainty-aware U-Mamba for cardiovascular segmentation. arXiv preprint arXiv:2409.14305 (2024)
21. Tsai, T.Y., Lin, L., Hu, S., Zhu, H., Wang, X., et al.: UU-Mamba: uncertainty-aware U-Mamba for cardiac image segmentation. arXiv preprint arXiv:2405.17496 (2024)
22. Wang, X., Hu, S., Fan, H., Zhu, H., Li, X.: Neural radiance fields in medical imaging: challenges and next steps. arXiv preprint arXiv:2402.17797 (2024)
23. Wang, X., et al.: Deep reinforcement learning for image-to-image translation. arXiv preprint arXiv:2309.13672 (2023)
24. Wang, X., Zhu, H.: Artificial intelligence in image-based cardiovascular disease analysis: a comprehensive survey and future outlook. arXiv:2402.03394 (2024)
25. Xu, Z., et al.: Codabench: flexible, easy-to-use, and reproducible meta-benchmark platform. Patterns **3**(7), 100543 (2022)
26. Zhang, C., et al.: Faster segment anything: towards lightweight SAM for mobile applications. arXiv preprint arXiv:2306.14289 (2023)
27. Zhang, Z., Cai, H., Han, S.: EfficientViT-SAM: accelerated segment anything model without performance loss. In: CVPR Workshop: Efficient Large Vision Models (2024)
28. Zhao, X., Chen, F., Hu, S., Cho, J.H.: Uncertainty aware semi-supervised learning on graph data. In: Advances in Neural Information Processing Systems, vol. 33, pp. 12827–12836 (2020)
29. Zhao, X., Hu, S., Cho, J.H., Chen, F.: Uncertainty-based decision making using deep reinforcement learning. In: 2019 22th International Conference on Information Fusion (FUSION), pp. 1–8. IEEE (2019)

Modality-Specific Strategies for Medical Image Segmentation Using Lightweight SAM Architectures

Thuy Dao[1]( ), Xincheng Ye[1], Joshua Scarsbrook[1],
Gowrienanthan Balarupan[1], Fernanda L. Ribeiro[1],
and Steffen Bollmann[1,2]

[1] School of Electrical Engineering and Computer Science, University of Queensland, Brisbane, Australia
thanhthuy.dao@uq.edu.au
[2] Queensland Digital Health Centre, University of Queensland, Brisbane, Australia

Abstract. Medical image segmentation tasks are often intricate and require medical domain expertise. Recent advancements in deep learning have expedited these demanding tasks, transitioning from specialized models tailored to each task to versatile foundation models capable of accommodating various image modalities. However, many of these foundation models are optimized for GPU computation, necessitating significant computational resources and constraining their practical utility in clinical settings. Furthermore, their variable accuracy across modalities and novel domains undermines their reliability in clinical practice. To address these limitations, we undertake a comparative investigation into deploying medical image segmentation models on CPU, focusing on accuracy and runtime efficiency, as part of the "*CVPR 2024: Segment Anything In Medical Images On Laptop*" challenge. Our methodology employs different models customized for each modality, including pre-trained EfficientViT-SAM and LiteMedSAM to yield the most precise and efficient outcomes. Additionally, to bolster model performance for datasets featuring small regions of interest, such as PET scans, we integrate a majority voting mechanism. We optimize runtime using the OpenVINO format within a C++ inference script. This approach improves inference runtime while maintaining competitive accuracy, achieving an average DSC score of **0.86** on the validation set and **0.75** on the testing set with an average runtime of **4.61 s** on the testing set. Notably, given that most modalities are evaluated in a zero-shot manner, our findings suggest that the zero-shot capability of foundation models can be further refined through dataset-specific inference strategies.

Keywords: Multi-modality · Zero-shot · OpenVINO · CPU Deployment

---

T. Dao and X. Ye—These authors contributed equally to this paper. F. L. Ribeiro and S. Bollmann—These authors contributed equally to this paper

© The Author(s), under exclusive license to Springer Nature Switzerland AG 2025
J. Ma et al. (Eds.): MedSAM on Laptop 2024, LNCS 15458, pp. 218–231, 2025.
https://doi.org/10.1007/978-3-031-81854-7_15

1 Introduction

Medical image segmentation, which involves manually delineating regions of interest (ROI), is a time-consuming endeavor. Furthermore, it requires a significant level of domain expertise for the precise identification of relevant landmarks and segmentation. The advent of deep learning marks a significant step forward to an automated solution for medical image segmentation [9]. Nevertheless, the variance between different medical image modalities and segmentation tasks makes developing a general segmentation model challenging [19]. However, recent advances in leveraging foundation models [1] have the potential to address these challenges. For example, by leveraging these pre-trained foundation models with prompt engineering techniques, one can optimize model performance without the need for model fine-tuning using large-scale medical image datasets.

Notably, the Segment Anything model (SAM) [5], a vision foundation model trained on a billion masks from 11 million natural scene images, has demonstrated immense potential to automate segmentation tasks. SAM is a promptable model—that is, it accepts prompts to guide segmentation, such as points, bounding boxes, or masks. While SAM shows strong zero-shot segmentation capabilities, differences in data statistics (intensity ranges and distributions) and inhomogeneity of medical images compared to natural scene images pose significant challenges, potentially limiting its performance [2,4,13].

Accordingly, MedSAM has been proposed to address the limited generalizability of SAM for medical image segmentation. It is a SAM-based model finetuned on one million medical image-ground truth segmentation pairs across 10 modalities [11]; it demonstrates a significant improvement in zero-shot medical image segmentation tasks in comparison to the original SAM. Nevertheless, given the large architecture footprint inherited from SAM, inference (or mask generation) requires GPU resources to perform efficiently and timely. This computing infrastructure requirement impedes the deployment of MedSAM in real-world scenarios, such as in clinical settings.

Therefore, there is a need for lightweight, promptable medical image segmentation models that can be deployed on laptops or edge devices without relying on expensive and scarce GPU resources. Accordingly, significant effort has been invested in various optimization techniques, such as model distillation, quantization, and pruning [12]. For example, LiteMedSAM consists of a distilled [8,15] version of MedSAM resulting in a more compact and efficient model, with reduced model size and, hence, inference time. Similarly, EfficientViT-SAM [18] replaces the heavy encoder of SAM with EfficientViT [7] through distillation. These studies have demonstrated the effectiveness of transferring knowledge to lightweight image encoders, showcasing their ability to reduce model size and runtime while maintaining accuracy to a considerable extent. However, their efficacy for zero-shot transfer to the medical imaging domain remains to be further investigated.

Here, we leverage these lightweight foundation models for efficient medical image segmentation using an edge device with limited memory and hardware (a 3.6GHz Intel CPU with 8G of RAM). To date, there is no one-size-fits-all solution for medical image segmentation; hence, we opt to use multiple lightweight foundation models in conjunction. Specifically, we explore the performance of different models—EfficientViT-SAM [18], EfficientSAM [16], and LiteMedSAM—across medical image modalities by comparing their accuracy and runtime. We further enhance model performance for 3D data with small regions of interest, such as PET scans, by integrating multiple-view knowledge and employing a majority voting strategy to combine segmentations across anatomical views. To reduce the model size, we converted the model into a lightweight format using OpenVINO. Finally, to accelerate deployment efficiency, we use a C++ inference script with an embedding caching mechanism that reduces runtime compared to the Python-based approach due to its compiled nature, optimized memory management, and direct hardware interaction [6]. This combination of strategies results in significant improvement in runtime while maintaining comparable accuracy on the validation set and testing set, demonstrating the potential of our solution to make advanced medical image segmentation models more accessible and efficient in practice without requiring an immense amount of labeled data for model fine-tuning.

2 Methods

2.1 Pre-processing

In the pre-processing phase, the intensity of each grey-scale 2D image (or 2D slices from 3D medical images) was normalized to the range of [0, 255]. Then, Gaussian normalization (which may produce negative values) was applied for EfficientSAM and EfficientViT-SAM, while min-max normalization (values are in the range of [0,1]) was applied for LiteMedSAM-based inference. The normalized images are then either padded or resized to match the required input dimension from each model (EfficientSAM: input image size of 1024×1024; EfficientViT-SAM: input image size of 512×512; LiteMedSAM: input image size of 256×256). Our models were validated using 3,278 images from the validation set (Table 1; see Sect. 3.1 for more information about the data).

Table 1. The validation set consists of both 2D images and 3D volumes across various modalities. The 2D data includes images from CT, MR, Microscopy, Dermoscopy, Endoscopy, Fundus, X-Ray, and Ultrasound—US, while the 3D data comprises volumetric scans from CT, MR and PET.

Modality	Microscopy	Dermoscopy	Endoscopy	Fundus	X-ray	US	PET	MR	CT
Number of Subjects	50	66	200	10	581	600	3	628	1140

2.2 Proposed Method

Our approach (Fig. 1) involves a tailored selection of SAM-based models for each medical image modality, combined with prompt engineering techniques designed to enhance segmentation accuracy. By customizing the model and prompts based on the specific characteristics of each modality, we aim to optimize performance across diverse imaging types and improve the overall robustness of the segmentation process.

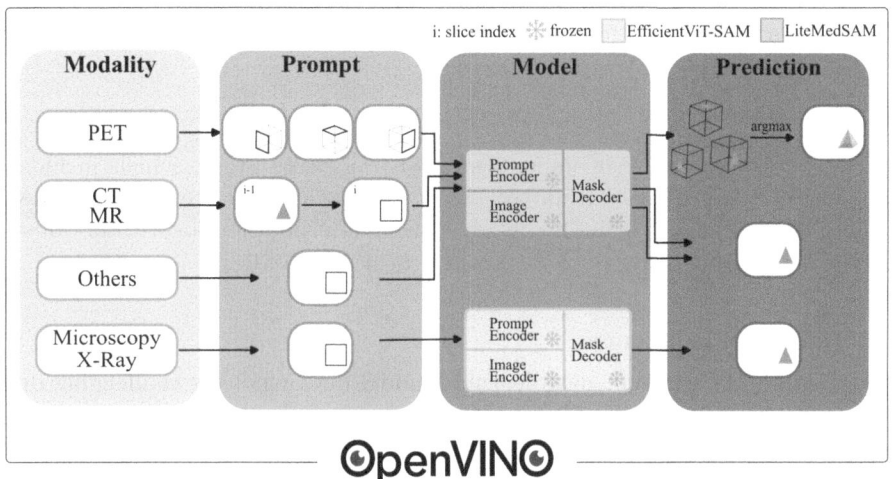

Fig. 1. Modality-specific strategy for medical image segmentation in edge device deployment.

Model Selection. Our approach combines modality-specific strategies that leverage the potential of zero-shot generalizability of lightweight, pre-trained SAM-based foundation models. We found that EfficientViT-SAM [18], LiteMedSAM, and EfficientSAM [16] demonstrated different generalizability across medical imaging modalities, requiring an empirical selection of inference models based on their performance.

Prompt Engineering. To enhance the zero-shot performance of foundation models, one promising approach is to explore different model prompts [14]. Prompts—a click (point) or a bounding box—provide the spatial priors for target location and segmentation. Specifically for 3D medical data, an ROI within the current inference slice shares a similar spatial location with the same ROI in adjacent slices. Given that these foundation models only take 2D images as input, it is possible to use the mask prediction of the current inference slice to generate a bounding box for the next inference slice. This strategy can be leveraged to improve the prompt by narrowing the bounding box to include only the ROI in an automated fashion.

3D Data Segmentation. Another challenge in deploying foundation models is the potential lack of consideration for 3D spatial information. A single anatomical view (or plane) of 3D images, specifically the axial view, is commonly used for inference with 2D foundation models. However, some regions of interest may be easier to segment by considering other anatomical views. Here, we also leverage a majority voting mechanism to integrate segmentation from multiple views for PET image segmentation.

2.3 Post-processing

The model-generated mask underwent post-processing steps, which included cropping the padded space from the pre-processing step and resizing the mask to the original image dimensions using a linear interpolation algorithm. Subsequently, the output logits were thresholded at a value of 0.

2.4 Inference Efficiency

Model Format. Efficient deep learning model deployment is challenging due to dependencies on specific frameworks, libraries, and computational environments. Moreover, large amounts of model weights and intricate architectures make model deployment take an extensive time to run without GPU accelerators. Thus, we leveraged the Open Visual Inference and Neural Network Optimization (OpenVINO) project to enhance model efficiency. OpenVINO stores model graphs in a lightweight format and provides a C++ API optimized for Intel hardware, reducing initialization and runtime. We exported our model to the ONNX format, taking advantage of its graph optimization features, and then converted the ONNX graph to OpenVINO for execution with a C++ pipeline.

Embedding Cache. Given that the image encoder is the most computationally expensive part of SAM-based models, we cache the image embedding for 3D inference with multiple ROIs to avoid recalculation.

Docker Image. Regarding runtime evaluation, our results include Docker image loading time, which is significantly impacted by the Docker image size. We adjusted the base image to include only the operating system, system libraries, and necessary libraries for imaging processing and model inference as the initial layer for building a Docker image. This adjustment notably decreased loading time compared to the original Docker image provided by the CVPR challenge.

3 Experiments

3.1 Dataset and Evaluation Measures

The "CVPR 2024: Segment Anything In Medical Images On Laptop" challenge dataset consists of three subsets: 1) more than one million image-ground truth segmentation pairs of pre-processed training data; 2) 3,278 image-bounding box pairs of pre-processed validation data; 3) 10 testing set demos from 10 different modalities with image-bounding box-ground truth segmentation triads. The accuracy and runtime were evaluated on the validation set and **final** testing set (as per the challenge).

We evaluated segmentation accuracy using two distinct metrics, Dice Similarity Coefficient (DSC) and Normalized Surface Dice (NSD), and the runtime as our deployment efficiency measure. Models were deployed using CPU restrained within 8GB of memory by Docker. These metrics collectively contribute to the ranking computation of the challenge.

3.2 Implementation Details

Environment Settings. Table 2 presents the development environment and general requirements.

Table 2. Development environments and requirements.

System	Ubuntu 20.04.6 LTS
CPU	AMD EPYC-Milan Processor@2.6 GHz
RAM	120GB
GPU (number and type)	One NVIDIA A100 40 GB
CUDA version	12.0
Programming language	Python 3.10
Deep learning framework	torch 2.0.1, torchvision 0.15.2
Specific dependencies	N/A
Code	https://github.com/NeuroDesk/cvpr-sam-on-laptop-2024

Training Protocols. To improve the performance of LiteMedSAM for specific modalities, including PET and microscopy, we explored model fine-tuning using Sharpness-aware Minimization [3] for loss optimization. Sharpness-aware Minimization considers regions in the loss landscape with uniformly low values instead of solely focusing on achieving the lowest possible loss value. This strategy aims to improve the robustness of model performance given our small training set. However, given the memory-performance gain trade-off, we did not include the fine-tuned model in our final challenge submission.

Initially, we converted 3D PET images into 2D slices and augmented these alongside microscopy images using random flips. Considering training efficiency, we only fine-tuned the image encoder of LiteMedSAM, keeping the remaining parameters frozen. Detailed training protocols are listed in Table 3.

Table 3. Training protocols.

Pre-trained Model	LiteMedSAM
Batch size	16
Patch size	16 × 16 × 3
Total epochs	50
Optimizer	AdamW [10], Sharpness-aware Minimization [3]
Initial learning rate (lr)	0.00005
Lr decay schedule	ReduceLROnPlateau
Training time	20 h
Loss function	DiceLoss + BCEWithLogitsLoss + MSELoss
Number of model parameters	9.79M*
Number of flops	147.57 GFLOPS*
CO_2eq	1 Kg**

* https://github.com/MrYxJ/calculate-flops.pytorch.
** https://github.com/lfwa/carbontracker/.

4 Results and Discussion

The runtime and DSC scores were compared across nine modalities using LiteMedSAM, EfficientSAM, and EfficientViT-SAM models on 450 images sampled from the training set (50 images for each modality), for which ground-truth masks were available. The results (Fig. 2) indicate that LiteMedSAM demonstrated great performance while maintaining a competitive runtime for most modalities. However, for microscopy and X-Ray data, EfficientViT-SAM outperformed LiteMedSAM by 10.31% DSC and 6.12% DSC, respectively, even though LiteMedSAM was trained using these data. Based on these findings, EfficientViT-SAM was selected for microscopy and X-Ray images, while LiteMedSAM was selected for the rest of the modalities.

As LiteMedSAM performed worse on PET images, we explored two methods to further improve segmentation accuracy: 1) fine-tuning LiteMedSAM with PET data; 2) using the pre-trained LiteMedSAM with a majority voting mechanism that incorporates 3D spatial information across segmentations generated from each anatomical view (axial, sagittal, and coronal). As shown in Fig. 3, the majority voting mechanism using LiteMedSAM improved the DSC score and NSD by 9% and 22.28% compared to the pre-trained LiteMedSAM model as the baseline model, respectively. However, the fine-tuned and EfficientViT models with majority voting yielded little to no accuracy improvement. These results (Fig. 3) demonstrate the effectiveness of incorporating 3D spatial information to improve segmentation accuracy without further training.

Given these initial findings, we proposed a solution that includes multiple models and techniques tailored for different imaging modalities rather than having a one-size-fits-all solution. EfficientViT-SAM is applied to microscopy and X-ray images using a bounding box as the prompt. The original LiteMedSAM

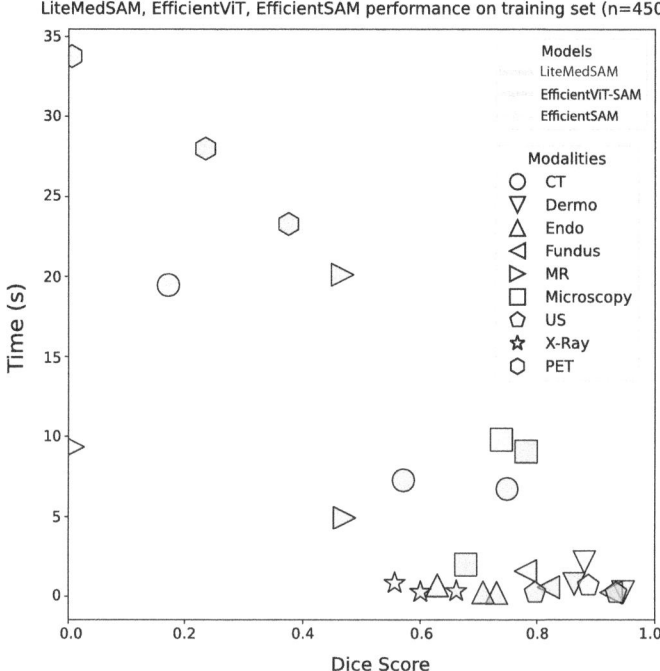

Fig. 2. Runtime as a function of DSC score across models—LiteMedSAM, EfficientViT-SAM, and EfficientSAM—and 9 modalities sampled from the training set. All models were converted to OpenVINO graphs for C++ inference pipeline.

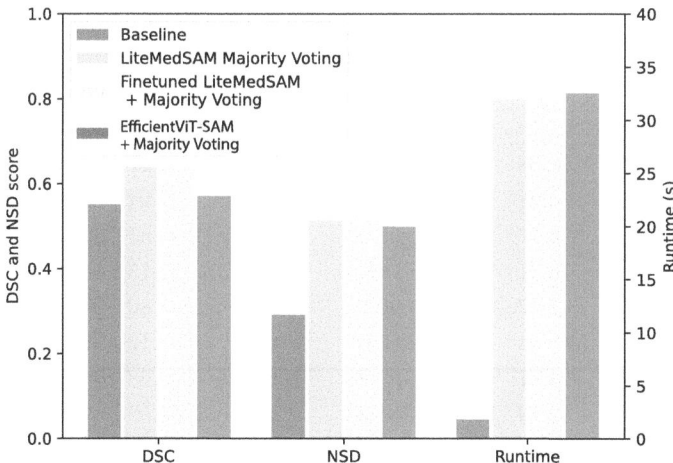

Fig. 3. DSC and NSD scores for PET validation data (n = 3) segmentation, as well as the runtime, are shown for three distinct approaches: baseline model, pre-trained LiteMedSAM with majority voting to incorporate 3D spatial information, finetuned LiteMedSAM with majority voting and EfficientViT-SAM with majority voting. The baseline model is in the Pytorch framework; the other three are OpenVINO models in the C++ pipeline.

model is utilized for other modalities, with bounding boxes automatically generated from previous slice segmentation for 3D MR and CT data. To improve segmentation accuracy for PET, a majority voting mechanism is applied to integrate 3D spatial information.

4.1 Quantitative Results on Validation Set

Our proposed method was evaluated in PyTorch, ONNX, and OpenVINO implementation, comparing DSC and NSD scores across all modalities to further understand the impact of different frameworks.

Overall, OpenVINO has a lower average DSC score than PyTorch and ONNX but achieves the highest average NSD score (Table 4). The performance variation among the three formats may be attributed to differences in the preprocessing step. OpenVINO's inference script used OpenCV's bilinear interpolation with fixed coefficients for faster processing, while PyTorch and ONNX employed bilinear interpolation with custom coefficients based on image dimensions.

While OpenVINO showed only marginal differences in accuracy compared to ONNX and PyTorch for 2D images, it exhibited significant discrepancies for 3D images, where bounding boxes were derived from masks in previous slices (Table 4). Its accuracy dropped by approximately 2% for CT and 3% for MR, while gaining notable improvement on PET images, achieving approximately 3% higher DSC and 8% higher NSD scores.

Table 4. Accuracy on the validation set using our proposed approach (a combination of models) in Pytorch, ONNX and OpenVINO frameworks.

Target	DSC (%)			NSD (%)		
	PyTorch	ONNX	OpenVINO	PyTorch	ONNX	OpenVINO
CT	92.19	92.19	90.05	94.71	94.74	92.66
MR	88.88	88.85	85.85	92.19	92.17	89.49
PET	60.68	60.33	63.87	43.21	42.94	51.40
US	94.77	94.77	94.50	96.81	96.83	96.56
X-Ray	76.31	76.13	76.46	81.52	81.15	81.49
Dermotology	92.47	92.41	92.2	93.86	93.80	93.58
Endoscopy	96.04	96.05	96.07	98.11	98.12	98.16
Fundus	94.81	94.77	93.28	96.42	96.38	94.88
Microscopy	82.79	83.03	83.25	89.67	89.58	89.96
Average	86.55	86.50	86.17	87.39	87.3	87.57

4.2 Qualitative Results on Training Set

The resulting segmentations for PET images from the training set, obtained using the pre-trained LiteMedSAM model with fixed 3D bounding box prompts and majority voting across anatomical views, are shown in Fig. 4. In some instances, the model under-segments, generating a segmentation that is much smaller than ground truth (upper panel in Fig. 4; DSC = 0.39, NSD = 0.45). However, the segmentation quality is considerably better in other cases, accurately capturing the target regions (lower panel in Fig. 4; DSC = 0.91, NSD = 0.93). This indicates that while the majority voting mechanism generally improves segmentation accuracy, there are still scenarios where the model's performance could be enhanced, especially for smaller ROIs.

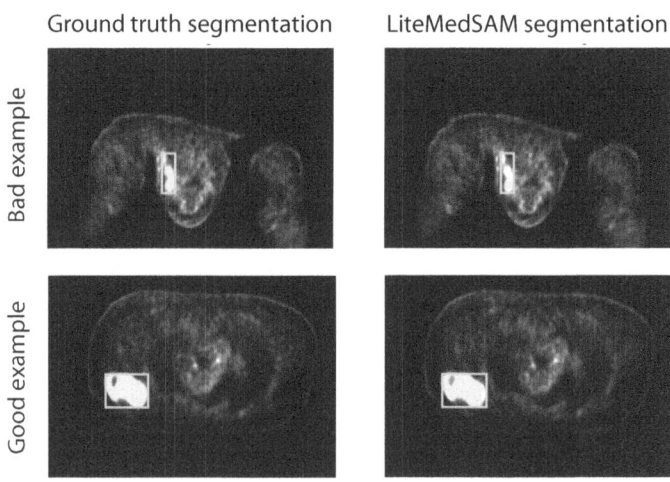

Fig. 4. Ground truth (left) and predicted segmentations (right) using majority voting with pre-trained LiteMedSAM model on PET images: 3D_PET_Lesion_PETCT_185da4c8b6 (upper panel) and 3D_PET_Lesion_PETCT_01140d52d8 (lower panel) in the training set.

As for microscopy images, the EfficientViT-SAM model prompted with a bounding box, demonstrated reasonable segmentation performance as in Fig. 5. Similarly to LiteMedSAM, in some instances, EfficientViT-SAM underperformed at the segmentation of small ROIs, leading to inaccurate segmentation (upper panel in Fig. 5; DSC = 0.53, NSD = 0.71). In contrast, the EfficientViT-SAM model performs exceptionally well for larger targets, delivering highly accurate segmentations (lower panel in Fig. 5; DSC = 0.90, NSD = 0.91). This suggests that the model's effectiveness is influenced by the size of the segmentation target, and while it excels with larger regions, additional refinement may be needed for smaller targets.

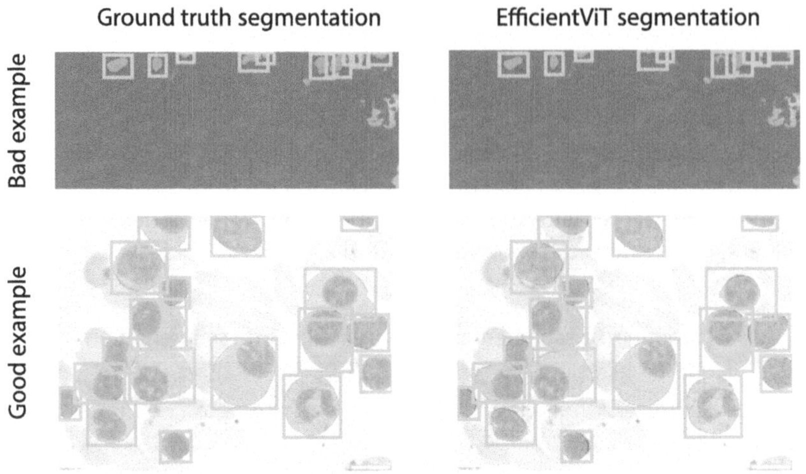

Fig. 5. Ground truth (left) and predicted segmentations (right) using EfficientViT-SAM model with bounding box prompt on microscopy images: 2D_Microscope_NeurIPS22CellSeg_cell_00020 (upper panel) and 2D_Microscope_NeurIPS22Cell Seg_cell_00020 (lower panel) in the training set.

Overall, our results suggest that the selected strategies exhibit promising performance in their respective modalities.

4.3 Segmentation Efficiency Results on Validation Set

The runtime measurement starts from loading the Docker image and ends with saving the segmentation. The OpenVINO models in the C++ pipeline consistently outperform the same approach using PyTorch and ONNX framework regarding runtime across all examples (Table 5).

4.4 Results on Final Testing Set

Table 6 presents the DSC, NSD, and runtime metrics for our proposed approach using OpenVINO, compared to the baseline model. While the DSC and NSD scores of the proposed approach are marginally lower than the baseline, it offers a significant advantage with respect to runtime, achieving inference speed over three times faster. This highlights a trade-off between segmentation accuracy and computational efficiency, demonstrating that the proposed method substantially improves inference speed with a slight compromise in performance.

4.5 Limitation and Future Work

Despite LiteMedSAM being trained on microscopy data and EfficientViT-SAM having no medical image training data, the zero-shot generalizability of

Table 5. Quantitative evaluation of segmentation efficiency in terms of runtime (s) on 12th Gen Intel® Core™ i7-12700 × 20 @ 2.10 GHz RAM 32 GB, Docker version 26.0.0. PyTorch is our proposed approach (a combination of models) using PyTorch framework within a Python inference pipeline, ONNX represents the converted graph of our PyTorch approach inferred using a Python script, and OpenVINO is the converted model from ONNX that is inferred using C++ script.

Case ID	Size	No. Objects	PyTorch	ONNX	OpenVINO
3DBox_CT_0566	(287,512,512)	6	330.18	208.05	45.46
3DBox_CT_0888	(237,512,512)	6	85.81	56.96	16.75
3DBox_CT_0860	(246,512,512)	1	15.33	9.46	5.24
3DBox_MR_0621	(115,400,400)	6	133.41	88.25	16.57
3DBox_MR_0121	(64,290,320)	6	88.01	57.26	10.59
3DBox_MR_0179	(84,512,512)	1	13.86	9.14	4.52
3DBox_PET_0001	(264,200,200)	1	42.54	31.72	10.23
2DBox_US_0525	(256,256,3)	1	3.62	2.04	1.13
2DBox_X-Ray_0053	(320,640,3)	34	3.27	2.67	1.49
2DBox_Dermoscopy_0003	(3024,4032,3)	1	4.03	2.33	1.52
2DBox_Endoscopy_0086	(480,560,3)	1	3.60	2.04	1.10
2DBox_Fundus_0003	(2048,2048,3)	1	3.64	2.07	1.18
2DBox_Microscope_0008	(1536,2040,3)	19	4.63	2.52	1.49
2DBox_Microscope_0016	(1920,2560,3)	241	12.81	7.82	7.01

Table 6. Accuracy on the **testing set** using our proposed approach (a combination of models) in the OpenVINO framework.

Target	DSC (%)		NSD (%)		Runtime (s)	
	Baseline	Our solution	Baseline	Our solution	Baseline	Our solution
CT	55.75	49.13	58.48	52.12	38.78	11.50
MR	64.80	58.80	62.75	59.07	18.57	5.55
PET	76.94	71.36	66.98	60.11	14.90	12.24
US	85.24	83.54	89.73	89.30	8.96	2.37
X-Ray	85.51	78.17	94.40	88.97	9.95	1.98
OCT	73.31	67.29	80.20	73.75	8.39	1.89
Endoscopy	94.41	94.40	96.95	96.93	7.56	1.81
Fundus	87.47	87.49	89.58	89.57	8.77	1.91
Microscope	84.36	87.61	86.15	89.35	16.34	2.19
Average	**78.64**	**75.31**	**80.58**	**77.69**	**14.69**	**4.61**

EfficientViT-SAM for this modality outperformed LiteMedSAM. Considering expensive training costs and the difficulty of collecting medical image data at a large scale, this finding motivates further exploration of zero-shot capabilities of foundation models trained on large-scale natural scene images to segment medical images without further fine-tuning.

In our current implementation of the majority vote mechanism for PET scans, all anatomical views have the same weight. Future work may consider the effect of weight adjustment on the final prediction to understand the contributions of each anatomical view in the overall segmentation improvement. To further optimize runtime for PET scans, one may test reducing the number of anatomical views for inference, for example, from three to two. This may lead to minor segmentation accuracy degradation but substantial runtime gains.

5 Conclusion

In conclusion, our solution includes various models customized for distinct imaging modalities: EfficientViT-SAM for microscopy and X-ray; the original LiteMedSAM for other modalities with an automatic bounding box generation mechanism for 3D data and majority voting to integrate 3D spatial information for PET data. Overall, the runtime of OpenVINO with the C++ inference script outperformed the baseline provided by the challenge. While accuracy on Microscopy images surpassed the baseline on the testing set, accuracy for other modalities remains suboptimal and requires further improvement.

Acknowledgements. We thank all the data consortiums and researchers involved in data acquisition for making the training medical imaging data publicly available, CodaLab [17] for hosting the challenge platform, and the CVPR 2024 challenge organizers. The authors acknowledge funding through an ARC Linkage grant (LP200301393).

Disclosure of Interests. The authors have no competing interests to declare that are relevant to the content of this article.

References

1. Bommasani, R., et al.: On the opportunities and risks of foundation models (2022). http://arxiv.org/abs/2108.07258, arXiv:2108.07258 [cs]
2. Deng, R., et al.: Segment anything model (SAM) for digital pathology: assess zero-shot segmentation on whole slide imaging. In: Medical Imaging with Deep Learning, Short Paper Track (2023). https://openreview.net/forum?id=lUZGyTRzxq
3. Foret, P., Kleiner, A., Mobahi, H., Neyshabur, B.: Sharpness-aware minimization for efficiently improving generalization. In: International Conference on Learning Representations (2021). https://openreview.net/forum?id=6TmlmposlrM
4. Huang, Y., et al.: Segment anything model for medical images? Med. Image Anal. **92**, 103061 (2024). https://doi.org/10.1016/j.media.2023.103061
5. Kirillov, A., et al.: Segment anything (2023). https://doi.org/10.48550/arXiv.2304.02643, http://arxiv.org/abs/2304.02643, arXiv:2304.02643 [cs]

6. Le, B.H., Nguyen-Vu, D.K., Nguyen-Mau, T.H., Nguyen, H.D., Tran, M.T.: MedficientSAM: a robust medical segmentation model with optimized inference pipeline for limited clinical settings. In: Submitted to CVPR 2024: Segment Anything In Medical Images On Laptop (2024). https://openreview.net/forum?id=aa0f77RKI0, under review
7. Liu, X., Peng, H., Zheng, N., Yang, Y., Hu, H., Yuan, Y.: EfficientViT: memory efficient vision transformer with cascaded group attention. In: Proceedings of the IEEE/CVF Conference on Computer Vision and Pattern Recognition, pp. 14420–14430 (2023). https://arxiv.org/abs/2305.07027
8. Liu, Z., et al.: Swin transformer: hierarchical vision transformer using shifted windows. In: Proceedings of the IEEE/CVF International Conference on Computer Vision, pp. 10012–10022 (2021). http://arxiv.org/abs/2103.14030
9. Liyanage, H., et al.: Artificial intelligence in primary health care: perceptions, issues, and challenges: primary health care informatics working group contribution to the yearbook of medical informatics 2019. Yearbook Med. Inform. **28**(01), 041–046 (2019). https://doi.org/10.1055/s-0039-1677901, http://www.thieme-connect.de/DOI/DOI?10.1055/s-0039-1677901
10. Loshchilov, I., Hutter, F.: Decoupled weight decay regularization (2019). http://arxiv.org/abs/1711.05101, arXiv:1711.05101 [cs, math]
11. Ma, J., He, Y., Li, F., Han, L., You, C., Wang, B.: Segment anything in medical images. Nat. Commun. **15**(1), 654 (2024). https://doi.org/10.1038/s41467-024-44824-z, https://www.nature.com/articles/s41467-024-44824-z
12. Marinó, G.C., Petrini, A., Malchiodi, D., Frasca, M.: Deep neural networks compression: a comparative survey and choice recommendations. Neurocomputing **520**, 152–170 (2023). https://doi.org/10.1016/j.neucom.2022.11.072, https://linkinghub.elsevier.com/retrieve/pii/S0925231222014643
13. Mazurowski, M.A., Dong, H., Gu, H., Yang, J., Konz, N., Zhang, Y.: Segment anything model for medical image analysis: an experimental study. Med. Image Anal. **89**, 102918 (2023). https://doi.org/10.1016/j.media.2023.102918
14. Roy, S., et al.: SAM.MD: zero-shot medical image segmentation capabilities of the Segment Anything Model (2023). http://arxiv.org/abs/2304.05396, arXiv:2304.05396 [cs, eess]
15. Wu, K., et al.: TinyViT: fast pretraining distillation for small vision transformers. In: Avidan, S., Brostow, G., Cissé, M., Farinella, G.M., Hassner, T. (eds.) ECCV 2022. LNCS, vol. 13681, pp. 68–85. Springer, Cham (2022). https://doi.org/10.1007/978-3-031-19803-8_5
16. Xiong, Y., et al.: EfficientSAM: leveraged masked image pretraining for efficient segment anything (2023). http://arxiv.org/abs/2312.00863, arXiv:2312.00863 [cs]
17. Xu, Z., et al.: Codabench: flexible, easy-to-use, and reproducible meta-benchmark platform. Patterns **3**(7), 100543 (2022)
18. Zhang, Z., Cai, H., Han, S.: EfficientViT-SAM: accelerated segment anything model without accuracy loss (2024). http://arxiv.org/abs/2402.05008, arXiv:2402.05008 [cs]
19. Zhou, T., Ruan, S., Canu, S.: A review: deep learning for medical image segmentation using multi-modality fusion. Array **3-4**, 100004 (2019). https://doi.org/10.1016/j.array.2019.100004, https://linkinghub.elsevier.com/retrieve/pii/S2590005619300049

Gray's Anatomy for Segment Anything Model: Optimizing Grayscale Medical Images for Fast and Lightweight Segmentation

In Kyu Lee[1], Jonghoe Ku[1], and YoungHwan Choi[2,3](✉)

[1] Medipixel Inc, Seoul, Korea
[2] Department of Dermatology, Samsung Medical Center, Sungkyunkwan University School of Medicine, Seoul, Korea
soulkest@skku.edu
[3] Department of Medical Device Management and Research, Samsung Advanced Institute for Health Sciences and Technology, Sungkyunkwan University, Seoul, Korea

Abstract. Advancements in medical image segmentation are critical for enhancing diagnostic accuracy in clinical settings, particularly when operating on edge devices like CPU-only laptops. In this context, we have developed a medical image segmentation model that is specifically designed for efficient deployment on such devices. Our approach leverages the EfficientViT-SAM architecture integrated with dynamic quantization to optimize both accuracy and computational efficiency. The model has been trained on a diverse dataset that includes over one million image-mask pairs from 10 different medical imaging modalities along with additional data for underrepresented anatomies. Performance evaluations show that our model achieves a dice score of 88.54% and a normalized surface dice of 98.28%, showing improvements of 4.37% and 2.85%, respectively, over the baseline model. The implementation of dynamic quantization not only preserves accuracy but also boosts inference speeds, making the model exceptionally viable for real-time clinical applications. This study affirms the potential of advanced segmentation technologies to operate effectively on non-specialized hardware, thereby expanding the accessibility of high-quality medical imaging analysis in environments constrained by resources. With its robust performance across various imaging scenarios and enhanced processing efficiency, the model promises substantial improvements in clinical workflows and patient outcomes. The code is available at https://github.com/Ninebell/GraysAnatomySAM.

Keywords: Medical imaging · Segmentation · Lightweight

I. K. Lee and J. Ku—Both authors contributed equally. Names are listed in alphabetical order.

1 Introduction

Medical imaging plays a critical role in the diagnosis, treatment planning, and monitoring of various diseases. Segmentation, the process of delineating regions of interest (ROIs) such as organs, lesions, and tissues in medical images, is fundamental to many clinical applications. Traditionally, manual segmentation has been the gold standard, but it is time-consuming, labor-intensive, and requires significant expertise. The advent of deep learning has brought substantial improvements, with models now capable of delivering accurate segmentation results across diverse tasks. However, these models are often task-specific, and their performance can degrade when applied to new tasks or different types of imaging data. This limitation has spurred interest in developing universal models for medical image segmentation that can generalize across various tasks.

The Segment Anything Model (SAM) [2] is a groundbreaking foundation model in the realm of image segmentation, demonstrating remarkable versatility and performance in natural image tasks. Despite its success, applying SAM directly to medical image segmentation presents challenges due to the inherent differences between natural and medical images. These differences necessitate adaptations to leverage SAM's strengths while addressing its limitations in the medical domain.

Recent studies have explored various adaptations of SAM to medical imaging, including MedSAM [5], which fine-tunes SAM on extensive medical image datasets to enhance its performance. Nonetheless, a significant barrier to the widespread adoption of these models in clinical settings is their computational intensity. SAM, in particular, requires substantial computational resources, making it impractical for time-sensitive and resource-constrained applications such as real-time diagnosis and mobile health applications.

To address this challenge, several lightweight versions of SAM have been proposed, such as FastSAM [10], MobileSAM [8], and EfficientSAM [6]. These models aim to reduce the computational burden while maintaining performance, often by employing techniques like model distillation and leveraging more efficient architectures. However, these adaptations still encounter trade-offs between performance and computational efficiency.

In this paper, we adopt EfficientViT-SAM [9] that combines the EfficientViT [1] architecture with SAM to create a fast and lightweight model for medical image segmentation. EfficientViT-SAM aims to retain the high performance of SAM while significantly reducing the computational requirements. In addition, we dynamically quantized our EfficientViT-SAM model for faster inference. Through comprehensive experiments on various medical imaging tasks, we demonstrate that our quantized EfficientViT-SAM achieves remarkable performance while being significantly faster and more efficient than existing models. Furthermore, we incorporate insights from recent research [3] on enhancing grayscale medical images to improve segmentation outcomes. By using the method we term "Gray's Anatomy", which processes grayscale medical images to optimize contrast and smoothness, we aim to boost the efficiency and accuracy of our model.

This work represents a step forward in making advanced medical image segmentation tools more accessible and practical for clinical use, highlighting the potential of combining foundation models with lightweight architectures and enhanced image preprocessing techniques.

2 Method

We introduce a comprehensive methodology for developing a lightweight medical image segmentation model. We start from preprocessing, including a three-channel enhancement technique that enriches input data essential for robust segmentation. Consequently, we elaborate on our adoption of the EfficientViT-SAM architecture, tailored for both accuracy and computational efficiency on edge devices. Finally, the post-processing subsection introduces dynamic quantization for fast and resource-efficient inference.

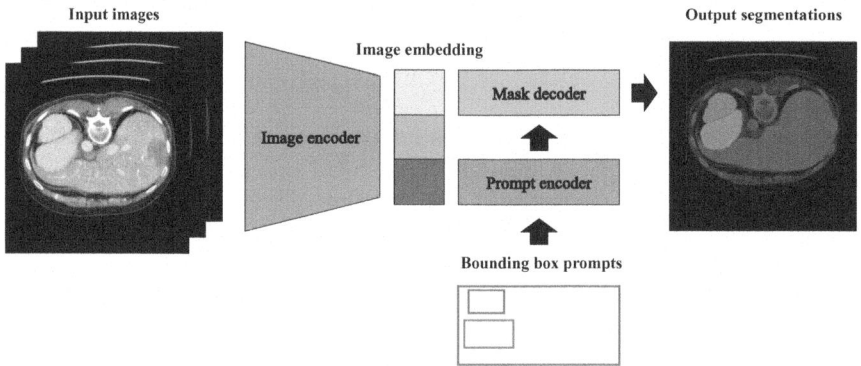

Fig. 1. Overview of the Image Segmentation Pipeline. The input is a three-channel constructed image, which is processed by the EfficientViT-SAM model to extract features across the entire image. Simultaneously, bounding box prompts specify regions of interest, guiding the model to focus its resources on specific areas. The final output is a segmentation mask applied within the regions defined by the prompts.

2.1 Preprocessing

Data Management. Given the challenge of processing over a million image-mask pairs, data management and preprocessing are critical for efficient training and validation. To standardize the input data and optimize the use of computational resources, we preprocessed and saved data in a new format.

To ensure consistency across the dataset, which includes images of varying dimensions from different medical imaging modalities, we resized all images to have the same dimensions. Each image was first padded to make its height and width equal, preserving the aspect ratio and ensuring that no anatomical information was distorted or lost. Subsequently, we resized the images to a size of

256 × 256 pixels. This resizing not only helps in maintaining computational efficiency but also ensures uniformity in the input data for our segmentation models.

To manage the large volume of segmentation masks accompanying the images, we employed run-length encoding (RLE) for the masks. RLE is a simple form of data compression where sequences of data (in this case, pixels of the same value) are stored as a single data value and count. This approach significantly reduced the size of our mask files, making them easier to store and faster to transmit.

The preprocessed images were saved in PNG format, which offers lossless compression, ensuring that no image data is lost after compression. The masks, encoded in RLE, were saved in Pickle (PKL) format, a Python-specific binary format, which facilitates easy loading and saving of large amounts of structured data. It was driven by the need for efficiency in both storage and speed during the training phase of our models.

Channel Construction and Enhancement. The preprocessing stage is crucial for ensuring that the medical images are in an optimal format for segmentation while preserving essential diagnostic features. Considering the diverse characteristics of medical imaging modalities such as CT, X-ray, and MRI, which are primarily in a single-channel grayscale format, we adopted a multi-channel preprocessing approach to enhance segmentation accuracy and robustness.

Instead of replicating the grayscale image across three channels, we tailored each channel to capture different aspects of the image data, enhancing both the model's input variability and its capacity to identify relevant features. The first channel retains the original raw image data, serving as a baseline representation of the anatomical structure without any modifications. To reduce noise while preserving edge integrity, which is critical for delineating regions of interest, we applied anisotropic diffusion in the second channel. Anisotropic diffusion is particularly effective in environments with high levels of noise, as it smooths the image while maintaining sharp edges, crucial for accurate segmentation. The third channel builds upon the smoothed image from Channel 2. Here, we apply histogram equalization to maximize the contrast. This step is particularly beneficial for enhancing the visibility of subtle features within the image, which are often crucial for accurate and segmentation.

Figure 2 illustrates the transformation of a single grayscale image through these preprocessing steps, demonstrating the distinct contribution of each channel to the overall enhancement of the image. This preprocessing strategy not only standardizes the input data but also enriches the information the model receives, equipping it to more effectively differentiate between relevant features for segmentation tasks across various medical imaging modalities.

2.2 Proposed Method

Architecture. To meet the challenge of developing a general and lightweight medical image segmentation model capable of running efficiently on laptops without GPU support, we adopted the EfficientViT-SAM model, specifically its smallest variant, EfficientViT-SAM-L0. This architecture combines the strengths of scalable architecture modeling with an efficient version of the Vision Transformer, tailored for speed and low-resource consumption.

EfficientViT-SAM incorporates a hybrid approach that leverages the power of Vision Transformers while alleviating their traditional computational inefficiencies. The architecture begins with a series of MBConvolution (Mobile inverted Bottleneck Convolution) layers, which are specifically designed for mobile and edge devices due to their reduced parameter count and efficient computation. These layers preprocess the input image, effectively reducing its dimensionality while retaining crucial spatial hierarchies necessary for feature extraction. The processed features are then fed into the EfficientViT module. We initialized our image encoder with weights that are knowledge distilled from the SAM-ViT model. In this way, our EfficientViT-SAM image encoder retains the robust feature recognition capability of more resource-intensive models while operating within the constraints of CPU-only environments.

Building on the EfficientViT-SAM's efficient feature extraction, the model incorporates MedSAM's bounding box prompt encoder and mask decoder. The bounding box prompt encoder enables the model to understand and process specific regions of interest within the image, focusing the segmentation task on areas highlighted by clinical relevance. The mask decoder then utilizes the features and spatial cues provided by the EfficientViT-SAM to generate precise segmentation masks, adapting dynamically to the varied shapes and sizes of medical anomalies.

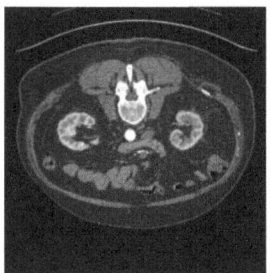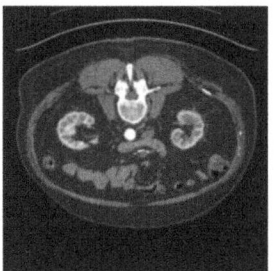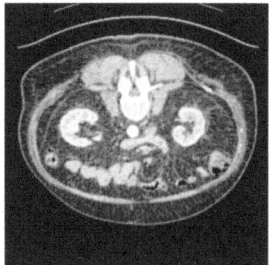

Fig. 2. Preprocessing Steps for Medical Image Segmentation. The left image displays the original raw grayscale image, showcasing the standard input format. The middle image illustrates the result of applying anisotropic diffusion, aimed at reducing noise while preserving critical edge details. The right image presents the histogram equalized image, where contrast has been enhanced to highlight subtle features and improve visibility, facilitating more accurate segmentation.

2.3 Post-processing

In the final stage of our model's deployment, we focus on optimizing the inference time and computational efficiency through the application of quantization techniques. Quantization reduces the precision of the numerical values in a model, which decreases the model's memory footprint and speeds up the processing time-essential traits for models intended for use on CPU-only laptops in clinical environments.

Quantization can be done in two ways: static quantization and dynamic quantization. Static quantization involves the conversion of both the weights and activations of the model to a lower precision format, such as int8, prior to deployment. This process requires the determination of quantization parameters, which are fixed during the initial calibration phase using a subset of the training data. While this method enhances the speed of operations by allowing the use of integer mathematics during inference, it suffers from a lack of flexibility. The predetermined scaling factors may not always accurately represent the range of values seen during actual model use, potentially leading to inaccuracies when processing data that differ significantly from the calibration dataset.

In contrast to static quantization, dynamic quantization offers a more adaptable solution for handling the variability inherent in medical imaging data. This approach involves quantizing the model's weights before deployment, while the activations are quantized dynamically at runtime. As a result, the quantization parameters for the activations are recalculated based on the actual data presented during inference. This dynamic adjustment allows the model to adapt to the specific characteristics of each image it processes, providing flexibility and accuracy crucial for medical applications where image diversity is high.

Opting for dynamic quantization using torch.qint8 enabled our model to maintain high segmentation accuracy while achieving substantial reductions in computational demands. This approach simplifies the deployment process by eliminating the need for extensive pre-calibration, thereby ensuring that the model can operate efficiently on a wide range of hardware, including the less powerful CPUs typical of many clinical settings. The dynamic nature of this quantization method enhances the model's usability and effectiveness, particularly in real-time clinical applications, making it a superior choice for ensuring robust performance across varied medical imaging scenarios.

3 Experiments

3.1 Dataset and Evaluation Measures

To comprehensively assess the performance of our segmentation model, we utilized a large-scale challenge dataset, which encompasses a diverse array of medical imaging modalities and cancer types. This dataset includes over one million image-mask pairs and covers 10 distinct imaging modalities, such as CT, MRI, and X-ray, providing a robust foundation for training our model. The dataset is also diverse in terms of anatomical coverage, featuring images of various body parts including the lungs, skin, and eyes, which are critical for a wide range of clinical applications.

Recognizing the need to enhance our model's capability in handling less common anatomies and modalities, we supplemented the challenge dataset with external datasets. These additional datasets focus on anatomies and modalities not extensively covered in the challenge dataset, such as hip X-rays and ultrasound images of the prostate. The inclusion of these datasets ensures a more comprehensive training process, enabling our model to perform well across a broader spectrum of medical scenarios. Table 1 summarizes the external datasets incorporated into our training. This comprehensive approach to data collection allows our model to learn from a wide variety of image characteristics and clinical conditions, enhancing its generalizability in real-world applications.

To assess the performance of the segmentation models, this challenge measured Dice Similarity Coefficient (DSC), Normalized Surface Dice (NSD), and inference time as our primary evaluation metrics. DSC measures the volumetric overlap between the predicted segmentation and the ground truth, providing a quantitative indicator of the segmentation accuracy. It is used to evaluate the agreement between the two segmentations, where a value of 1 indicates perfect overlap and 0 indicates no overlap. In addition, NSD focuses on the accuracy of the segmentation boundaries rather than their volumetric correspondence. By measuring the similarity of the surfaces, NSD measures how well the segmentation contours align with the anatomical boundaries, which is crucial for applications requiring precise delineation of complex anatomical structures. Lastly, inference time is considered for the ranking computation. It ensures that they not only are accurate but also fit well within the operational constraints of medical environments.

Table 1. External training dataset.

Dataset Name	Modality	Segmentation Targets	Annotated Images
Nuclei Segmentation	Microscopy	Nucleus	5426
HipXRay	X-ray	Bones	140
BTCV	CT	abdominal organs	30
Micro-Ultrasound	Micro-Ultrasound	Prostate	75
ToothSeg	X-ray	Teeth	598

3.2 Implementation Details

Environment Settings. The development environments and requirements are presented in Table 2.

Training Protocols. Training a model for medical image segmentation with over one million image-mask pairs presents unique challenges and constraints.

Table 2. Development environments and requirements.

System	Windows 11
CPU	AMD Ryzen 7 3700X 8-core Processor
RAM	16 × 2 GB; 2.67 MT/s
GPU (number and type)	NVIDIA RTX 4090 24G
CUDA version	11.0
Programming language	Python 3.12
Deep learning framework	torch 2.0, torchvision 0.2.2
Specific dependencies	N/A
Code	https://github.com/Ninebell/GraysAnatomySAM

Our approach to training was carefully designed to optimize resource use while maintaining relevance to clinical applications.

Given the standardized nature of medical imaging and the critical importance of anatomical positions, conventional data augmentation techniques like flipping or random cropping are less suitable. For instance, anatomical landmarks such as the heart are consistently located in specific positions (e.g., the left side of the chest), making such transformations potentially misleading for a segmentation model. Therefore, our augmentation focused solely on adjusting the bounding box positions and sizes. This approach preserves the integrity and relevance of the anatomical information in the images, ensuring that the model learns to recognize and segment based on realistic variations in patient anatomy.

To evaluate our model effectively, we allocated 1% of the images from each modality to a validation set and reserved the remaining 99% for training. This split was designed to provide a robust dataset for training while ensuring that the validation set was representative of the diversity and challenges present in the larger dataset.

Due to the extensive size of our dataset and limitations in computational resources, completing even one epoch of training required more than a day. To manage this efficiently, we adopted a sampling strategy during training where only 1000 samples from each 2D imaging modality and 1000 samples from each 3D imaging submodality were used per epoch. This approach not only facilitated faster iterations but also made monitoring and saving model checkpoints more manageable. Model checkpoints were evaluated based on the performance on the validation set, with a focus on minimizing the validation loss. The model that demonstrated the smallest validation loss was selected for our final submission (Table 4).

4 Results and Discussion

4.1 Quantitative Results on Validation Set

Our proposed model demonstrated significant enhancements in segmentation performance on the validation set compared to the baseline model, particularly

Table 3. Training protocols.

Pre-trained Model	Efficient-ViTSAM [9]
Batch size	32
Patch size	256×256×3
Total epochs	300
Optimizer	AdamW [4]
Initial learning rate (lr)	5e−5
Lr decay schedule	ReduceLROnPlateau
Training time	113.2 h
Loss function	BCE, MSE, Dice
Number of model parameters	34.79M[4]
Number of flops	602G[5]
CO_2eq	7 Kg[6]

[4] https://github.com/sksq96/pytorch-summary
[5] https://github.com/facebookresearch/fvcore
[6] https://github.com/lfwa/carbontracker/

Table 4. Quantitative evaluation results.

Target	Baseline		Quantized Baseline		Proposed		Quantized Proposed	
	DSC (%)	NSD (%)	DSC (%)	NSD (%)	DSC (%)	NSD (%)	DSC (%)	NSD (%)
CT	72.47	88.49	72.71	89.15	84.46	97.74	84.80	98.05
MR	76.40	93.02	77.12	93.22	80.92	95.86	82.69	97.22
PET	70.56	95.71	70.91	95.93	79.22	98.61	79.15	98.56
US	94.80	98.41	95.10	98.93	94.91	98.38	95.01	98.42
X-Ray	96.04	99.30	95.82	99.12	95.21	98.67	95.17	98.66
Dermoscopy	94.23	98.09	94.41	98.09	94.60	98.12	94.62	98.14
Endoscopy	91.47	98.46	91.45	98.34	91.38	98.60	91.40	98.57
Fundus	92.68	98.90	92.93	98.30	89.93	98.6	90.15	98.73
Microscopy	65.80	86.43	66.10	86.83	83.24	97.90	83.86	98.23
Average	83.83	95.20	84.06	95.32	88.20	98.05	88.54	98.28

in terms of DSC and NSD. Overall, improvements of 4.37% in DSC and 2.85% in NSD were observed. While the baseline model showed stronger results in specific modalities such as X-ray, endoscopy, and fundus imaging, our proposed model excelled across a broader range of modalities, indicating its versatility and robustness. A significant improvement was observed in microscopy images, where the DSC dramatically increased from 65.80% to 83.24%. This substantial enhancement underscores the robustness of our model in handling various datasets.

Furthermore, the performance of both quantized versions of the baseline and the proposed models was evaluated to compare dynamic quantization. Remarkably, the quantized models did not exhibit a performance drop compared to their non-quantized counterparts, maintaining similar DSC and NSD scores. This result highlights the effectiveness of dynamic quantization as a post-processing step, confirming its potential to preserve the model's accuracy while significantly reducing the computational load during inference.

Table 5. Quantitative evaluation of segmentation efficiency in terms of running time (s).

Case ID	Size	Num. Objects	Baseline	Proposed
3DBox_CT_0566	(287, 512, 512)	6	210.98	**51.85**
3DBox_CT_0888	(237, 512, 512)	6	53.35	**11.22**
3DBox_CT_0860	(246, 512, 512)	1	7.50	**2.51**
3DBox_MR_0621	(115, 400, 400)	6	83.16	**16.92**
3DBox_MR_0121	(64, 290, 320)	6	51.20	**9.84**
3DBox_MR_0179	(84, 512, 512)	1	6.92	**1.6**
3DBox_PET_0001	(264, 200, 200)	1	3.50	**0.78**
2DBox_US_0525	(256, 256, 3)	1	0.40	**0.11**
2DBox_X-Ray_0053	(320, 640, 3)	34	0.90	**0.72**
2DBox_Dermoscopy_0003	(3024, 4032, 3)	1	**1.41**	2.09
2DBox_Endoscopy_0086	(480, 560, 3)	1	0.43	**0.09**
2DBox_Fundus_0003	(2048, 2048, 3)	1	0.72	**0.38**
2DBox_Microscope_0008	(1536, 2040, 3)	19	1.05	**0.66**
2DBox_Microscope_0016	(1920, 2560, 3)	241	6.27	**6.19**

4.2 Qualitative Results on Validation Set

The qualitative evaluation of our model on the validation set further demonstrated its capability to accurately identify and segment regions of interest within bounding box prompts, particularly when a single region of interest is included within the prompt. For instance, as illustrated in the first and second rows of Fig. 3, our model achieved precise segmentation of mammography and head CT images, respectively. In these cases, the bounding box prompts effectively covered the entire region of interest, allowing the model to correctly delineate the boundaries without interference from adjacent structures.

However, the model's performance was less consistent when faced with bounding box prompts containing multiple regions of interest. These scenarios often led to incorrect segmentations, as the model sometimes prioritized one region over another or misinterpreted the intended area of focus. Examples of such failures are displayed in the third and fourth rows of Fig. 3. In one case involving an X-ray image of the lung, the model was prompted to segment the pneumothorax region but erroneously focused on the entire right lung. Another example includes a prompt covering both lungs and bones; here, the model incorrectly segmented the bone structure when the ground truth required segmentation of the entire lungs.

4.3 Segmentation Efficiency Results on Validation Set

An integral aspect of our evaluation focused on the efficiency of the segmentation process, particularly how dynamic quantization affects performance and inference speed. According to the results presented in Table 4, our dynamically quantized model maintained the accuracy of its non-quantized counterpart, with no degradation in DSC or NSD. This result underscores the effectiveness of dynamic quantization in preserving the integrity of the model's predictive capabilities while optimizing computational efficiency.

More importantly, the impact of quantization on inference speed was substantial. The dynamically quantized version of our proposed model demonstrated a remarkable increase in processing speed compared to the baseline model. Specifically, our proposed quantized model achieved up to five times faster inference times in certain scenarios and on average three times faster across all tested conditions.

These efficiency gains are further detailed in Table 5, which provides an overall comparison of inference times. This comprehensive overview underscores the significant speed advantages offered by our approach. Such improvements are particularly valuable in resource-constrained environments, aligning with our goal to develop a model that is both effective and efficient on edge devices.

4.4 Results on Final Testing Set

We submitted our proposed model for evaluation using the final testing set. Overall, DSC and NSD metrics decreased by 9.6% and 16.6% respectively. Particularly in three-dimensional datasets, including CT, MR, and PET scans, our model performed poorly. The results from the final test set are presented in (Table 6).

4.5 Limitation and Future Work

Our model faces challenges with bounding box prompts leading to segmentation ambiguities, such as whether to segment organs or bones in CT images. To improve clarity, future works could integrate more detailed prompting techniques, such as scribble-based input, where users provide direct annotations within the image, guiding the model more precise segmentation. Additionally, while our preprocessing methods successfully enhanced grayscale images, they proved less effective for color images. Future research can be focused on developing preprocessing techniques that improve feature recognition in color images as well, ensuring consistent performance across different imaging types. These refinements will boost the model's precision and expand its clinical utility.

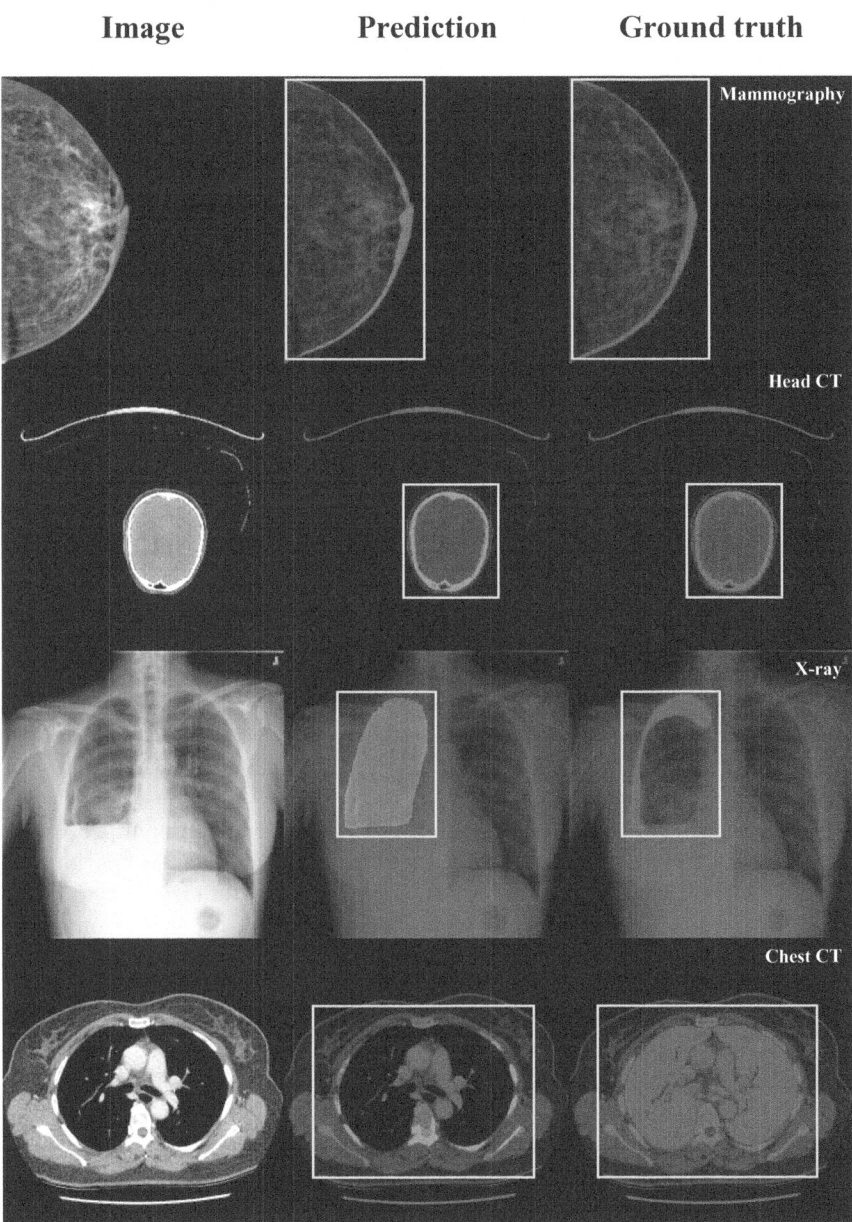

Fig. 3. Qualitative segmentation results. It illustrates examples of segmentation predictions made by our model. The top two rows display cases of successful segmentations. The third and fourth rows illustrate unsuccessful segmentations, where the predicted areas significantly diverge from the ground truth masks. Yellow bounding boxes represent prompts given to the model. (Color figure online)

Table 6. Quantitative evaluation results on the test set.

Target	Quantized Proposed	
	DSC (%)	NSD (%)
CT	62.63	65.49
MR	67.17	68.44
PET	77.73	68.50
US	86.02	90.42
X-Ray	74.16	85.62
Endoscopy	92.80	95.66
Fundus	90.61	92.64
Microscopy	82.14	84.43
OCT	77.30	84.39
Average	78.95	81.73

5 Conclusion

In this study, we introduced a novel approach for medical image segmentation that leverages an efficient transformer-based architecture, EfficientViT-SAM, combined with dynamic quantization to achieve robust performance on edge devices, including laptops without dedicated GPU resources. Our methods addressed key challenges in medical imaging by providing a lightweight yet powerful solution capable of handling a diverse imaging modalities and anatomical structures.

Our results demonstrate that our proposed model significantly improves upon the baseline in terms of DSC and NSD, particularly showing notable performance enhancements in microscopy imaging where the segmentation accuracy increased dramatically. Importantly, the implementation of dynamic quantization ensured that these improvements did not come at the cost of computational efficiency. On the contrary, our quantized model achieved up to five times faster inference speeds, making it highly suitable for real-time clinical applications where rapid image processing is crucial.

Furthermore, our model's efficiency highlight its potential for widespread adoption in clinical settings, especially in scenarios where high computational resources are not available. This capability opens up new possibilities for deploying advanced medical imaging technologies in resource-limited environments, potentially enhancing patient care by providing quicker and more accurate diagnostic tools.

Acknowledgements. We thank all the data owners for making the medical images publicly available and CodaLab [7] for hosting the challenge platform. This research was supported by a grant of the MD-Phd/Medical Scientist Training Program through the Korea Health Industry Development Institute (KHIDI), funded by the Ministry of

Health & Welfare, Republic of Korea. Finally, we would also like to thank Medipixel, especially Danny and Andy, for their support and encouragement.

Disclosure of Interests. The authors have no competing interests to declare that are relevant to the content of this article.

References

1. Cai, H., Li, J., Hu, M., Gan, C., Han, S.: EfficientViT: multi-scale linear attention for high-resolution dense prediction (2024)
2. Kirillov, A., et al.: Segment anything. In: Proceedings of the International Conference on Computer Vision, pp. 4015–4026 (2023)
3. Kong, L., Huang, M., Zhang, L., Chan, L.W.C.: Enhancing diagnostic images to improve the performance of the segment anything model in medical image segmentation. Bioengineering **11**(3) (2024). https://doi.org/10.3390/bioengineering11030270, https://www.mdpi.com/2306-5354/11/3/270
4. Loshchilov, I., Hutter, F.: Decoupled weight decay regularization (2019)
5. Ma, J., He, Y., Li, F., Han, L., You, C., Wang, B.: Segment anything in medical images. Nat. Commun. **15**(1), 654 (2024)
6. Xiong, Y., et al.: EfficientSAM: leveraged masked image pretraining for efficient segment anything. arXiv:2312.00863 (2023)
7. Xu, Z., et al.: Codabench: flexible, easy-to-use, and reproducible meta-benchmark platform. Patterns **3**(7), 100543 (2022)
8. Zhang, C., et al.: Faster segment anything: towards lightweight SAM for mobile applications. arXiv preprint arXiv:2306.14289 (2023)
9. Zhang, Z., Cai, H., Han, S.: EfficientViT-SAM: accelerated segment anything model without performance loss. In: CVPR Workshop: Efficient Large Vision Models (2024)
10. Zhao, X., et al.: Fast segment anything (2023)

Author Index

A
Ali, Qasim   195

B
Balarupan, Gowrienanthan   218
Bollmann, Steffen   218

C
Chen, Shuqing   57
Chen, Ye   83
Chen, Yuhao   195
Choi, YoungHwan   232

D
Dai, Bingze   151
Dao, Thuy   218

F
Fu, Yujie   137

G
Gao, Ruochen   70
Guan, Haotian   151

H
Hu, Shu   206
Huang, Peng   206
Huang, Pu   206
Hutter, Frank   15

J
Jaus, Alexander   39, 101
Jeong, Seoi   180

K
Kim, Kwangtai   180
Kirchhoff, Yannick   167
Kleesiek, Jens   39, 101
Kong, Hyoun-Joong   180

Kong, Youngbin   180
Ku, Jonghoe   232

L
Le, Bao-Hiep   1
Lee, In Kyu   232
Lee, Kyu Eun   180
Li, Yizhou   83
Liu, Xiaoyu   206
Lu, Haisheng   137
Lyu, Donghang   70

M
Maier-Hein, Klaus   167
Marinov, Zdravko   39, 101

N
Nguyen, Hai-Dang   1
Nguyen-Mau, Trong-Hieu   1
Nguyen-Vu, Dang-Khoa   1

O
Okutomi, Masatoshi   83

P
Pfefferle, Alexander   15
Purucker, Lennart   15

R
Ravindran, Ashis   167
Ribeiro, Fernanda L.   218
Rokuss, Maximilian R.   167

S
Scarsbrook, Joshua   218
Staring, Marius   70

Stiefelhagen, Rainer   39, 101
Stock, Raphael   167

T
Tran, Minh-Triet   1

W
Wang, Shuai   126
Wang, Xin   206
Wang, Yaqi   126
Wei, Muxin   57
Wong, Alex   195

Wu, Silin   57
Wu, Zhuofeng   83

X
Xu, Dabin   57

Y
Yang, Songxiao   83
Ye, Xincheng   218

Z
Zhang, Fan   137
Zhang, Jiajing   151
Zhang, Le   137
Zhi, Li   126
Zhu, Hongtu   206

The manufacturer's authorised representative in the EU is Springer Nature Customer Service Centre GmbH, Europaplatz 3, 69115 Heidelberg, Germany. If you have any concerns regarding our products, please contact ProductSafety@springernature.com

Printed and bound by CPI Group (UK) Ltd, Croydon, CR0 4YY
26/03/2026
02078935-0008